The Strained Alliance

U.S.–EUROPEAN RELATIONS FROM NIXON TO CARTER

Using a wide array of recently declassified archival materials in the United States and Western Europe, this collection offers new insights into the changing dynamics of transatlantic relations during the era of détente (1969–1980). Whereas prior studies of this decade have focused on the end of the Vietnam War or U.S.-Soviet relations, this volume reveals why bitter conflicts developed between the United States and its European allies, and how, contrary to conventional wisdom, European integration evolved less as a consequence of Washington's support than as a result of America's relative decline and growing U.S.-European discord. Taking into account the developments in various bilateral and multilateral settings, such as the European Community, the Helsinki process, and the G-7 summits, the contributions show that a common alliance strategy has always been a difficult undertaking, often the result of bitter confrontation and painful compromises. With clear overtones to more recent disputes, this collection demonstrates that there was never a golden age of transatlantic harmony.

Matthias Schulz is currently Professor of History of International Relations and Transnational History, Département d'Histoire Générale, Université de Genève, Switzerland. He is the author of *Regionalismus und die Gestaltung Europas* (1993), *Deutschland, der Völkerbund und die Frage der europäischen Wirtschaftsordnung, 1925–1933* (1997), and *Normen und Praxis: Das Europäische Konzert als Sicherheitsrat, 1815–1860* (2009).

Thomas A. Schwartz is Professor of History at Vanderbilt University. He is the author of *America's Germany: John J. McCloy and the Federal Republic of Germany* (1991) and *Lyndon Johnson and Europe: In the Shadow of Vietnam* (2003), as well as numerous articles on various aspects of American foreign relations.

PUBLICATIONS OF THE GERMAN HISTORICAL INSTITUTE

Edited by Hartmut Berghoff
with the assistance of David Lazar

The German Historical Institute is a center for advanced study and research whose purpose is to provide a permanent basis for scholarly cooperation among historians from the Federal Republic of Germany and the United States. The Institute conducts, promotes, and supports research into both American and German political, social, economic, and cultural history; into transatlantic migration, especially in the nineteenth and twentieth centuries; and into the history of international relations, with special emphasis on the roles played by the United States and Germany.

Recent books in the series:

Michaela Hoenicke Moore, *Know Your Enemy: The American Debate on Nazism, 1933–1945*

Suzanne L. Marchand, *German Orientalism in the Age of Empire: Religion, Race, and Scholarship*

Manfred Berg and Bernd Schaefer, editors, *Historical Justice in International Perspective: How Societies Are Trying to Right the Wrongs of the Past*

Carole Fink and Bernd Schaefer, editors, *Ostpolitik, 1969–1974: European and Global Responses*

Nathan Stoltzfus and Henry Friedlander, editors, *Nazi Crimes and the Law*

Joachim Radkau, *Nature and Power: A Global History of the Environment*

Andreas W. Daum, *Kennedy in Berlin*

Jonathan R. Zatlin, *The Currency of Socialism: Money and Political Culture in East Germany*

Peter Becker and Richard F. Wetzell, editors, *Criminals and Their Scientists: The History of Criminology in International Perspective*

Michelle Mouton, *From Nurturing the Nation to Purifying the Volk: Weimar and Nazi Family Policy, 1918–1945*

The Strained Alliance

U.S.–EUROPEAN RELATIONS FROM NIXON TO CARTER

MATTHIAS SCHULZ
Université de Genève

THOMAS A. SCHWARTZ
Vanderbilt University

GERMAN HISTORICAL INSTITUTE

Washington, D.C.
and

CAMBRIDGE
UNIVERSITY PRESS

CAMBRIDGE UNIVERSITY PRESS
Cambridge, New York, Melbourne, Madrid, Cape Town, Singapore,
São Paulo, Delhi, Dubai, Tokyo

Cambridge University Press
32 Avenue of the Americas, New York, NY 10013-2473, USA

www.cambridge.org
Information on this title: www.cambridge.org/9780521899994

First published 2010

Printed in the United States of America

A catalog record for this publication is available from the British Library.

Library of Congress Cataloging in Publication data
Schulz, Matthias, 1964–
The strained alliance : U.S.-European relations from Nixon to Carter / Matthias Schulz,
Thomas A. Schwartz.
p.   cm. – (Publications of the German Historical Institute)
Includes bibliographical references and index.
ISBN 978-0-521-89999-4 (hardback)
1. Europe – Foreign relations – United States.   2. United States – Foreign relations – Europe.
3. Detente – History – 20th century.   4. European cooperation – History –
20th century.   5. Europe – Economic integration – History.   6. European federation – History –
20th century.   7. European Economic Community – History.   I. Schwartz, Thomas Alan, 1954–
II. German Historical Institute in London.   III. Title.   IV. Series.
D1065.U5S293   2009
327.730409′047 – dc22   2009028742

ISBN 978-0-521-89999-4 Hardback

Contents

Contributors

Ronald J. Granieri, Department of History, University of Pennsylvania

William G. Gray, Department of History, Purdue University

Claudia Hiepel, Historisches Institut, Universität Duisburg-Essen

Fabian Hilfrich, School of History, Classics, and Archaeology, University of Edinburgh

Werner D. Lippert, Department of History, Indiana University of Pennsylvania

Daniel Möckli, Center for Security Studies, ETH Zurich

Gottfried Niedhart, Historisches Institut, Universität Mannheim

Alastair Noble, Foreign and Commonwealth Office, London

Joe Renouard, Department of History, The Citadel

Raj Roy, independent scholar and in-house counsel, Vodafone Group

Bernd Schaefer, Cold War International History Project, Woodrow Wilson International Center for Scholars

Joachim Scholtyseck, Institut für Geschichtswissenschaft, Rheinische Friedrich-Wilhelms-Universität Bonn

Matthias Schulz, Département d'Histoire Générale, Université de Genève

Thomas A. Schwartz, Department of History, Vanderbilt University

Sarah B. Snyder, Department of History, Yale University

D. Nathan Vigil, Department of History, Emory University

Hubert Zimmermann, Institut für Politikwissenschaft, Philipps-Universität Marburg

Preface

This is a book about transatlantic relations from the Nixon to the Carter years. During the 1970s, the U.S. war in Vietnam, the European integration process, different strategic preferences with a view to détente between the two blocs, the oil crunch and instability in the Middle East, economic and monetary globalization, and the renewed arms race challenged and, in many ways, transformed U.S.-European relations. It is the purpose of this collection to shed light on and characterize those changes from multiple perspectives. Most of the essays assembled here go beyond the classical bilateral approach and take into account, as much as possible, interactions on multilateral levels such as between the European Community and the United States, within NATO, in the Conference on Security and Cooperation in Europe (CSCE), and at the World Economic Summits that began in 1975. In addition, almost all the contributors could use recently declassified archival materials on either side of the Atlantic.

As Keith Middlemas wrote, "Without contemporary history, studies in the contemporary world – by political scientists, lawyers, economists, or specialists in international relations – rest on a dangerously relative foundation, and students are faced with a blind spot for the 'years not taught.'"[1] The book hopes to help overcome this difficulty for transatlantic relations and European integration in the 1970s. It provides rich material for courses on U.S. foreign policy, European integration in its transatlantic context, and the West's policy choices in dealing with the wider but interdependent world. It also hopes to stimulate further research on this important phase that foreshadowed the end of the Cold War.

---

[1] Keith Middlemas, *Orchestrating Europe: The Informal Politics of European Union, 1973–1995* (Hammersmith, 1995), xii.

The collection grew out of a conference on transatlantic relations held at Vanderbilt University, September 17–19, 2004. It was sponsored by the German Historical Institute, Washington, D.C.; the German Academic Exchange Service (DAAD), New York; and, at Vanderbilt University, the College of Arts and Science, the Robert Penn Warren Center for the Humanities, the Center for European Studies, the Chancellor's Office for Public Affairs, the Department of History, and the Department for Political Science.

For their support for this conference and the volume, respectively, we thank those institutions as well as our friends and colleagues there, in particular, at Vanderbilt, Richard McCarty, Michael Schoenfeld, Mona Fredericks, Marshall Eakin, Daniel Usner, Neal Tate, Joel Harrington, Ann Oslin, Rowena Olegario, Donald Hancock, Michael Bess, and Daniel Breck Walker; at the DAAD New York, Barbara Motyka, Britta Baron, and Ulrich Grothus; and at the German Historical Institute in Washington, D.C., Christof Mauch and Bernd Schaefer. We also thank the anonymous referees invited by Cambridge University Press. A special thanks goes to David Lazar, whose input and support of this project as the German Historical Institute's senior editor has been absolutely crucial, and, of course, to the contributors to this volume.

Matthias Schulz and Thomas A. Schwartz

Introduction

THOMAS A. SCHWARTZ AND MATTHIAS SCHULZ

Angry recriminations from political leaders fly across the Atlantic. A crisis builds within NATO. Street protests take place in European cities against an unpopular American war. Western countries face shortages of oil and sharp price increases for energy. The United States and Europe disagree strongly about policy in the Middle East. The threat of terrorism plagues the West.

One might guess that this would be a description of recent events, especially those concerning the American and European conflict over the Iraq War in 2003. Actually, those features are meant to characterize the 1970s.

As Mark Twain is reputed to have said, "History doesn't repeat itself, but it does rhyme a lot." In many respects, the era of the "long 1970s," that period from 1969 to 1983, seems like a not-so-distant mirror of our own time, with many of the same problems, phenomena, and protests. Indeed, the 1970s era in transatlantic relations offers us many rhymes for today, and the essays in this volume demonstrate the degree to which today's events have influenced our perspective on this recent past.

From an American point of view, the historiography of this time period is still in the shadow of the Vietnam War. The slow release of the larger documentary record has resulted in very few serious historical studies of the latter 1970s and early 1980s, and this latter period is still largely dominated by the memoir literature.[1] Vietnam remains central to the serious studies of the earlier years of the 1970s. Even Henry Kissinger's attempt to define this history with his monumental, if problematic, memoirs, was largely seen

---

1 Among the most important memoirs on the American side for the late 1970s and early 1980s are Jimmy Carter, *Keeping Faith: Memoirs of a President* (New York, 1982); Cyrus Vance, *Hard Choices: Critical Years in America's Foreign Policy* (New York, 1983); Zbigniew Brzezinski, *Power and Principle: Memoirs of the National Security Advisor, 1977–1981* (New York, 1985); Ronald Reagan, *An American Life* (New York, 1990); Alexander Haig, *Caveat: Realism, Reagan, and Foreign Policy* (New York, 1984); and George P. Shultz, *Turmoil and Triumph: My Years as Secretary of State* (New York, 1993).

1

as an attempt to explain and justify American policies in Southeast Asia, although Kissinger provided many arguments and much raw material for historians interested in other regions of the world.[2] In recent years, most historical writing on the early 1970s continues to concern America's slow exit from the war in Indochina and the Nixon administration's fruitless search for a "peace with honor."[3] Most of these books have been highly critical of Nixon's policies, either for extending the war, temporally and geographically, or from a different political perspective, for the cynical search for a decent interval before abandoning the South Vietnamese. Indeed, some of this literature accuses American leaders like Kissinger with war crimes and calls for their trial before international tribunals.[4] Only slowly and fitfully have other foreign policy issues of this era received anywhere near the same attention.

The dominant book in dealing with non-Vietnam issues, which received fulsome praise when it was first published in the Reagan era, was Raymond Garthoff's *Détente and Confrontation: American-Soviet Relations from Nixon to Reagan*. Garthoff, a foreign service officer with more than two decades of experience in Soviet affairs, provided both a historian's and an insider's perspective on U.S.–Soviet relations from 1969 to the Reagan era. He took a highly nuanced view of Nixon and Kissinger's approach to foreign policy, praising their efforts to achieve détente but critical of their inability to root détente firmly enough in American domestic politics so that it could survive the challenges faced in the Carter and Reagan years. Highly critical of Reagan's confrontational policy toward the Soviets in the early 1980s, Garthoff's history of the period tended to fault more heavily American diplomacy and American leaders for their failures. He praised European leaders for the degree to which détente in Europe "became much more of an organic process" and revived "the conception of Europe rather than the distinction between Western and Eastern Europe." He also saw in this period the beginning of a certain "American estrangement" from Europe because of the different attitudes toward détente.[5] Garthoff's book captured the prevailing orthodoxy among most scholars, an orthodoxy that remained dominant until the sudden end of the Cold War shook its foundations.

---

2 Henry Kissinger, *White House Years* (Boston, 1979); *Years of Upheaval* (Boston, 1982); and *Years of Renewal* (New York, 1999). Kissinger's book *Crisis* (New York, 2003) provides important materials on both the 1973 Yom Kippur War and the fall of Saigon in 1975.

3 Among the most recent works dealing with Vietnam in this era are Jeffrey Kimball, *Nixon's Vietnam War* (Lawrence, KS, 1998); Larry Berman, *No Peace, No Honor: Nixon, Kissinger, and Betrayal in Vietnam* (New York, 2001); and Lewis Sorley, *A Better War* (New York, 1999).

4 Christopher Hitchens, *The Trial of Henry Kissinger* (New York, 2001).

5 Raymond Garthoff, *Detente and Confrontation* (Washington, 1985), 500–1. A revised edition was published in 1994.

Garthoff's magisterial volume set the tone for many subsequent treatments of the era. In 1998, shortly before his death, William Bundy, another foreign policy official from the Kennedy and Johnson era and the brother of National Security Adviser McGeorge Bundy, published *A Tangled Web: The Making of Foreign Policy in the Nixon Presidency*. Bundy's very title captured one of his principal themes, namely that the Nixon-Kissinger foreign policy, which frequently employed secrecy and deception, was ultimately undermined by those methods, especially when it misled the American people and Congress. Echoing Garthoff's conclusions, Bundy argued that secrecy and deception were major reasons why Nixon's détente policy ultimately foundered. On other European issues, however, Bundy was less critical. Although hesitant with any praise for Nixon, Bundy concluded that, "during the Nixon era, the Alliance was strained but in the end came back together." He tended to credit other officials, like Treasury Secretary George Shultz, for this success with Europe, seeing them as having brought relations back from "an all-time low."[6] He did acknowledge that the Nixon years pioneered new structures for consultation, and that President Gerald Ford, with Kissinger's help, was able to build on those to mend alliance relations after Nixon's resignation.

Other historians also engaged in this debate, which had overtones at times of a referendum on the Kissinger style. John Lewis Gaddis, one of the preeminent American diplomatic historians, provided a more positive assessment of the Nixon-Kissinger foreign policy. Both in his still-seminal *Strategies of Containment* published originally in 1982 and in an essay on Kissinger more than a decade later for the collection *The Diplomats, 1939–1979*, Gaddis gave high marks to Nixon and Kissinger for "imparting intellectual coherence to the conduct of American foreign policy."[7] Although critical of Kissinger for his lack of appreciation for the role of ideas in foreign policy and for his inadequate understanding of economics and such developments as the information revolution, Gaddis was nevertheless sympathetic to Kissinger's attempts to educate the American public to the limits of American power. More critical assessments of Nixon, Kissinger, and détente were contained in the works of Robert Schulzinger and Keith Nelson. Schulzinger's short biography of Kissinger criticized the degree to which Kissinger's personal style, the celebrity image he created and cultivated, undermined his own effectiveness over time. "Jealous of sharing power with

6 William Bundy, *A Tangled Web* (New York, 1998), 527.
7 John Lewis Gaddis, *Strategies of Containment* (New York, 1982), 343; and "Rescuing Choice from Circumstance: The Statecraft of Henry Kissinger," in *The Diplomats 1939–1979*, ed. Cordon A. Craig and Francis L. Loewenheim (Princeton, NJ, 1994), 564–92.

others, it became nearly impossible for him to bequeath a legacy to successors," Schulzinger concluded, and "his diplomacy represented an end of an era more than it heralded a new beginning in American foreign relations."[8] For his part, Nelson criticized Nixon and Kissinger's conservative approach and continuing adherence to Cold War formulations, and he called the "detente of the 1970s . . . one of the truly great missed opportunities for reforming international relations in recent history."[9] Jussi Hahnimäki's richly documented, full-scale study of Kissinger as a policy maker, *The Flawed Architect*, echoes this criticism, seeing Kissinger's unwillingness to "grasp the intrinsic significance of local and regional circumstances to the unfolding of the Cold War," as the central weakness in his approach to foreign policy.[10]

The most recent innovative, yet highly controversial treatment of this era comes from a student of Gaddis at Yale. Jeremi Suri's *Power and Protest: Global Revolution and the Rise of Detente* is a provocative book, seeking to link the changes in diplomacy of this period with larger social and domestic forces. Suri examines developments in five countries – the United States, France, West Germany, the Soviet Union, and China – during the 1960s and early 1970s, and argues that, as a result of similar social problems, they all contended with widespread dissent and the global revolution of their young people in 1968. In response, the governments sought to construct a détente to reestablish a conservative world order to control their citizens and contain these revolutions. Détente, in Suri's view was a counterrevolution from elites when faced with mass public protest. "The promise of detente became a stick with which to beat domestic critics," he concludes. The result of this has been widespread public apathy and a loss of interest in politics, a "cynical environment," where "we are still living with the dissent and detente of a previous generation."[11]

Critics have pointed out that Suri's sweeping and ambitious argument makes little room for the enormous differences between the types of protest that developed within liberal industrialized and developed Western countries, and the movements of small groups of dissidents in the Soviet Union or government-instigated Red Guards in China. Nevertheless, Suri's daring approach to international history has provided a new paradigm for historians of the period to consider. Many of the articles in this collection take

8 Robert Schulzinger, *Henry Kissinger: Doctor of Diplomacy* (New York, 1989), 241–2.
9 Keith Nelson, *The Making of Detente* (Baltimore, 1995), 152.
10 Jussi Hahnimäki, *The Flawed Architect* (New York, 2004), 491.
11 Jeremi Suri, *Power and Protest: Global Revolution and the Rise of Detente* (Cambridge, MA, 2003), 258–9.

his account into consideration but find it lacking in explanatory power. The transatlantic relationship of the 1970s reflects the similar social and economic problems that Western democracies confronted, but the foreign policy changes that occurred do not seem directly connected to the issue that Suri isolates.

Until archival records from the 1970s started recently to become available for research, historians interested in the inner workings of Western European policy making during that decade were heavily dependent on the memoirs and published writings of leading political and diplomatic figures.[12] Those accounts are now being supplemented by a growing scholarly literature based on archival research and newly published volumes in documentary series such as the U.S. State Department's *Foreign Relations of the United States*; the *Akten zur Auswärtigen Politik der Bundesrepublik Deutschland*, edited by the Institut für Zeitgeschichte on behalf of the German Foreign Office; and the British Foreign and Commonwealth Office's *Documents on British Policy Overseas*. Because many of the official records of the later portion of the period covered by this volume are still not accessible to researchers, there are still gaps in the scholarly literature. Any review of the historiography must, by necessity, be selective.

As Max Kaase and Andrew Kohut have shown recently in *Estranged Friends? The Transatlantic Consequences of Societal Change*, Western Europeans' admiration and sympathy for the United States declined markedly from the early 1960s to the Nixon years.[13] European opinion of the United States improved briefly at the outset of the Carter presidency, only to turn

---

12 A selection of the most important ones would include Georges Pompidou, *Entretiens et discours, 1968–1974*, 2 vols. (Paris, 1975); Michel Jobert, *Mémoires d'avenir* (Paris, 1974) and *L'autre régard* (Paris, 1976); Valéry Giscard d'Estaing, *Le pouvoir et la vie* (Paris, 1988); Edward Heath, *The Course of My Life: My Autobiography* (London, 1998); Harold Wilson, *Final Term: The Labour Government 1974–1976* (London, 1979); Tony Benn, *Against the Tide: Diaries* (London, 1989), James Callaghan, *Time and Chance* (London, 1987); Margaret Thatcher, *The Downing Street Years* (New York, 1993); Giulio Andreotti, *The U.S.A. Up Close: From the Atlantic Pact to Bush* (New York, 1992); Willy Brandt, *Begegnungen und Einsichten* (Hamburg, 1976) [English: *People and Politics: The Years 1960–1975* (Boston, 1976)]; Egon Bahr, *Zu meiner Zeit* (Munich, 1996); Helmut Schmidt, *Menschen und Mächte* (Berlin, 1999 [1987]), *Deutschland und seine Nachbarn: Menschen und Mächte II* (Berlin, 1990), and *Weggefährten: Erinnerungen und Reflexionen* (Berlin, 1996); Hans-Dietrich Genscher, *Erinnerungen* (Berlin, 1999); Roy Jenkins, *A Life at the Centre* (London, 1991) and *European Diary 1977–1981* (London, 1989); Horst Ungerer, *A Concise History of European Monetary Integration: From EPU to EMU* (Westport, CT, 1997); and Bino Olivi, *L'Europe difficile: Histoire politique de la Communauté européenne* (Paris, 1998).

13 The percentage of people holding a favorable view of the United States hit postwar highs in 1964 after the tragic death of President John F. Kennedy, reaching 84 percent in West Germany, 74 percent in Italy, 66 percent in Britain, and 41 percent in France. A low point was reached in West Germany in 1973, when only 45 percent had a favorable view of the United States. In Great Britain, Italy, and France, the figures had sunk even lower by 1976, to 24, 25, and 28 percent, respectively. See Max Kaase and Andrew Kohut, *Estranged Friends? The Transatlantic Consequences of Societal Change* (New York, 1996), 55.

more critical once again. It was only in the mid-1980s, as Ronald Reagan became more enthusiastic about détente, that views of the United States in Western Europe became more favorable. It is not surprising that some contemporary scholars and observers thought that the Atlantic alliance was in "crisis" or that the allies might drift apart.[14] Scholarly discussion of the causes and consequences of the strains within the alliance during the 1970s has focused on the bilateral relations between the United States and the individual European states, West Germany's *Ostpolitik*, and European integration. Here, we concentrate on recent studies of European governments' dealings with Washington, which have centered in large part on the leading personalities, and on European integration.

In Western Europe, three long-term processes during the 1960s and 1970s influenced the intra-European balance, the dynamics of European integration, and transatlantic relations. First, President Charles de Gaulle's decision in 1966 to take France out of the integrated military structures of NATO made West Germany the United States' most important European ally next to Britain. Second, in the wake of decolonization, the geopolitical orientation of France and Britain became more European. And third, Italy and West Germany both enjoyed a boost in international status from their strong economic growth up until 1973. Having entered the 1970s as Western Europe's strongest economy, West Germany was able to weather the oil crisis better than most other Western nations.

The era of Social Democratic–Liberal coalition governments under Willy Brandt (1969–1974) and Helmut Schmidt (1974–1982) marks an important transition in West Germany's relations with its allies.[15] A more self-assured West Germany strengthened its diplomatic status by establishing closer relations to Moscow through a new Ostpolitik.[16] At the same time, Bonn

---

14 Walter Hahn and Robert L. Pfaltzgraff Jr., eds., *Atlantic Community in Crisis: A Redefinition of the Transatlantic Relationship* (New York, 1979); Richard C. Eichenberg, ed., *Drifting Together or Apart? U.S.-European Relations in the Paul-Henri Spaak Lectures Harvard University 1981–1984* (Lanham, MD, 1986).

15 See, e.g., Detlef Junker, ed., *Die USA und Deutschland im Zeitalter des Kalten Krieges 1945–1990: Ein Handbuch*, vol. 2, *1968–1990* (Stuttgart, 2001); Klaus Larres and Torsten Oppelland, eds., *Deutschland und die USA im 20. Jahrhundert: Geschichte der politischen Beziehungen* (Darmstadt, 1997); Kathleen Burk and Melvyn Stokes, *The United States and the European Alliance since 1945* (Oxford, 1999); Georges-Henri Soutou, *L'alliance incertaine: Les rapports politico-stratégiques franco-allemands, 1954–1996* (Paris, 1996); Gilbert Ziebura, *Die deutsch-französischen Beziehungen seit 1945* (Stuttgart, 1997); Klaus Larres and Elizabeth Meehan, eds., *Uneasy Allies: German-British Relations and European Integration since 1945* (Oxford, 2000).

16 E.g., Peter Bender, *Neue Ostpolitik: vom Mauerbau zum Moskauer Vertrag* (Munich, 1986); M. E. Sarotte, *Dealing with the Devil: East Germany, Détente, and Ostpolitik, 1969–1973* (Chapel Hill, NC, 2001); Markus Bernath, *Wandel ohne Annäherung: die SPD und Frankreich in der Phase der neuen Ostpolitik 1969–1974* (Baden-Baden, 2001); and David C. Geyer and Bernd Schaefer, eds., *American Détente and German Ostpolitik, 1969–1972: Bulletin of the German Historical Institute, Supplement 1* (2004).

distanced itself from Washington, where both Brandt and Ostpolitik were eyed with some skepticism. Unjustly so, argues Peter Merseburger in what could be described as the first scholarly biography of the chancellor.[17] It was, after all, Brandt who brought Bonn more into line with the détente policy Washington had pursued since the Cuban missile crisis.[18] Without calling the Atlantic alliance into question, the Brandt government began to look for political means to improve German security; by normalizing of relations with Moscow, it hoped to establish closer links with the East German state. Merseburger concludes that Brandt's Ostpolitik was crucial in giving West Germany the "capacity for action" in the international arena.[19]

West Germany's capacity for action was also enhanced through European integration. Haig Simonian argues that Brandt's enthusiasm for European integration was partly due to the need to "balance and enhance" his Ostpolitik by developing closer links to the West.[20] Andreas Wilkens contends, by contrast, that Brandt's *Westpolitik*, especially his European integration policies, probably would have been much the same without Ostpolitik.[21] In any case, Bonn's closer cooperation with France on European integration suggests that it was moving somewhat closer to a Gaullist vision of Europe and seeking a measure of independence in foreign policy from the United States.

Under Brandt's Atlanticist successor in the Chancellery, relations between Bonn and Washington improved during Gerald Ford's brief tenure but then became more strained than ever before during the presidency of Jimmy Carter. Barbara Heep attributes the difficulties in German–American relations in the late 1970s in large part to the differing personalities of the pragmatist Schmidt and the idealist Carter.[22] Klaus Wiegrefe goes so far as to speak of a "rupture" (*Zerwürfnis*) in German–American relations during the Schmidt–Carter years.[23] Wiegrefe, who had access to some of Schmidt's papers, argues that neither Schmidt nor Carter wanted German–American relations to deteriorate, but a variety of factors led to that result. In addition

17 Peter Merseburger, *Willy Brandt 1913–1992: Visionär und Realist* (Stuttgart, 2002). On Washington's view of Brandt, see 622ff. Other recent biographies include Hartmut Soell, *Helmut Schmidt 1918–1969: Vernunft und Leidenschaft* (Munich, 2003) and Michael Schwelien, *Helmut Schmidt: Ein Leben für den Frieden* (Hamburg, 2003).
18 Merseburger, *Willy Brandt*, 623.   19 Ibid., 856.
20 Haig Simonian, *The Privileged Partnership: Franco-German Relations, 1969–1984* (Oxford, 1985), 82, 94.
21 Andreas Wilkens, "Westpolitik, Ostpolitik and the Project of the Economic and Monetary Union: Germany's European Policy in the Brandt Era," *Journal des Économists et des Études Humaines* 5, no. 1 (1999): 100.
22 Barbara Heep, *Helmut Schmidt und Amerika: Eine schwierige Partnerschaft* (Bonn, 1990).
23 Klaus Wiegrefe, *Das Zerwürfnis: Helmut Schmidt, Jimmy Carter und die Krise der deutsch-amerikanischen Beziehungen* (Berlin, 2003).

to the end of the golden age of postwar economic growth with the oil crisis, Wiegrefe points to Bonn's efforts to gain influence within the Atlantic alliance at a time when Washington was looking to Western Europe for greater support on the international stage. A certain German disillusionment about the often invoked German-American friendship, Schmidt's arrogance, and Carter's lack of foreign policy experience and insensitivity to issues of concern to West Germany also contributed to the deterioration in relations between the two countries.[24] The argument that Bonn was seeking to play a more prominent international role fits well with Inge Schwammel's contention that Schmidt's European policy was motivated by the wish to transform West Germany into a great power. European integration was instrumentalized by Schmidt, according to Schwammel, to gain leverage in Washington.[25] Herbert Dittgen, in contrast, argues that despite the "irritations" between Schmidt and Carter, German-American cooperation was, given the considerable economic, political, and military challenges of the period, very "successful."[26]

West Germany's growing stature explains the end of French resistance to British entry into the European Community. Haig Simonian and Georges-Henri Soutou emphasize that Britain became a welcome balance to West Germany in French eyes, especially as Bonn took the initiative in improving relations with Moscow.[27] President Georges Pompidou, as Andreas Wilkens has pointed out, was ready to welcome Britain into the European Community from the moment that British Prime Minister Edward Heath gave his assurance that he, too, was opposed to the idea of a supranational Europe.[28] Franco-British agreement on the bases of European integration left West Germany an isolated proponent of a federal Europe.

Ostpolitik and West Germany's growing international prominence also help explain, Soutou argues, why Pompidou attempted to establish something like a special relationship with the United States, especially in the area of nuclear arms.[29] That initiative failed, however, because, first, Pompidou remained too Gaullist, insisting on France's independence in political and security matters, and refused to cooperate in NATO. Second, Kissinger

24 Wiegrefe, *Das Zerwürfnis*, 371–94.
25 Inge Schwammel, *Deutschlands Aufstieg zur Großmacht. Die Instrumentalisierung der europäischen Integration 1974–1994* (Frankfurt am Main, 1997).
26 Herbert Dittgen, "Die Ära der Ost-West-Verhandlungen und der Wirtschafts- und Währungskrisen (1969–1981)" in Larres and Oppelland, *Deutschland und die USA im 20. Jahrhundert*, 178–203.
27 Simonian, *The Privileged Partnership*, 117–20, 153–5. Soutou, *L'alliance incertaine*, 316–17.
28 Wilkens, "Westpolitik, Ostpolitik," 84.
29 Georges-Henri Soutou, "Georges Pompidou and U.S.-European Relations" in *Between Empire and Alliance: America and Europe during the Cold War*, ed. Marc Trachtenberg (Lanham, MD, 2003), 157–200.

and Nixon, despite "their proclaimed vision of a multipolar world," Soutou argues, "never really abandoned the notion of a U.S.-led Atlantic world."[30] The relationship between France and the United States thus remained, in the words of Frank Costigliola, a "cold alliance."[31] Nonetheless, as Costigliola points out, the 1970s saw a "slow thaw" between the two governments after the deep freeze of the de Gaulle era, due in large part to the end of the Vietnam War and the ascent of Valéry Giscard d'Estaing to the French presidency in 1974.[32] Giscard's attitude toward the United States varied according to circumstances, as Hélène Miard-Delacroix has argued. In some instances, Giscard was in favor of close policy coordination among the members of the Atlantic alliance, especially on monetary matters. At other times, he resisted the United States in the name of French independence.[33] Giscard, holding to a policy of "multipolarity," thought France's power would be enhanced through an independent Europe.[34] Still, France did join the European Planning Group in NATO during his presidency, and he strongly supported NATO's dual-track decision in 1979.

Studies dealing with British foreign policy in the 1970s frequently focus on either London's often-difficult dealings with Europe[35] or its "special relationship" with the United States.[36] The Europhile Edward Heath brought Great Britain into the European Community in 1973. Heath's memoirs not only attest to his love affair with Europe but also stand as the broadest firsthand British account of European politics in the 1960 and 1970s.[37] A major question was – and remains – how far Heath was willing to commit Britain to Europe at the expense of relations with the United States. He was challenged by members of his own Conservative Party and of the Labour

---

30 Soutou, "Georges Pompidou and U.S.-European Relations," 194.
31 Frank Costigliola, *France and the United States: The Cold Alliance since World War II* (New York, 1992).
32 Ibid., 160–86. See also Charles Cogan, *Oldest Allies, Guarded Friends: The United States and France since 1940* (Westport, CT, 1994).
33 Hélène Miard Delacroix, *Partenaires de choix? Le chancelier Helmut Schmidt et la France (1974–1982)* (Bern, 1993), 172–206.
34 Simonian, *Privileged Partnership*, 240.
35 See, e.g., Hugo Young, *This Blessed Plot: Britain and Europe from Churchill to Blair* (London, 1998). See also David Gowland and Arthur Turner, *Reluctant Europeans: Britain and European Integration 1945–1998* (Harlow, U.K., 2000); and John W. Young, *Britain and European Unity 1945–1999* (Houndsmills, U.K., 2000). On the historiography, see Oliver J. Daddow, *Britain and Europe since 1945: Historiographical Perspectives on Integration* (Manchester, U.K., 2004): Daddow concentrates on the 1950s and 1960s, where there is a historiography properly speaking.
36 See, e.g., John Baylis, *Anglo-American Defense Relations 1939–1984: The Special Relationship* (New York, 1981); C. J. Bartlett, *"The Special Relationship": A Political History of Anglo-American Relations since 1945* (London, 1992); and John Dumbrell, *A Special Relationship: Anglo-American Relations in the Cold War and After* (Houndsmills, U.K., 2001).
37 Heath, *Course of My Life*. On this period, see also Wilson, *Final Term*; Benn, *Against the Tide*; and Jenkins, *A Life at the Centre*.

opposition alike who wanted to "defend the Atlantic and Commonwealth links at all costs."[38] In Heath's view, though, as he told Pompidou, "there could be no special partnership between Britain and the United States, even if Britain wanted it, because one was barely a quarter the size of the other." He was in favor, rather, of a "strong Europe . . . speaking with one voice" that would be able to exert influence in the world.[39] Personality may also have played a part in London's tilt toward Europe under Heath. He and Nixon, a recent study notes, did not get along well with one another.[40] In his memoirs, Heath also criticizes Kissinger for his "lack of sensitivity" toward the concerns of the Europeans.[41]

Harold Wilson's renegotiation of the terms of Britain's entry into the European Community (EC) and the referendum on membership after the country had already joined the EC brought the British-European honeymoon to an end and Paris and Bonn closer together.[42] Although Wilson campaigned in favor of continued EC membership during the referendum, he did so unenthusiastically. James Callaghan's attitude to Europe was similarly ambiguous. Seeing himself as a devout Atlanticist,[43] he had opposed British entry in 1971–72 while in the opposition.[44] He became a reluctant supporter of EC membership, however, while serving as foreign secretary in Wilson's cabinet, which was deeply divided on the issue. Membership in the EC, he believed, was "only marginal" to Britain's economic success or failure.[45] Reversing his earlier position, Callaghan came to see the European Community as a vehicle for Western Europe to assert itself vis-à-vis the superpowers,[46] but he nonetheless preferred to deal with the United States bilaterally in the interest of maintaining the special relationship.[47] Callaghan saw Britain as a mediator between Europe and the United States,

---

38 Young, *This Blessed Plot*, 225.
40 Dumbrell, *A Special Relationship*, 62, 73–8.
42 Young, *This Blessed Plot*, 281–5.
44 Ibid., 273.

39 Heath, *Course of My Life*, 370.
41 Heath, *Course of My Life*, 492.
43 Ibid., 285.

45 Ibid., 326. This can easily be contested, of course. Despite its rather dismal economic performance and economic policies during the 1970s, Britain quickly overtook West Germany and France in foreign direct investment (FDI) inflows after it entered the European Community. Even before Thatcher became prime minister, the level of FDI in Britain was much greater than that of France and West Germany combined. In Britain, from 1971 to 1980, FDI totaled US$40.5 billion: in the same period, France received $16.5 billion and West Germany $14 billion in FDI. This had largely to do with the changed location of Britain – being inside rather than outside of the European Community. See data in Ziebura, *Die deutsch-französischen Beziehungen,* 318; cf. Matthias Schulz, "Vom Atlantiker zum Europäer? Helmut Schmidt, deutsche Interessen und die europäische Einigung," in *Die Bundesrepublik und die europäische Einigung 1949–2000: Politische Akteure, gesellschaftliche Kräfte und internationale Erfahrungen,* Mareike König and Matthias Schulz, eds. (Stuttgart, 2004), 213.

46 Callaghan, *Time and Chance*, 330.

47 See Matthias Schulz, "The Reluctant European: Helmut Schmidt, the European Community, and Transatlantic Relations," in this volume.

and during his tenure as prime minister, Britain was, as David Gowland and Arthur Turner conclude, "semi-detached" from Europe.[48]

Margaret Thatcher, by contrast, thought that Britain had "underrated the potential advantage to Britain of access to the Common Market"[49] and that a special relationship with neither the United States nor the Commonwealth could serve as a substitute for EC membership. In the referendum of 1975, she led the Tory's campaign in favor of continued membership. Her support for the European Community notwithstanding, however, Thatcher's negotiating style and the long-running dispute over Britain's rebate from the EC budget were sources of tension within the community and impeded progress on a number of issues.[50] Moreover, Thatcher showed little of the warmth toward Europe that she clearly felt for the United States.[51]

The memoirs of figures like Callaghan and Thatcher are now being supplemented by scholarly studies based on research in newly accessible archival records, and the history of European integration has emerged as a major topic in contemporary history. Studies of the European Community and the process of integration in the 1970s have centered on two questions: First, was the 1970s a "stagnant decade"[52] or a period of fundamental transformation for Europe? Second, how far was European integration during the decade a continuation of what Geir Lundestad has called American empire by integration? How far, in other words, were the Europeans able to redress the inequality and asymmetry of power that were, according to Lundestad, the precondition of American predominance?[53]

The balance of economic power had certainly begun to tip more in Europe's favor as the 1970s opened. By the late 1960s, Harm Schröter argues, the Americanization of the European economy was waning because "Europeans had caught up with, or even overtaken, their former teachers."[54] During the 1970s, the European Community outpaced the United States

---

48 Gowland and Turner, *Reluctant Europeans*, 214–29.
49 Margaret Thatcher, *The Path to Power* (New York, 1995), 126.
50 See Schulz, "Vom Atlantiker," 209–13.
51 See also Paul Sharp, *Thatcher's Diplomacy: The Revival of British Foreign Policy* (Houndsmills, 1997).
52 Even the skeptical Keith Middlemas, who labels the period from 1973 to 1983 a "stagnant decade," admits that "EC institutions sustained the idea of integration with an often surprising momentum," and that the substantial progress toward European union achieved later, from 1985 to 1992, was the result of an "accumulation of long-planned strategies at different levels within the Community." Keith Middlemas, *Orchestrating Europe: The Informal Politics of European Union, 1973–1995* (Hammersmith, 1995), 73–110, quote at 73.
53 Geir Lundestad, *"Empire" by Integration: The United States and European Integration, 1945–1997* (Oxford, 1998).
54 Harm G. Schröter, *Americanization of the European Economy: A Compact Survey of American Economic Influence in Europe since the 1880s* (Dordrecht, 2005), 206.

in economic growth, steel production, trade, and development aid.[55] It was against this background that advocates of European integration embarked on the establishment of a "second-generation Europe."[56] This new Europe built upon but went beyond the Common Market. As envisaged at its summit in the Hague in December 1969,[57] the EC was to be enlarged and its institutions strengthened. Europe would pursue economic and monetary union, and it would gain a voice in international affairs. Western Europe, in other words, would translate its growing economic power into political influence by transforming the European Community into a European Union. In the years after the summit in the Hague, the European Community implemented policies designed to increase European economic competitiveness and internal cohesion and began to explore new areas of cooperation, most notably foreign policy and development aid.[58]

---

55 From 1949 to 1969, annual growth averaged 4.1 percent in Western Europe and 2.7 percent in the United States. In the period from 1965 to 1980, the average growth rate in the nine EC countries (3.7 percent) also surpassed that of the United States (2.7 percent). It is difficult to compare gross domestic products because of the dollar fluctuations in the 1970s. In 1969, the EC Six had a combined GDP lower than that of the United States. In May 1977, just before the dollar began its second major decline, Roy Jenkins put the United States' GDP at just about 40 percent of the EC Nine; in 1987, when the dollar was trading at higher rates against European currencies, the U.S. GDP was about 70 percent of the EC Twelve's. Steel production in the EC Nine came to 144 million metric tons in 1973 and 134 million tons in 1979; in the United States, the figures were 137 and 123 million tons, respectively. In 1965, the United States still exported 50 percent more merchandise than the second-largest exporting nation, West Germany; by 1971, the difference had dropped down to 11 percent, and by 1978, to 1.4 percent. In 1960, the original members of the European Community – Belgium, France, Germany, Italy, Luxembourg, and the Netherlands – accounted for 23 percent of world trade; by 1970, the figure had risen to 32 percent. After Britain, Ireland, and Denmark joined in 1973, the European Community's share of world trade came to 40 percent. The European Community's exports to the rest of the world were roughly a third higher than those of the United States in 1973. The differences in development aid are also striking. In 1965, the United States spent $4 billion on aid, more than twice as much as the EC Six ($1.4 billion); by 1980, the EC Nine spent twice as much as the United States ($13 billion against $7.1 billion). See Christoph Buchheim, "Von der aufgeklärten Hegemonie zur Partnerschaft: Die USA und Westdeutschland in der Weltwirtschafts 1945–1968," in *Die USA und Deutschland im Zeitalter des Kalten Krieges 1945–1990: Ein Handbuch,* ed. Detlef Junker (Stuttgart, 2001), 1:401–23, 402; Gerold Ambrosius, *Wirtschaftsraum Europa: Vom Ende der Nationalökonomien* (Frankfurt am Main, 1996), 96l; Nicholas V. Gianaris, *The European Community and the United States: Economic Relations* (New York, 1991), 67, 70, 163; Claudia Hiepel, "The Hague Summit of the European Community, Britain's Entry, and the 'New' Atlantic Partnership, 1969–1970," in this volume; Jenkins, *European Diary,* 99; B[rian] R. Mitchell, *International Historical Statistics: Europe 1750–1988* (New York, 1992), 460, and *International Historical Statistics: The Americas, 1750–1988* (New York, 1992), 356; and Harold James, *International Monetary Cooperation since Bretton Woods* (Washington, D.C., 1996), 473–4.

56 Franz Knipping and Matthias Schönwald, eds., *Aufbruch zum Europa der zweiten Generation: Die europäische Einigung 1969–1984* (Trier, 2004).

57 See *Journal of European Integration History* 9, no. 2 (2003), which is devoted to the summit in the Hague.

58 See Ingeborg Trömmel, "Die EG in den Jahren 1970–1984: Neue Politikmuster als Katalysatoren der Integration," in Knipping and Schönwald, *Aufbruch zum Europa,* 269–84.

Scholars are at odds on whether the European Community adapted successfully to the weakened position of the United States and its more nationalist policies during the 1970s. Gustav Schmidt argues that, despite some progress, the EC failed to take advantage of the opportunities open to it.[59] The EC, according to Schmidt, was unable to develop the means to exert political influence because the member states were unwilling to give up sovereignty or to develop the kind of hard power the United States had. Historians and political scientists more alert to the potential of soft power, in contrast, have argued that, halting as progress toward a common foreign policy may have been, Europe could claim a measure of success on the international stage – for example, in assisting the détente process, in contributing to the abolition of apartheid in South Africa, and in reaching out to developing nations.[60] As Christopher Piening has pointed out, the European Community's global ambitions found expression in a large number of interregional cooperation and development agreements during the 1970s.[61] At the same time, it also embarked on a new kind of multilateral diplomacy. In 1971, for example, the European Community and the United States established regular meetings between members of the European Parliament and the U.S. Congress. Since the Ford administration, the holder of the European Council's rotating presidency and the U.S. president have likewise met on a regular basis.[62] The European Commission has been represented by its president at the summit meetings of the major industrial powers since 1977.

American leaders often found it difficult to understand what was going on in the European Community. But although uncertain whether European integration was good for American interests or whether they should

59 Gustav Schmidt, "Europa und die Welt: Transatlantische Beziehungen und 'Dritte Welt' in den 1970er Jahren," in Knipping and Schönwald, *Aufbruch zum Europa*, 96.
60 Elfriede Regelsberger, "Die EPZ in den achtziger Jahren: Ein qualitativer Sprung?" in *Die Europäische Politische Zusammenarbeit in den achtziger Jahren: Eine gemeinsame Aussenpolitik für Westeuropa?*, eds. Alfred Pijpers, Elfriede Regelsberger, and Wolfgang Wessels (Bonn, 1989), 21–70; Frank R. Pfetsch, "Die Entwicklung der Europäischen Politischen Zusammenarbeit: Zwischen Identität und Handlungsfähigkeit," in Knipping and Schönwald, *Aufbruch zum Europa*, 115–30. See also the following collections of documents: Christopher Hill and Karen Smith, eds., *European Foreign Policy: Key Documents* (London, 2000); and Auswärtiges Amt, ed., *Europäische Politische Zusammenarbeit (EPZ) auf dem Weg zu einer Gemeinsamen Aussen- und Sicherheitspolitik (GASP): Dokumentation* (Bonn, 1992).
61 See Christopher Piening, *Global Europe: The European Union in World Affairs* (Boulder, 1997); Kurt Düwell, "Die Entwicklungspolitik der Europäischen Gemeinschaft zwischen Jaundé und Lomé (1969–1984)," in Knipping and Schönwald, *Aufbruch zum Europa*, 187–200; William Brown, *The European Union and Africa: The Restructuring of North-South Relations* (London, 2002), 31–72; Martin Holland, *The European Union and the Third World* (Houndsmills, U.K., 2002), 25–51; Søren Dosenrade and Anders Stubkjaer, *The European Union and the Middle East* (London, 2002), 52–119.
62 Lundestad, *"Empire" by Integration*, 107.

actively support it, they did not try deliberately to impede the Europeans. And although Western Europe's leaders differed as to how close transatlantic ties should be and how independently Europe should act on the international stage, there was a basic consensus in Europe during the 1970s that the Atlantic partnership remained necessary and desirable. Consequently, the Europeans made sure that EC initiatives in monetary, development, and foreign policy were compatible with the goals and policies of the Atlantic alliance. In trade policy, its major area of responsibility, the EC also tried to accommodate U.S. interests during the Tokyo Round of GATT (General Agreement on Tariffs and Trade) negotiations.[63] The European integration process did not call the alliance into question, but it did create a new diplomatic culture that, on the one hand, made it more difficult for Washington to assert its leadership and to have its way in political and economic conflicts and, on the other hand, allowed the Europeans to safeguard their interests and voice their concerns more effectively.[64] Adapting to this change in culture has proved a long and difficult process for Washington.

The articles assembled here, using newly available archival material from both the United States and Western Europe, cover the major transatlantic issues during the long 1970s: growing superpower détente, increasing European integration, and a changing transatlantic environment in financial and monetary structures. They also record the problems within these developments, the rise and fall of détente, the complex nature of alliance politics, the difficulties within the European integration process, and the challenges posed by terrorism to Western democracies. This was also a time when the Middle East, along with energy and oil issues, became central questions to the West, and led to a type of trial separation between Europe and the United States in a way that, despite its length and all of the protests, the Vietnam War had never done. Many of the authors see the roots of some contemporary differences between Europe and the United States in this decade.

Gottfried Niedhart begins the first chapter with an overview of one of the main issues of contention during the early part of this era. Drawing on his comprehensive knowledge of the origins of Ostpolitik, as well as on the archives in the United States, Britain, and Germany, Niedhart presents

---

63 Andreas Falke, "Zwischen liberalem Multilateralismus, Neoprotektionismus und regionaler Integration: Amerikanische und deutsche Handelspolitik," in Junker, *Die USA und Deutschland*, 341–52, 345.
64 The best history of NATO is the three-volume *A History of NATO: The First Fifty Years*, ed. Gustav Schmidt (New York, 2001).

Ostpolitik as a central stimulus to America's pursuit of détente, the "engine of peaceful change" that led the Nixon administration, not always willingly, toward engagement with the Soviet Union. Recognizing the historically based distrust within the United States and other Western countries of any German initiatives in foreign policy, Niedhart nevertheless argues for the basic compatibility of Ostpolitik with integration into the Western alliance. He concludes that, despite NATO's guarantee of the containment of West Germany, Nixon and Kissinger dramatically overreacted to Brandt's efforts, fearing German flexibility. Ultimately, in Niedhart's view, the final peaceful outcome of 1989 vindicated the vision of Willy Brandt and, especially, Egon Bahr.

Bernd Schaefer's contribution follows in a similar vein as Niedhart's, providing a wealth of additional detail concerning the West German political battles set off by Ostpolitik. His chapter makes it clear how strongly Christian Democratic leaders lobbied Washington leaders against Brandt's policies, feeding Nixon and Kissinger's fears about the ultimate intentions of the Social Democratic leader. Schaefer shows how deep the resentment and dislike of Brandt was among American officials, especially Nixon, who associated the German chancellor with the Kennedys, liberalism, and all manner of things he hated. Still, in Schaefer's view, the Americans held their noses and supported Ostpolitik because it served American interests in regard to improving relations with the Soviet Union, especially in 1972, when Nixon and Kissinger recognized that the peacemaker image would be essential to electoral victory in November. He concludes that the American record displays "to a surprising extent a pragmatic, cooperative, and sometimes even friendly approach." Where Schaefer differs from Niedhart is in his argument that neither détente nor Ostpolitik really aimed to challenge Soviet power in Eastern Europe and that both sought stability and security more than political transformation in the East.

Werner Lippert and Ronald Granieri provide very different and contrasting perspectives on Ostpolitik. Lippert's emphasis on the deliberate use by Brandt of economic incentives for West German business to trade with the Soviet Union leads him to argue that Brandt was trying to achieve real autonomy for the Federal Republic from the United States. Ultimately, Brandt sought reunification by changing the dynamic of Soviet-German relations. In particular, the gas pipeline deal that Brandt would advocate risked making Germany energy dependent on the Soviet Union. Taking issue with Niedhart and Schaefer, Lippert argues that Nixon and Kissinger did not grasp how threatening Brandt's approach was to the alliance and that they failed to see the "inherent dangers of such close economic cooperation," in large measure because both leaders underestimated the role of trade and economic issues in German politics. In many respects, Lippert's argument sees the roots for the contemporary U.S.-German problems, so in evidence during the Iraq War, as rooted in Brandt's drive for separation from American hegemony. In contrast, Granieri's essay on the Christian Democrats in opposition during this period paints them as placing almost blind faith in their American patron. The problem was that the United States no longer saw the Christian Democratic Union (CDU) as essential to its interests in Europe. Granieri argues that the Nixon administration played "both sides against each other, using the Union as a possible brake on Brandt, while also working with Brandt and Bahr to advance an American détente agenda." In effect, the Americans were able to manipulate Ostpolitik and banish vestiges of Gaullism from the CDU, so when it returned to power with Helmut Kohl in 1982, the party was reliably Atlanticist. In contrast to Lippert's view of an American defeat and an assertion of a more independent Germany, Granieri argues that the Americans had achieved a victory over those Europeans who wanted closer European integration and more autonomy, asserting a "hollow hegemony" in a condition that continues to bedevil the U.S.-European relationship.

Did the Atlantic widen in the early 1970s? The four authors in the second section cover the relaunching of the movement toward European integration, the collapse of the Bretton Woods international monetary system, and the Anglo-American special relationship with a view to this overarching question. The contributions reflect on our understanding of Atlanticism, European integration, and the crises faced during this era. Claudia Hiepel emphasizes the importance of the Hague summit in reenergizing the European movement in late 1969. The changes in leadership in France and West Germany, with Georges Pompidou and Willy Brandt coming to power, offered a new opportunity to restart Europe. Unlike de Gaulle, Pompidou was prepared to accede to European enlargement, most importantly British membership in the European Community, in part to offset Germany's increasing power. Hiepel's chapter also makes clear that, even had the Nixon administration not been preoccupied with Vietnam, the European project itself was in such a fragile state of transition that there were "hardly any signals from the community that it would take up the new Atlantic partnership" that Nixon had suggested. As she rightly notes, the European community of this time was a "'shackled giant' whose hands were bound and who did not know what to do with his power and potential."

The collapse of the Bretton Woods international monetary order is the subject that concerns both Hubert Zimmerman and William Gray, though their approaches to this question differ. Zimmerman emphasizes the degree to which the collapse of Bretton Woods contributed to the evolution of a European monetary order and stimulated the strengthening of European institutions. Although in the short run the United States benefited from Nixon's decision to end the gold-dollar link, it failed in its "core monetary objective" of "keeping Europe open to American trade." It also inadvertently stimulated a process that would contribute to the creation of a powerful rival to the dollar in the development of a single European currency. Both Zimmerman and Gray see an important and critical change in German policy during this period, away from its previous cooperation with the United States and toward a Franco-German alignment on monetary issues. Both stress the degree to which Willy Brandt used a pro-French European monetary policy as a way to "defang Christian Democratic attacks against his foreign policy," namely Ostpolitik, "by reaffirming his administration's good citizenship in Western Europe." Although Brandt did have domestic political motives for his turn toward Europe, Gray argues that American policy played into his hands. Gray is particularly critical of the way in which the American unilateralism of August 1971, perhaps best symbolized by Treasury Secretary John Connally's "screw them before they screw you" attitude toward the Europeans, compromised the position of German leaders like Karl Schiller who wanted to cooperate with the United States on monetary policy. American policies, designed for the domestic audience and to produce results favorable for Nixon's reelection in 1972, helped drive Paris and Bonn together. With Schiller's successor Helmut Schmidt, forging a Franco-German consensus, even if that meant "pandering to French vanity—allowing Paris to 'save Europe' again," was more important than insisting on West Germany's own economic priorities within the European Community.

Raj Roy's case study of the Rolls-Royce–Lockheed crisis provides a window into understanding why the British, even under their most pro-European of prime ministers, were still drawn toward the special relationship with the United States, often to the great annoyance of their continental European counterparts. As Roy makes clear, the extraordinary degree of Anglo-American economic interdependence, which had also created webs of personal and institutional connections between the two countries, made it very difficult for Prime Minister Edward Heath not to act to help save Rolls-Royce's contract with Lockheed in 1971. Heath may not have liked Nixon – it seems few European leaders actually did – but he still had to take seriously his pleas for action, as well as the domestic political impact in the United States of British policy. Heath was also aware of these implications because of the network of informal connections between British and American companies. What Roy presents in his case study can be viewed as a rejoinder to the frequently facile comments of diplomatic historians about the preferences of leaders such as Heath – yes, he was pro-European, but this didn't mean he could act in disregard of many years of previous history and the development of alliance relations. As Roy argues, "Wherever the two countries shared a community of interest, the unique relationship between them would be likely to survive any challenges which lay ahead." The special relationship survived Heath and would prosper again under Wilson, Callaghan, and Thatcher, and Roy's chapter helps make clear why it was so durable.

The major transatlantic crisis that followed on the heels of the end of Bretton Woods and developed from the Year of Europe initiative taken by the U.S. National Security adviser and future secretary of state Henry Kissinger in April 1973, and its consequences up until 1975, are analyzed in the third section of this collection. On the basis of recently declassified European archival sources, Daniel Möckli argues that Kissinger, disconcerted by U.S.-European disputes over détente and trade, wanted a "new consensus on security" and more interallied political and economic cooperation. Because he also seemed to confine the Europeans to a regional role, and underlined U.S. global leadership, virtually all West European governments reacted, at first, negatively. Yet, depending in varying degrees on the United States, Britain, France, and West Germany had difficulties in maintaining unity after the oil crisis hit in the fall of 1973. Möckli provides a general picture with an emphasis on French sources, Alastair Noble works from British sources, and Fabian Hilfrich analyzes the wrangling about the U.S. attempt to reassert its leadership on the basis of West German sources. Although their conclusions still leave room for argument, it becomes clear that the initiative was a catalyst for reenforcing European foreign policy cooperation; and that the United States was initially put under substantial diplomatic pressure, yet in the end a clear majority in the Community favored co-opting the European edifice with transatlantic partnership.

Looking at a different issue, Sarah Snyder underlines, on the basis of recently declassified U.S. sources, the difficulties the United States had, parallel to the turbulent Year of Europe, in restoring U.S. leadership and controlling the negotiations for the Helsinki Conference on Security and Cooperation in Europe. She also reveals how the United States collaborated, behind the backs of the Europeans, with Moscow, to make sure the European demands did not go too far for the Soviets such that the conference would break down.

In the fourth section on the search for a new consensus in the alliance during the waning of détente, Matthias Schulz begins the discussion with an analysis of the consolidation of the transatlantic partnership in the mid-1970s before looking at the major conflict that arose in 1977–78. He highlights the European strategies used by West German Chancellor Helmut Schmidt in close cooperation with the French President Valéry Giscard d'Estaing aimed at binding the United States to Europe. Drawing on the Schmidt papers archived at the Friedrich Ebert Foundation, Schulz documents Schmidt's strong preference for multilateralism as a means to frame West Germany's exertion of its influence, and he discusses the reasons why Schmidt opted for transatlantic frameworks in some cases and European ones in others.

Schulz's study of Schmidt's foreign policy course is complemented by Joseph Renouard and D. Nathan Vigil's analysis of the Carter administration's policies and attitudes toward Europe. Covering the row within NATO over the neutron bomb in 1977–78, transatlantic economic conflicts, the Iran hostage crisis, and the Soviet invasion of Afghanistan in December 1979, they consider the motivations behind Carter's policies and point to the disparities between objectives and outcomes.

The section concludes with an essay on the growing missile gap between the Soviets and the Western alliance at the end of the 1970s. Confronted by the possibility of a realistic Soviet first-strike capability in Europe, NATO responded with the so-called dual-track decision, which envisioned the deployment of intermediate-range nuclear missiles. That decision gave rise to protest movements throughout Western Europe, which in turn prompted concern among political leaders that the European–American partnership might unravel under the pressure of popular opposition to the alliance's plans. In his contribution to this volume, Joachim Scholtyseck looks at the role played by West Germany in NATO's dual-track decision and the deployment of the controversial missiles in 1983. He questions the view that Schmidt had been crucial in bringing about the dual-track decision and underscores instead the immense pressure brought to bear on him to uphold détente. But Scholtyseck also credits Schmidt, together with his successor Helmut Kohl, for holding the line and thereby helping save the Western alliance at a crucial moment.

PART ONE

Disturbing American Leadership?

Détente and German Ostpolitik

1

U.S. Détente and West German Ostpolitik

Parallels and Frictions

GOTTFRIED NIEDHART

It is in large measure on account of Germany that we can refer to a post-1945 Atlantic community. The United States had already intervened in Europe during World War I in order to forestall German hegemony. But only after 1945, once a renewed German bid for power was stopped, did the United States bind itself firmly, by treaty, to Europe and thus become a "European" power. This is not to say, however, that the revolutionary change in American policy following World War II was due exclusively to Germany. To the contrary: another crucial factor was the transformation of the Soviet Union from ally to enemy. The North Atlantic Treaty Organization accordingly served two purposes, namely containing the Soviet Union and containing the newly founded Federal Republic of Germany.

The strategy of "double containment," as it was called, lost its urgency during the East-West détente of the late 1960s.[1] Not only had the Federal Republic proved itself a reliable partner in the Atlantic alliance, it had also set an example through its readiness to bind itself into the multilateral structures of the West. At the same time, the Soviet Union had become interested in reducing tensions and was prepared to enter into negotiations. But although the East-West conflict eased during the era of détente, it by no means came to an end. And as the global political rivalry among the superpowers continued, the Federal Republic — without asking its protector, the United States, for permission — began to assume a leadership role in the policy of détente in Europe. The new West German *Ostpolitik* was

---

1 Wolfram F. Hanrieder, *Deutschland, Europa, Amerika. Die Außenpolitik der Bundesrepublik Deutschland 1949–1994* (Paderborn, 1995), 29.

This essay grew out of a research project on the role of Germany in East-West relations (1968–1974) that was financed by the Fritz Thyssen Foundation and directed by the author in conjunction with Oliver Bange at the University of Mannheim.

based on NATO's strategy as laid down in the Harmel Report, namely, the strategy of pursuing détente while maintaining a military deterrent.[2] Thus, as Geir Lundestad concluded in his recent analysis of transatlantic relations in this period, "Ostpolitik did not lead to any real crisis in American-European relations."[3]

Indeed, there was no real crisis. Yet there was some uncertainty among Washington's decision makers as to the possible consequences of Ostpolitik for West Germany's anchoring in the West and German-American relations. In the following pages, I examine the dissonance occasioned by Ostpolitik within an otherwise relatively stable transatlantic relationship. I begin by considering the first year of the new Ostpolitik under Chancellor Willy Brandt. Then transatlantic relations are set against the background of the global political changes that were taking place in the era of détente. Finally, the role of the Federal Republic in East-West relations, the American perspective on the resulting German "problem," and Washington's resolution "to contain German dynamism toward the East" are analyzed.[4]

THE FIRST YEAR OF SOCIAL-LIBERAL OSTPOLITIK

In May 1970, Kenneth Rush, the American ambassador in Bonn, gave his impressions of the Federal Republic in a private letter. "The change of government," he wrote, "with the new Ostpolitik of the Brandt government, along with Germany's new approach to the West, and her also very important new steps in domestic policies, have created an atmosphere of change and excitement even greater than that of the New Deal thirties in our country."[5] Writing roughly half a year after the West German election, Rush did not yet speak of a Brandt era, but his brief account indicated that the Federal Republic was entering a new phase in its still short history. His allusion to the New Deal is quite revealing. With the formation of the "social-liberal" coalition of the Social Democratic Party (Sozialdemokratische Partei Deutschlands, SPD) and the Free Democratic Party (Freie Demokratische Partei, FDP) in October 1969, Willy Brandt became the country's first Social Democratic chancellor. The coalition

2 Andreas Wenger, "Crisis and Opportunity: NATO's Transformation and the Multilateralization of Détente 1966–1968," *Journal of Cold War Studies* 6 (2004): 22–74.
3 Geir Lundestad, *The United States and Western Europe since 1945: From "Empire" by Invitation to Transatlantic Drift* (Oxford, 2003), 173.
4 Memorandum from Kissinger to Nixon, Dec. 10, 1971. National Archives and Records Administration, College Park (NARA), Nixon Presidential Materials (Nixon), National Security Council (NSC), President's Trip Files (PTF) 473.
5 Rush in a private letter to F. L. Jennings, May 22, 1970. NARA, Record Group 59: General Records of the Department of State (RG 59), Lot Files, Entry 5406, Box 4.

itself was also unprecedented. The two parties differed considerably in their positions on economic and social policy. It was foreign policy that served as the glue binding them together. Walter Scheel, the FDP's chairman, became foreign minister and vice chancellor.

Even though the Brandt government began its work with numerous reform initiatives, which Rush found remarkable,[6] Ostpolitik became its trademark. Both coalition parties had developed this policy during the 1960s, and those who had conceived it now held positions of authority. Foremost among them was Brandt's closest collaborator, Egon Bahr. Bahr became state secretary in the Chancellery, and he would eventually represent Bonn in its negotiations with the Soviets and the East Germans.[7]

Rush, for one, quickly grasped the importance both of Bonn's hopes of achieving a "normalization" of relations with the Soviet Union and the other Warsaw Pact states and of its new approach to the West. He was not alone in the view that the Federal Republic had in recent years become more self-confident in its dealings with the other Western powers and was promoting its national interests more openly. His counterparts from Paris and London, too, had come to the conclusion that the Federal Republic had entered a new phase in its foreign policy and had become a "major actor in international politics."[8] This view stemmed in part from Bonn's refusal to comply with the wishes of its partners in late 1968 that it revalue the D-mark. "The Germans are flexing their muscles again," the French ambassador to Bonn commented.[9] In May 1969, the British ambassador noted a "new trend" and a "new consciousness of national interest and power" in West Germany's foreign policy. "Among its features are a greater self-reliance, a feeling that the period of atonement for the war is over, [and] impatience with restraints on German liberty of action."[10]

Rush's receptiveness to developments in his host country was matched by the White House's skepticism. President Richard Nixon had been alarmed by the first phase of the new Ostpolitik introduced by the so-called grand coalition of Christian Democrats and Social Democrats headed by Chancellor Kurt Georg Kiesinger (Christlich Demokratische Union, CDU). In June 1969, Nixon warned Scheel, whose party still belonged to the

---

6 For Brandt's first governmental declaration, see Peter Merseburger, *Willy Brandt 1913–1992. Visionär und Realist* (Stuttgart, 2002), 578ff.
7 Egon Bahr, *Zu meiner Zeit* (Munich, 1996), 268ff.
8 Karl Kaiser, *German Foreign Policy in Transition: Bonn Between East and West* (London, 1968), 1.
9 François Seydoux, *Botschafter in Deutschland. Meine zweite Mission 1965 bis 1970* (Frankfurt, 1978), 152.
10 Dispatch by Roger Jackling to Foreign and Commonwealth Office (FCO), Apr. 9, 1969, "Towards a National Foreign Policy." National Archives, Public Record Office, Kew (PRO), FCO 33/566.

parliamentary opposition at that point, to be extremely careful in pursuing a policy of understanding with the Soviet Union. "This was a 'spongy road' and great care would have to be taken in going down this road." Nixon himself favored a policy of détente, yet his perception of the Soviet Union was still shaped by the Cold War. "The Soviet Union had not yet changed," he told Scheel. For this reason, he insisted on extreme caution. In searching for new approaches to East–West relations, he argued, Bonn must not accept a deal "which might impair the forces built up in the [Federal Republic of Germany]. The FRG would have to keep its integrity." Scheel, in response, used the opportunity to reaffirm West Germany's commitment to NATO.[11] Whether that commitment was actually compatible with an active West German Ostpolitik was, from the White House's perspective, an open question. It seemed to Washington that the intrinsically ambiguous German question was about to be reopened: the Federal Republic's role as part of the West would be up for discussion again along with the issue of the eventual unification of the two postwar German states.

Leaders in Washington grew increasingly alarmed following the change of government in Bonn in the fall of 1969. When British Prime Minister Harold Wilson visited the United States in January 1970, Nixon asked him whether he thought the West German commitment to NATO "might be gradually eroded by Herr Brandt's new policy of promoting better relations with Eastern Europe." Would Brandt be "capable of managing a détente"? Wilson replied that he was convinced of "Brandt's loyalty" and his ability to master the dynamic that might arise from a policy of détente: "He can manage it. He's unfrozen the situation; he's gotten the troops out of the trenches; he's done away with stale, cold-war rhetoric."[12]

Wilson's assurances notwithstanding, Nixon's views were strongly influenced by his national security adviser, Henry Kissinger. In February 1970, Kissinger delivered a memorandum on West Germany's foreign policy to Nixon. He summarized what Brandt's government had explained to him and had declared in public, namely that the Federal Republic was "strongly committed to NATO and West European integration." Brandt was convinced that Ostpolitik "can be successful only if Germany is firmly anchored in the West." Kissinger was nonetheless worried that Bonn's "Eastern policy is acquiring its own momentum and will lead Brandt into dangerous concessions." Although he did not doubt Brandt's "basic Western orientation,"

11 Memorandum of a conversation between Nixon and Scheel, June 13, 1969. NARA, Nixon, NSC, Country Files Europe (CFE) 681.
12 Conversation between Nixon and Wilson, Jan. 27, 1970. PRO, FCO 7/1823; NARA, Nixon, NSC, Presidential-HAK Memcons (PresHAK) 1023.

Kissinger feared that a "longer term danger" could arise. In the margin, Nixon described Kissinger's memorandum as "a very perceptive piece."[13]

Kissinger remained ambivalent about Ostpolitik. When Ostpolitik yielded its first results in late 1970 with the signing of the Moscow and Warsaw treaties, Kissinger distinguished "between the things that had already happened in Ostpolitik and the long term dangers" during a meeting with Edward Heath, Wilson's successor. "What had happened up to now was not dangerous. What the long-term change might be was another matter," he told the new prime minister.[14] Kissinger was qualifying a simple statement made by Nixon, which was recorded in the British minutes of the discussion. Ostpolitik, the president had said, was a "dangerous affair." The U.S. government "would do nothing to encourage it."[15] That was not to be Nixon's final word on the subject, however. It would soon become clear that U.S. détente and West German Ostpolitik were not only compatible but also interdependent: the success of Nixon's summit meeting with Leonid Brezhnev in May 1972 to sign an antiballistic missile treaty rested on the Bundestag's ratification of the Moscow and Warsaw treaties.

Shortly after Wilson's meeting with Nixon and Kissinger, Washington and Bonn found themselves at odds as a result of divergent perceptions of the Soviet Union and of differing national interests. The Brandt government was pushing for an acceleration of the Four Powers' negotiations on Berlin: a successful conclusion to those negotiations was, from the outset, Bonn's conditio sine qua non for the ratification of the Moscow and Warsaw treaties. While Bonn was optimistic about the chances of progress on Berlin, Washington had a bleak view of the Soviet Union. The evident improvement in West German–Soviet relations stood in contrast to the stagnation in U.S.-Soviet relations. Washington had endured an autumn of crises, finding itself in conflict with its rival superpower around the globe.[16]

---

13 Memorandum for the President, Feb. 16, 1970, with Nixon's handwritten remark. NARA, Nixon, NSC, CFE 683. See also Henry Kissinger, *White House Years* (Boston, 1979), 408, 529.

14 Kissinger in the course of a conversation between Nixon and Heath, Dec. 17, 1970. NARA, RG 59/2657.

15 PRO, FCO 7/1842. The basis for the American position on Ostpolitik was the National Security Decision Memorandum 91, Nov. 6, 1970: "United States Policy on Germany and Berlin." Concerning Ostpolitik, it says: "Our approach to specific question raised by the FRG's Eastern policy should continue to be one of general support for the avowed objectives, without obligating ourselves to support particular tactics, measures, timing or interpretations of the FRG's policies. We approve the establishment of normal relations between the FRG and the states of Eastern Europe. We should not conceal, however, our longer range concern over the potentially divisive effect in the western alliance and inside Germany of any excessively active German policy in Eastern Europe as well as our concern over the potential risks of a crisis that such a policy might create in relations between Eastern European states and the USSR." NARA, RG 273/NSDM.

16 Kissinger, *White House Years*, 594ff.

Moscow's intentions in the Middle East were opaque, and its positions on Vietnam and in the Strategic Arms Limitation Talks (SALT) were not as constructive as the U.S. government had hoped. There were even problems at Washington's own front door. Soviet plans to build a submarine base in Cienfuegos, Cuba, revived memories of the most dangerous crisis ever in U.S.-Soviet relations. In addition, Washington's leaders were shocked by Salvador Allende's victory in Chile.

This accumulation of conflicts stood in contrast with Moscow's siren songs to the Federal Republic and the other Western European states.[17] Consequently, détente carried negative associations in Washington at the end of 1970. The discourse featured terms like "reduction of tensions" or "avoidance of confrontation."[18] The effects of this attitude were felt in Bonn. On December 16, 1970, the U.S. envoy Russell Fessenden paid a visit to the chancellor's office and suggested that Bonn slow the pace of Ostpolitik. There were, he said, "major concerns at a high level" in Washington.[19] Kissinger, too, expressed his apprehension to the German ambassador, telling him that "too pronounced an engagement for improved relations with the Soviet Union might make the Federal Republic increasingly dependent on Soviet behavior and deprive it of its room for maneuver."[20] When Minister of the Chancellery Horst Ehmke met with Kissinger in Washington a few days later, the secretary of state noted that there were, indeed, "minor differences of opinion" between Bonn and Washington. He then cautioned Ehmke that Bonn should not try to go it alone in dealing with the Soviets. It would be important that "we do not allow [the Soviets] to play us off against each other." The Soviets were currently dealing "nicely" with the Federal Republic and "harshly" with the Americans. It had become clear in recent months, Kissinger continued, that the Soviets were not interested in negotiated settlements on all important issues — the Middle East, Vietnam, and SALT — and that they were speculating about the divisibility of détente. Kissinger's assessment of the international situation was, Ehmke thought,

17 Helmut Sonnenfeldt in a conversation with Berndt von Staden, Oct. 4, 1970. Note by Sonnenfeldt, Oct. 16, 1970. NARA, Nixon, NSC, CFE 684. On U.S.-Soviet tensions at this time, see the recapitulation in William Bundy, *A Tangled Web: The Making of Foreign Policy in the Nixon Presidency* (New York, 1999), 179ff.
18 Martin Hillenbrand, Director of the Section for European Affairs in the State Department, to Hervé Alphand, General Secretary in the French Ministry of Foreign Affairs, Dec. 12, 1970. NARA, RG 59/2263.
19 Ulrich Sahm, Head of the Foreign Policy Section in the Chancellor's Office, about a conversation with Fessenden, Dec. 16, 1970. Archiv der sozialen Demokratie der Friedrich Ebert Stiftung, Bonn (AdsD), Depositum Ehmke, 1/HE AA 000788.
20 Note by Botschafter Pauls, Dec. 18, 1970, about a conversation with Kissinger the day before. *Akten zur Auswärtigen Politik der Bundesrepublik Deutschland (AAPD)* 1970, 2294.

defined by the global interests of the United States. As a representative of a regional power, he could point out only that the progress already achieved in Europe should be extended in the form of an arrangement on Berlin and that such an arrangement might have positive effects on other areas of conflict.[21]

The disagreements between Bonn and Washington were not confined to confidential exchanges; the media took an active interest, too. As is often the case, politicians provided information to particular journalists for tactical reasons. In the case of Ostpolitik, the figures who tried to intervene via the media were not simply critical of a policy of détente with the Soviets but were fundamentally opposed to it. The Chancellery in Bonn learned from American sources that "a storm" was brewing "in the American right wing on the subject of Germany's policy toward the East."[22] An alliance of opponents to détente took shape on both sides of the Atlantic. The diverse critics of Ostpolitik included the American labor organization AFL–CIO, as well as West Germany's Christian Democratic opposition parties, the CDU and CSU (Christlich-Soziale Union, Christian Social Union). Christian Democratic politicians took advantage of long-standing contacts to American officials, members of Congress, and journalists to lobby against Ostpolitik.[23] No less prominent a figure than former Secretary of State Dean Acheson, for example, called on Bonn to "slow down the mad race to Moscow," as the *Washington Post* reported after Acheson and other noted members of the American foreign policy "old guard" met with Nixon and Kissinger at the White House.[24]

On December 10, 1970, the same day the *Post* quoted Acheson, Secretary of State William Rogers appeared before the Senate Foreign Relations Committee. The Committee's chairman, J. William Fulbright, told Rogers he was "distressed to see one of the prominent advisers to the President... criticize Willy Brandt because Willy Brandt was seeking some way for better relations with Russia." In response, Rogers emphasized that

---

21 Note by Ehmke, Dec. 23, 1970, about conversation with Kissinger on Dec. 21, 1970. AdsD, Dep. Ehmke, 1/HE AA 000788. See also the note by Pauls, Dec. 22, 1970. *AAPD* 1970, 2305ff. and Horst Ehmke, *Mittendrin. Von der Großen Koalition zur deutschen Einheit* (Berlin, 1994), 141–2.

22 Memorandum by Blumenthal for Ehmke, Dec. 10, 1970. AdsD, Depositum Bahr 81/A1. The New York public relations company, Roy Blumenthal International Associates: Public Relations and Advertising, had a contract with the government in Bonn. Ibid.

23 Bernd Schaefer, "'Washington as Place for the German Campaign': The U.S. Government and the CDU/CSU Opposition, 1969–1972," in *American Détente and German Ostpolitik 1969–1972: Bulletin of the German Historical Institute Supplement 1,* eds. David C. Geyer and Bernd Schaefer, 98–108.

24 See the photo in Kissinger, *White House Years,* after 744: "Nixon meets with the Old Guard (Lucius Clay, Thomas E. Dewey, Dean Acheson, John McCloy)." The meeting took place on Dec. 7, 1970. Douglas Brinkley, *Dean Acheson: The Cold War Years 1953–71* (New Haven, CT, 1992), 293. And thus it could be read in the *Washington Post* on Dec. 10, 1970.

Acheson "is not a member of this Administration and does not reflect our views." He went on to declare:

We have supported the German policy of Ostpolitik, we have had a very great degree of cooperation with that Government. I just returned from a NATO meeting and assured Minister Scheel again of our full support that we not only support it, but we have encouraged them. So I think it would be most unfortunate if the impression were created that the statement represents our views.[25]

What Rogers did not know, and what Kissinger concealed from his German interlocutors, was that Acheson's sharp criticism of Ostpolitik had been prompted by Kissinger himself. Acheson had asked him whether "there was anything you would want from us" during a telephone conversation. "Some concrete suggestions on leadership we could exercise in Europe right now especially with respect to Ostpolitik which I think is a disaster," Kissinger replied. "Brandt is sincere but there are a lot of sincere fools in the world."[26]

The Nixon administration was clearly speaking in different voices on Ostpolitik depending on the audience and circumstances. Nixon's statement that he "would do nothing to encourage" Ostpolitik stands in sharp contrast to Roger's assurance before the Foreign Relations Committee that the administration had been encouraging the Brandt government's efforts. The reported strains in German-American relations did not, in the end, lead to a "crisis of confidence" between Bonn and Washington in late 1970.[27] Washington's mounting reservations about Ostpolitik soon gave way to a more "optimistic outlook," as Ambassador Rolf Pauls reported back to Bonn.[28] Indeed, the picture would change considerably in January 1971. A German journalist in Washington could report that the rather unpleasant debate on Ostpolitik had come to an abrupt end.[29] One indication of the change that had occurred was Kissinger's invitation via envoy to Bahr for a face-to-face meeting in Washington.[30] The meeting would focus on the Berlin negotiations. Although the issue of Berlin's status fell solely under the jurisdiction of the Four Powers, Washington wanted to integrate Bonn into

---

25 State Department to U.S. Embassy, Bonn, Dec. 11, 1970. NARA, RG 59/2265. See also Memorandum of conversation between Hillenbrand and Pauls, Dec. 10, 1970. Hillenbrand "noted that Mr. Acheson is given to use colourful language. He could clearly not be governed by us in any way. Unfortunately, some German correspondents might link Acheson's views to the White House." NARA, RG 59/2264.
26 Phone call between Acheson and Kissinger, Dec. 9, 1970. NARA, Nixon, Henry Kissinger Telephone Conversation Transcripts, Box 8.
27 "Strain in U.S.-Bonn Relations Reported," *New York Times*, Dec. 20, 1970.
28 Pauls to Auswärtiges Amt (hereafter AA), Dec. 18, 1970. *AAPD* 1970, p. 2295.
29 Klaus Bölling to Helmut Schmidt, Jan. 24, 1971. AdsD, Depositum Schmidt 5701.
30 Kissinger to Bahr, Jan. 25, 1971. NARA, Nixon, NSC, HAK Office Files (HAK) 57.

the negotiations, albeit on a top-secret level. Kissinger and Bahr developed an elaborate system of back-channel communications in which Rush and Soviet diplomats in Washington and Bonn played part. It was, however, kept secret not only from the public but also from the State Department and the West German Foreign Ministry as well as from the French and British governments.[31]

The creation of a secret triangular diplomatic network is an indication that the superpowers saw détente and Bonn's Ostpolitik as intertwined. There was not always perfect harmony between Washington and Bonn, but they concurred on the major strategic questions. If the White House kept its distance from Ostpolitik, that was due, as one British diplomat speculated, to its "comparative lack of confidence in the socialist government in Germany." This attitude had been intensified, he suggested, by "a certain amount of poison by their long-standing friends in the CDU."[32] Indeed, Nixon believed that "any non-socialist government would be better."[33] That does not mean, though, that Washington intended to block Ostpolitik. It could have done so had it wanted to. For its part, Bonn was careful not to call the Four Powers' responsibility for Berlin into question. The Brandt government had no intention of pursuing Ostpolitik at the expense of the Federal Republic's integration within the political, military, and economic structures of the West. To the contrary, the Federal Republic acted as a "balancing power which was intertwined in multiple ways"[34] while remaining solidly anchored in the West. There was, then, a continuity in West German foreign policy from Adenauer to Brandt even as Bonn took the initiative in East-West relations and thereby embarked into new territory. In doing so, the Brandt government met with a wide variety of reservations both at home and in the United States. What mattered ultimately were not the undercurrents of disagreement but the open affirmations of commitment to the German-American strategic partnership. As Kissinger indicated to Nixon before a meeting with opposition leader Rainer Barzel, "We are interested in keeping our lines to the CDU open"; but he was quick to

---

31 David C. Geyer, "The Missing Link: Henry Kissinger and the Back-Channel Negotiations on Berlin," in Geyer and Schaefer, *American Détente*, 80–97.
32 Minutes by Assistant Under-Secretary Bendall, Jan. 27, 1971. PRO, FCO 33/1416.
33 Handwritten remark by Nixon to an undated memorandum of Kissinger, in preparation for a conversation with Foreign Minister Scheel, July 18, 1970. Kissinger argued that, because of the narrow majority in the federal parliament, a CDU government would not be in a strong position either. NARA, Nixon, NSC, CFE 683. See also memorandum by Kissinger for Nixon, July 15, 1970. NARA, Nixon, White House Special Files (WHSF), Confidential Files 1969–74 (CF), Box 6.
34 Hanrieder, *Deutschland*, 448.

add, "You have told Chancellor Brandt, quite frankly, that you will not take sides, but will do nothing that might embarrass his government."[35]

THE TRANSATLANTIC WORLD IN TIMES OF GLOBAL POLITICAL CHANGE

The simultaneity of interdependence within the alliance and interallied conflict in the late 1960s and early 1970s was neither new nor limited to West German–American relations. Even during the Adenauer era there had repeatedly been periods of discord between Bonn and Washington.[36] Adenauer's fear of a possible American-Soviet condominium over Europe and, in particular, divided Germany was profound. Toward the end of his chancellorship, he irritated the United States with the Franco-German Treaty of 1963. Furthermore, Bonn's orthodox position on the German question was seen in Washington as unrealistic and, from the time of the Kennedy administration, as an impediment to efforts to ease East-West tensions.[37]

In the wake of the Berlin crisis and the building of the Berlin Wall in 1961, it was West Berlin Mayor Willy Brandt who, in opposition to Adenauer, was ready to adapt to the international political situation and allow détente between East and West to take priority over a quick resolution of the German question. Brandt became leader of the SPD in 1964, and he seemed capable of leading the party beyond the decidedly nationalist orientation it had adopted after the war – of persuading the party to abandon the view that the Federal Republic was a provisional political entity and to accept the territorial status quo in Europe, including the existence of two German states.

Previously seen as a symbol of hope, Brandt was viewed as a risk in Washington after the Republicans regained the White House and Brandt took over at the Chancellery in Bonn. This change of attitude stemmed only in part from the assumption that Ostpolitik would weaken the Federal Republic's commitment to the West. It also reflected a more general uncertainty about the new era that was opening in Europe.[38] In Washington, the fundamental question was what role the United States would play on the

---

35 Memorandum of Kissinger for Nixon, Jan. 27, 1972. NARA, Nixon, WHSF, CF, 6.

36 Ronald J. Granieri, *The Ambivalent Alliance: Konrad Adenauer, the CDU/CSU and the West, 1949–1966* (New York, 2003). An overview on the state of research can be found in Detlef Junker, ed., *The United States and Germany in the Era of the Cold War, 1945–1990: A Handbook. Vol. I: 1945–1968* (Cambridge, 2004).

37 Thomas A. Schwartz, *Lyndon Johnson and Europe: In the Shadow of Vietnam* (Cambridge, MA, 2003) 22, 134–5.

38 Willy Brandt, *Erinnerungen* (Frankfurt, 1989) 204.

international stage after the Vietnam disaster, as it found itself matched
in military strength by the Soviet Union. From a Western European perspective, the uncertainty about whether the United States would maintain
its military presence in Europe provided additional rationale for trying to
reduce tension with the Eastern bloc.

The American debate on possible troop reductions in Europe had a considerable impact on thinking in Bonn. Brandt noted in June 1970 that the
United States "is staying but cutting back."[39] Minister of Defense Helmut
Schmidt likewise observed, "It is not holy writ that U.S. forces will have
to remain in Europe at present strength forever and ever."[40] Bonn saw the
United States as an irreplaceable but overstretched ally whose future role was
not yet clearly defined. This impression was confirmed when Washington
abandoned the gold standard in August 1971 without consulting or even
informing its European allies beforehand. One of Brandt's advisers commented several months later on the "temporary chaos" besetting relations
among the Western allies. The "United States' ability to function within the
Western alliance," he predicted, would be "diminished for a long period of
time." And if there was instability within the alliance, he argued, it was the
result not of Ostpolitik but rather of the "American situation."[41]

The postwar period had not yet come to a close, but its structures were
beginning to unravel. The worldwide reform and protest movement linked
to the symbolic year of 1968 were one sign of the changes under way, as was
the transformation of the Cold War by the move away from the rigid East-
West confrontation toward détente.[42] The so-called empires of the Cold War
showed visible cracks.[43] In Eastern Europe, the Soviets attempted labori-
ously to reassert their hegemony with the Brezhnev doctrine, their response
to the Prague Spring. The Brezhnev doctrine did not, however, result in
the long-term stability the Soviets had sought.[44] In Western Europe, the call
for an easing of East-West tensions and the open sympathy for any sign of

---

39 Willy Brandt Archives in the AdsD (WBA), Bundeskanzler 91.
40 Helmut Schmidt, "Germany in the Era of Negotiations," *Foreign Affairs* 49 (1970/71): 43.
41 Richard Löwenthal, Professor of Political Sciences in Berlin, addressing a group of foreign policy
    experts of the Social Democratic Party, Feb. 2, 1972. Quoted in Gottfried Niedhart, "Ostpolitik:
    The Role of the Federal Republic of Germany in the Process of Détente," in *1968: The World
    Transformed*, eds. Carole Fink, Philipp Gassert, and Detlef Junker (Cambridge, 1998), 185.
42 Carole Fink, Philipp Gassert, and Detlef Junker, eds., *1968: The World Transformed* (Cambridge,
    1998); Jeremi Suri, *Power and Protest: Global Revolution and the Rise of Détente* (Cambridge, MA,
    2003); Jussi M. Hanhimäki, "Ironies and Turning Points: Détente in Perspective," in *Reviewing the
    Cold War: Approaches, Interpretations, Theory*, ed. Odd Arne Westad (London, 2000), 326–42.
43 On Cold War empires, see John L. Gaddis, *We Now Know: Rethinking Cold War History* (Oxford,
    1997), 26ff.
44 Matthew J. Ouimet, *The Rise and Fall of the Brezhnev Doctrine in Soviet Foreign Policy* (Chapel Hill,
    NC, 2003).

liberalization in the Eastern bloc combined with a resurgent European integration process. This surge began in December 1969 in the Hague and soon had an impact on U.S.-European relations. The European Community, like Japan and China, was a rising power in the international system. Although the Soviet-American bipolarity continued, a new trend toward multipolarity was clearly visible. Western Europe continued to depend on the United States in the area of security, but it was striving for political emancipation. And even if the Europeans' growing self-confidence was no substitute for power, it added an increasing degree of competition to the traditional cooperation with the United States.[45]

The Federal Republic was not unaffected by this trend. Quite the contrary: its effects were felt all the more clearly after the SPD-FDP coalition took office in 1969. The Brandt government, as one scholar has aptly written, developed a "semi-Gaullist, seemingly more independent style."[46] While foreign minister in the Kiesinger government, Brandt had pleaded for "more self-reliance" with respect to the United States."[47] As chancellor, he held to this maxim, but he never underestimated the structural asymmetry in the relations between the regional power and the global power. On occasion, he commented bitterly on that asymmetry. After the outbreak of war in the Middle East in October 1973, the United States loaded weapons stored in West Germany onto Israeli ships in Bremerhaven for delivery to Israel — without informing the Bonn government, which was officially neutral in the conflict. Brandt felt that the Federal Republic had been treated "like a colony."[48]

The transformation in transatlantic relations also became visible in the new approach pursued by the United Kingdom. Britain continued to maintain special links with the United States in the areas of nuclear weapons and intelligence. The British withdrawal from east of Suez after 1968 led to the "decline of the British contribution to world peace keeping"[49] and signified the end of Britain's role as junior partner to the United States on the international political stage. At the same time, Britain's reorientation toward

45 Marc Trachtenberg, ed., *Between Empire and Alliance: America and Europe during the Cold War* (Lanham, MD, 2003); Hartmut Kaelble, "Wie die Europäer Amerika sahen. Die USA und das europäische Selbstverständnis im 19. und 20. Jahrhundert," in *Amerika und Europa. Mars und Venus? Das Bild Amerikas in Europa*, eds. Rudolf von Thadden and Alexandre Escudier (Göttingen, 2004), 43.
46 Werner Link, "Ostpolitik: Détente German-Style and Adapting to America," in *The United States and Germany in the Era of the Cold War, 1945–1990: A Handbook*, ed. Detlef Junker (Cambridge, 2004), 2:36.
47 Note dated Jan. 3, 1967. AAPD 1967, 15.
48 Klaus Harpprecht, Im Kanzleramt. *Tagebuch der Jahre mit Willy Brandt, Januar 1973-Mai 1974* (Reinbek, 2000), 369, 375, 404.
49 FCO briefing paper "Anglo/United States Relations," Sept. 23, 1970. PRO, FCO 7/1839.

Europe entailed economic disadvantages for the United States. Heath made clear to the Americans that he wanted to avoid having Britain viewed as "an American Trojan Horse" in Europe.[50] Kissinger later recalled that "no previous British Prime Minister would have considered making such a statement to an American President... We were witnessing a revolution in Britain's post-war foreign policy."[51] At this point, the Federal Republic and Ostpolitik also entered the picture. The British "revolution" led to both "greater distance" between the Britain and the United States,[52] and rapprochement between London and Bonn. Heath, although not an enthusiastic supporter of détente, had no choice when he took office in 1970 but to follow the advice of the Foreign and Commonwealth Office that Britain maintain "the present excellent Anglo-German relations." The Federal Republic had become "the strongest member of the EEC [European Economic Community]," a senior Foreign Office official wrote in a memorandum for the newly elected prime minister, and functioned as "a key both to our entry [into the EEC] and to East-West relations."[53]

The transatlantic relationship did not unravel, but it did gradually change in the early 1970s. The European project, which would hardly have been launched without the impulse the United States provided, began to take on ambiguous features in American eyes. The policies of individual Western European countries also caused headaches in Washington. That France under President Georges Pompidou continued to claim a special role in international affairs, albeit in more modest fashion than it had under Charles de Gaulle, had become a routine aspect of transatlantic relations.[54] It was rather unusual, though, that Britain tried to extricate itself from the "special relationship"[55] with the United States and that the Federal Republic,

---

50 Heath in a conversation with Nixon and Kissinger, Dec. 17, 1970. NARA, RG 59/2657.

51 Kissinger, *White House Years*, 937. See also David Reynolds, *Britannia Overruled: British Policy and World Power in the Twentieth Century*, 2nd ed. (Harlow, 2000), 224.

52 Lundestad, *United States*, 181.

53 Memorandum by Permanent Undersecretary Denis Greenhill, June 1970 (no exact date), on the occasion of the change of government. PRO, PREM 15/64. See also a long dispatch by Ambassador Jackling to Douglas Home, June 25, 1970. After having enumerated the priorities of British policy (security, prosperity, strength of NATO, entry into the European Community), he concluded: "It is against this background that Her Majesty's Government have hitherto thought it wise to support the Federal Republic's Ostpolitik, not only because we too favour the relaxation of tensions, which is its main aim, but also because of our interest in developing as close bilateral relations as possible with the Federal Republic for a number of reasons, of which our negotiations for membership of the European Communities are prominent." PRO, FCO 28/916.

54 On this topic, see Georges-Henri Soutou, "Le Président Pompidou et les relations entre les États-Unis et l'Europe," *Journal of European Integration History* 6 (2000): 111–46. English version in Trachtenberg, *Between Empire and Alliance*, 157–200.

55 On EEC versus special relationship, see C. J. Bartlett, *The "Special Relationship": A Political History of Anglo-American Relations since 1945* (London, 1992), 130.

which took close collaboration with the United States as the cornerstone of its foreign policy, pursued Ostpolitik quite independently.[56] From the American perspective, these developments were partially counterbalanced by a cautious French move toward rapprochement with Washington. As the Federal Republic gained in political stature and Ostpolitik developed a dynamic of its own, the French government deemed it necessary to resume regular consultations with the United States. The newly installed Nixon administration responded positively.[57]

The new developments in U.S.–Western European relations came at a time when the United States found itself having to adapt to fundamentally new realities. The international situation was undergoing profound change. From the American perspective, the decisive factor was the loss of the position of dominance in the international area it had held since 1945. Washington had to find new ways to bring its influence to bear in crisis regions around the world. It was confronted with a problem it had not encountered since the end of the World War II, namely the danger of "global overstretch."[58] Nixon was clearly preoccupied with the relative loss of power. "Is the United States going to continue to be a great nation, number one?" he asked nervously in April 1971.[59] During his first year in office, Nixon signaled, in the doctrine named after him, that he wanted to limit the country's global obligations. It was all too evident that the United States had experienced the limits of its power in Vietnam. The war did not produce the desired result and consumed human lives and resources, placing an intolerable burden on government finances, the economy, and American society. With respect to the Soviet Union, which had reached military parity with the United States, Nixon believed that the "era of confrontation" should give way to an "era of negotiation" to contain the ruinously expensive arms race. In short, the leadership in Washington was on the defensive and trying to secure international stability while maintaining the United States' position as the global "number one" despite the relative decline of its power. Although American economic dominance remained unchallenged, Washington had no choice but to accept the Soviet Union as a military equal. After the U.S.-Soviet summit in 1972, Nixon, the former

---

56 In his memoirs, Ehmke talks of a "standing leg for defense" [*Standbein der Verteidigung*] and a "playing leg for détente" [*Spielbein der Entspannungsbemühungen*]. Ehmke, *Mittendrin*, 121.

57 Gottfried Niedhart, "Frankreich und die USA im Dialog über Détente und Ostpolitik 1969–1970," *Francia. Forschungen zur westeuropäischen Geschichte* 31, no. 3 (2004): 65–85.

58 Paul Kennedy, *The Rise and Fall of the Great Powers: Economic Change and Military Conflict from 1500 to 2000* (London, 1988), 360.

59 H. R. Haldeman, *The Haldeman Diaries: Inside the Nixon White House* (New York, 1994), 344 (Aug. 13, 1971). On the American self-perception of relative decline, see Warren I. Cohen, *America in the Age of Soviet Power, 1945–1991* (Cambridge, 1993), 183; Lundestad, *United States*, 168.

Cold Warrior, even held out the prospect for a "lasting peace" between the superpowers.[60]

With an eye to the upcoming election, the Nixon administration presented the 1972 summit to the public as a success.[61] But that was not the full story, as Nixon acknowledged behind the scenes. A day after returning from Moscow, Nixon and Kissinger gave congressional leaders a blunt assessment of the international situation as they tried to win their support for American-Soviet détente. More than at any point since 1945, the United States had to recognize that it had to share power on the world stage. Nixon's central message was that the Cold War paradigm was no longer valid. "The world has changed," he told the congressional leaders. China and the Soviet Union remained ideological adversaries, yet they followed pragmatic courses in their foreign policies. A change in American policy would simply follow from the new realities. As Kissinger explained, "We are facing a new international situation compared to the one that obtained through most of the postwar period, and therefore it would be wrong for the United States, not in keeping with the opportunities before it, if we had simply continued the traditional pattern." He pointed out that the Berlin agreement and the conclusion of SALT demonstrated the success of the new approach in East-West relations.[62] Nixon and Kissinger did not mention Ostpolitik or the détente policies of other European countries. Ostpolitik was indirectly important for the administration's argument, however, because Bonn had insisted on a linkage between the German Eastern treaties and the successful conclusion of the Four Powers' Berlin talks.[63]

The change in the international political situation meant a curtailment of Washington's freedom of maneuver. Because the United States had lost its military advantage over the Soviet Union, it had no alternative to a policy of coexistence. "We either deal with them or live with them or we are going to die with them," Nixon said in summing up the constraints of the nuclear age. It had become imperative to end the Cold War arms race. "If we continue the arms race, it is a race in which neither can win." This crucial insight implicitly acknowledged the United States' own weakness. In the future, Nixon told the congressional leaders, the best way for Washington

---

60 Nixon before Congress, immediately after his return from Moscow on June 1, 1972. Jussi Hanhimäki, *The Flawed Architect: Henry Kissinger and American Foreign Policy* (Oxford, 2004), 226.

61 See also the assessment by Kissinger, *White House Years*, 1252ff.

62 Remarks of the President at Leadership Breakfast, June 2, 1972. NARA, Nixon, WHSF, President's Office Files, Box 90.

63 See, e.g., Bahr during the American-German talks in Washington, Apr. 10, 1970. The negotiations with Moscow, Warsaw, and East Berlin and on Berlin "are all linked together. If the FRG should succeed in negotiating an agreement with the Soviet Union but the Berlin talks do not succeed, the whole process would be stopped." NARA, RG 59/2304.

exercise its influence would be to reach compromises by negotiation. The self-assurance that had been a hallmark of American foreign policy was relegated to the past: "Never assume," Nixon warned, "that it is inevitable that in any contest we will eventually come out ahead."[64]

In this context, it was imperative that the United States maintain its existing alliances. When Bonn protested covert American arms deliveries to Israel from depots in West Germany during the Yom Kippur War of 1973, Washington feigned incomprehension.[65] The West Germans, backed by the other Western European governments, demanded consultations; the Americans responded with calls for loyalty. Washington appealed to the Europeans to understand that its foreign policy was shaped above all by the East-West conflict. That conflict may have lost some of its explosiveness in Europe, the Nixon administration argued, but it continued unabated in other regions of the world. Bonn received a familiar admonition: "A differentiated détente in which the Allies hope to insulate their relations with the USSR can only divide the Alliance and ultimately produce disastrous consequences for Europe."[66]

THE GERMAN PROBLEM AND CONTAINMENT OF THE GERMANS

Toward the end of Kissinger's abortive "Year of Europe," the usual complaints about European-American relations could be heard on both sides of the Atlantic. Washington criticized the Europeans' incomprehension of the global conceptualization underlying American foreign policy. The leading power of the West expected the support of its European allies. In Western Europe, there was widespread frustration about Washington's unwillingness to include its weaker NATO partners in strategic planning. These differences between the Western superpower and its European allies, whose outlook was global on economic matters but regional on defense and security, were simply unavoidable.

Thus, not a year went by without transatlantic dissonance. At the same time, though, it must be stressed that the overarching agreement on common Western interests was never called into question. That was clearly evident

---

64 Remarks of the President at Leadership Breakfast, June 2, 1972. NARA, Nixon, WHSF, President's Office Files, Box 90.

65 AAPD 1973, 1638ff., 1647ff., 1662ff.

66 Nixon to Brandt, Oct. 30, 1973. Henry Kissinger, *Years of Upheaval* (Boston, 1982), 716. This was a response to a letter from Brandt to Nixon dated Oct. 28, 1973. Brandt underlined that the Middle East was not part of the alliance's zone of "common responsibility" [*gemeinsame Verantwortung der Allianz*] and confirmed his criticism of the American actions. Moreover he contradicted "any suspicion that the Federal Republic was lacking loyalty to the Alliance" [*jeder Vermutung, die Bundesrepublik Deutschland könnte es an Bündnissolidarität fehlen lassen*], AAPD 1973, 1669.

in German-American relations. As noted previously, Ostpolitik provoked arguments about timing and fears about its potential consequences. Yet the decisive element is that Bonn not only needed reassurance in Washington but also never lost sight of the central importance of the Federal Republic's partnership with the United States.[67] Ostpolitik was certainly intended to make West Germany more independent, but it did not impinge on the foundations of the Federal Republic's integration within the West. In hindsight, Kissinger recognized this: "It was a tremendous achievement of Brandt that he dared to raise the question of German national interests and attempted to relate them and indeed succeeded in relating them to the common interests of the West."[68]

From Washington's perspective, West Germany's integration within the West meant the containment of Germany. One purpose of NATO, "to keep the Germans down," in Lord Ismay's oft-quoted words, still had its justification. This task appeared particularly pressing when the SPD-FDP government in Bonn assumed a rather autonomous character and pressed forward in East-West relations. That prompted an overreaction on Kissinger's part that could almost be called traumatic. He perceived Ostpolitik not in the actual context of West German foreign policy but as a new manifestation of the eternal "German problem." Every generation had been confronted with the German problem, he pointed out just before the Moscow Treaty was signed in August 1970. It would have been too good to be true had the current generation been spared.[69] His perception was based upon an image of Germany that was influenced more by the past than by the present. The other member of the National Security Council with a German background, Helmut Sonnenfeldt, also emphasized in a conversation with a German diplomat how the past was still very much a part of the present: "There was no magic that could make German history disappear and consequently none that could wipe away people's memories of it or the inferences they drew from it." Sonnenfeldt pointed out that the German past "was almost universally viewed with dismay and skepticism."

---

67 The guideline was written down by Bahr in a memorandum dated Sept. 18, 1969: "The United States will remain our most important partner, eventually our security is based upon our relationship with them" [*Unser wichtigster Partner werden nach wie vor die Vereinigten Staaten bleiben; auf dem Verhältnis zu ihnen beruht letztlich unsere Sicherheit*], *AAPD* 1969, p. 1050.

68 Kissinger on the occasion of the unveiling of a portrait of Willy Brandt in the German Historical Institute, Washington, D.C., Mar. 18, 2003. Bundeskanzler-Willy-Brandt-Stiftung, ed., *Remembering Willy Brandt. Egon Bahr, Henry Kissinger und die deutsch-amerikanischen Beziehungen* (Berlin, 2003), 44.

69 Kissinger to the French ambassador, Aug. 7, 1970. *Archives du Ministère des Affaires Etrangères, Paris (AMAE)*, Série Europe 1944–1970. Sous-Série République Fédérale d'Allemagne (Allemagne), 1542.

It was this past that "weighed heavily on people's minds when Germany made itself the engine for change in Central Europe and the source of a new fluidity and uncertainty in European politics and East-West relations."[70]

On account of their history, the Germans were kept under surveillance, and they were still suspected of being unpredictable. Too little time had passed since the war to exclude the danger of a renationalization of German politics. Moreover, since the rise of the protest movements culminating in 1968, in which neo-Marxist groups played a major role, Washington was worried by the current of anti-Americanism within the West German protest movements, especially in the opposition to the war in Vietnam. Although Bonn's policies were not directly influenced by those protests, the Federal Republic appeared — like the United States itself — to be a divided society. For Kissinger, that impression was reinforced by the intense debate over Ostpolitik. He believed that the polarization of West German society could threaten the stability of the Federal Republic and, in turn, of Europe.[71]

Another factor made Bonn's claim to freedom of maneuver in East-West relations seem risky to Kissinger. The Federal Republic lacked an attribute he considered essential for its Ostpolitik to succeed: power. At a seminar with senior State Department staff in early October 1969, Kissinger cited this factor, which he, as a follower of the realist school of international relations, considered crucial, in critiquing Bonn's foreign policy. Refusing to endorse the "enthusiasm of some people for greater German flexibility," he argued:

Considering the objective weakness of Germany in dealing with today's world, I am not sure Germany is the one to take the lead. The Federal Republic simply cannot afford massive intervention into the affairs of the world. And the more they go in this direction, the less they move towards an integrated Europe . . . Although the Germans can ease their problems temporarily, you also have to ask where they will be five years from now. Of course, you can't tell them that. You can't tell them they won't be able to sustain their present course.[72]

Kissinger did not voice his true convictions a few days later when he met with Brandt's emissary, Egon Bahr. Even before Brandt assumed the chancellorship, Bahr traveled to Washington to inform the American leadership about the incoming government's plans for Ostpolitik. Bahr

---

70 Note by Sonnenfeldt dated Oct. 16, 1970, about a conversation with Berndt von Staden, Oct. 4, 1970. NARA, Nixon, NSC, CFE 684.
71 Kissinger to the French ambassador, Aug. 7, 1970 (see note 70 above).
72 NARA, Nixon, NSC, PresHAK, 1026 (Oct. 8, 1969).

informed the Americans that the Brandt government would appear self-confident and sometimes even irksome with its policies. It had no intention of asking Washington "every two months" whether it was "still loved." "Thank God," Kissinger reportedly responded.[73] Events would show that Bonn did in fact hold to its present course in a way that impressed even the American leadership. It did not try, as Kissinger might have feared, to go solo in relations with Moscow. Bonn did not see itself as an intermediary between East and West but rather as a member of the West interested in advancing dialogue with the East.[74] The United States would retain its "old friend" status, while the Soviet Union was to be recruited as a "new partner."[75] Even Nixon came to view Bonn's efforts positively.

Ostpolitik was not supposed to be simply an adaptation to the trend of détente led by the superpowers. To the contrary: it had, according to Brandt, "its own roots and its own justification."[76] It was rooted in two wars: World War II, which Germany had conducted as a war of annihilation in the East, and the Cold War, which posed a threat that had to be brought under control. The reasons behind Ostpolitik were thus more comprehensive than those behind Washington's American détente policy. With Ostpolitik, Bonn strove not only to create a stable foundation for East-West coexistence but also to achieve reconciliation with the nations of Eastern Europe. There was an additional motivation behind Ostpolitik that was specifically German and that was thus a cause of skepticism in Washington. Ostpolitik was also a new approach to the German question, an approach that allowed Bonn to pursue the goal of German national unity after the construction of the Berlin Wall. This dimension of Ostpolitik had been voiced already in 1963 when Bahr coined the formula "change through rapprochement" (*Wandel durch Annäherung*) and Brandt spoke of the "transformation of the other side" (*Transformation der anderen Seite*).[77] More broadly, however, Ostpolitik

---

73 *AAPD* 1969, 1115f. (Oct. 13, 1969). For the wider context, see Gottfried Niedhart and Oliver Bange, "Die 'Relikte der Nachkriegszeit' beseitigen. Ostpolitik in der zweiten außenpolitischen Formationsphase der Bundesrepublik Deutschland im Übergang von den Sechziger- zu den Siebziger-jahren," *Archiv für Sozialgeschichte* 44 (2004): 415–48.

74 In a conversation with Golda Meir on Mar. 13, 1973, Nixon assessed the dialogue with the Soviet Union as an appropriate means to deescalate the East-West-conflict. Meir congratulated him on "revolutionizing the world and creating for the first time hope in the hearts of people." Nixon responded, "We have changed the world because of this dialogue and these agreements." At the same time, he warned against illusions. The antagonism between East and West continued to exist. "It doesn't mean we're still in the Cold War, but we must be realistic." NARA, Nixon, NSC, PresHAK, 1026.

75 Bahr, *Zeit*, 333.   76 Brandt, *Erinnerungen*, 190.

77 In July 1963 in Tutzing at the Starnberger. See, Brandt and Bahr made programmatic declarations about how they envisioned the future policies concerning Germany and Eastern Europe. The texts of both speeches are in *Dokumente zur Deutschlandpolitik*, 4th ser., 9:565ff. and 9:572ff.

was addressed to the entire Eastern bloc. Recognition of the status quo served as the preliminary step in a long-term process designed to overcome the absence of contact between the two blocs. The acceptance of postwar realities was intended to allow for East-West contacts on the political, economic, and cultural levels. In this way, the communist systems in the Soviet sphere of influence could be opened step by step, with their gradual change as a consequence. Ostpolitik was a strategy of transformation through which Brandt sought to achieve national unity in Germany and to overcome the division of the Europe.

The intellectual architect of and most prominent spokesman for this strategy was without doubt Egon Bahr. Of course, the idea of East-West rapprochement was not unique to Bahr. But like no one else, he brought analytical rigor to political practice. Time and time again, he underscored the connection between East-West détente and the liberalization of the East: "We have to promote the process of change in the Eastern bloc," he wrote in 1965. "For this purpose, economic and cultural communications, as well as common projects will be useful."[78] Bahr's objective was the "disintegration of the Soviet bloc.[79] For this strategy to succeed, staying power was required. As he explained to Kissinger in 1973, he put his stakes on "a systematic but selective expansion of economic East-West relations." That would "increase the contradictions in the communist-governed countries, and contribute to further modifications of the system." But with the suppression of the Prague Spring fresh in memory, Bahr also warned that care had to be taken "that this development does not lead to an explosive and uncontrollable turn of events."[80]

The personal contacts between Kissinger and Bahr developed quite well between 1969 and 1973, not least because of the "back channel" between the White House and the Chancellery created after Bahr's trip to Washington in October 1969.[81] Kissinger certainly had doubts about whether change in Eastern Europe could be brought about and controlled as Bahr envisioned and, in particular, about whether the Federal Republic had the influence needed to achieve its goals. Moreover, Kissinger was confronted with international political questions that permitted little room for the

78 Note by Bahr, Nov. 11, 1965. AdsD, Dep. Bahr, 1/EB AA 000030.
79 Bahr during a meeting of the American, British, and German planning staffs in Washington, Apr. 18, 1969. Note by the British participant R. A. Burroughs, Apr. 25, 1969. PRO, FCO 49/265.
80 "Dass diese Entwicklung keinen explosiven und nicht kontrollierbaren Umschlag erfährt": Bahr to Kissinger, Apr. 14, 1973. AdsD, Dep. Bahr 439/1.
81 Stephan Fuchs, *"Dreiecksverhältnisse sind immer kompliziert." Kissinger, Bahr und die Ostpolitik* (Hamburg, 1999).

subtleties of Bonn's Ostpolitik. But it was not enough to sneer about the "eternal optimism of the Germans," however.[82] By late 1972, the tone in the White House had changed substantially. Helmut Sonnenfeldt took up Bahr's terminology. He found it

astonishing in how many areas the East Germans have agreed to open themselves up to dealings with the FRG. Brandt has gone a long way toward achieving the *Annäherung* which Bahr set out as a policy objective a decade ago. The East German regime, to ensure his [Brandt's] success at the polls, has decided to take the risk that this will cause some *Wandel* in its internal structure too and in its relations with West Germany.[83]

How far the West German strategy of transformation could have an impact in Eastern Europe remained to be seen. But it could not be denied that East–West relations had been set in motion, and that the Federal Republic had become an engine for peaceful change.

Bonn had been pushed in that direction by the Kennedy and Johnson administrations well before it had learned to walk on its own. Johnson left no doubt that his policy of détente had priority over older West German positions like the Hallstein doctrine. Moreover, he encouraged the Federal Republic to improve its relations with the Soviet Union. From his experience as mayor of West Berlin and foreign minister, Brandt knew that his strategy of transformation and Johnson's concept of economic and cultural bridge building were essentially identical.[84] Apparently, Johnson was more optimistic than Nixon that West German Ostpolitik could be integrated into American détente policy.[85] Yet even during Johnson's presidency, the Federal Republic's ambassador in Washington reported that general American support for Bonn's Ostpolitik did not preclude "certain fears with respect to its practical execution."[86]

Those concerns increased after Nixon came to office, as has been shown here. At the same time, it became clear that those fears – and the sharp terms used to voice them – were unfounded. Ostpolitik was neither a "disaster" (Kissinger) nor a "dangerous affair" (Nixon). American perceptions of this sort sounded dramatic but did not lead to a veto of Ostpolitik. In the

---

82 Kissinger in a memorandum for Nixon, Sept. 1, 1970. NARA, Nixon, NSC, CFE 684.
83 Sonnenfeldt in a memorandum for Kissinger, Nov. 7, 1972. NARA, Nixon, NSC, CFE 687.
84 For Johnson's approval of Ostpolitik, see Schwartz, *Johnson*, 150–1, 230. Oliver Bange, "Ostpolitik und Détente in Europa. Die Anfänge 1966–1969" (Mannheim, 2004).
85 Frank Costigliola, "Lyndon B. Johnson, Germany and 'the End of the Cold War,'" in *Lyndon Johnson Confronts the World: American Foreign Policy, 1963–1968*, eds. Warren I. Cohen and Nancy Bernkopf Tucker (Cambridge, 1994), 197.
86 Knappstein to AA, Jan. 30, 1968, *AAPD* 1968, p. 117.

final analysis, this could be attributed to the fact that Washington saw not only the dangers of Ostpolitik but also the means to respond to them if they ever erupted. To maintain Western integration, Washington could use NATO. Not only in Nixon's eyes, NATO remained the guarantee for the containment of Germany.[87]

87 Nixon to Pompidou, Feb. 26, 1970. Memorandum of a conversation by Haig, Mar. 2, 1970. NARA, Nixon, NSC, PresHAK 1024.

2

The Nixon Administration and West German Ostpolitik, 1969–1973

BERND SCHAEFER

It was not until long after the building of the Berlin Wall in 1961 that a government of the Federal Republic of Germany felt confident enough to pursue an innovative policy in its relations with the Soviet Union, the states of Eastern Europe, and "the other German entity" – the German Democratic Republic (GDR). As the parliamentary elections of September 1969 demonstrated, the prerequisite was the replacement of the conservative Christian Democratic Union (Christlich Demokratische Union Deutschlands, CDU) and its Bavarian sister party, the Christian Social Union (Christlich-Soziale Union, CSU), by the Social Democratic Party (Sozialdemokratische Partei Deutschlands, SPD) at the government's helm. Despite small differences in their approaches toward the East, the Christian Democratic chancellors Konrad Adenauer, Ludwig Erhard, and Kurt Georg Kiesinger, together with the influential CDU-CSU parliamentary caucus, prolonged a legalistic stalemate through the 1960s. Policy debates within the conservative parties did not lead to any fundamental departures from the policy established under Adenauer. Under the Christian Democrats, there was no indication that Bonn might be willing to recognize the GDR or that it might enter into real negotiations with the Soviet Union, and thus there were no major agreements between the Federal Republic and the Eastern states and nor was there any easing of the division of Germany.[1]

The situation changed immediately – and profoundly – when a coalition of the SPD and the Free Democratic Party (Freie Demokratische Partei, FDP) came to power in Bonn after winning a slim Bundestag majority in the 1969 elections. The incoming government of Chancellor Willy Brandt was eager to build on the preliminary talks with Moscow initiated during

---

1 Daniela Taschler, *Vor neuen Herausforderungen. Die acumen- und deutschlandpolitische Debatte in der CDU/CSU-Bundestagsfraktion während der Großen Koalition (1966–1969)* (Düsseldorf, 2001).

Brandt's tenure as foreign minister. Brandt and his policy adviser Egon Bahr wanted to open negotiations with Moscow, Warsaw, Prague, and East Berlin as quickly as possible. They did so with surprising speed and with a self-assertiveness unprecedented in a West German government. For geopolitical and economic reasons, the Soviet leadership was looking forward to the opportunity of working with a SPD-led West German government. In an extraordinary development, it soon offered an additional secret channel of negotiations via KGB officers Valerij Lednev and Vyacheslav Kevorkov to bypass the influence of the rather Germanophobic foreign minister Andrej Gromyko.[2]

By recognizing the political status quo in Europe, Bonn hoped to lay the groundwork for easing and, in the long run, overcoming the division of Germany. That seemed a distant prospect in the early 1970s, but the East German leadership was nonetheless worried about Brandt's real intentions. Those fears proved justified as *Ostpolitik* gradually spurred dissent within the so-called Soviet bloc. "Change through rapprochement" was not merely a by-product of Bonn's Ostpolitik but rather an essential element of it from the outset. Ostpolitik had a strongly revisionist focus aimed ultimately at ending the division of Germany,[3] and it was only secondarily concerned with alleviating the consequences of Soviet predominance for the countries of Eastern Europe.[4]

Before this revolutionary change in policy was implemented, the White House had been expecting business as usual in its dealings with West Germany. That sometimes complicated but otherwise reliable and docile ally had not hitherto challenged the status quo in Europe in any serious way.[5] After taking office in early 1969, the Nixon administration established what seemed to be a smoother relationship with Bonn than that of the previous

2 Wjatscheslaw Keworkow, *Der geheime Kanal. Moskau, der KGB und die Bonner Ostpolitik. Mit einem Nachwort von Egon Bahr* (Berlin, 1995). See Kevorkov's statement of May 2002 in David Geyer and Bernd Schaefer, eds., *American Détente and German Ostpolitik, 1969–1972: Bulletin of the German Historical Institute Supplement 1* (2004): 143–6.

3 "Geyer and Schaefer, "American Detente and German Ostpolitik"; Gottfried Niedhart, "Revisionistische Elemente und die Initiierung friedlichen Wandels in der neuen *Ostpolitik* 1967–1974," *Geschichte und Gesellschaft* 28, no. 2 (2002): 233–66; Bundesministerium des Innern and Bundesarchiv, eds., *Dokumente zur Deutschlandpolitik*, 6th ser., vol. 1, Oct. 2, 1969–Dec. 31, 1970 (Munich, 2002) and vol. 2, Jan. 1, 1971–Dec. 31, 1972 (Munich, 2004).

4 Timothy Garton Ash, *In Europe's Name: Germany and the Divided Continent* (New York, 1993). See also Carole Fink and Bernd Schaefer, eds., *Ostpolitik, 1969–1974: European and Global Responses* (Cambridge, 2009).

5 Thomas A. Schwartz, *Lyndon Johnson and Europe: In the Shadow of Vietnam* (Cambridge, MA, 2003); Ronald J. Granieri, *The Ambivalent Alliance: Konrad Adenauer, the CDU/CSU and the West, 1949–1966* (New York, 2003).

administration. Nixon, Henry Kissinger, and Kiesinger got along rather well and were largely in agreement in their assessments of the European political situation. During their conversations, the West German leader dismissed the idea that Bonn might need its own Ostpolitik toward the Soviet Union or GDR.[6] On September 24, the night of the West German election, Nixon called Bonn to congratulate Kiesinger on his electoral victory – prematurely, as it turned out. Although they had indeed won the largest block of seats in the Bundestag, the CDU and CSU were ousted from power by an SPD-FDP coalition led by Brandt. "The worst tragedy," Kissinger observed in a conversation with Nixon on June 16, 1971, "is that election in '69. If this National Party, that extreme right wing party, had got three-tenths of one percent more, the Christian Democrats would be in office now."[7]

THE NIXON ADMINISTRATION AND THE CDU-CSU OPPOSITION

American administrations and the embassy in Bonn for many years had cultivated a close relationship with the leaders of the CDU-CSU and generally perceived them as mostly loyal backers of American policy. Washington maintained those ties after the 1969 change of government in Bonn, not least because Brandt's slim majority in the Bundestag was gradually eroding. For almost three years, it looked as if the CDU-CSU might be within reach of a return to power. In July 1970, Kissinger sent a memorandum to the president arguing that the United States should avoid being held responsible for a possible collapse of the SPD-FDP coalition in Bonn; "I do not agree – any non-socialist government would be better," Nixon wrote in longhand in the margin.[8]

---

6 Records of Conversations between Nixon and Kiesinger, Feb. 26, 1969 (Bonn), Aug. 7–8, 1969. (Washington, D.C.), in *Akten zur Auswärtigen Politik der Bundesrepublik Deutschland* 1969 (hereafter *AAPD*), eds. Hans-Peter Schwarz et al. (Munich, 2000), 1:273–91, 2:881–98, 2:906–13.

7 Recording of Conversation between Nixon and Kissinger, 16 June 1971, National Archives and Records Administration (hereafter NARA), Nixon Presidential Materials Project (hereafter NPMP), White House Tapes, Conversation 523–4. Kissinger was referring to the National Democratic Party of Germany (NPD), an openly neo-Nazi party that had won 4.3 percent of the national vote. It thus fell short of the 5 percent minimum required under the Federal Republic's constitution for a party to gain seats in the Bundestag. Had the NDP cleared the 5 percent hurdle, thereby bringing the number of parties represented in the Bundestag to four, Brandt could not have formed a coalition against the CDU-CSU, which had won the single largest block of seats in the September 1969 election. During a talk with Kiesinger in Washington on Aug. 8, 1969, Kissinger had described the contemporary student protest movements as "more Nazi" than the NDP: *AAPD* 1969, 2:907.

8 Memorandum for the President, from Henry A. Kissinger, n.d., NARA, NPMP, National Security Council (hereafter NSC) Files, Country Files – Europe, Box 684.

Having learned his lesson, Kissinger referred to the Christian Democrats as "our friends" in a September 13, 1970, memorandum to Nixon and insisted that the administration not "demoralize" them by openly supporting the policy of the SPD-led government.[9] In a conversation with Kissinger in the Oval Office on May 29, 1971, the president expressed his preference for the CDU over Brandt in his own fashion: "I don't want to hurt our friends in Germany by catering to that son-of-a-bitch."[10] According to CDU chairman Rainer Barzel, Nixon reaffirmed that stance less profanely in January 1972, when he told him off the record, "We stand by our old friends."[11]

This loyalty notwithstanding, the Nixon administration had been forced to sacrifice political, sometimes even personal, friendships to overarching American interests since late 1969. And maintaining good working relations with the sitting government of a crucial ally like West Germany was certainly in America's interest. At the same time, however, the Nixon administration maintained close contacts with the opposition parties in Bonn and, in light of the volatile majorities in the Bundestag, treated them as a government in waiting. More than once between 1970 and 1972, CDU-CSU leaders told U.S. officials that they might be able to bring down the Brandt government by dealing it a major parliamentary defeat or through a vote of no confidence. That may have been merely self-deluded, wishful thinking up until late 1971. On his return from a special mission to Washington in November of that year, the CDU envoy Kurt Birrenbach reported that the U.S. government expected Brandt's coalition to maintain its parliamentary majority and ratify the Eastern treaties. Washington, he said, considered it impossible to infringe upon the sovereignty of West Germany by taking sides in an internal political debate. Birrenbach later speculated that Washington's position was explained by its desire to maintain a "low profile" in foreign policy in the wake of its military retreat from Vietnam.[12] By early 1972, CDU-CSU leaders were very hopeful that continuing defections from the SPD and FDP Bundestag caucuses would soon allow them to bring down the Brandt government. In February of that year, Barzel was looking forward with guarded optimism to supplanting Brandt; indeed, he

---

9 Memorandum for the President, from Henry A. Kissinger. Sept. 3, 1970, NARA, NPMP, NSC Files, Country Files – Europe, Box 684.
10 Recording of Conversation between Nixon and Kissinger, May 29, 1971, NARA, NPMP, White House Tapes, Conversation 507–14.
11 Rainer Barzel, *Im Streit und umstritten. Anmerkungen zu Adenauer, Erhard und den Ostverträgen* (Frankfurt, 1986), 172.
12 Kurt Birrenbach, *Meine Sondermissionen. Rückblick auf zwei Jahrzehnte bundesdeutscher Außenpolitik* (Düsseldorf, 1984), 336–7.

went so far as to share his preliminary cabinet list with the U.S. embassy in Bonn.[13]

During Brandt's chancellorship, Washington attempted a show of neutrality toward West German domestic political fights. Internally, the White House had settled on a double strategy of offering public support for neither Brandt's policy nor his Christian Democratic rivals. This stance was complicated, however, by the differing views within the administration of Bonn's Ostpolitik, and those differences eventually led to mixed signals from Washington to Bonn. There was much goodwill toward Ostpolitik at the pragmatic State Department. Secretary William Rogers and his deputy Elliot Richardson were also personally in favor of Brandt and trusted him fully. In their first postelection meeting on December 6, 1969, Rogers told Brandt that the American government would welcome West German initiatives toward the Eastern bloc: "In Washington there haven't been the slightest doubts about German intentions at any time," he assured the newly elected chancellor."[14]

At the White House, by contrast, Nixon was not alone in his doubts about Brandt and the Social Democrats. Kissinger and his National Security Council colleague and fellow German immigrant Helmut Sonnenfeldt were also skeptical about the new government in Bonn. Leaving no tracks and denying any involvement when asked, they capitalized on criticism by U.S. Embassy Minister Russell Fessenden in Bonn or public figures from the occupation period, such as Dean Acheson, John J. McCloy, and Lucius D. Clay, to sow doubts about aspects of Brandt's policy.[15] In November 1970, Kissinger arranged for Acheson and McCloy to meet with Nixon; afterward, the two elder statesmen spoke critically of Brandt and Ostpolitik before the press. When confronted by the angry and suspicious Rogers, Kissinger distanced himself from the meeting he had organized.[16]

---

13 Bernd Schaefer, "'Washington as a Place for the Geman Campaign': The U.S. Government and the CDU/CSU Opposition, 1969–1972," in ed. Geyer and Schaefer, *American Détente and German Ostpolitik, 1969–1972*: 98–108.

14 Note from Egon Bahr (Dec. 8) on meeting between Brandt and Rogers on Dec. 6: *AAPD* 1969, 2:1384. See also the remarks by John S. Sutterlin, Director of Office of German Affairs in the Department of State, from Feb. 16, 1970, quoted in Note (Feb. 17, 1970) from Ambassador Rolf Pauls on a meeting with Elliot Richardson and John Sutterlin, Feb. 16, 1970.

15 Notes from Ministerialdirektor Ruete, Nov. 27, 1969, on conversation with Fessenden on 26 November 1969: *AAPD* 1969, 2:1338–41; Note from Egon Bahr on a conversation with Fessenden, 28 November 1969: *AAPD* 1969, 2:1347–8; Note from Rolf Pauls (Dec. 18, 1969) on conversation with Henry Kissinger, Dec. 17, 1970, *AAPD* 1969, 3:2293–5; Note from Pauls (Dec. 22, 1970) on meeting of Minister of State Horst Ehmke with Henry Kissinger, Dec. 21, 1970: *AAPD* 1969, 3:2305–6. See also Horst Ehmke, *Mittendrin. Von der Großen Koalition zur deutschen Einheit* (Reinbek, 1996), 140–1.

16 NARA, NPMP, Henry A. Kissinger Telephone Conversation Transcripts (*Telcons*), Box 7.

Nonetheless, U.S. officials generally tried to avoid being dragged into West German public debates or pushed into showing favor to a particular party. Often, they resisted the temptation to follow personal inclination. National Security Decision Memorandum (NSDM) 91 bound all U.S. government departments and agencies to a position of neutrality on West German political issues.[17] During consultations with Brandt on December 28–29, 1971, Nixon scrupulously avoided voicing either support for or criticism of the Eastern treaties. He limited himself to endorsing the Four Power Agreement on Berlin and informing Brandt of an upcoming meeting with Barzel.[18] Even as the political atmosphere grew ever more heated during April 1972, the Nixon administration showed remarkable self-discipline in not taking sides in the lead-up to the failed no-confidence vote on Willy Brandt on April 28.

The bitter, divisive, and often-vicious West German debate over Ostpolitik was worrisome to Washington. Not surprisingly, it was Kissinger who invoked the German past in commenting on the debate under way in the Federal Republic. In a memorandum to Nixon dated February 16, 1970, he warned that the controversy over Ostpolitik "could in time produce the type of emotional and doctrinaire political argument that has paralyzed political life in Germany and some other West European countries in the past. It is this possibility that we must obviously be troubled about ourselves."[19] Nixon used his meetings with Barzel on September 4, 1970, and April 18, 1971, to urge restraint on the part of the CDU-CSU for the sake of political stability and West German democracy.[20]

Washington's show of neutrality notwithstanding, Nixon and Kissinger's foreign policy gave Bonn the opportunity to pursue its Ostpolitik with de facto American backing. Nixon apparently decided in late 1970, following the disappointing midterm elections in November, to make foreign policy, above all progress with the Soviet Union, China, and Vietnam, a central element in his bid for reelection. This strategy had major implications for West German Ostpolitik. Nixon claimed credit in public for the 1971 Four Power Berlin Agreement and hailed it as an important milestone

---

17 NSC, NSDM 91, Subject: United States Policy on Germany and Berlin, Nov. 6, 1970, NARA, NPMP, NSC Files, Country Files – Europe, Box 685.

18 See records of conversation between Nixon and Brandt on Dec. 28–29, 1971, *AAPD* 1971, 3: 1980–97, 3: 2008–19; for comments on the Eastern treaties, see *AAPD* 1971, 3:2013–14.

19 Memorandum for the President from Henry A. Kissinger, Feb. 16, 1970, NARA, NPMP, NSC Files, Country Files – Europe, Box 683.

20 Memorandum of Conversation, Rainer Barzel, Ambassador Rush, Jonathan Dean, Apr. 18, 1971, NARA, RG 59, Lot 74 D 430, Box 13.

in U.S.-Soviet relations. Moscow, in turn, linked its implementation to ratification of the Eastern treaties in Bonn. The debate on the treaties was thus not simply a German domestic issue that Washington could regard disinterestedly. Leaving aside the question of whether Nixon and Kissinger were sincere in their professed neutrality toward the West German debate, their larger foreign policy aims – and thus Nixon's reelection – presupposed Bundestag ratification of the Eastern treaties. Under Secretary of State John Irwin was absolutely to the point when, on November 30, 1971, he said that the result of nonratification would be "chaos."[21]

Abandoning its initial reluctance, Washington laid claim to the dominant role in incorporating the Berlin Agreement into Bonn's new Ostpolitik. An account of how the United States used the Brandt government and parliamentary opposition to negotiate this agreement would demonstrate just how futile the Christian Democrats' hopes of exploiting their ties to Washington for domestic political advantage were. Even more so than the State Department, the West German opposition parties had been kept in the dark about the highly secret back-channel negotiations between the White House, the Kremlin, and the Brandt government.[22] At one point, CDU leaders complained to the U.S. embassy in Bonn about "unacceptable" drafts of the Berlin Agreement and blamed Brandt for them; even some American officials were not aware that the drafts were in fact of American origin and had been approved by the White House.

The CDU-CSU's foreign policy setbacks in 1971–72 came hard on the heels of the parties' 1969 electoral defeat. As the parties tried to regroup in the wake of that defeat, Barzel established himself as the CDU's rising star. He consolidated his position as leader of the opposition in 1971, when he succeeded Kiesinger as chairman of the CDU. Looking back on this period in his three published memoirs, Barzel described Washington as one stop in the CDU's campaign to regain power in Bonn. Had Washington been able to decide West German elections, Barzel might have had a chance of replacing Brandt at the Chancellery. Referring to those years, Barzel later described Washington in one of his three memoirs as another place for fighting German electoral campaigns.[23]

---

21 Record of Conversation between State Secretary Paul Frank and Undersecretary of State John Irwin in Washington, Nov. 30, 1971: *AAPD* 1971, 3: 1861.
22 David Geyer, "The Missing Link: Henry Kissinger and the Back-Channel Negotiations on Berlin," *Bulletin of the German Historical Institute* (2004, suppl. 1): 80–97.
23 Barzel, *Im Streit und umstritten*, 173; Schaefer, "'Washington as a Place for the German Campaign.'"

Despite his poor command of English, Barzel maintained closer ties to American leaders and officials than any other German politician. He asked his American contacts regularly for advice and was always eager to share his thoughts and concerns with them. He generally presented himself as a supporter of bipartisanship on foreign policy and as more sympathetic to Brandt's Ostpolitik than most of his party colleagues. By supporting the sensible aspects of Ostpolitik and laying claim to credit for correcting its flaws, Barzel hoped to win international recognition as a statesman. He wanted to reap the benefits of Ostpolitik and to use domestic issues to bring down his Social Democratic rival.

Had Barzel voiced such thoughts to his fellow Christian Democrats even behind closed doors, he would have lost his leadership positions instantly. From early 1970 to his failed no-confidence motion in the Bundestag in April 1972 and the ratification of the Eastern treaties a month later, he held to his party's increasingly militant position in public while trying to restrain his colleagues in internal party debates by echoing his American partners' concerns. Unable to formulate a coherent CDU-CSU alternative to Brandt's Ostpolitik that a majority in his own party would support, the opposition leader adopted the lowest common denominator: he welcomed the Eastern treaties in general but called the SPD-FDP versions unduly hasty and sloppily negotiated. The treaties disregarded vital West German positions, he argued, and were bound to be modified by the next West German government – a government under his leadership. Barzel's private statements made to his American contacts in this period, by contrast, were devoted mainly to his complaints about his party and its Bavarian sister party, about his party rivals, and about the difficulties of deciding on the line for the CDU-CSU to pursue. Explaining Barzel's situation to Washington, Kenneth Rush said the CDU chairman could take as his motto Mahatma Gandhi's observation, "I have to catch up to my people, for I am their leader."[24]

The many memoranda of conversations between Barzel and U.S. officials in Bonn and Washington between 1969 and 1973 contribute to the true story of this ambitious politician who ended up being soundly defeated at the West German polls in November 1972, and a few months later by partisan competitors led by his successor Helmut Kohl, whom he heartily disliked. Barzel did not realize that he was a comparatively minor player in Washington's strategy and maneuvering during the early 1970s. The

---

24 American Embassy Bonn to Department of State: The CDU's Increasing Militancy, Mar. 26, 1970, NARA, RG 59, Central Files, POL 12 GER W.

substance of Nixon and Kissinger's foreign policy and their secret diplomacy were hidden from him and most of his American confidants. Realpolitik kept Washington from offering Barzel the support he sought in his battle with Brandt and the SPD-FDP coalition. Indeed, Barzel on several occasions weakened his leadership position in the CDU when he followed American advice and attempted to calm down his party. He thought he deserved outright American acknowledgment for such efforts, but his pleas in this vein to U.S. officials went unheard.

THE SPD-FDP GOVERNMENT AND THE NIXON ADMINISTRATION

Following the 1969 Bundestag elections, Egon Bahr called Henry Kissinger and received an apology for Nixon's premature congratulatory message to Kiesinger.[25] The Nixon administration would show no partisan preferences, Kissinger assured Bahr, and looked forward to cooperating fully with the Brandt government.[26] The two had known each other since 1966, when Kissinger was still teaching at Harvard and Bahr was serving as the policy planning chief in the West German Foreign Ministry.[27] Their ties took real effect on October 13, 1969, at their first White House meeting. On Kissinger's suggestion, they agreed to establish a confidential back channel for direct communication between themselves and between Nixon and Brandt. Having been literally smuggled into the White House through the back door to Kissinger's basement office to "freeze out" the State Department,[28] Bahr was excited about this "great success" for the new Bonn government.[29] In an October 20 memorandum on this meeting to Nixon, Kissinger emphasized that Washington should expect "posture of greater independence toward us in Bonn" and added that he had told Bahr that "we want to deal with Germany as a partner, not a client." Nevertheless, he conveyed deep skepticism and pessimism about the Federal Republic's domestic stability and the continuation of its ties to the West in the wake of moves to negotiate with the East.[30] In his account of the same conversation, Bahr

25 See Andreas Vogtmeier, *Egon Bahr und die deutsche Frage. Zur Entwicklung der sozialdemokratischen Ost- und Deutschlandpolitik vom Kriegsende bis zur Vereinigung* (Bonn, 1996).
26 Egon Bahr, *Zu meiner Zeit* (Munich, 1996), 269.
27 See Stephan Fuchs, *"Dreiecksverhältnisse sind immer kompliziert". Kissinger, Bahr und die Ostpolitik* (Hamburg, 1999).
28 Martin J. Hillenbrand, *Fragments of Our Time: Memoirs of a Diplomat* (Athens, GA, 1998), 286–7; Henry A. Kissinger, *White House Years* (Boston, 1979), 411.
29 Bahr, *Zu meiner Zeit*, 272.
30 Memorandum for the President, from Henry A. Kissinger. Subject: Visit by Willy Brandt's Emissary, Egon Bahr, Oct. 20, 1969, NARA, NPMP, NSC, Country Files – Europe, Box 682.

stressed his own insistence that Bonn did not intend to ask Washington to renew its commitment to West Germany every two months and for reassurance that it was still loved (Kissinger reportedly responded, in German, "Thank God!"). Bahr also indicated that he did not hide the fact that the new government, led by figures without compromising pasts, might be more assertive and "maybe somewhat more inconvenient" than its predecessor. It had been his intention, Bahr reported, to make clear that he had come to Washington not to consult but to inform the Nixon administration of the Brandt government's plans. According to Bahr's account, Kissinger advised the West Germans to "act quickly" and start negotiations with the Russians before the end of the year. "Your success will be our success," he told Bahr at the close of their discussion.[31]

The establishment of the Kissinger-Bahr back channel opened a period of intensive communication between Bonn and Washington. Its success was due in large part to both men's secretiveness and their pride in "protecting" each other from the State Department and Foreign Ministry "bureaucrats" they so despised.[32] A channel of this sort was unprecedented in German-American relations. It facilitated highly substantive communication that was increasingly characterized, Bahr noted in 1972, by "intensity and intimacy." Washington, for instance, received valuable information about and analyses of certain members of the Soviet leadership, as Brandt and Bahr were the first Western politicians to meet and become acquainted with them.[33] During a meeting in late March 1972, Kissinger suggested to Bahr that the two of them meet in person every three months. Given Kissinger's personality, it was quite meaningful when Bahr wrote in memorandum on the meeting, "For the first time, the conversation with Kissinger could be described as cordial."[34]

Communication via the back channel, most intensive during 1971–72, continued well into 1974, when Brandt and Nixon both resigned office amid political scandals. In the years that the back channel was active, Bahr later wrote, Nixon and Kissinger never voiced political concerns about either the substance or the tempo of Ostpolitik, nor did they attempt to

31 *AAPD* 1969, 2:1114–18; Bahr, *Zu meiner Zeit*, 271–3; Kissinger, *White House Years,* 410–12.

32 Bahr, *Zu meiner Zeit*, 351. "It was part of my obligations to protect Henry" (from his bureaucracy), Bahr wrote in his memories. Bahr's protection proved reliable. Although Kissinger had first been somewhat skeptical, as, according to his opinion before their meeting in October 1969, Bahr did not have "a reputation for discretion."

33 Bahr, *Zu meiner Zeit*, 409. See, e.g., Bahr's back-channel message to Kissinger from 20 September 1971, providing information on Leonid Brezhnev after Willy Brandt's Crimea meeting with the Soviet leader Sept. 16–18, 1971. *AAPD* 1971, 2:1432.

34 Notes by Egon Bahr from 1 April 1972 on his meeting with Henry Kissinger in Washington on Mar. 28, 1972. *AAPD* 1972, 1:349.

make Bonn modify it.[35] To the contrary: Bahr recounted that, on occasion, he sensed genuine appreciation on Kissinger's part for Bonn's initiatives.[36] When Brandt and Nixon met for the first time in Washington in April 1970, Bahr was encouraged by the atmosphere of their talks; he did not realize how adept the president was at hiding the animosity he felt toward his West German guests (and later confessed to Kissinger). The head of the CIA showed the German guests, in a closed session, spectacular photos of military and civilian spots in the Soviet Union, taken from U.S. reconnaissance satellites. In his memoirs, Bahr acknowledged that he liked to be "among friends" and favorably contrasted his experiences in Washington to his dealings with the Soviet leadership.[37]

After initial American reluctance to support negotiations between the FRG and Moscow, from late 1970 the pending quadripartite agreement on Berlin had moved the United States into a situation where it began to work for the success of such negotiations and thus inadvertently legitimized Brandt's Ostpolitik, of which a Berlin accord was an essential cornerstone. By late 1970, the pending Four Power Agreement had put Washington into a position to set aside its initial reluctance and actively support Bonn's negotiations with Moscow.[38] Kissinger put it bluntly in a note to Richard Nixon, which the president rated as an "excellent perceptive analysis (and somewhat ominous)": "Brandt has maneuvered the situation so that *we* have been pushed into the position of being responsible both for Berlin, *and* for the success of his Eastern initiative."[39]

In correlation with Washington's policy moves toward China and the Soviet Union, by 1971 everything had been more or less linked: a U.S.-Soviet summit in Moscow; an agreement in the Strategic Arms Limitation Talks (SALT); an agreement on Berlin; Moscow's treaty with the FRG; and, first on the White House's' list, the reelection of Richard Nixon in 1972 and the ending of the Vietnam War. Like it or not, the White House

---

35 Bahr, *Zu meiner Zeit*, 278. Although this was correct in a technical sense, concerns over the conduct of German Ostpolitik did not go unnoticed with Bahr, who subsequently attempted to raise them with Kissinger: "If you have any questions, please ask them." *AAPD* 1970, 2:1232 (top secret message from Bahr to Kissinger via back channel on July 24, 1970); *AAPD* 1970, 3:1901 (top secret message from Bahr to Kissinger via back channel on Nov. 3, 1970).

36 *AAPD* 1970, 2:1487–91 (record of conversation between Bahr and Kissinger on Aug. 17, 1970 in Washington by Ambassador Pauls; Memorandum from Bahr to Foreign Minister Walter Scheel of Aug. 20, 1970 forwarding Pauls' report).

37 Bahr, *Zu meiner Zeit*, 313–14.

38 Memorandum for the President, from Henry A. Kissinger. Subject: Conversation with Brandt's Foreign Policy Advisor, Egon Bahr. Various Aspects of Soviet and European Policy, Aug. 20, 1970, NARA, NPMP, NSC, Country Files – Europe, Box 684.

39 Memorandum for the President, from Henry A. Kissinger, Sept. 1, 1970, NARA, NPMP, NSC, Country Files – Europe, Box 684.

had to take an interest in the success of Ostpolitik, and Bonn realized that.[40]

The secret talks between the White House and Brandt's Chancellery reached a new level of intensity during the negotiations on the Four Power Agreement on Berlin.[41] From the perspective of State Department officials, the Kissinger-Bahr connection presented "the rather absurd picture of a White House scheming with the Soviets and the Germans against the president's chosen secretary of state (as well as our British and French allies) in a way that could only humiliate Rogers and weaken the effectiveness of American diplomacy."[42] In January 1971, Kissinger issued an innocent-sounding invitation to Bahr via Vice President Spiro Agnew to attend an Apollo moon launch in Cape Canaveral, Florida. The two then used their *Jet Star* return flight from Florida to hold a substantive discussion of the Berlin negotiations.[43] From that point on, the Kissinger-Dobrynin, Kissinger-Bahr, and Bahr-Kevorkov channels provided the background for the Berlin negotiations in Bonn between Bahr, Rush, and Valentin Falin, the Soviet ambassador to West Germany. These three musketeers, as they called themselves, worked out most of the Four Power Agreement on Berlin. In his last back-channel message on the subject, Bahr informed Kissinger "also in the name of Ken [Rush]: No worries any more. Relax! . . . Many factors had to come together for a successful Berlin agreement. Maybe our hotline wasn't the least important one."[44]

Richard Nixon happily took public credit for the successful outcome of the Berlin negotiations at a staged event with Kissinger and Rush at the so-called Western White House in San Clemente, California, on August 27, 1971. According to Bahr, his "new friend" Rush, still basking in the afterglow of success, wanted to stay in Bonn to work for the reelection of Nixon and Brandt and help bring them together personally as well. The U.S. ambassador enthusiastically expressed the conviction that the three musketeers would also be able to conclude successful negotiations on the

40 Ambassador Pauls, Washington, to the Foreign Office. Mar. 20, 1972; idem., Mar. 25, 1972, in *AAPD* 1972, 1:281–5, 1:327–30.

41 See pars pro toto Bahr's secret back-channel messages to Kissinger from Aug. 16–17, 1971, *AAPD* 1971, 2:1245–7.

42 Hillenbrand, *Fragments of Our Time*, 287, 292–3; James S. Sutterlin and David Klein, *Berlin: From Symbol of Confrontation to Keystone of Stability* (New York, 1989).

43 Memorandum for the President's File, from Henry A. Kissinger, Conversation of Dr. Kissinger with Egon Bahr Aboard the Jet Star Going from Cape Kennedy to New York, Jan. 31, 1971; Memorandum for the President, from Henry A. Kissinger, Meeting with Egon Bahr, Jan. 31, 1971, Feb. 4, 1971, NARA, NPMP, NSC, Kissinger Office Files, Box 60.

44 *AAPD* 1971, 2:1247.

reduction of conventional military forces in Europe.[45] Yet Rush later returned to Washington, D.C., as deputy secretary of defense and was replaced as U.S. ambassador in Bonn in April 1972 by Martin J. Hillenbrand, formerly assistant secretary of state for European affairs.

In the first half of 1972, with the Beijing and Moscow summits on the horizon and another North Vietnamese offensive underway, Nixon and Kissinger grudgingly had to recognize that the survival of the Brandt government and Bundestag ratification of the Eastern treaties were very much in America's interest. Although the administration abstained from formally taking sides, Kissinger's support for Bahr in their back-channel communications was unequivocal. Nonetheless, Bahr did not succeed in persuading his American counterpart to induce Nixon to write a letter to Brandt declaring the compatibility of the Eastern treaties with American foreign policy goals.[46] After the defeat of Barzel's no-confidence motion on April 24, 1972, by a tie vote, Kissinger congratulated Brandt via his back channel to Bahr.[47] After both Nixon and Brandt scored impressive personal victories in their countries' November 1972 elections, Kissinger and Bahr discovered further parallels, notably that Brandt's inaugural policy speech before the Bundestag and Nixon's State of the Union address would be taking place almost simultaneously in January 1973. They mused that it would be quite advantageous for the two countries to hold elections in the same month in the future. It now appeared that the president and the chancellor would have four more years to get much accomplished.[48]

Less than two years later, both politicians were out of office. Although always skeptical about the White House's professed trust and goodwill, Brandt considered the letter Nixon sent following his (Brandt's) resignation in May 1974 to be sincere. The president wrote that, whatever the future might bring, Brandt could be assured of his close personal friendship. Looking back in 1989, Brandt described Nixon's gesture as honest and voiced

---

45 Bahr, *Zu meiner Zeit*, 370. On Berlin negotiations, see also Valentin Falin, *Politische Erinnerungen* (Munich, 1993).

46 Maybe it was not this helpful with Richard Nixon that Bahr wrote to Kissinger how Leonid Brezhnev had already sent to Willy Brandt a letter in that vein. Memorandum of State Secretary Bahr, Apr. 1, 1972, State Secretary Bahr to Security Adviser Kissinger, Apr. 1, 1972. *AAPD 1972*, 1:349–53.

47 Memorandum for Mr. Kissinger, from Helmut Sonnenfeldt. Subject: Barzel on Fate of Eastern Treaties. Wants a Message From Us, Apr. 28, 1972, NARA, NPMP, NSC Files, Box 686, Country Files – Europe, Germany (Bonn).

48 Bahr, *Zu meiner Zeit*, 426.

his confidence that the president had not harbored mistrust of either him or his government.[49]

THE WHITE HOUSE AND OSTPOLITIK

Nixon had in fact disliked Brandt from the outset of his tenure as chancellor, even if that was not readily apparent. Sonnenfeldt was wrong when he told Bahr in October 1969 that he was encouraged about the prospects for cooperation between Bonn and Washington on account of the supposedly good chemistry between Brandt and Nixon, who had long known one another.[50] The opposite was the case, however, and not simply because the president viewed the chancellor as a socialist. More important was Brandt's assertive and self-reliant Ostpolitik, which won him widespread recognition as a statesman. No West German chancellor, in Nixon's view, should have such a prominent international profile, least of all Brandt. Nor did it help Brandt's standing in the Nixon White House that he had been close to the Kennedys and that many of Nixon's domestic critics and much of the American press lauded him, especially after he was awarded the Nobel Peace Prize in 1971.[51] *Time* magazine declared Brandt its 1970 "Man of the Year," hailing him as an "innovator" who, in contrast to "most political leaders," shaped events rather than merely reacted to them. "He has projected the most exciting and hopeful vision for Eastern Europe since the Iron Curtain crashed down," the weekly wrote. "It's a daring vision, full of opportunity and danger."[52]

Kissinger inadvertently made clear the jealous, hierarchical mind-set of the Nixon administration when he pointedly warned a senior West German official in June 1970, "There is one thing I want to tell you: If there has to be any détente with the Soviet Union at all, then *we* will do it."[53] Echoing many contemporary observers both inside and outside the administration, one scholar notes, "Kissinger probably meant to say that the greatest offense of the West German *Ostpolitik* was that he personally was not in charge of it."[54]

---

49 Willy Brandt, *Erinnerungen* (Frankfurt, 1989), 193.

50 *AAPD* 1969, 2:1115.

51 See, e.g. (by *New York Times* correspondent in Bonn at the time) David Binder, *The Other German: Willy Brandt's Life and Times* (Washington, D.C., 1975); see also highly positive assessments of Brandt and Ostpolitik by a prominent former Kennedy and Johnson administration official and long-term editor of *Foreign Affairs*, William Bundy, *A Tangled Web: The Making of Foreign Policy in the Nixon Presidency* (New York, 1998).

52 "On the Road to a New Reality," *Time*, Jan. 4, 1971. 6.

53 Paul Frank, *Entschlüsselte Botschaft. Ein Diplomat macht Inventur* (Stuttgart, 1981), 287. Italics are in the original.

54 A. James McAdams, "The New Diplomacy of the West German *Ostpolitik*," in *The Diplomats: 1939–1979*, eds. Gordon Craig and Francis L. Loewenheim (Princeton, NJ, 1994), 551.

Nixon, encouraged by reports from CDU politicians, hoped in vain that Brandt's government would soon fall. In a March 1970 comment on the upcoming state elections in West Germany, Kissinger noted that the outcome could jeopardize the SPD-FPD coalition on the federal level. "If Brandt continues his soft headed line – This would be in our interest," Nixon wrote in the margin.[55]

Obliged to live with the Brandt government, however, Nixon had to hide his true feelings and could voice his true opinions only in private conversations or in his notes on Kissinger's memoranda. He felt slighted, for example, by the toast Brandt offered during a White House visit on June 15, 1971. The chancellor, who "owed a lot" to the United States in Nixon's view, had been "presumptuous" and had "lectured" the president on Pakistan and Vietnam. To calm Nixon down, Kissinger was forced to call and complain to Bahr.[56]

On December 20, 1972, Kissinger wrote in a memorandum to the president, "Our interest in good relations with [Brandt's] government on East-West security issues generally dictates maximum accommodation to Brandt on East Germany, where our interests, except for Berlin, are minor." Infuriated, Nixon wrote an emphatic "no" in the margin. He then instructed Kissinger, "Do *absolutely* nothing which plays to Brandt (regardless of his election)" (emphasis in original). He ordered that all decisions pertaining to Germany henceforth be submitted for his approval and concluded with a diatribe against the State Department: "The State Bureaucracy is *pro* Brandt and *pro* Socialist – I *totally* disagree with their approach" (emphasis in original).[57] After Nixon's 1972 electoral triumph, conspiracy theories about the West German chancellor's true intentions to neutralize Western Europe in collaboration with his socialist friends in other European governments, his deference to Soviet interests, and his efforts to weaken transatlantic ties with the United States became steadily more popular in a White House that found itself increasingly under siege as a result of the Watergate scandal. Substantive policy differences and personal jealousy are inextricably interwoven in Nixon's rants against Brandt, which White House staffers and Brandt's political opponents did nothing to discourage.

---

55 Memorandum for the President's File, from Henry A. Kissinger. Subject: The Current Status of Brandt's *Ostpolitik*, Mar. 10, 1970, NARA, NPMP, NSC, Country Files – Europe, Box 683.
56 NARA, NPMP, White House Tapes, recordings of (three different) conversations between Nixon and Kissinger, June 16, 1971.
57 Memorandum for the President, from Henry A. Kissinger. Subject: Initial Contacts with East Germany, Dec. 20, 1972, NARA, NPMP, NSC, Country Files – Europe, Box 60.

"That Henry Kissinger expressed himself with different emphasis in my absence than in my presence has often been claimed but never substantiated," Willy Brandt wrote in 1989,[58] apparently dismissing the polemic against him that had appeared seven years earlier in the second volume of Kissinger's memoirs.[59] Further evidence of Kissinger's views of Brandt and Ostpolitik became available a decade and a half after Brandt's death in 1992 with the release of the content of Kissinger's taped telephone conversations during his time in the Nixon administration.[60] This material reinforces the impression that the account of these years that Kissinger offers in his memoirs is not always supported by the archival record.[61]

Although initially skeptical and prone to jealousy, Kissinger was not opposed to Bonn's Ostpolitik – in contrast to Nixon – nor was he as unfavorably disposed toward Brandt as he later claimed to be. How could he have been, after all, given his proclivity for realpolitik and equilibrium, his personal style of secretive diplomacy, and his interest in using leverage on Moscow and Beijing to facilitate the American exit from Vietnam? Washington's policy goals vis-à-vis the Eastern bloc were never incompatible with Bonn's. With the negotiations on the Berlin Agreement linked to the SALT talks, and the Moscow summit somehow linked to the ratification of the Eastern treaties, Ostpolitik and détente became intertwined.[62] Much as he might have ranted against it, Nixon did not have the means to intervene against Brandt's Ostpolitik or to torpedo it. Moreover, the Polish riots of December 1970 and especially the U.S.-Chinese opening since 1971 had made dealings with the Soviet Union easier. Both Washington and Bonn opted for very cautious and only implicit exploitation of Soviet problems and did so jointly, as this further induced Moscow to strive for stability and predictability at its Western front in Central Europe.

CONCLUSION

The Nixon administration pursued its own course toward détente with the Soviet Union, even if it did not use that term in public. Washington and Paris had both made moves to improve relations with Moscow before Brandt took office as chancellor in 1969. Without these Western models, it is unlikely the SPD–FDP coalition would have dared to undertake such a bold, almost frantic approach to Ostpolitik. In their conversations with

58 Brandt, *Erinnerungen*, 192.
59 Henry A. Kissinger, *Years of Upheaval* (Boston, 1982), 143–6.
60 See *Foreign Relations of the United States*, vol. 40, *Germany and Berlin, 1969–1972* (Washington, D.C., 2008).
61 Kissinger, *White House Years*, 409–10.   62 McAdams, *New Diplomacy*, 551.

their West German counterparts, American officials from the president on down emphasized the "encouraging parallel," in Nixon's words, between Washington's stance toward Moscow and Bonn's.[63] Kissinger later deliberately and misleadingly overstated Bonn's influence on American policy. In his memoirs, he tried to justify the Nixon administration's disputed détente policy by arguing that the administration had had to act preemptively to outflank Brandt's overtures to Moscow.[64] Kissinger also claimed that he saw a potential threat posed by "German nationalism" in Bonn's Ostpolitik, but there is little indication in his comments at the time that he gave much thought to this threat. Having criticized Bahr mildly in rather tongue-in-cheek fashion in his memoirs,[65] Kissinger praised him in 1992 after German reunification had been realized: "I don't know of any politician with greater analytical faculties. He well deserved the highest honor to be bestowed on a statesman – the fulfillment of his dreams of the sixties in the nineties."[66]

Kissinger had pragmatically sought to engage Bonn in intensive communication and consultation to obtain information about the specifics of its Ostpolitik, a policy concept he regarded as inevitable.[67] He acknowledged the pivotal role of the United States in safeguarding and promoting Brandt's Ostpolitik by facilitating American involvement in a quadripartite agreement on Berlin. Kissinger later justified Washington's intensive part in those negotiations with a need to constrain "nationalistic undercurrents" in Germany, although he did not make this argument explicitly in contemporary circumstances. Given the symbolic importance of Berlin and overall German-American relations, the United States hardly could have afforded to stay out of negotiations about the divided city or even to work toward their failure. The American government was very well aware of that and acted accordingly. Actually it proved wiser, as Kissinger was to recall later from hindsight, to let Germany "pursue its own identity" than to insist on its division and therefore undermine the Western alliance.[68]

The U.S. policy vis-à-vis West Germany after 1969 was not a relationship of pretended confidentiality "to prevent the worst" from happening and

63 *AAPD* 1970, 2:1202 (notes from Ambassador Pauls of July 19, 1970 on conversation between President Nixon and Foreign Minister Walter Scheel on July 18).
64 Kissinger, *Years of Upheaval*, 146.   65 Kissinger, *White House Years,* 410–11.
66 Henry A. Kissinger, "Seine Träume der sechziger Jahre wurden in den Neunzigern Wirklichkeit," in *Das Undenkbare denken. Festschrift für Egon Bahr zum siebzigsten Geburtstag,* ed. Dieter Dowe (Baden-Baden, 1992), 119.
67 Holger Klitzing, *The Nemesis of Stability: Henry A. Kissinger's Ambivalent Relationship with Germany* (Trier, 2007).
68 Henry A. Kissinger, Statement on Occasion of Unveiling a Willy Brandt Portrait by Johannes Heisig, German Historical Institute, Washington, D.C., Mar. 18, 2003, http://www.ghi-dc.org/Kissinger.html.

curb the "resurgence of German nationalism." Viewing the FRG as in potential danger of floating freely in the center of Europe between West and East like in the period "from Bismarck to Rapallo," to quote one of Henry Kissinger's later historical parallels,[69] does not illuminate much beyond historical erudition. Such was not Washington's actual policy toward Bonn during the Nixon and Brandt years.

It is a distortion of the historical record to characterize the policy of Brandt and Bahr between 1969 and 1973 with allusions to later positions of both politicians. Bearing in mind the transatlantic rift over the deployment of intermediate-range nuclear weapons and misgivings about the Reagan administration, as well as the implicit role of Brandt and Bahr in bringing down Helmut Schmidt's SPD-led government in 1982, Ostpolitik was portrayed in the 1980s as a long-term strategy for European "neutralism," accommodation, and, ultimately, dependence on the Soviet Union. Back then, Henry Kissinger ascribed to the Soviet Union a successful prospect of "selective détente" to split the Western alliance and an almost mythical attractiveness to the Germans in particular. About twenty years down the road, though, in 2003, Kissinger called it "a tremendous achievement of Brandt that he dared to raise the question of German national interests and attempted to relate them, and indeed succeeded in relating them to the common interests of the West."[70]

Despite Nixon's misgivings about Brandt, his administration's approach to U.S.–West German relations was on the whole pragmatic, cooperative, and sometimes even friendly. This seeming paradox points to the necessity of distinguishing between a political actor's personality traits and political skills. In substance, the communication between the "totally different personalities," as Kissinger described them, heading the governments in Bonn and Washington was without precedent in the history of U.S.–West German relations. Kissinger has more recently observed, "There has never been a better period in the relationship on the issues that mattered." Speaking on the same occasion, Bahr added that "a trust developed between Washington and Bonn that proved itself in an intimate cooperation that was rarely matched or surpassed later."[71]

69 Kissinger, *White House Years*, 409.   70 Ibid.

71 Henry A. Kissinger, Statement on Occasion of Unveiling a Willy Brandt Portrait by Johannes Heisig, German Historical Institute, Washington, D.C., Mar. 18, 2003, http://www.ghi-dc.org/Kissinger.html; Egon Bahr, Statement on Occasion of Unveiling a Willy Brandt Portrait by Johannes Heisig, German Historical Institute, Washington, D.C., Mar. 18, 2003, http://www.ghi-dc.org/Bahr.htm.

A common element of both West German Ostpolitik and American détente was the acknowledgment of realpolitik in dealing with the de facto Soviet domination over Eastern Europe. "Change through rapprochement" implied a gradual evolution in Eastern Europe, brought on by trade and openness to the West, but not necessarily a change in the so-called status quo. Détente and Ostpolitik, despite their sometimes revisionist rhetoric, did not really aim to help the Eastern European countries gain more autonomy from the Soviet Union.

Avoiding the destabilizing of Eastern European governments and bolstering the Soviets' sense of security were key elements in the policies of both Washington and Bonn. With the Soviet invasion of Czechoslovakia fresh in memory, Bahr and his American partners did not want to do anything that might ultimately lead to another Soviet crackdown within the Warsaw Pact. In December 1970, Pauls reported from Washington that Sonnenfeldt was worried that Ostpolitik might lead to a greater demand for Western goods and technologies in Eastern Europe and thus cause dangerous instability or even revolution.[72] Bahr voiced much the same concerns two months later in a back-channel message to Kissinger on the situation in Poland. General Secretary Władysław Gomułka had recently been forced to resign after the violent suppression of strikes and protest demonstrations resulted in hundreds of deaths. Attributing the unrest to low living standards, Bahr openly expressed his worries about the Polish government's attempts to liberalize the country's political system to Kissinger: "We know how it will start. . . . If the situation in Poland takes off like a wildfire, the Soviet Union will have to intervene earlier than in Prague to avoid repercussions for the Soviet leadership. In any event, such a development would lead to blockade of East-West-relations like after Prague."[73] Kissinger identified the Polish riots of early 1971 as the final reason why Moscow had moved toward détente with the United States. He did not have to mention that Washington had no intention of trying to exploit the Polish situation against the Soviet Union.

Europe was spared the proxy wars and superpower-backed coups that afflicted other regions of the world during the 1970s and early 1980s. That was in no small measure a result of détente and Ostpolitik. With the Conference on Security and Cooperation in Europe's Helsinki Final Act of 1975, the two blocs committed themselves to peaceful coexistence at least

---

72 Ambassador Pauls to Foreign Ministry, Dec. 18, 1970, *AAPD* 1970, 3:2295.
73 Top Secret Message from Bahr to Kissinger on Feb. 18, 1971, *AAPD* 1971, 1:340–1.

within Europe. That commitment, in turn, gave Mikhail Gorbachev the confidence eleven years later to embark on a foreign policy very different from that of his predecessors. It was thus anything but a coincidence that after his consolidation of power in 1986 Gorbachev took encouragement from his talks with elder Western statesmen like Brandt, Bahr, and Kissinger for his new Soviet *Westpolitik*.

3

The Economics of Ostpolitik

West Germany, the United States, and the Gas Pipeline Deal

WERNER D. LIPPERT

On the first day of February 1970, at the Hotel Kaiserhof in Essen, Soviet Trade Minister Nicolai Patolichev and West German Economics Minister Karl Schiller signed the largest trade deal between their two countries up to that point. This agreement, Schiller pointed out in his speech for the occasion, reinvigorated the century-old export of German technology and finished products to Russia, a tradition that had stalled in the confrontational climate of the Cold War.[1] This agreement, later known as the first natural gas pipeline deal, was the first of many the government of Chancellor Willy Brandt backed and helped finance to build closer economic cooperation between the two nominally hostile countries: from Bonn's perspective, *Osthandel* (trade with the East) was intended to serve as a cornerstone of *Ostpolitik*. The Nixon administration's failure to recognize and act on the dangers inherent in such close economic cooperation prompted a significant divergence in West Germany's strategic interests that ultimately would collide with American visions and ideas.

Superficially, Bonn's interest in increasing cooperation with the Soviet Union was very much in line with Western détente efforts of the early 1970s. Exhausted by military expenditures, proxy wars, and an escalating arms race, both superpowers and their respective allies sought a reprieve from the confrontational policies of the early Cold War.[2] President Richard M. Nixon had declared that his term of office would be "an era of negotiation." In this context, trade deals with the Soviet Union seemed eminently sensible.

---

1 The first German steel pipes were shipped to the Soviet Union in 1867.
2 Keith Nelson, *The Making of Détente: Soviet-American Relations in the Shadow of Vietnam* (Baltimore, 1995).

65

For Brandt, though, trade with the Soviet Union meant more than boosting the West German economy or protecting German jobs. Expanding West German–Soviet economic ties was, rather, the first step in implementing his foreign policy vision of a new era of peaceful cooperation in Europe that would eventually make German unification possible. Brandt's need for Soviet cooperation, reinforced by the political and strategic imbalances between the two countries, contributed to a West German trade policy heavily in favor of the Soviet Union. That was necessary, however, as it was only through trade that Brandt could overcome Soviet antagonism to the Federal Republic and persuade the Soviet leadership to engage in high-level talks. Osthandel, therefore, became the cornerstone of a visionary Ostpolitik that was aimed at transforming the status quo.

The Nixon administration ignored Bonn's economic overtures to Moscow and, blind to the importance of trade other than as a short-term means of securing political concessions, failed to establish a similar trade relationship before the Jackson-Vanik amendment repoliticized Soviet-American trade.

Against the background of the debate on the effectiveness of trade as an instrument of foreign policy, this chapter explores how differing policies on technology and energy trade within an alliance system can severely undermine its integrity. This is a case study of the West German–American alliance during the Nixon–Brandt era and delineates the structural differences caused by Willy Brandt's successful incorporation of trade in his détente policies vis-à-vis the Soviet Union and the failure of the Nixon-Kissinger team to achieve the same for the United States.[3] The diverging strategic interests, then, resulted in conflicts within the alliance during the Yom Kippur War and the pipeline constructions projects in 1975 and 1981, and are one of the root causes for the troubles the transatlantic alliance faced during the 1970s and beyond.

As foreign minister in the Christian Democratic–Social Democratic "grand coalition" government, Brandt had been able to secure trade agreements with some Eastern European states by 1968. Building economic ties

---

3 Even though an entire school of thought on U.S. foreign policy was inspired by William Appleman Williams's concepts of economic perceptions, little research has been done on the effect of trade on German-American alliance politics during the Nixon era. Some of the best ones to cover economic history from either the U.S. or the German side are Angela E. Stent, *From Embargo to Ostpolitik: the Political Economy of West German–Soviet Relations, 1955–1980* (Cambridge, MA, 1985); Alan P. Dobson, *U.S. Economic Statecraft for Survival, 1933–1991: Of Sanctions, Embargoes, and Economic Warfare* (New York, 2002); Karsten Rudolph, *Wirtschaftsdiplomatie im Kalten Krieg: Die Ostpolitik der westdeutschen Großindustrie 1945–1991* (Frankfurt am Main, 2004); and Diane B. Kunz, *Butter and Guns: America's Cold War Economic Diplomacy* (New York, 1997).

with the Eastern bloc states was the common denominator in his and Chancellor Kurt Georg Kiesinger's foreign policy visions. The key to achieving Brandt's vision of a new European peace order lay, however, with the Soviet Union.[4] But given the animosity and public confrontation that marked West German–Soviet relations in the wake of the Soviet invasion of Czechoslovakia, Brandt found it difficult to establish high-level contacts within the Soviet leadership.

Driven by a desperate "search for a new connection to Soviet politicians," Egon Bahr, Brandt's right hand in dealing with the Soviets, floated the idea of inviting Soviet Foreign Trade Minister Nikolai Patolichev to the Hanover trade fair in April 1968.[5] After repeated inquiries to the Economics Ministry, Bahr finally ignored Schiller's instructions to hold off on the invitation unless Patolichev agreed in advance to attend and instructed the embassy in Moscow to convey a verbal invitation.[6] Patolichev proved as difficult as the officials at the Economics Ministry in Bonn. He insisted on a formal invitation, which Brandt's Foreign Ministry obtained after another two weeks of interministerial wrangling, only to turn it down in the end.[7]

The Warsaw Pact invasion of Czechoslovakia in August 1968 certainly did not increase the chances of improving contacts, particularly as the Soviet Union perceived West Germany's growing trade with Eastern Europe as an expression of German revanchism: "The new Ostpolitik is to play the role of a battering ram, which will smash a hole in the Socialist community and open legal paths for an economic and ideological, and, later, political invasion of West German imperialism in the lands of Eastern Europe."[8] Despite the public outrage over the invasion of Czechoslovakia and the threat in September that the Kremlin might also invade West Germany to curb revanchism, in early November, Brandt broached the idea of trying to entice the Soviets with the prospect of trade in nuclear technology to expand West German–Soviet cultural, economic, and technical exchange.[9]

---

4 Willy Brandt, *A Peace Policy for Europe* (New York, 1969), 110–11.
5 Memo, VC5, Dr. Steidle, to L1 Herrn MinRat Dr. Moltrecht, Bonn, Feb. 15, 1968, betr: Hannover-Messe 1968, Bundesarchiv Koblenz (BA) 102/100025.
6 Memo, Foreign Ministry Undersecretary Harkort to Economics Ministry Undersecretary Schiettinger, "Einladung des sowjetrussischen Außenhandelsministers Patolitschew zu diesjährigen Hannover-Messe," Mar. 13, 1968, BA 102/100025.
7 Memo, Foreign Ministry Undersecretary Harkort to Economics Ministry Undersecretary Schiettinger, "Einladung des sowjetischen Außenhandelsministers Patolitschew," Apr. 9, 1968, BA 102/100025; Memo, Deputy Undersecretary Toepfer to Secretary von Dohnanyi, "Einladung des sowjetischen Außenhandelsministers," Apr. 11, 1968, BA 102/100025.
8 Prawda article, as cited in Michael Kreile, *Osthandel und Ostpolitik* (Baden-Baden, 1978), 103.
9 Letter, Secretary Duckwitz to German Embassy in Moscow, Nov. 8, 1968: *Akten zur Auswärtigen Politik der Bundesrepublik Deutschland* [hereafter *AAPD*] 1968, #370; MemCon, "Gespräch des Bundesministers Brandt mit dem sowjetischen Botschafter Zarapkin," Jan. 10, 1969: *AAPD* 1969, #8.

Yet the Soviets remained reserved. When Brandt raised the issue of East-West trade during a lunch with Soviet Ambassador Zarapkin on February 11, 1969, Zarapkin only rehashed the old line that oil import quotas would need to be increased before West German companies could be considered for sizable Soviet orders.[10] The issue of heating oil import quotas was, however, a dead end. Heating oil was the only energy product the Soviets produced in surplus, but the Western European market was saturated. The import quota was already at the maximum level the West German market could absorb, thus leaving no real scope for expansion. Brandt may thus have seen the invitation to Patolichev as an opportunity to explore other options for expanding West German–Soviet trade.

Brandt's overtures came at a time when the Soviet leadership was growing increasingly frustrated with its largest trading partner in Western Europe, France. France's trade with the Soviet Union had grown rapidly during the 1960s. By 1969, however, a continuously expanding trade relationship seemed less and less likely. Chronic Soviet difficulties in financing French imports created tensions between Moscow and Paris. The French had hoped to make the Soviet economy more productive by pushing for more transparency, a wider flow of information, and increased human interactions. The Soviets saw those efforts as a form of political interference that went beyond the acceptable level of Western influence.

Other Western European countries had also been trading with the Soviets and, like France, were becoming disillusioned with the Soviet market. The troubles experienced by the Italian automaker Fiat served as a warning to other Western companies. Fiat had entered into an agreement to build an automobile factory in the Soviet Union. Soviet authorities were cooperative in spirit, as evidenced by their renaming the town where the factory was to be built after the Italian Communist leader Palmiro Togliatti. But delays and poor workmanship in the construction of the infrastructure for the plant had turned the entire project into a nightmare. As the other Western European countries became less enthusiastic about doing business with the Soviets, West Germany began to look more appealing in Moscow's eyes.

In the end, it was not Brandt who managed to tame the Russian bear with some visionary scheme. Rather, the Soviets needed West Germany for their economic strategy. After Brandt's personal intervention with Zarapkin, Patolichev agreed to attend the Hanover fair. There, he outlined a proposal that would solve the Soviet Union's hard currency troubles and provide a

---

10 MemCon, "Gespräch des Staatssekretärs Duckwitz mit dem sowjetischen Botschafter Zarapkin," Apr. 8, 1969, *AAPD* 1969, #117, n. 2.

basis for future West German–Soviet trade: a natural gas pipeline.[11] The proposal had very firm boundaries: Patolichev made clear to Schiller that the deal would not be linked to any political concessions on Moscow's part.[12] Despite that insistence, Brandt and his advisers saw the pipeline proposal as the only means to cultivate a working relationship with the Soviet Union, and thus gave it their full backing for the sake of its potential political benefits.

Concerns within the West German government about becoming dependent on Soviet energy exports were pushed aside with the argument that the volume of the proposed deal was not large enough to pose a serious threat. Nor was there any questioning of the wisdom of making a huge infrastructure investment in a Communist country that had recently threatened to invade the Federal Republic.[13] The most striking aspect of the deal was Bonn's utilization of trade for strictly political ends. The gas the Soviets would be supplying was of little commercial interest to the West Germans. According to assessment of the Economics Ministry in Bonn, the proposed pipeline would be economically feasible only if it connected southern Germany, Italy, France, Austria, and Czechoslovakia. In the north, the Federal Republic could count on natural gas from the Netherlands and Norway for the foreseeable future. The south of the country was also well supplied, but the Economics Ministry believed that the market there could possibly absorb an additional 2 to 3 billion cubic meters of natural gas as of 1975. Even that relatively small increase in supply would, however, require price discounts and the creation of strong incentives for consumers to switch from oil to natural gas.[14] In short, the Soviets were offering something the West Germans had no need for.

In a reversal of the usual situation in their economic dealings with West Germans, during the 1970s the Soviets had the upper hand in trade negotiations. That might have been a consequence of their recognition that Brandt's political vision depended on Soviet cooperation. It probably also helped that the KGB was able to inform the Soviet negotiators of Bonn's negotiating positions.[15]

---

11 Memo, "Eventuelle Einladung des sowjetischen Außenministers Patolitschew," Apr. 16, 1969, BA 102/100025.

12 Letter, Economics Minister Schiller to Chancellor Kiesinger, Apr. 29, 1969, BA 102/100021, 2.

13 Talking Points Memo, Secretary v. Dohnanyi trip to the Soviet Union, "Einfuhr sowjetischen Erdgases nach Bayern," May 20, 1969, BA 102/100021, 2.

14 Ibid.

15 Arkady N. Shevchenko, *Breaking with Moscow* (New York, 1985), 224. Shevchenko recalls KGB information on the German negotiating positions to be "surprising in the quality and quantity."

West German Ambassador Allardt, thus, assured a very reserved Patolichev on May 26, 1969, that the Economics Ministry would try to assist
the Soviets in selling its natural gas in West Germany on the terms the Soviets
had envisioned. Providing additional incentives to continue the dialogue,
the ambassador also suggested an industrial-technological exchange between
the two countries.[16]

Not everyone in Bonn was happy with the manner in which this trade
deal was being negotiated. Otto-Axel Herbst, the director of the Foreign Ministry's trade department, pointed to a majority in-house opinion
according to which the West German government should seek to use the
deal for political leverage. Because the annual Soviet revenues from the
natural gas deliveries would allow the Soviet Union to finance one-fifth of
its total imports from West Germany, Herbst thought that the government
could wrestle a long-sought-after comprehensive trade agreement from the
Soviets.[17] This trade agreement, which had last been discussed in negotiations in October 1966, had failed because of the Soviet refusal to include
West Berlin in the agreement. Herbst and the foreign trade section of the
Foreign Ministry therefore argued for tougher negotiations with the Soviet
delegation on the natural gas pipeline deal. Foreign Ministry State Secretary
Günther Harkort concurred with Herbst's assessment and further consid-
ered a 20 percent cap on Soviet natural gas, as proposed by the Economics
Ministry, to be surprisingly high.[18]

Apparently concerned by the criticism of the proposed deal within the
government, Brandt intervened personally with Schiller. He outlined the
great commercial and political significance of the deal and said that he was
not worried by the prospect of large imports of Soviet natural gas. "Our
interest lies in the expansion of trade," he told Schiller, "which requires an
increase of export capabilities by the Soviet Union." Brandt used Herbst's
trade agreement proposition but only as a basis for a future trade deal rather
than a contingency.[19]

Schiller agreed with Brandt in general on the desirability of a trade agreement but did not show the same readiness to sacrifice commercial interests
for political. With a vague reference to interministerial coordination at the
appropriate time, Schiller blocked Brandt's interference and referred him

16 Memo, German Ambassador in Moscow Allardt to German Foreign Office, May 26, 1969, *AAPD* 1969, #176.
17 Memo, German Foreign Office Undersecretary Herbst to Economics Ministry Undersecretary Döring, "Sowjetisches Erdgas," July 3, 1969, BA 102/99987.
18 Memo, German Foreign Office, Herbst, June 27, 1969: *AAPD* 1969, #213, nn. 4 and 6.
19 Letter, Foreign Minister Brandt to Economics Minister Schiller, July 10, 1969, B102/99987.

to the Economics Ministry staff should he have further questions.[20] It is clear that the discourse within the West German government on trade with the Soviet Union was marked by caution and reservations. Even some of Brandt's fellow Social Democrats in the cabinet, such as Schiller, did not share his enthusiasm for pursuing trade deals with the Soviets. It is thus not surprising that, as chancellor, he had to bypass a reluctant government bureaucracy and rely on individuals like Bahr in negotiations with Moscow.

This rift within the government bureaucracies did not stem simply from differences on negotiation strategy. At its core lay the debate over how to deal with the Soviet Union and its foreign policy ambitions. Much like Bonn's later differences with the Nixon administration, the internal conflicts had occurred because Brandt had abandoned the image of the Soviet Union as a dangerous enemy and now tried to court it as a potential partner in his vision of a European peace order with a "Marshall Plan for the East."[21]

With Brandt's election to the chancellorship in October 1969, the pro-Osthandel faction gained significant ground. Under Bahr's auspices as minister without portfolio, the chancellor's office was able to move the talks along at such a pace that in January 1970 the deal would be finalized. Herbst could do little more than voice his concern that West Germany had not managed to "obtain a basic set of rules, regulating trade deals between Western countries and the Soviet Union" in its negotiations over the pipeline deal. What Herbst criticized most, albeit indirectly, was Brandt and Bahr's style of policy making. Pointing to the significance of the pipeline deal, he argued that the Foreign Ministry should have been involved in the negotiations and that there should have been an intense discussion of the negotiations, because they threatened to undercut internationally agreed-on procedures. He pointed to the unprecedented levels at which West German banks had extended loan guarantees to the Soviet Union, more than doubling the customary five-year cap. The West German government also secured the loan with an unusually large export guarantee covering 50 percent of the value of the deal. Even the repayment procedures proved extraordinary. The Soviet Union would provide only one-eleventh of the value of the trade deal as down payment and did not have to start repaying the loan until roughly three years after completion, and then at an interest rate that was one and a half percentage points below the market rate. The installments would increase significantly toward the end of the loan, providing further financial flexibility for the Soviet Union.[22] In short, the Brandt government had

---

20 Letter, Economics Minister Schiller to Foreign Minister Brandt, Aug. 26, 1969, B102/99987.
21 See Brandt, *Peace Policy*, 122.
22 Memo, German Foreign Office, Herbst, Jan. 26, 1970: *AAPD* 1970, #23.

bent over backward to make the deal as favorable as possible for the Soviet Union and quietly made the German taxpayers responsible for the difference between the customary market interest rate of 6.5 percent and the 5 percent the Soviet Union had insisted on.[23]

Harkort voiced an even stronger condemnation of the terms of the deal. He attributed the unusually generous terms Bonn offered Moscow to political reasons – "because they are deals with the East" – and saw disadvantages for Western trade in such favoritism. In addition, he believed that this deal broke a decade-old understanding among Western powers that they coordinate their export credit rates and conditions so they would not be played off one another.[24] While other European nations had previously broken the five-year cap on loans, the combination of subsidized interest rates, the long duration of the loan, and low initial payments that Bonn had agreed to were heavily criticized by the Federal Republic's neighbors.[25]

Here, Brandt's policies ran counter to Nixon's ideas about dealing with the Soviets. Nixon, too, sought to liberalize trade with the Communist bloc and commissioned Secretary of Agriculture Clifford M. Hardin to explore possible economic ties with the countries of Eastern Europe during a visit to the region. But trade was for Nixon little more than a political tool to continue the struggle against an ideological adversary.[26] The Communist regimes were still enemies, and trade was seen as a political weapon.[27] National Security Council staffer Fred Bergstein summed up Nixon's early views on trade with the Soviet Union pointedly when he wrote to Kissinger: "I fully recognize that he wishes to avoid giving the Soviets anything at this time."[28] The era of negotiation that Nixon had announced during the campaign would thus be one of quid pro quo: increases in trade would be contingent on political concessions.

The Brandt government was fully aware of this approach, as evidenced by West German Ambassador Rolf Friedman Pauls's observation, "When Nixon talks about an era of negotiation, he does not mean an era of

23 Randall Newnham, *Deutsche Mark Diplomacy: Positive Economic Sanctions in German-Russian Relations* (University Park, PA, 2002), 159.
24 Memo, German Foreign Office, Herbst, Jan. 26, 1970: *AAPD* 1970 #23, n. 5.
25 Memo, Dr. Henze, "Lastwagenprojekt in der UdSSR," Sept. 16, 1970, BA 102/100011, 2.
26 Memo, C. Fred Bergsten (NSC) to President's Assistant for National Security Affairs (Kissinger), Apr. 14, 1969, *Foreign Relations of the United States [FRUS]* 1969–1976, 3:19.
27 Richard M. Nixon, *The Memoirs of Richard Nixon* (New York, 1978), 343–44.
28 Memo, C. Fred Bergsten (NSC) to President's Assistant for National Security Affairs (Kissinger), July 3, 1969, *FRUS* 1969–1976, 4:303. In July 1971, Nixon's view would change to a highly mercantilist view of international trade. His subsequent pursuit of economic nationalism brought him no closer to Brandt's economic policies with the Soviet Union. For further details, see Allen J. Matusow, *Nixon's Economy: Booms, Busts, Dollars, and Votes* (Lawrence, KS, 1998), 132–7.

agreement at all costs but a phase of exchange on the basis of give and take."[29] He also reported that Nixon rejected an "as if" approach, like Brandt's, of making overtures of cooperation even if the Soviets failed to follow suit.[30] Given such reports from Washington, Brandt was consciously disregarding American tutelage when he decided to intensify West Germany's economic contacts with the Soviet Union. West Germany, long the loyal ally, broke with its strict allegiance to U.S. leadership and pursued its own foreign policy. Even though the National Security Council had found trade with the Soviet Union of little economic value, it was nonetheless construed as "an instrument of negotiation."[31] By offering the Soviets the Western goods and technology that Nixon sought to use in a quid pro quo, Brandt, in essence, stole the American thunder.

Lack of American economic leverage with the Soviet Union was especially significant with regards to Vietnam, as Nixon intended to encourage the Russians to "show greater willingness to be helpful on some of the more vexing problems between us."[32] He and Kissinger were hoping that limiting exports to the Soviet Union and China "would put pressure on them to help in Vietnam and would signal that we are prepared to deal with them after the war."[33] As the carrot, Nixon had decided that the United States "should be prepared to move generously to liberalize our trade policy toward the Soviet Union and the other Eastern European countries whenever there is sufficient improvement in our overall relations with them."[34] As Kissinger put it, "Expanding trade without a political quid pro quo was a gift; there was little the Soviets could do for us economically."[35]

Washington's ability to use trade to gain political leverage was undercut, however, by the willingness of its allies to supply the Soviet Union with Western goods. Western European business deals with the Eastern bloc states were, indeed, a source of frustration to Nixon:

At the heart of the problem is the fact that in our East-West trade policy as it relates to peaceful trade we are going it alone. Today only American industry has such heavy bureaucratic governmental licensing requirements and controls for the

---

29 Memo, German Ambassador in Washington (Pauls) to German Foreign Office, "Bemerkungen zur amerikanischen Außenpolitik," Dec. 21, 1970, BA 102/111915.
30 Ibid.
31 Paper prepared by the National Security Council Staff, [n.d., but between Apr. 16 and May 15], *FRUS* 1969–1976, 5:292.
32 Memo, Undersecretary of State (Richardson) to President's Assistant for National Security Affairs (Kissinger), June 21, 1969, *FRUS* 1969–1976, 4:300.
33 Ibid. See also Editorial Note, *FRUS* 1969–1976, 4:313.
34 National Security Decision Memorandum #15, May 28, 1969, *FRUS* 1969–1976, 4:299. Also Dobson, *U.S. Economic Statecraft for Survival*, 200.
35 Kissinger, *White House Years*, 152. See also Dobson, *U.S. Economic Statecraft for Survival*, 99.

export of many kinds of peaceful goods to Eastern Europe. If the governments of the European industrial nations of NATO followed a policy similar to ours, it would be one thing. . . . But European NATO and other free-world governments are actively supporting their business communities to expand exports to East Europe by assisting in long-term credits, subsidizing export, encouraging barter arrangements, etc. . . . Our policy of denial denies very little and simply forces the satellite nations to obtain comparable products from Britain, France, West Germany, Italy and other European nations, and Japan at the expense of American business and industry.[36]

Why, then, did Nixon and Kissinger not object to the pipeline deal or try to exert pressure on the Brandt government? First and foremost, they were probably surprised by the speed with which the negotiations were finalized after Brandt took office. It must have come as a surprise that such a monumental deal would be completed within three months after negotiations had been dragging on for years.

Nixon's relative quietness on Brandt's Ostpolitik in the winter of 1969–70 must also be viewed in light of his other priorities. Vietnam was undoubtedly the White House's main concern. Having failed, on the one hand, to satisfy the antiwar movement with his pledge to secure an "honorable" withdrawal and, on the other hand, to make any headway in the negotiations with the North Vietnamese, Nixon faced a conflict that affected not only the American economy but also his popularity.[37] He was taking a much bigger political gamble with the troop withdrawals announced in September 1969 and the Paris peace talks than Brandt was with Ostpolitik. In addition, arms control negotiations with the Soviet Union, the Strategic Arms Limitation Talks (SALT), began in Helsinki in November: these negotiations were of more direct bearing on U.S. policy and interests than was Bonn's pipeline deal. After Brandt had removed Germany as an obstacle to superpower détente, the Nixon administration viewed Brandt's Ostpolitik with a grandfatherly benevolence: out of line but ultimately doomed to failure. Nixon did not think that Ostpolitik would succeed and summed it up the following way: "It looks like Brandt is over his head. He has very little to offer + they have a great deal."[38] Taking the long view, interfering in negotiations on a single trade deal must have seemed unwise.

Most importantly, neither Nixon nor Kissinger saw trade as an important part of international relations. Apart from gaining political concessions from

---

36 Letter, U.S. Embassy Vienna (MacArthur) to Deputy Undersecretary of State for Economic Affairs (Samuels), Apr. 4, 1969, *FRUS 1969–1976*, 4:289.

37 George C. Herring, *America's Longest War: The United States and Vietnam, 1950–1975* (New York, 1979), 225–32.

38 Memo, Kissinger to President Nixon, "*Ostpolitik*," Mar. 10, 1970, folder "Germany Vol. IV. 12-69-9 Apr 70," Box 683, NSCF, Country Files – Europe, NPMS, NA.

the Soviets, Nixon's interest in trade with the East extended little beyond acquiring a market for U.S. agricultural products, which would help him politically in the Midwest. He was convinced that trade, removed from politics, mattered little: "Trade policy is a case in point. This is something where it just isn't going to make a lot of difference. . . . Oil import is also a case in point. While it has some political consequences it is not something I should become deeply involved in."[39] As Kissinger also tended to restrict his views of international relations to high politics, neither of the men who directed U.S. foreign policy paid much attention to the trade policies of other countries.

Yet it was the long-term effects of this new trade policy that Nixon and Kissinger underestimated. For all its fear of Soviet influence on West Germany, the Nixon administration failed to recognize the potential for influence that came with trade. If we can believe former Soviet diplomat Arkady Shevchenko, Moscow saw trade as an important tool to foster political change:

Gromyko and others often remarked that although the Federal Republic belonged to the West, its geopolitical interests would gradually push it toward neutrality and eventually perhaps closer to the Soviet Union than to the United States. . . . Soviet policy was to encourage Bonn to think that only the U.S.S.R. – not the United States – could alleviate the terror of nuclear war. We intended to support the theme with a refrain that Moscow was Germany's natural and historic economic partner.[40]

Undoubtedly, ever-stronger economic ties with the Soviet Union and the political capital Brandt had invested in Ostpolitik drove Bonn to increase cooperation with the Soviet Union and, at the same time, to disregard American leadership. It often tolerated or consented to Soviet anti-American rhetoric as part of the business negotiations. When Schiller visited Moscow in September 1970, Alexi Kosygin immediately tried to sow discord within the Western alliance. "The Dutch sell their gas pretty expensively," he told Schiller early in their discussion. "We took note of this but of course do not mind."[41] This was followed later by an abrupt change in topic with the question as to whether the West German payments for U.S. troops were a heavy burden on Bonn's budget. To Schiller's objection that these were measures to balance payments, a well-informed Kosygin

39 Memo, President Nixon to President's Assistant for National Security Affairs (Kissinger), Mar. 2, 1970, folder "HAK/RN Memos 69–70," Box 341, NSCF, Subject Files, NPMS, NA.
40 Shevchenko, *Breaking with Moscow*, 226.
41 MemCon, Visit of Economics Minister Schiller with Prime Minister Kosygin, Sept. 26, 1970, BA 102/100023, 3.

countered that Bonn's offset purchases were used to acquire weapons and U.S. bonds that it could not resell.[42] While Kosygin's statement was not entirely true, it nonetheless demonstrated a strong preoccupation with the German-American relationship and a readiness to remind his West German visitor of sore points in the transatlantic alliance.

Kosygin also went a step further and outlined his vision of a future German-Soviet nuclear energy policy that would alleviate the "one-sided orientation towards the West in these matters." He recalled Brandt's offer of cooperation in the development of nuclear technology after the signing of the Moscow treaty. Without mentioning the United States by name, Kosygin noted "that other countries might be angered by such cooperation or might fear it" and suggested that "we can work without much noise and want to build our economic relations on a firm basis."[43] Schiller actually played along and reiterated the Federal Republic's interest in nuclear cooperation with other countries and "agreed with [Kosygin's] presentation of economic issues and declared bravery and patience as necessary preconditions for the solution of economic and political tasks of the treaty of August 12 [i.e., the Moscow treaty]."[44]

On another occasion, Kosygin explained that continued U.S. devaluation of the dollar was putting Western Europe at a competitive disadvantage. Through the uniting of resources between European countries such as West Germany, France, Italy, and Great Britain, however, a solid foundation for continued East-West trade would be created.[45] Furthermore, he elaborated on the monetary situations in which "today, the FRG credits the USA – just like a reverse Marshall Plan." After sufficiently discrediting the Western economic system, he portrayed the Soviet Union as the steady rock that would continue to expand according to plan and that, benevolently, would continue to engage in trade with the Federal Republic even if the devaluation of the dollar adversely affected the competitiveness of West German products.[46]

While it is questionable whether Soviet rhetoric in these talks had any impact on West German foreign policy per se, it is evidence of Soviet intentions to disrupt the German-American partnership. The Brandt government did recognize American fears about Soviet divide-and-conquer

---

42 Ibid., 5–6.   43 Ibid.
44 Ibid.
45 Telegram, German Embassy in Moscow, Sahm, to German Foreign Office, "Gespräch O. A. Friderichs mit Kossygin," Oct. 5, 1973, BA 102/135258.
46 Letter, Otto A. Friedrich to Economics Minister Friderichs, "Zusammenfassende Notiz über einen Besuch in Moskau vom 1. bis 5. Oktober 1973," Oct. 17, 1973, BA 102/135258, 2–3.

tactics.[47] Nonetheless, despite its clear recognition of an aggressive Soviet "Smiles for Europe, Frown for Washington" policy, Bonn continued in its course of intense economic cooperation with the Soviet Union.[48]

It was the sense of ownership in the new Osthandel and Ostpolitik, the necessity of its success, that was perhaps the most profound effect of the pipeline deal. No one could seriously argue that the annual delivery of 2 to 3 million cubic meters of natural gas would put the Federal Republic in a position of dependency on the Soviet Union. However, by tying German business and governmental interests to the successful development of the Soviet economy and the Soviet–West German relationship, the Federal Republic had a vested interest in the prosperity of the Soviet Union and a continuation of the relationship. As the old adage aptly illustrates, "Lend a man a dollar and he owes you; lend him a million and he owns you." No such dependency or even interest in East-West trade existed within the Nixon administration until mid-1971. Following an ill-fated report by then Assistant to the President for International Economic Affairs Peter Peterson, Nixon began to recognize the importance of trade and international economics for his domestic purposes. Along with Treasury Secretary John Connally, Peterson convinced Nixon in July 1971 of a highly mercantilist view of international trade in which the decline of U.S. economic strength was directly linked to unfair import practices by foreign allies. Pairing the concept of economic warfare with illustrations on how declining U.S. exports fostered domestic unemployment, Nixon began to foster economic nationalism.[49] In this light, West Germany's overtures toward the Soviet Union became that of an economic competitor rather than a misguided ally. As if exemplifying Alexandre Auguste Ledru-Rollin's famous quotation, "There go the people. I must follow them, for I am their leader," Nixon, the supposed leader of the Western world, now sought to catch up with his European allies. Snatching a piece of the East-West trade pie became the wisdom of the day.

Progress in the Paris Peace Talks on Vietnam and in arms control talks with the Soviet Union now allowed Nixon to change course without losing face. Making good on his promise to liberalize East-West trade in return for Soviet support on Vietnam, Nixon signed a generous economic package during his summit with Leonid Brezhnev in Moscow in 1972.

47 Telegram, German Ambassador in Washington, Pauls, to German Foreign Office, "Bemerkungen zur amerikanischen Außenpolitik," Dec. 21, 1970, BA 102/111915, 2–3.
48 Joseph C. Harsch, "Smiles for Europe, Frown for Washington" *Christian Science Monitor,* Dec. 21, 1970, 23.
49 Matusow, *Nixon's Economy*, 132–7.

Kissinger, for his part, started to praise the benefits of East–West trade for the remainder of Nixon's tenure as well as Gerald Ford's presidency: "Over time trade and investment may leaven the autarkic tendencies of the Soviet system, invite gradual association of the Soviet economy with the world economy and foster a degree of interdependence that adds an element of stability to the political equation."[50] Whether Kissinger had indeed come to believe in the importance of trade in cementing political relationships is open to doubt. Ultimately, his cavalier attitude toward economic issues prevented Nixon from duplicating Brandt's success in harnessing trade for political ends. After all, it was Congress that held final sway over economic issues, and it was here that Kissinger's failure to prioritize East–West trade became most evident.

To the Soviet Union, the main obstacle to Soviet–American trade was gaining most favored nation (MFN) status. Without MFN status, Soviet gas imports, its main export commodity to the United States, would be subject to a 20 percent tariff. Coming on top of the expense of liquefying the gas for transport, that tariff would have effectively priced the Soviets' only exportable commodity out of the American market. Instead of using the elation over the Nixon–Brezhnev summit to gain congressional approval for MFN, Kissinger displayed a cavalier attitude to trade and postponed a major initiative in this regard. This allowed members of Congress to hijack East–West trade for their own political purposes. Ironically, when the White House had begun to pursue East–West trade liberalization, Congress sought to apply Nixon and Kissinger's quid pro quo approach to trade policy to influence the behavior of the Soviet Union. In mid-1972, Senator Henry Jackson and Representative Charles Vanik introduced the Jackson–Vanik amendment, a piece of legislation that would link the granting of MFN status to Soviet policy on allowing Soviet Jews to emigrate. In the ensuring debate, Jackson pressed for ever-greater demands on the Soviets, in part on account of his own political ambitions, while Kissinger hesitated to expend political capital to win MFN status for the Soviet Union. Hesitation, however, would prove a fateful move. As Jussi Hanhimäki has demonstrated, the domestic influence of the White House was crucial in implementing necessary foreign policy legislation. As the Watergate scandal steadily undermined the president's credibility and political position, opposition to his policies, such as trade liberalization with the Soviet Union, grew proportionally in strength.[51]

50 Testimony by Henry A. Kissinger to the Senate Foreign Relations Committee, Sept. 19, 1974, as quoted in Henry A. Kissinger, *American Foreign Policy* (New York, 1977), 158–9.
51 Jussi Hanhimäki, *The Flawed Architect* (New York, 2004), 340–4.

Clearly indicating how much the Soviets wanted MFN status, Brezhnev told Kissinger in the course of preparations for the Soviet leader's 1973 visit to the United States that "all those [Soviet Jews] who want to can go."[52] Kissinger, however, dismissed the issue as "peripheral" and assured Brezhnev rather flippantly that MFN status for the Soviet Union was a sure thing, yet he did nothing to prevent it from becoming the subject of a political tug of war in Washington.[53] Kissinger's failure to recognize the central importance of MFN status to the Soviet leadership as a determining factor in its foreign policy seems outright negligent. Yet the criticism must be levied not so much on Kissinger's lack of decisive action in May 1973 before Brezhnev's visit to the United States. Arguably, Nixon's domestic weakness would have called for a more cautious approach on the matter at that time. Rather, had Kissinger accepted the importance of trade in international relations, he would have shored up MFN status for the Soviet Union in mid-1972, when Nixon's visit to Moscow had created the necessary public support.

By an ironic turn of events, the first Soviet natural gas pipeline to West Germany was completed the same week that the Yom Kippur War thrust the world into the 1973 energy crisis. As a result of the divergence in interests that had developed with West Germany's energy deals, the two allies found themselves entirely at odds as they sought to formulate a unified response to the war.

Nixon, seeing his suspicions of the Soviet Union confirmed, backed Israel in this proxy war and expected the European allies to demonstrate support for the Western cause. With no permanent economic ties to act as a restraint, it was easy for the Nixon administration to be very critical of Soviet intervention in this conflict. Naturally, Soviet-American relations took a nosedive in light of this military clash, and improvements in East-West trade would be a dead issue for some time to come.

For West Germany, by contrast, there was much more at stake in a possible cooling of East-West relations over the Middle East crisis. Support for the American intervention on behalf of Israel might have alienated not only the Organization of Petroleum Exporting Countries member states but also the Soviet Union. Unlike the Nixon administration, the Brandt government – and many West German firms – had a substantial interest in maintaining good relations with the Soviets. One gas pipeline had already

52 MemCon, Henry A. Kissinger to President Nixon, May 11, 1973, folder "Kissinger's Conversations at Zavidovo, May 5–8, 1973," Box 75, NSC Files, NPMS, NA.
53 Ibid.

been completed with West German funding and loan guarantees, and a second was under construction. Good East-West relations were essential to Bonn not only to ensure continued Soviet gas deliveries but also to maintain the dynamics of Ostpolitik.

Thus, the Federal Republic would have liked to follow the example of other Western European countries. Other NATO states – Spain, Greece, Turkey, France, and Great Britain – tried to keep a low profile and refused to allow the United States to supply Israel from bases on their territories. Yet, with West Germany not fully sovereign and acutely aware of its military dependence on the United States, Bonn pursued a "don't ask, don't tell" policy toward the American bases in the Federal Republic. On October 24, it became public knowledge that Israeli ships had docked in Bremerhaven to receive military supplies from the United States. Having to take a public stance, the Brandt government publically condemned the United States for providing military aid to Israel from German soil. Reporting to Brandt, Bahr wrote that Soviet journalist Valery Lednev, his back-channel contact to Moscow, had commented excitedly that "this stance of the government of the Federal Republic vis-à-vis the U.S. was not only brave but also helped the cause of the General Secretary [Brezhnev] in this difficult situation." In exchange for this help, Bahr added, "we could have gotten anything we wanted on Berlin."[54]

On October 26, Nixon, flanked by Secretary of Defense James R. Schlesinger, publicly chastised the West European allies for their lack of support in a crisis that would have affected them even more than the United States. They conducted the supposedly first direct criticism of the European allies since NATO's founding. Schlesinger even hinted at a partial withdrawal of U.S. forces from West Germany on the grounds that "the reaction of the Foreign Ministry in Germany raises some questions about whether they view enhanced readiness in the same way that we view enhanced readiness."[55] While the issue of military shipments from German soil would largely be resolved within a couple days with a face-saving compromise, the divergence between the strategic interests of West Germany and the United States remained.

For the remainder of the 1970s and 1980s, the Americans and Western Europeans would both contribute to the persistence of this rift. The Ford, Carter, and Reagan administrations each sought Western European support for its foreign policy but ignored the allies' economic interests. Despite the

---

54 Letter, Minister Bahr to Chancellor Brandt, Nov. 9, 1973, Mappe 190, Bundeskanzler, WBA, 1.
55 David Binder, "Bonn Is Singled Out," *New York Times*, Oct. 27, 1973, 65.

two energy crises of the 1970s, Washington failed to take Western Europe's energy needs into its foreign policy calculations. Part of the Western European response to those crises, meanwhile, was to increase Soviet energy imports. West Germany signed pipeline deals in 1972 and 1975. When Carter called for a Western trade boycott of the Soviet Union in 1979, the Europeans, defending their own interests, refused to comply. The ferocity of the 1981–82 conflict over another pipeline deal with the Soviet Union demonstrated not only how dependent Western Europe had become on Soviet natural gas but also, more importantly, how far the two sides of the Atlantic alliance had drifted apart.[56]

It is still open for debate whether increased political, economic, and cultural ties with the West were a factor to the collapse of the Eastern bloc in 1989 and subsequent dissolution of the Soviet Union. It is clear, however, that Brandt's Ostpolitik had a major economic component that not only made Ostpolitik possible but also created a rift between the Federal Republic and the United States that was to persist through the Cold War and beyond.

Nixon and Kissinger's failure to recognize trade as more than a negotiating tool, as an avenue of interchange in its own right, left them unaware of the importance the Soviets attributed to trade and unable to appreciate the impact the Soviet–West German pipeline deals would have on American dominance within the Western alliance. This disregard for trade was also reflected in the failure of the Nixon administration to counter the Jackson–Vanik amendment and engage in a significant superpower détente.

The first natural gas pipeline deal was a milestone in West German foreign policy. It created a more permanent bond and trust between Bonn and Moscow than any political treaty could have done on its own. It also represents the beginning of a shift in West Germany's strategic interests that relied on a peaceful, cooperative relationship with the Soviet Union that permeated West German policy throughout the 1970s. With no similar economic interdependence between the United States and the Soviet Union, the Nixon, Carter, and Reagan administrations were much quicker and forceful in their response to Soviet policies than West Germany. This difference in their approach to the Soviet Union went far beyond the Yom Kippur War and hampers the Western alliance to this day.

---

56 Bruce Jentleson, *Pipeline Politics: The Complex Political Economy of East-West Energy Trade* (Ithaca, NY, 1986).

4

Odd Man Out?

The CDU-CSU, Ostpolitik, and the Atlantic Alliance

RONALD J. GRANIERI

The Christian Democratic Union (Christlich Demokratische Union, CDU) and its Bavarian sister party, the Christian Social Union (Christlich-Soziale Union, CSU), collectively "the Union," achieved political predominance during the Federal Republic of Germany's first two decades by contrasting their willingness to accept American leadership of the West with the seminationalist Social Democrats (Sozialdemokratische Partei Deutschlands, SPD). By the mid-1960s, however, this bargain broke down as a result of changing American attitudes toward Germany and Europe, the reorientation of the SPD, and growing dissent within the Union about the proper balance between Europe and the Atlantic community. After electoral defeat in 1969, the Union tried to reclaim power (and reduce the appeal of right-wing nationalist alternatives to Christian Democracy) through opposition to the *Ostpolitik* of Willy Brandt. Out of a mixture of economic interests, party-political calculation, and sincere doubts about détente, the CSU was especially determined, according to its chairman Franz Josef Strauss, to be "the last Prussians" defending German national interests.

Union opposition to Ostpolitik has been the subject of significant scholarly analysis since the 1970s. Most works focus on such dramatic moments as the failed no-confidence vote against Brandt in April 1972, the Bavarian government's attempt to have the Basic Treaty with the German Democratic Republic declared unconstitutional in 1973, and the Union's symbolic rejection of the Helsinki Accords in a nonbinding Bundestag resolution in 1975. These studies often present the Union's failure to accept international realities (and the internal debates that raged over the proper form of opposition) as the cause of their thirteen-year exile from government. Until they accepted these new realities under the pragmatic leadership of CDU chair Helmut Kohl, the Union remained the odd man out in international relations.[1] The eventual "conversion" of the Union has become the common trope, symbolized by the title of Clay Clemens's influential book *Reluctant Realists*.[2]

This emphasis on the Union's gradual acceptance of international realities made analytical sense in works written while East-West détente was at the top of the political agenda. A post–Cold War perspective, however, suggests that it is not the only story that emerges from his period, and perhaps not the most important one, either. From this new perspective, what happened during the 1970s was less a tug-of-war between two positions than a multipartner dance involving Brandt's government, the Union opposition, and the Federal Republic's allies, especially the Americans. It was not a Newtonian relationship between competing forces and fixed points of reference but rather a relativistic system, where all actors and reference points were in motion. Parties and individuals may have had firm ideals and interests, but the movements of other actors, and the system as a whole, created new uncertainties requiring continuous adjustment. To understand the implications of this dance, it is necessary to look beyond the debate on Ostpolitik and consider its relationship to disputes within the Atlantic alliance about the future of NATO, the European Economic Community, and the European-American relationship that were indirectly related to détente but also had long-term significance in themselves. This essay offers a first effort at that reconsideration, exploring the Union's adaptation to Ostpolitik with special attention to its impact on the Atlantic alliance and European-American relations.

THE SETTING: CONTINUITY, CORPORATISM, AND AMERICAN INFLUENCE ON GERMAN POLITICS

The Union's adaptation to new policies was not completely unique. Rather, it mirrored the SPD's shift from neutralism to Atlanticism a decade earlier.[3] In opposition, the SPD and Union both proceeded in a series of

1 Most recent is Andreas Grau, *Gegen den Strom: Die Reaktion der CDU/CSU Opposition auf die Ost- und Deutschlandpolitik der sozial-liberalen Koalition, 1969–1973* (Düsseldorf, 2005). Christian Hacke, *Die Ost- und Deutschlandpolitik der CDU/CSU: Wege und Irrwege der Opposition seit 1969* (Cologne, 1975) has inspired much subsequent scholarship. For an interesting East German angle, see Michael Lemke, *CDU/CSU und Vertragspolitik der Bundesrepublik Deutschland in den Jahren 1969–1975* (Saarbrücken, 1992), written in 1985 but banned from publication until after 1989.

2 Clay Clemens, *Reluctant Realists: The CDU/CSU and West German Ostpolitik* (Durham, NC, 1989), esp. 172–234.

3 Kurt Klotzbach, *Der Weg zur Staatspartei: Programmatik, praktische Politik und Organisation der deutschen Sozialdemokratie 1945 bis 1965* (Berlin/Bonn, 1982); Beatrix W. Bouvier, *Zwischen Godesberg und Großer Koalition* (Bonn, 1990).

dialectical stages, from "You can't do that!" to "You shouldn't do that!" to "You shouldn't do it like that!" to, finally, "I can do that better than you, so you should let me do it!" Fundamental opposition, including constitutional challenges, eventually leads to the presentation of alternatives and then switches to criticism of specifics, indicating a willingness to accept the broad outlines of what had been a taboo policy. At the end of the process, the opposition surrenders, but charges that the government has strayed from the proper path, and claims to offer a more appropriate version of what is now the consensus policy. The corporatist structure of West German politics, with strong party discipline and generally stable coalitions, encouraged this pattern. With little chance to change policy, but clearly defined roles for the leaders of Bundestag parliamentary caucuses and party chairs who constantly seek public attention (what Timothy Garton Ash calls the sport of *sich Profilieren* ["sharpening one's profile"], the opposition enjoys wide latitude for its members to float and reject ideas while positioning themselves for further adjustments once in government.

All German politicians were aware of the parallels between the 1950s and the 1970s, even as they argued over their applicability. Brandt's supporters often emphasized the connection between Ostpolitik and Konrad Adenauer's *Westbindung* and went so far as to suggest that one naturally led to the other, to force Union critics to accept the futility of fundamental opposition. Union leaders, rejecting the parallel, claimed that they were sticking by their traditions as they gradually adapted to the new situation. Eventually, adaptation prevailed, and the same Franz Josef Strauss who demanded a constitutional challenge to Ostpolitik declared with characteristically self-styled classicism, *pacta sunt servanda* ("agreements must be kept"). Once the treaties were a reality, the question was not whether but how they would be respected by any future Union government, especially as the initial high hopes for radical changes in East–West relations faded into more pragmatic cooperation after Brandt's resignation in 1974.

Thus, the Union, by following the SPD's pattern, was not exactly an odd man out. As the Union moved toward the center under the force of circumstances, circumstances moved toward it as well. Terms such as "reluctant realists," which suggest the existence of a single universal version of détente, are thus rather misleading. The political scientist Christian Hacke, who had worked on the CDU-CSU Bundestag staff in the 1970s, has noted that the Union never had a single coherent position on Ostpolitik.[4] Nor, as it turned out, had the SPD. Rather, the long process of adjusting to

---

4 Hacke, *Ost- und Deutschlandpolitik*, identifies five different positions in the Union, ranging from fundamental rejection to enthusiastic acceptance. See also Geoffrey Pridham, "The *Ostpolitik* and the

Ostpolitik helped the Union modify untenable positions and develop new ones, while the SPD continued to be pulled leftward by its own successes. By the early 1980s, a more unified and pragmatic Union overtook an SPD torn by internecine rivalries and policy disagreements.

Its unique role as both protector and occupier made the United States a crucial factor in German politics. Beginning with Adenauer's 1953 pre-election visit to North America and the barely concealed endorsement he received from John Foster Dulles, courting American support became a key to West German electoral success. In 1957, SPD chair Erich Ollenhauer sought a preelection photo opportunity in the White House as well, and by 1961, Willy Brandt modeled his political style on John F. Kennedy, even claiming that the SPD was better equipped to deal with the Americans than the hidebound Adenauer government.[5] The United States was not, however, immobile. In shifting from confrontation to détente, and in encouraging its allies to shift with it, the United States influenced both the Atlantic alliance and German domestic politics.

An understanding of the structure of West German political life, and the American role in it, is crucial for appreciating the debates about Ostpolitik. American support allowed Brandt a degree of freedom when his policies corresponded to American plans for Europe. At the same time, concern about Brandt's ultimate goals led the Americans to maintain close relations with the Union as a guarantee against radical change, as the Union exploited the limited but real opportunities available to the opposition within the German system. American encouragement, however, also required the Union to alter its attitude toward the Atlantic alliance and abandon visions of European autonomy, a change that continues to resonate after the end of the Cold War.

THE UNION AND THE ATLANTIC ALLIANCE BETWEEN ADENAUER AND OSTPOLITIK

By the time Konrad Adenauer retired as chancellor in October 1963, the Union was embroiled in a conflict between Atlanticists, who advocated a foreign policy based on close German-American relations, and Gaullists, who emphasized Franco-German relations to build a Europe more

---

Opposition in West Germany," in *The Ostpolitik and Political Change in Germany*, ed. Roger Tilford (Lexington, MA, 1975), 45–58.

5 Ronald J. Granieri, "Political Parties and German-American Relations: Politics beyond the Water's Edge," in *The United States and Germany During the Cold War: A Handbook*, 2 vols., ed. Detlef Junker (Cambridge, 2004), 1:141–8.

independent of American leadership. German Gaullists advocated European autonomy in large part because they came to mistrust the Kennedy administration, which they accused of pursuing a superpower condominium to cement the European status quo. Thus, they opposed American initiatives for détente, even as Foreign Minister Gerhard Schröder, a leading Union Atlanticist, advocated a "policy of movement" in Eastern Europe that protected West German and Western European interests while also working closely with the Americans. Whether Atlanticist or Gaullist, however, Union leaders only imagined Ostpolitik in conjunction with *Westpolitik*, tying the idea of progress in one to their visions of the other. This preference placed limits on their policy options and led to a noticeable estrangement between the Union and the Americans in the latter 1960s. Tensions within the Union made the SPD more attractive to Washington and contributed to the collapse of the Union's governing coalition with the Free Democratic Party (Freie Demokratische Partei, FDP) government in 1966, opening the door to SPD participation in the "grand coalition" under Kurt Georg Kiesinger of the CDU.[6]

The grand coalition does not attract much attention or respect from scholars or the public, though a few recent studies have tried to highlight its importance as a transitional stage in West German politics.[7] It certainly provided an opportunity for SPD chair and Foreign Minister Willy Brandt and his adviser Egon Bahr to formulate policies that provided the groundwork for the Ostpolitik they pursued after Brandt became chancellor in 1969. Many in the Union, including Kiesinger, worried that Brandt was moving too far too fast, which led to open warfare within the cabinet by the election year 1969.[8] This conflict has contributed to the impression that Union positions during the grand coalition were primarily negative, hindering Brandt with their refusal to recognize existing realities.[9] To a certain extent this was true, as the Union did hold to traditional legal positions on German borders, for example, and their reluctance to abandon the Hallstein Doctrine prohibiting relations with states that recognized the GDR.[10]

---

6 Ronald J. Granieri, *The Ambivalent Alliance: Konrad Adenauer, the CDU/CSU, and the West, 1949–1966* (New York, 2003), esp. 191–227. On Schröder, see Franz Eibl, *Politik der Bewegung: Gerhard Schröder als Aussenminister 1961–1966* (Munich, 2001); and Torsten Oppelland, *Gerhard Schröder 1910–1989: Politiker zwischen Staat, Politik und Konfession* (Düsseldorf, 2003).

7 Reinhard Schmoeckel and Bruno Kaiser, *Die Vergessene Regierung* (Bonn, 1991). Daniela Taschler, *Vor neuen Herausforderungen: Die außen- und deutschlandpolitischen Debatte in der CDU/CSU Bundestagsfraktion während der Großen Koalition (1966–1969)* (Düsseldorf, 2001).

8 Karl Theodor zu Guttenberg, *Fussnoten* (Stuttgart, 1971), 138–40.

9 This is the position of Taschler, *Herausforderungen*, 385–405.

10 On the debates over the Hallstein doctrine, see William Glenn Gray, *Germany's Cold War: The Global Campaign to Isolate East Germany, 1949–1969* (Chapel Hill, NC, 2003).

Nevertheless, the charge of immobility overlooks the area in which Union leaders, especially Strauss and fellow Gaullist Theodor zu Guttenberg, but also Kiesinger, spent a great deal of time developing new ideas, namely the question of West Germany's role in Europe. Their attempts to fashion a new Westpolitik made the Union the source of most experimental ideas about the future of the Atlantic alliance in the 1960s.

Strauss was especially active in arguing for new economic and political structures in Europe. In his introduction to the German edition of Jean-Jacques Servan-Schreiber's international best seller, *The American Challenge*, Strauss railed against "a mentality that inclines toward assigning the Europeans in their relations with the USA the role of the Greeks opposite the Roman Empire." Calling the idea of an Atlantic Union a "pious self-deception" and a "pretty illusion," he argued that the Europeans needed to recognize their common interest rather than allow themselves to be dominated by the Americans. Once Western Europe, building on a Franco-German core, formed strong political and military-strategic institutions, Strauss argued, Europe and the United States could operate at a level of true partnership and negotiate a peaceful resolution of the division of Europe with the Soviets and Eastern Europeans.[11]

This vision sprang from the assumption that the Americans, motivated by their problems in Vietnam and a general desire to achieve détente with the Soviets (itself a return to "Yalta," the buzzword chosen by de Gaulle and his supporters to epitomize superpower dominance), had begun naturally to become less interested in European integration, and even to advance policies contrary to European interests.[12] Cooperation with de Gaulle's France was essential to escape from American hegemony, despite concerns about de Gaulle's reliability. As Guttenberg wrote: "Many warn that de Gaulle intends to establish French hegemony in Europe. Actual American hegemony seems to bother them much less than this theoretical French hegemony, which the relative size and power of the European states reveals as an empty fear."[13]

---

11 Franz Josef Strauss, introduction to *Die Amerikanische Herausforderung*, by Jean-Jacques Servan-Schreiber (Stuttgart, 1968), 17–18. See also Detlef Bischoff, *Franz Josef Strauss, die CSU, und die Außenpolitik: Konzeption und Realität am Beispiel der Großen Koalition* (Meisenheim am Glan, 1973), 124n; Strauss, *The Grand Design: A European Solution to German Reunification* (New York, 1965); and Strauss, *Herausforderung und Antwort: Ein Programm für Europa* (Stuttgart, 1968), esp. 73–4.

12 Kiesinger discussion with Swedish Prime Minister Erlander, April 17, 1969. *Akten zur Auswärtigen Politik der Bundesrepublik Deutschland* [*AAPD*] 1969, 2 vols. (Munich, 2000), 1:494. See also Richard Coudenhove-Kalergi to Strauss, May 22, 1966. Archiv für Christlich Soziale Politik [ACSP] CSU LG 5. WP Folder 135, endorsing the "Pan-European rebellion against Yalta."

13 Karl Theodor zu Guttenberg, *Wenn der Westen Will: Plädoyer für eine mutige Politik* (Stuttgart, 1964), 164.

The emphasis on Western European integration as the first step in the creation of a European peace order led Strauss and Guttenberg to confront existing international realities in novel ways. Central to their thinking was overcoming traditional nationalism. As Strauss told the CSU convention in 1965: "The unification of Germany in justice and freedom can only happen by overcoming the European status quo of Yalta, within the framework a United States of Europe."[14] A year later, he told the same audience: "The real issue is the restoration of Germany, not the reestablishment of a great German national state, whatever its borders. Only when reunification no longer appears in the guise of the restoration of the national state can it be brought closer to reality."[15] Strauss called this the "Europeanization of the German question," and through the 1960s, he emphasized the priority of Europe over traditional German nationalism, even going so far as to declare, "I do not believe in the reestablishment of a German national state, even within the borders of the four occupation zones."[16]

Guttenberg tried to clarify this position in a 1967 discussion with Egon Bahr, when they were both junior ministers in the grand coalition. Bahr, trying to gain Guttenberg's support, claimed that conservatives misunderstood him: "I am actually a nationalist," he said. Guttenberg was unmoved, however, declaring: "You see, Herr Bahr, that's where we part ways; I am not a nationalist – I am an advocate of freedom."[17] While Bahr und Brandt pursued policies they believed would best reunite the German nation, even if that meant weakening European integration,[18] Union Gaullists were more interested in maintaining and strengthening those European ties, arguing that this stronger West would bring the Germans together under a European roof. Within that Europe, Germany could play the decisive international role otherwise impossible for a middle-sized state in a world of superpowers.

Critics pointed out the illusions in Strauss and Guttenberg's European visions, especially they reliance on the unreliable de Gaulle, and their emphasis on the need for an independent European nuclear deterrent. But

---

14 Strauss speech, July 17, 1965, in Dieter Halfmann, *Das Konzept der deutschen Rechten: Aus den Reden und Schriften des F.J. Strauss* (Cologne, 1971), 75.

15 Strauss speech, Oct. 9, 1966, in Halfmann, *Konzept*, 180. See also *Herausforderung*, 136–40 and 163ff.

16 Strauss interview with *Die Zeit*, Apr. 8, 1966. Halfmann, *Konzept*, 179. See also Bischoff, *Franz Josef Strauss*, 68, and Strauss to Josef Klaus, May 26, 1966, ACSP CSU-LG 5, WP Folder 139.

17 Guttenberg, *Fussnoten*, 140. Ronald J. Granieri, "Thou Shalt Consider Thyself a European: Catholic Supranationalism and the Sublimation of German Nationalism after 1945," in *Religion und Nation/Nation und Religion: Beiträge zu einer unbewältigten Geschichte*, ed. Michael Geyer and Hartmut Lehmann (Göttingen, 2004), 336–63.

18 Timothy Garton Ash, *In Europe's Name* (New York, 1994), emphasizes Brandt and Bahr's nationalism.

these were certainly challenging, creative ideas. This European transformation was for them the first condition for any active Ostpolitik. While the Germans continued to defend their legal positions, France would act as Germany's representative, to soften the German image in Eastern European capitals. Strauss called this, with his traditional combination of sophistication and cynicism, a "game with divided roles." Kiesinger argued

Ostpolitik . . . would have more weight together with France. . . . [Who] would . . . act as a guarantee for the eastern lands that the Germans did not plan any wild adventures. . . . The question of America would not play as great a role, as long as those of us on both sides of the Rhine were determined to do everything that they could under their own power.[19]

It is therefore not completely correct to say that the Union did not have any new ideas in the 1960s, but the Union's vision of Ostpolitik was centered on an autonomous Europe rather than on a stable Soviet-American condominium. These theoretical considerations had practical consequences for German-American relations in the late 1960s. One controversial issue was the Nuclear Nonproliferation Treaty (NPT). Nonproliferation, a central issue for the superpowers, posed a direct threat to the conception of an autonomous Europe with its own deterrent. (Indeed, that was exactly what made NPT attractive to the superpowers in the first place.) Germans who opposed NPT cited France's resistance as proof the treaty was bad for Europeans. Strauss tirelessly attacked what he called a "Versailles of cosmic proportions." The NPT "would not only deepen the dividing lines of Yalta, but would destroy the decisive criterion for European self-defense." Kiesinger concurred, arguing that German promises not to produce ABC weapons were made under *rebus sic stantibus* and could be modified if conditions warranted. The NPT would close off that possibility, which made it unacceptable.[20]

Despite pressure from the Johnson administration, Kiesinger refused to sign the NPT, delaying a formal decision by demanding modifications and clarifications (on issues such as the possible intervention rights of the four powers under the UN Charter, and the possibility that a future European Union could absorb existing national nuclear forces), much to the frustration

19 Strauss, *Herausforderung*, 128. Kiesinger conversation with French Ambassador François Seydoux, Jan. 30, 1969. AAPD 1969, 1:126–7.

20 Strauss made the Versailles comment to Harold Wilson in 1967, cited in Halfmann, *Konzept*, 149. See also Strauss, *Entwurf für Europa* (Stuttgart, 1965), 128; Strauss notes on cabinet meeting of Nov. 29, 1967, ACSP Nachlass Franz Josef Strauss, BMF 567; and Kiesinger comments to Seydoux, Jan. 30, 1969. *AAPD* 1969, 1:128.

of official Washington.[21] While Brandt hinted that he would sign the NPT if he were in charge, Strauss told one interviewer in 1969: "For us the NPT is not immediately necessary, no matter what others believe or try to argue."[22]

The Union vision of a more self-assured Germany within a more autonomous Western Europe also had economic consequences in the question of a possible revaluation of the D-mark. Its strength and resulting German trade surpluses threatened the economic stability of the West, and the Germans came under heavy pressure to revalue, a position supported by Economics Minister Karl Schiller of the SPD. Finance Minister Strauss, however, seconded by Kiesinger, argued that the Germans should resist this pressure. In an interview with *Die Welt* in September 1969, Strauss, responding to criticism of "D-mark imperialism," asserted: "We Germans were driven out of the world [economy] by our own actions. Now it is the task of our policy to open the way into the world economy for [German] sales representatives, industrialists, and the younger generation."[23] Kiesinger went so far as to argue that the Americans should consider revaluing their own currency, sarcastically remarking that the Americans seem to think "the dollar orbits around gold like the earth around the sun."[24] Although Kiesinger and Brandt tried to downplay the issue during the latter states of the campaign, the Union rejected revaluation, both to protect the economic interests of friendly industries and to avoid giving right-wing radicals a campaign issue, even in the face of American criticism.[25]

After Nixon's election, Kiesinger hoped for closer relations with Washington, but that did not lead him to change the Union's position on either NPT or revaluation, nor did it remove fears that détente would cement a superpower condominium over Europe.[26] American observers such as Henry Cabot Lodge were disturbed by what they considered the lack of clear leadership in Bonn and the "chill" in German-American relations, and

---

21 Fessenden (Bonn) to State, Jan. 28,1969. Nixon Presidential Materials [NPM], National Security Council Files [NSC], Box 681.

22 Strauss, interview with *Publik*, Jan. 24, 1969, Halfmann, *Konzept*, 149. See also Bahr to Brandt, Aug. 6, 1968, *AAPD* 1968 (Munich, 1999), 2: 967–72.

23 Strauss interview with *Die Welt*, Sept. 18, 1969, in Halfmann, *Konzept*, 209. See also Bischoff, *Franz Josef Strauss*, 124–30; and Kiesinger conversation with Seydoux, May 7, 1969, *AAPD* 1969, 1:560–1. See generally Francis J. Gavin, *Gold, Dollars, and Power: The Politics of International Monetary Relations, 1958–1971* (Chapel Hill, NC, 2004).

24 Kiesinger conversation with Japanese Prime Minister Sato, May 20, 1969, *AAPD* 1969, 1:615–16.

25 Brandt to Kiesinger, Sep. 25, 1969, and Kiesinger to Brandt, Sept. 25, 1969, *AAPD* 1969, 2: 1080–1; State Department Intelligence Note, May 15, 1969, NPM NSC Box 681.

26 Kiesinger discussion with Iranian Prime Minister Hoveyda, Apr. 28, 1969, *AAPD* 1969, 1:525. See also Kissinger to Nixon, June 16, 1969, and Bonn to State, Jan. 21, 1969, evaluating German-American relations. NPM NSC Box 681.

encouraged Nixon to make a strong statement in favor of strengthening the relationship.[27]

Nixon and Kiesinger met twice in 1969, in Bonn in February and Washington in August. Although they developed a personal rapport, they were not able to heal the German-American relationship. Interestingly enough, Strauss had surprised American officials in June by asking whether a preelection visit to Washington was worthwhile at all. Although he admitted that such visits were "a standard part of Adenauer's election routine in the 1950s," he wondered whether forgoing the "pilgrimage" might signal German maturity, and thus enhance the Union's image as the true defender of German interests.[28] These musings, at a time when most analysts assumed the Union was likely to be part of any future government, indicated how far some in the Union were willing to go in their reconsideration of European-American relations. Events in the years to come would reveal the practical limits to such speculations.

THE UNION, THE AMERICANS, AND OSTPOLITIK, 1969–1972

The elections of 1969 opened a new era in West German politics. Willy Brandt's success in building a coalition between the SPD and FDP meant that the Union, despite remaining the largest party in the Bundestag, was forced into opposition for the first time in two decades. The Union's initial response to their loss was a sullen belief that they had been robbed of their rightful prize, missing an absolute majority by less than one percentage point.[29] For the next three years, Union leaders treated their opposition status as a temporary annoyance, which fueled their determination to oppose every initiative from a government they considered illegitimate.

The Americans, however, were willing to work with Brandt, which hindered Union attempts to regain power. Nixon anticipated "continued close cooperation with the German government, regardless of party composition." The Americans were cautious about Brandt's tendency to act without prior consultation, leading Kissinger to note sourly on the bottom of one memo, "We will come to regret German '*flexibility.*'"[30] At the same time, however, Kissinger and Nixon were eager to meet SPD leaders,

27 Henry Cabot Lodge, memorandum on Germany (late 1968), NPM NSC Box 681.
28 "The German Domestic Situation," July 16, 1969; State Department Intelligence Note, Aug. 1, 1969. On Strauss, see Morris (Bonn) to State, June 20, 1969, NPM NSC Box 917.
29 Daniel Hoffmann, "Verdächtige Eile": Der Weg zur Koalition aus SPD und F.D.P. nach der Bundestagswahl vom 28. September 1969" *Vierteljahreshefte für Zeitgeschichte* 48, no. 3 (2000): 515–64.
30 Sonnenfeldt to Kissinger, Sept. 29 and Nov. 25, 1969; Kissinger to Nixon, Sept. 29 and Oct. 6, 1969. For Kissinger's quote, see Sonnenfeldt for Kissinger, Oct. 29, 1969, NPM NSC Box 682.

declaring that the administration had "no trouble at all with the idea of a more mature partnership" and quickly denying any implications that the Americans mistrusted Brandt's policy, even when CDU friends leaked critical comments to the press.[31] American policy aimed "to develop a sense of confidence and trust in relations with the FRG" by avoiding "to the fullest extent feasible any involvement, either indirectly or directly, in the internal political affairs of the FRG and, in particular, to avoid any impression that we favor or support any political party in the FRG."[32] Nixon and Brandt agreed to "look to the future in the light of realities, unclouded by the shibboleths of the past."[33]

Brandt's government quickly demonstrated its distance from the Union and its willingness to smooth over relations with Washington by satisfying American desires on the NPT and revaluation. In November 1969, they announced their intention to sign the NPT after a vitriolic Bundestag debate produced a narrow majority in favor. That same autumn, they revalued the mark, earning Washington's gratitude.[34] Whatever doubts they may have had about Brandt's intentions, both Kissinger and Nixon were willing to support him as long as German actions fit with American desire for détente in Europe. Kissinger found a kindred spirit in Brandt's adviser Egon Bahr, with whom he developed a series of "back channels" allowing them to bypass foreign policy bureaucracies on both sides. At their first meeting after the 1969 elections, Kissinger assured Bahr of American support, declaring, "Your success will be our success."[35] Bahr, who claimed that Brandt and the SPD were "representatives not of the defeated, but the liberated Germany," promised "that we would also not ask every two months for repetitions of guarantees, or ask if we were still loved," leading Kissinger to the "spontaneous comment: Thank God!"[36] Cooperation between Bahr and Kissinger bore fruit with the Berlin Agreement of September 1971, where

31 Sonnenfeldt for Kissinger, Nov. 5, 1969, NPM NSC Box 682. See also Kissinger's marginalia on a memo from Sonnenfeldt, Dec. 3, 1969, and Kissinger, memorandum for the record, Dec. 5, 1969, about a subsequent article in the *New York Times*. NPM NSC Box 683.

32 National Security Decision Memorandum 91, Nov. 6, 1970, NPM Henry Kissinger Office Files [HAK], Box 58.

33 State to Kissinger, Mar. 27, 1970; Sonnenfeldt to Kissinger, Apr. 9, 1970, NPM NSC Box 917.

34 Rush (Bonn) to State, Nov. 28, 1969; memo, Kissinger to Nixon, Oct. 29, 1969, NPM NSC Box 682.

35 Bahr memorandum on a meeting with Kissinger in Washington, Oct. 14, 1969, *AAPD* 1969, 2:1114–18. Kissinger and Bahr maintained a voluminous correspondence, in both English and German. Unfortunately, the entire Bahr file in the Kissinger papers at the National Archives remains closed to researchers, though several communications are included in the *AAPD*.

36 Ibid., 1116. Kissinger's report on the conversation, identical on most particulars, did not include either the alleged comment on "your success being our success" or his "Thank God!" Kissinger to Nixon, Oct. 20, 1969, NPM NSC Box 682.

Bahr was more likely to consult with Kissinger than his own foreign minister, Walter Scheel. Some conservative Americans, such as Kissinger aide Helmut Sonnenfeldt, complained that cooperation with Bahr slighted old friends in the Union. Ultimately, however, Sonnenfeldt was "set straight" by Kissinger on the administration's priorities, which focused on making Ostpolitik serve American interests.[37]

American willingness to work with Brandt made things difficult for Rainer Barzel, former floor leader of the Union's Bundestag caucus, who became CDU chair in 1971. Barzel, who had tilted toward Gaullism in the early 1960s, now tried to balance the factions within his own party and also to claim that the Union offered a preferable alternative to Brandt. Working within the existing tradition of opposition behavior, Barzel called his approach a *so nicht* ("not like that") strategy, which was intended to make him appear more open to dialogue with the government than "fundamentalists" such as Guttenberg or Strauss.[38] Barzel encouraged the Union to defend traditional German policy but also to work their way back into American good graces, thus abandoning Gaullist suspicions. He regularly visited the American embassy in Bonn to emphasize his moderation and his commitment to close German-American relations and traveled so often to Washington that officials joked he should apply for a green card.[39] Attempting to position the Union as defender of the Atlantic alliance, he warned Secretary of State Rogers and Ambassador Martin Hillenbrand that Brandt's and Bahr's negotiating tactics signaled a return to *Schaukelpolitik* ("seesaw policy"), claiming that they were not committed to preserving Western rights in Berlin and Germany. The Americans listened respectfully but were unmoved.[40] In general, the State Department praised Ostpolitik for creating a more relaxed atmosphere in Europe and dismissed Union criticism as a "political ploy."[41]

37 Haig to Kissinger, Feb. 6, 1971, NPM HAK Box 60.
38 Pridham, *"Ostpolitik."*
39 Comment by James Sutterlin in David C. Geyer and Bernd Schaefer, eds., *American Détente and German Ostpolitik, 1969–1972: Bulletin of the German Historical Institute, Supplement* 1 (Washington, 2004), 156; Bernd Schaefer, "Washington as a Place for the German Campaign: The U.S. Government and the CDU/CSU Opposition, 1969–1972," in ibid., 98–108. Rogers to Nixon, Jan. 5, 1970, includes a State Department analysis of Barzel's desire for close ties to the United States. NPM NSC Box 683. See also Sonnenfeldt to Kissinger, Aug. 13, 1970, NPM NSC Box 684.
40 Sonnenfeldt to Kissinger, Sept. 10, 1970; Kissinger to Nixon, Sept. 3, 1970; Arthur Downey to Kissinger, Sept. 2, 1970, and memorandum of conversation between Barzel and Kissinger on Sept. 5, 1970, attached to Winston Lord to Kissinger, Sept. 12, 1970, NPM NSC Box 684. On Schaukelpolitik, see State to Bonn Embassy, Sept. 8, 1970; for the conversation with Hillenbrand, see State to Bonn, Sept. 4, 1970, NPM NSC Box 683.
41 On NSC neutrality, see Sonnenfeldt to Kissinger, Apr. 3, 1970; for "political ploy," see State Department Intelligence Brief, Mar. 26, 1970, NPM NSC Box 917. For State Department praise of Ostpolitik, see Sonnenfeldt to Kissinger, Apr. 9, 1970, NPM NSC Box 683.

Union gains and FDP losses in key state elections in 1970 and 1971 created domestic difficulties for Brandt, and opportunities for the Union, which put the Americans on their guard. Kissinger reminded Nixon of the need to maintain connections to the CDU but remained cautious: "We should not of course interfere in German politics by questioning Brandt's policies. At the same time we should say nothing which would . . . appear overly supportive of the SPD and Brandt in such a way as to demoralize the CDU who are our friends."[42] The administration adopted formal guidelines by which the United States would support "the general policy of the FRG with respect to its relations with the East" but would "not involve itself in the specific negotiating details and tactics of the Federal Government, for it is confident that the Federal Republic fully understands the continuing need for the protection of Allied rights and responsibilities with respect to Berlin and Germany as a whole."[43] This American unwillingness to take sides left little room for Barzel's attempts at moderate manipulation.

Strauss was much less interested in displaying diplomatic moderation than Barzel, though he also found it hard to exercise influence. Drawing on a relationship with Kissinger that went back to the 1950s, Strauss peppered his "old friend" with letters and phone calls deeply critical of Brandt, joining Guttenberg in questioning the SPD's commitment to the West.[44] Kissinger's responses to Strauss were usually "polite and noncommittal," in part because his staff felt Strauss had "faded badly as a national figure in Germany," despite his continued influence in the CSU. After one such phone call, Kissinger ordered Sonnenfeldt to inform German Ambassador Rolf Pauls that Strauss "set forth the well-known reservations of his Party concerning the Federal Government's foreign policy," and that "Mr. Kissinger had taken note of Strauss' comments and had responded only that he would convey them to those concerned in the U.S. government."[45] In another meeting, Strauss offered withering criticism of Brandt and requested American support. Kissinger, however, refused to take the bait, shifting the conversation to the Berlin agreement, where détente served American purposes.[46]

---

42 Sonnenfeldt to Kissinger, Sept. 10, 1970; Kissinger to Nixon, Sept. 3, 1970; Kissinger to Nixon, June 18, 1970, NPM NSC Box 683.
43 Kissinger to Rogers, July 16, 1970; Kissinger to Nixon, July 13, 1970, NPM NSC Box 683.
44 Hacke, *Ost- und Deutschlandpolitik*, 39–44. See also Guttenberg, *Die Neue Ostpolitik: Wege und Irrwege* (Munich, 1971); and Paul Pulcher, *Reichs-Freiherr von und zu Guttenberg* (Freudenstadt, 1971), 49–50 and 85.
45 Sonnenfeldt to Kissinger, Oct. 13, 1970, included Strauss to Kissinger, Oct. 7, 1970, NPM NSC Box 684. See also Sonnenfeldt, memorandum for the record, July 15, 1970, NPM NSC Box 683.
46 Memorandum for the record, Strauss-Kissinger meeting, Oct. 16, 1970. Kissinger was equally noncommittal in a discussion with Günther Gaus and Rudolf Augstein of *Der Spiegel*. Sonnenfeldt to Kissinger, Nov. 24, 1970, NPM NSC Box 684.

The Nixon administration was certainly not unanimous or consistent in its support for Ostpolitik.[47] Nevertheless, their dominant position in the alliance, and their significance in German politics allowed the Americans to play both sides against each other, using the Union as a possible brake on Brandt while also working with Brandt and Bahr to advance an American détente agenda. When Barzel visited the White House in April 1971, for example, Nixon opened the meeting by declaring, "We are always glad to see members of what I understand is the majority party," and he reiterated American commitment to the presence of West German institutions in Berlin and opposition to East German control over access routes to Berlin. Barzel had requested those declarations to guarantee Union support for the Berlin agreement, even as it continued to oppose the Moscow and Warsaw treaties. Nixon studiously avoided making any statement on these treaties, "but we can express an opinion on Berlin."[48]

Such conversations certainly appealed to Barzel's vanity and his belief that his negotiations were significant in controlling both the Brandt government and the more rambunctious elements of his own party. But the American position was much more subtle. The Americans certainly wanted to see the Berlin agreement succeed, and it did not cost them anything to make the statements necessary to ensure that the Germans did not get in the way. American refusal to comment on the other aspects of Ostpolitik, however, meant that they were willing to allow Brandt a great deal of latitude. The Americans did not try to stop the Moscow and Warsaw treaties because they did not threaten American interests, no matter how much Barzel or Strauss warned about Brandt's abandonment of traditional West German legal positions.

As the Moscow and Warsaw treaties approached ratification in the spring of 1972, Barzel visited Washington even more often. Although the Americans wanted to "[keep] our lines to the CDU open," they carefully avoided the appearance of meddling in German affairs.[49] Even when the German ambassador worried about the impact of a possible rejection of the treaties on Nixon's planned visit to Moscow, Kissinger warned his staff, "I want us to express no opinion on ratification."[50] Kissinger was frank in off-the-record

---

47 For contrasting views, see Haig to Sonnenfeldt, Sept. 2, 1970; Rogers to Nixon, Aug. 10, 1970; and Eliot (State) to Kissinger, Aug. 11, 1970, NPM NSC Box 683.

48 Memorandum of Nixon–Barzel conversation, Apr. 14, 1971, NPM Nixon/Kissinger Memoranda of Conversations [RN/HAK Memcons] Box 1025.

49 Kissinger to Nixon, Jan. 27, 1972, included talking points for Nixon–Barzel meeting on Jan. 28, NPM NSC Box 686.

50 Kissinger's handwritten comment on a memo from Sonnenfeldt, Mar. 13, 1972. See also Rogers to all European stations, Mar. 11, 1972, included in Kissinger to Nixon, Mar. 20, 1972, NPM NSC Box 686.

conversations about the American desire to see the treaties ratified, but he refused to lobby either way, declining to accept last-minute telephone calls from Germany. Even when Barzel urgently requested an American endorsement of bipartisan compromise in the Bundestag, the Americans, considering ratification inevitable, demurred.[51]

The ratification process proved a harrowing experience for the Union in general and Barzel in particular. Squeezed between a small group advocating ratification and a much larger faction of rejectionists, Barzel's *so nicht* strategy fell apart. His confused position, and possibly his own ambition, led to the miscalculation of forcing a no-confidence vote in the Bundestag in late April 1972. The narrow defeat (by only three votes) of his attempt to bring down Brandt's government obscured the reality that even a victory would not have allowed him to build a stable government. To save face, he worked with the government on a bipartisan resolution and chaired tedious negotiations within the Union to secure an abstention that would allow the treaties to pass. In the end, however, differences between advocates of clear yes or no votes led to a fragmentation of the Union vote. Barzel's reputation suffered, and although he was able to remain leader of the CDU and chancellor candidate in the special election of November 1972, his position in the Union leadership was undermined.[52] Electoral defeat at the hands of the wildly popular Brandt in November spelled the end of his leadership career, and the CDU replaced him as chair in 1973, electing the stolid and moderate Helmut Kohl in his place. That change, combined with the death of Guttenberg in 1972, signaled a shift toward greater pragmatism. The Union had to accept that, despite its attempts to paint Brandt's policies as irresponsible, Ostpolitik enjoyed significant support both at home and from Germany's allies. This situation forced them to adjust further to the new world.

THE UNION AND OSTPOLITIK AFTER 1972

After the election of 1972, the Union had to abandon their fundamental opposition to Ostpolitik.[53] Instead, adopting Strauss's dictum, *pacta sunt*

---

51 Livingston to Kissinger, May 2, 1972, forwarded several cables from Bonn with Barzel's pleas; memorandum of conversation between Kissinger and Ambassador Rolf Pauls, May 8, 1972, NPM NSC Box 687. On American neutrality, see Sonnenfeldt to Kissinger, Apr. 28, 1972, NPM NSC Box 686.

52 Barzel reported his disappointment with the Union leadership in a discussion with a member of the U.S. embassy staff in Bonn on May 31, 1972. Bonn to State, June 1, 1972, NPM NSC Box 687.

53 The constitutional challenge to the Basic Treaty with the GDR, filed not by the Union Bundestag caucus but by the Bavarian state government, was a last gasp; rejecting the nonbinding Bundestag resolution on the Helsinki agreements in 1975, which Bahr and others criticize so heavily, was more

servanda, they adopted a new policy of positioning themselves for power in the future. The CDU's chair, Helmut Kohl, with his experience as a moderator in previous party quarrels and devotion to internal party reform, personified the new era.

The irony is that, at the same time, the Social Democrats were finding that they had reached the limits of Ostpolitik. What the Union considered the absolute limit of acceptable policy was for many in the SPD only the start; but after 1973, the Americans as well as the world situation got in the way. Just as the Union's hopes for a new Europe stalled in the 1960s, the SPD's left wing would also be frustrated in the 1970s. After Brandt's 1974 resignation, the SPD fell into increasing disarray on foreign policy. By 1979, when Chancellor Helmut Schmidt advocated deployment of new intermediate range missiles in Europe, open warfare erupted between factions within the SPD, leading to their loss of power in 1982.

As the SPD divided over the next steps in Ostpolitik, the Union busily positioned itself within the new political mainstream. One sign of the changing atmosphere was the 1974 decision by the editors of the series *Adenauer Studies*, who had close connections to the Union leadership, to publish a collection of essays and documents highlighting the Ostpolitik of Adenauer's later years in office.[54] One of Adenauer's confidantes, Heinrich Krone, offered excerpts from his diaries, and the volume also included the so-called Globke Plans of 1958 and 1961. Named after Adenauer's recently deceased chief of staff, to whom the volume was dedicated, these secret plans for reunification through negotiations were published to counteract the image of Adenauer as uninterested in the East. Moreover, they also demonstrated that Union officials were now more interested in showing that they had always been up to date rather than emphasizing their continuing commitment to older principles.[55]

Tensions in the Atlantic alliance during the Year of Europe in 1973, compounded by the political and economic repercussions of the Middle East war and the Organization of Petroleum-Exporting Countries oil embargo that same year, contributed to a growing sense of estrangement between the West German and American governments.[56] By March 1973, when

---

of a symbolic gesture than an attempt to change policy. See, e.g., the 1991 exchange between Bahr and Barzel in *Süddeutsche Zeitung*, reprinted in Rainer Barzel, *So Nicht! Für eine bessere Politik in Deutschland* (Düsseldorf, 1994), 19–29.

54 Rudolf Morsey and Konrad Repgen, eds., *Adenauer Studien III: Untersuchungen und Dokumente zur Ostpolitik und Biographie*, Veröffentlichung der Kommission für Zeitgeschichte Reihe B: Forschungen Band 15 (Mainz, 1974).

55 See the comments from former Adenauer aide Horst Osterheld, *"Ich gehe nicht leichten Herzens . . ." Adenauers letzte Kanzlerjahre: Ein Dokumentarischer Bericht* (Mainz, 1986), 155–8.

56 Sonnenfeldt to Kissinger, Apr. 19, 1973, and July 11, 1973, NPM NSC Box 687.

conservative writer Hans Habe wrote Kissinger charging that Brandt was planning a "divorce" within the Atlantic alliance, and that Brandt "was elected with the unsaid blessing of America," President Nixon, who called the letter "a very perceptive and very disturbing analysis . . . *too* close to the truth," scrawled in the margin: "One of our greatest mistakes. We must do everything possible to rectify it."[57]

In this atmosphere, Union strategists abandoned their focus on the wrongs of Ostpolitik and instead reasserted their belief in the alliance with Washington. In an essay he published near the end of 1973 in the CSU newspaper, the *Bayernkurier*, for example, Strauss denounced European anti-Americanism. Arguing that Europe needed to accept greater international responsibility, he advocated European integration, but this was a Europe stripped of its former Gaullist filigree. Now Strauss advocated close Atlantic relations, asserting: "Whoever rejects the Pax Americana must create a Pax Atlantica, if he wants to prevent a Pax Sovietica."[58] Where once Strauss had advocated distance from the Americans, he now declared, as in a 1980 book written to advance his unsuccessful run for chancellor: "In foreign policy we need again a firm position [*Verankerung*] in the Atlantic alliance, and the complete fulfillment of our security commitments."[59] The Union had returned to its roots, accepting American leadership as the SPD-led government in Bonn began to drift away from it.

CONCLUSION

Accepting Ostpolitik made as much sense politically for the Union in the 1970s as accepting Atlanticism did for the SPD in the 1960s. To regain lost political influence at home and abroad, the Union had to adapt to the new geopolitical realities, a move made easier by the decline of détente euphoria after 1973. Of greater long-term significance, however, which scholars have not yet fully appreciated, the Union also had to abandon visions of a politically autonomous, "Gaullist" Europe and accept continuing American predominance in the West.

Herein lies a significant historical irony. De Gaulle had advocated détente to overcome the superpower dominance of Europe, associated with Yalta.

---

57 Habe to Kissinger, Mar. 5, 1973, with Nixon's marginalia. Attached to Kissinger to Nixon, Mar. 15, 1973, NPM HAK Box 61. Emphasis in original.
58 Strauss, "Europa – Ende aller Träume," *Bayernkurier*, Dec. 1, 1973. Reprinted in Strauss, *Signale: Beiträge zur deutschen Politik* (Munich, 1978), 133–46, quote at 144. See also the references to Strauss in a discussion between State Secretary Paul Frank and Ambassador Hillenbrand, Oct. 29, 1973, *AAPD* 1973, vol. 3 (Munich, 2004): 1673.
59 Strauss, *Gebote der Freiheit* (Munich, 1980), 11.

By the 1970s, however, détente and Atlanticism had become linked, especially as the Americans encouraged their German allies to follow the American example by accepting the European status quo.[60] This transformation served American interests, both because it took away one of the General's arguments by reasserting the centrality of the superpowers and because it forced conservative Europeans to abandon their skepticism about American leadership before the perceived need to defend the Atlantic alliance against SPD neutralism. The Americans were more than happy to play the German government and opposition against each other to encourage the degree of détente they wanted while also limiting German and European autonomy. European integration was subordinated to détente, which now aimed not to transcend the bipolar world but to stabilize it.

The implications of Ostpolitik for East–West relations are obviously central in most previous studies. Its implications for the future of Europe within the Atlantic alliance, however, deserve closer attention. Despite rhetorical support for European integration, a closer Europe was simply not a priority for Brandt and Bahr, since such a Europe would only get in the way of German national policy.[61] Even today, Bahr argues that he is "glad that the European Union had not developed as well or as quickly [during the period of Ostpolitik] as its protagonists might have wanted and still want today."[62] Helmut Schmidt tried to reassert Franco-German cooperation and German economic influence within the West, but without notable success in creating strong political structures. The result was a Europe that was, despite its wealth, less able to assert itself as an independent political force than ever before.

The conflict within Germany was the clearest expression of European-American differences over the ultimate purpose of détente. Union Gaullists pursued Ostpolitik through Westpolitik; the Americans did the reverse, using Ostpolitik to force German conservatives to abandon experiments in Westpolitik and return to Atlanticism. Many of the same individuals who had called for a more autonomous Europe, such as Strauss, now criticized the SPD for weakening European-American ties. The taming of the Union was part of a larger process of taming Europe, which left the Europeans fragmented, weakened, and incapable of pursuing a common autonomous policy. The triumph of Ostpolitik and Atlanticism was a victory

---

60 Jeremy Suri, *Power and Protest* (Cambridge, MA, 2003); Marc Trachtenberg, *A Constructed Peace: The Making of the European Settlement, 1945–1963* (Princeton, NJ, 1999).
61 Livingston to Kissinger, Aug. 29, 1972, reporting on Bahr comments to Hillenbrand, NPM NSC Box 687.
62 Bahr comment in Geyer and Schaefer, 143.

for American short-term interests over long-term plans for European political reorganization. Economic weakness, however, and a lack of political will left the United States unable to develop a coherent program for the future of the alliance either, as demonstrated by the failure of the Year of Europe. As a consequence, the Americans were left with an increasingly hollow hegemony that was resented by Europeans, who offered no alternative vision of their own. This unhappy situation, maintained by a mutual lack of imagination, haunts the Atlantic community to this day.

PART TWO

A Widening Atlantic?

The Relaunching of Europe and the Collapse of the Transatlantic Monetary Order

5

The Hague Summit of the European Community, Britain's Entry, and the New Atlantic Partnership, 1969–1970

CLAUDIA HIEPEL

Writing three years after the event, former European Commission president Walter Hallstein lauded the summit meeting of the European Community's heads of state and government that had taken place in the Hague on December 1–2, 1969, as a "significant event in the life of the European Communities."[1] This assessment became the generally accepted view of the conference, and the gathering is widely celebrated in the literature on the history of European integration as a great success that made possible the relaunching of the integration process begun in the 1950s.[2] According to this view, the Hague summit represented a "qualitative leap in the work of unification,"[3] broke the logjam on the reform of the Community, and, from a long-term perspective, was a milestone on the road to the European Union.[4]

If the summit's contribution to ending the "chronic crisis of the Community" has been amply acknowledged, its failure to address the larger international context in which the Community operated has been largely overlooked.[5] The research on the summit reflects an accusation made against

1 Walter Hallstein, *Europe in the Making* (London, 1972), 99.
2 Cf. the judgment of the Nestor of integration research, Pierre Gerbet, *La construction européenne de 1945 à nos jours* (Brussels, 1999), 173ff. The French concept of *relance européenne* was widespread in the research.
3 Franz Knipping, *Rom. 25. März 1957. Die Einigung Europas* (Munich, 2004), 156; Gerhard Brunn, *Die europäische Einigung von 1945 bis heute* (Stuttgart, 2002), 182.
4 Jürgen Mittag and Wolfgang Wessels, "Die Gipfelkonferenzen von Den Haag (1969) und Paris (1972): Meilensteine für die Entwicklungstrends der Europäischen Union?" in *Aufbruch zum Europa der zweiten Generation. Die europäische Einigung 1969–1984*, eds. Franz Knipping and Matthias Schönwald (Trier, 2004), 3–27, here 27.
5 According to Katharina Focke, Parliamentary State Secretary for European Questions in the Chancellor's Office, "Europa-Politik nach Den Haag. Neubeginn in der europäischen Integration?" *Europa-Archiv* (hereafter *EA*) 25 (1970): 267–80; here, 270.

the Community by many contemporaries, and not only Americans. The European Community (EC) was seen as introverted and fixated on resolving its internal problems.[6] The unwieldy decision-making procedures, harmonization, and enlargement absorbed all of its energy. At the same time, however, the growing interdependence of the world economy had a profound impact on the Community, and the emerging monetary troubles as well as the "shift in the transatlantic balance as well as in the balance within" the Community were felt at the summit.[7] Nonetheless, external influences on intra-European harmonization efforts were hardly discussed at the summit. In fact, the decision of the summit "to progress in the matter of political unification, within the context of enlargement"[8] was announced "in a few lines tucked away in the final communiqué of the Hague meeting."[9] Questions of security and defense policy played no role at the meeting of the Six.

That is all the more surprising given that Richard Nixon, who had taken office as president of the United States in January 1969, was reshaping American foreign and security policy and envisioned a new role for Europe. If the relaunching of the European project and Nixon's proclamation of a new Atlantic partnership did not culminate in a fruitful joint initiative of the Western nations, this was because, on the one hand, Nixon's conception was not perceived as a constructive offer by the Europeans and, on the other hand, the Nixon administration did not make a genuine effort to transform it into a coherent policy.[10] As a result, the years 1969–70 saw European-American conflicts on monetary, economic, and trade policy, and those issues would continue to test transatlantic relations.

This essay will address the question of why the EC and the United States did not succeed in initiating a dialogue at the beginning of the Nixon era. I will argue that the problems that arose in 1969–70 can be seen as a prelude to the crises in transatlantic relations of the 1970s. It is in this context that Britain, having accepted the Community's regulations and treaties, ceased to be seen as a potential American Trojan horse within the EC. The decisions

---

6 According to Harald B. Malmgren, "Europa, die Vereinigten Staaten und die Weltwirtschaft," *EA* 27 (1972): 117–28, here 119. Malmgren served in the Nixon administration as deputy special adviser to the president on trade negotiations.

7 André Szász, *The Road to European Monetary Union* (Houndsville, 1999), 29.

8 "Final Communiqué of the Conference of the Heads of State or Government on 1 and 2 December 1969 at the Hague," Paragraph 15; reprinted in A.G. harryvan and J. Van der Harst, eds., *Documents on European Union* (New York, 1997), 168–9.

9 See Christopher Hill and Karen E. Smith, *European Foreign Policy: Key Documents* (London, 2000), 71–4.

10 It is amazing that this declaration met with little response. See the very positive reaction recorded in the files of the chancellor's office in Bonn. Bundesarchiv Koblenz [hereafter BaK], B 136 [Bundeskanzleramt], 3616.

made at the Hague did not create a basis for a transatlantic dialogue on either institutional or political matters. To the contrary, the resolution on the Common Agricultural Policy (CAP) adopted at the summit deepened the existing divide between the Europeans and Americans on trade policy.

NIXON'S NEW ATLANTIC PARTNERSHIP

In his inaugural address of January 20, 1969, Nixon outlined the overall aims of his foreign policy with the pledge that the previous "era of confrontation" would be replaced by an "era of negotiations."[11] Nixon took the process of coming to terms with the Soviets, a step initiated by his predecessors, a step farther in the summer of 1969, when he proposed the Strategic Arms Limitations Talks (SALT). By that time, the United States had realized that it had overextended itself with the responsibilities it had assumed around the world in the previous two decades, and the costs of its international commitments were burdening the U.S. economy.[12] Instead of being governed by the principle of superiority, defense policy was now determined by sufficiency – that is, the possession of sufficient means. Nixon thus asked the European allies to increase their contributions toward the defense of the West. His "new strategy for peace" included the offer of a "new trans-Atlantic partnership" within the framework of U.S. efforts at détente. Nixon's new foreign policy doctrine was presented in a comprehensive foreign policy report to Congress on February 18, 1970.[13] In the report, prepared by National Security Adviser Henry Kissinger,[14] Europe was designated one of many regions of the world in which U.S. interests would be pursued. It was, however, to play a central role: "The peace of Europe is crucial to the peace of the world. . . . Our efforts to pursue genuine relaxation of tensions between East and West will be a test of the new trans-Atlantic partnership."[15] Within the context of the era of negotiations in Europe, the efforts by Western European governments to ease tension with the Eastern bloc appeared to complement U.S. objectives and were looked on favorably.[16] Nixon and Kissinger were thus following

---

11 Quoted from Viktor E. Meier, "Nixon und die 'Ära der Verhandlungen,'" *EA* 25 (1970): 311–18, here 311.

12 Wolfram F. Hanrieder, *Deutschland, Europa, Amerika. Die Aussenpolitik der Bundesrepublik Deutschland 1949–1994* (Paderborn, 1995).

13 "U.S. Foreign Policy for the 1970's. A New Strategy for Peace. A Report to the Congress by Richard Nixon, President of the United States, February 18, 1970," *Department of State Bulletin* 62, no. 1602 (March 9, 1970): 273–332, here 275.

14 Henry A. Kissinger, *Memoiren 1968–1973* (Munich, 1979), 460.

15 "U.S. Foreign Policy for the 1970's," 284.   16 Ibid., 286.

in the tradition of President John F. Kennedy, who, in his proclamation of
Atlantic partnership on July 4, 1963,[17] envisaged that a Europe strengthened
politically and economically with the help of the United States would grow
to become an equal partner capable of assuming a fair share of economic
and military responsibility and a coshaper of the international order.[18]

Accordingly, Nixon declared in 1970 that the postwar period in international relations had ended once and for all and that a "new era" had
begun.[19] Transatlantic relations in the 1970s would rest on a different basis,
he maintained, from that of the 1940s and 1950s. The United States would
now expect a larger contribution toward maintaining peace from a politically and economically strengthened Western Europe. The core message of
the "Nixon Doctrine" was that "the United States will participate in the
defense and development of allies and friends, but that America cannot –
and will not – conceive all the plans, design all the programs, execute all
the decisions, and undertake all the defense of the free nations of the world.
We will help where it makes a real difference and is considered [to be] in
our interests."[20]

What this "new and mature partnership" on offer to the Western Europeans might mean in practice was left quite vague in Nixon's declaration.[21]
The only thing clearly indicated was that Washington intended to become
less involved in internal European affairs, especially in matters pertaining
to political integration under EC auspices. Indeed, Nixon confirmed his
fundamental support for the "strengthening and broadening of the European Community" and showed himself ready to accept the economic and
trade disadvantages that European integration might entail for the United
States for the sake of the West's geopolitical interests: "We recognize that
our interests will necessarily be affected by Europe's evolution, and we may
have to make sacrifices in the common interest. We consider that the possible economic price of a truly unified Europe is outweighed by the gain
in the political vitality of the West as a whole."[22] No longer, however,
did the United States want to be involved in the details of the unification

17 Presented in West Germany on the occasion of his visit to the Paulskirche in Frankfurt on July 25,
   1963: published in *EA* 18 (1963), D 352ff. See also Karl Kaiser, "Die neue Abhängigkeit der atlanti-
   schen Staaten. Präsident Kennedys Grand Design: Vorgeschichte und Entwicklungsmöglichkeiten,"
   EA 24 (1969): 815–30.
18 Nixon's declaration in February 1970 actually anticipated Kissinger's programmatic speech on the
   Year of Europe in April 1973 that incurred the displeasure of the Europeans. See, e.g., Karl Dietrich Bracher, Wolfgang Jäger, and Werner Link, *Republik im Wandel. 1969–1974. Die Ära Brandt*
   (Stuttgart, 1986), 246; and Henry A. Kissinger, *Memoiren 1973–74* (Munich, 1982), 2:181ff.
19 "U.S. Foreign Policy for the 1970's," 274.   20 Ibid., 275ff.
21 Ibid., 284.   22 Ibid., 285.

process: "The structure of Europe itself is fundamentally the concern of the Europeans." The United States would work with Western Europe within NATO and through the European institutions, but Nixon also indicated that Washington would willingly continue bilateral cooperation with individual European governments. Bilateral relations, he added, would remain the "essential transatlantic bonds" for the foreseeable future.[23]

THE EUROPEAN COMMUNITY AND THE SUMMIT IN THE HAGUE

Nixon's mention of bilateral negotiations reflected the fundamental mistrust in Washington of the EC and its institutions, which were as mysterious as the "Tibetan theocracy" in American eyes.[24] The U.S. ambassador to the Communities in Brussels, J. Robert Schaetzel, a critic of Nixon, initially thought he saw here a "new Nixon" who wanted to make earnest efforts to improve the relationship with the Community, but he soon found himself confronted with an incoherent U.S. policy toward Western Europe that still focused on bilateral negotiations and took no account of the European institutions.[25] Washington's plan for two-track negotiations with Western Europe revealed a lack of understanding of how Europe worked and little sensitivity to European sensibilities, but it also reflected an uncertainty about the European integration process and where it was leading that was not entirely unjustified.

The year 1969 ended with a breakthrough for Europe that fulfilled a long-standing demand of Washington's, namely that the EC agree to open negotiations on the admission of the United Kingdom.[26] The resolutions on the completion of the Common Market adopted at the Hague summit also meant the continuation of the CAP, heavy American criticism notwithstanding. Above all, the summit was disappointing – at least at first glance – as it demonstrated a lack of will and ambition on the part of the Community to develop and set goals for a common foreign and defense policy.

---

23 Ibid., 285.
24 J. Robert Schaetzel, *The Unhinged Alliance: America and the European Community* (New York, 1975), 143.
25 On his first trip to Europe as president, through Europe in February 1969, Nixon met with the heads of state and government of the most important countries and went to NATO headquarters in Brussels. The members of the Commission were, however, merely invited to an audience in his hotel suite even though the office of the Commission was only five minutes away from the hotel. Schaetzel, *Unhinged Alliance*, 49–51.
26 On the U.S. attitude toward European integration, see Geir Lundestad, *"Empire" by Integration: The United States and European Integration, 1945–1997* (Oxford, 1998); and Beate Neuss, *Geburtshelfer Europas? Die Rolle der Vereinigten Staaten im europäischen Integrationsprozess 1945–1968* (Baden-Baden, 2000).

The outcome of the Hague summit should, however, be considered against the background of the crises that had beset the EC in the preceding years. Despite some successes, such as the early finalization of the customs union in 1968, the EC had been experiencing a creeping "disintegration."[27] The West German Foreign Ministry warned in the summer of 1969 that "signs of the dissolution of European cooperation" could be expected if the disagreement over EC enlargement were not resolved within the next twelve to eighteen months.[28] The "accumulation of unresolved difficulties for some time" complicated the search for a solution.[29]

Three major crises had shaken the Community in the 1960s. The first was the failure of the Fouchet Plan that France put forward in 1962; it envisioned the creation of a political union of the six Community member states and the adoption of a common foreign and defense policy. The incompatibility of Charles de Gaulle's intergovernmental conception of political union and the more supranational views of the other five member states, together with the question of the EC's relations with NATO and the United States, had caused the collapse of the negotiations. The second crisis arose from conflicts over the Community's institutional structure and the envisaged introduction of majority decision making. These disagreements led to a severe constitutional crisis in 1965–66, during which France halted work in the Council of Ministers for six months.[30] A modus vivendi on these two issues was eventually found: the project of a political Europe was kept off the agenda. The constitutional crisis was resolved in January 1966 by the Luxembourg compromise, in effect a gentlemen's agreement to set aside majority voting in the Council of Ministers on issues that member states deemed to be of vital national interest.[31] The third crisis was prompted by the question of enlargement, and it was this issue above all that had poisoned the atmosphere within the Community and had the potential to destroy it altogether. The first British application for entry, submitted in 1961, had been unilaterally rejected by de Gaulle in January 1963.

---

27 Norbert Kohlhaas, "Die Europäische Gemeinschaft vor der Gefahr der Desintegration," *EA* 24 (1969): 263–8.
28 "Aufzeichnung des Ministerialdirektors Paul Frank, 26.8.1969, Betr. Europäische Politik," *Akten zur Auswärtigen Politik der Bundesrepublik Deutschland* (hereafter *AAPD*), 1969 (Munich, 2000), doc. 267.
29 "Aufzeichnung des Ministerialdirektors Frank, 21.8.1969, Betr. Europapolitik, hier: Anstehende Probleme und ihre Ursachen. Vorschläge für das Verfahren," *AADP* 1968, doc. 319, 1127.
30 On the Fouchet Plan, see Knipping, *Einigung Europas*, 127ff. On the empty-chair crisis, see the contributions in Wilfried Loth, ed., *Crises and Compromises: The European Project 1963–1969* (Baden-Baden, 2001), 157–243.
31 On the Luxembourg compromise, see N. Piers Ludlow, "The Eclipse of the Extremes: Demythologising the Luxembourg Compromise," in Loth, *Crises and Compromises*, 247–64.

The second, in May 1967, had not been rejected formally, but the French president refused to start negotiations on it.[32] His arguments against British entry rested on a combination of understandable policy concerns and rather bizarre prejudices. They culminated in the charge that Great Britain would be the Americans' Trojan horse in Europe; that it was not culturally European; and that it was, because of its special relationship with the United States, more committed to transatlantic relations than to building Europe. De Gaulle's intransigence increasingly isolated him from his partners, who were all strong supporters of enlarging the Community. Attempts to bring Britain in through the back door – for example, by defense cooperation within the framework of the Western European Union (WEU) – forced the self-isolation of France, which began employing the tactic of the "empty chair" at the WEU level.[33] The admission of Britain became a *conditio sine qua non* for further progress in European integration, and the French blockade led to stagnation in the Community. "For some, the zeal for internal construction was exhausted by the blocking of enlargement; for France, internal construction had precedence over enlargement."[34]

Italy, the Benelux countries, and, in particular, the Netherlands were the strongest advocates of enlargement. Alongside economic arguments, such as the opening of new export markets for Italian products,[35] and interest in reforming the CAP, political reasons stood in the foreground, such as the prevention of a joint Franco-German hegemony in Europe.[36] West Germany's Christian Democratic–Social Democratic governing coalition was divided on this issue. Out of consideration for France, Chancellor Kurt Georg Kiesinger (of the Christian Democratic Union) leaned toward deferring enlargement in favor of political union along the lines of the Fouchet Plan.[37] Social Democratic Foreign Minister Willy Brandt, by contrast, was among the most energetic proponents of enlargement. The Social

---

32 On the second and successful British application for membership, see Anne Deighton, "The Second British Application for Membership of the EEC," in Loth, *Crises and Compromises*, 391–405. On de Gaulle's attitude, see Gérard Bossuat, "De Gaulle et la seconde candidature britannique aux Communautés européennes (1966–1969)," in Loth, *Crises and Compromises*, 511–38.

33 Maurice Vaïsse, *La grandeur. Politique étrangère du Général de Gaulle 1958–1969* (Paris, 1998), 553ff.

34 This simple formulation is Katharina Focke's: Focke, "Europa-Politik nach Den Haag," 270.

35 See Frank's assessment, "Aufzeichnung des Ministerialdirektors Paul Frank, 26.8.1969, Betr. Europäische Politik." For an opposing view, see Maria Eleonora Guasconi, "Italy and the Hague conference of December 1969," *Journal of European Integration History* [hereafter *JEIH*] 9, no. 2 (2003): 101–16: Italy expected economic problems from the entry of Britain.

36 This was an important argument on the Dutch side. See Anjo Harryvan and Jan van der Harst, "Swan Song or Cock Crow? The Netherlands and the Hague Conference of December 1969," *JEIH* 9, no. 2 (2003): 27–40.

37 Expressed in a conversation with the French president on September 9, 1969, Archives Nationales, 5 AG 2 [Papiers présidentielles], 1010. See also Theo M. Loch, "Ausgangsposition für die europäische Gipfelkonferenz in Den Haag," *EA* 24 (1969): 707–16, at 708.

Democrats had been calling for enlargement since the founding of the European Economic Community (EEC) in 1957, and Brandt could be certain of wide support among the West German public in backing membership for Britain.

Kiesinger and Brandt were working in their own ways to strengthen the Community in response to the transformation of the international order. Kiesinger saw a stronger political union that included a common foreign and defense policy as a means to compensate for the expected reduction in U.S. troop strength in Europe. Brandt, for his part, believed that the Community could play role in reducing East-West tensions only after it had been strengthened by the inclusion of Britain. It "is in the common interest of the Community to enlarge at a time in which we are striving for the West and the East to grow more closely together," he argued at the Hague summit. Furthermore, "the Community must expand beyond the circle of the Six if it wants to compete economically and technologically with the giants and meet its worldwide political responsibilities."[38] Brandt received the opportunity to change Bonn's policy on Europe after becoming chancellor in the fall of 1969.[39] The other Western European governments were hoping Brandt would pursue a more active European policy than Kiesinger had and would put pressure on France. Paris, too, was anticipating a change in West German policy.[40] Brandt did not hesitate to touch on taboos. In the Hague, he played off French worries in arguing for the necessity of allowing Britain's entry into the EEC: "Whoever fears that the economic weight of the Federal Republic of Germany could have negative consequences for the balance within the Community should, for that reason, support enlargement, too."[41]

France's political standing within the Community had indeed deteriorated. After the enormous economic growth and political stability of the "good years of the Gaullist Republic," the unrest of May 1968 prompted widespread distress within French society and led to both capital flight and a weakening of the franc.[42] Inflation and trade deficits were feeding

---

38 Willy Brandt, "Appell an die europäische Solidarität. Erklärung des Bundeskanzlers auf der EWG-Gipfelkonferenz in Den Haag," *Bulletin des Presse- und Informationsamtes der Bundesregierung*, Dec. 2, 1969, 1241.

39 On Brandt's role in the preparations for the Hague summit, see Claudia Hiepel, "In Search of the Greatest Common Denominator: Germany and the Hague Summit Conference 1969," *JEIH* 9, no. 2 (2003): 63–81.

40 French Ambassador Francois Seydoux to Brandt's security adviser, Egon Bahr, in a conversation on Oct. 8, 1969: *AAPD* 1969, doc. 310.

41 Brandt, "Appell an die europäische Solidarität."

42 Serge Berstein and Pierre Milza, *Histoire de la France au XXe siècle*. Vol. 4, 1958–1974 (Brussels, 1992), 53–7.

latent French fears of West German predominance in the Community. For both political and psychological reasons, de Gaulle firmly refused to draw the necessary conclusions.[43] Only his resignation in April 1969 cleared the way for France's adjustment to the economic and political realities in Europe. His successor, Georges Pompidou, was a financial expert and prag- matist who understood the necessity of employing the Gaullist rhetoric of *grandeur* while cautiously pursuing the economic modernization of France.[44] Together with Minister of Finance Valéry Giscard d'Estaing, Pompidou pur- sued an ambitious program to overhaul the French economy and catch up to West Germany in the industrial sector. But until this modernization plan yielded visible success, Pompidou had to shield France's important agricultural sector.[45] That would be possible only within the framework of the Common Agricultural Market, which, pending negotiations, was to be in place by January 1, 1970. Paris was seeking to retain the system of agricultural financing agreed upon in 1962 and 1965–66 that had been ad- vantageous for French farmers – and had created an unequal burden within the Community.[46] Pompidou was fully aware that the other member states would use this issue during the negotiations on the Common Agricultural Market to break French resistance to enlargement.[47]

During the presidential campaign, Pompidou seized the initiative by proposing a conference of the heads of state and government of the Six to deal with the pressing issues confronting Europe.[48] He summed those issues up with the trio *achèvement, approfondissement, élargissement* – com- pletion, deepening, enlargement.[49] The order of Pompidou's key words indicated French priorities. The completion of the Common Agricultural Market was of the greatest importance to Paris. "Deepening" referred to

---

43 Robert Frank, "Pompidou, le Franc et l'Europe 1969–1974," in *Georges Pompidou et l'Europe. Colloque 25 et 26 novembre 1993*, ed. Association Georges Pompidou (Brussels, 1999), 339–70.
44 On Pompidou, see Eric Roussel, *Georges Pompidou 1911–1974* (Paris, 1994).
45 See the analysis by Frank: "Aufzeichnung des Ministerialdirektors Frank, 21.8.1969, Betr. Europa- politik, hier: Anstehende Probleme und ihre Ursachen. Vorschläge für das Verfahren."
46 Ann-Christina Lauring-Knudsen, "Defining the Policies of the Common Agricultural Policy: A Historical Study" (Ph.D. diss., European Univerity Institute, Florence, 2001).
47 "It is quite obvious that relations between the Common Market and England will be in the background of the discussions that will then start [on the financing of the agricultural market] because, on the one hand, the English will insist on their desire not to be left out of an area critical to their candidacy and on the other, because it is possible that our partners (Mr. Nenni will particularly insist on this) will want to establish a link between the two matters." Archives Nationales, 5 AG 2, 1035, note from Gaucher to Pompidou, June 24, 1969.
48 Marie-Thérèse Bitsch, "Le sommet de La Haye. L'initiative francaise, ses finalités et ses limites," *JEIH* 9, no. 2 (2003): 83–99, at 87.
49 As mentioned in the Council of Ministers session on Sept. 15, 1969. See "Aufzeichnung des Staatssekretärs Harkort, 18.9.1969, Arbeitsessen der EWG-Aussenminister in Brüssel am 15.9.1969," *AAPD* 1969, doc. 294.

the extensions of cooperation into new areas, such as monetary policy, technology, transportation, and energy. Completion and deepening would be the price Pompidou would demand for French consent to enlargement.

The other member states agreed in principle to the idea of a summit conference even though each had its own interests and priorities. Enlargement was the most important issue for all members except France, but their views on deepening varied.[50] Moreover, the smaller states and proponents of supranational integration objected that a summit conference of heads of state and government undermined the Community, in particular the Commission. The summit proposal also awakened memories of the Fouchet Plan.[51]

In the Hague, Willy Brandt played the role of cautious mediator and thereby helped prevent a collision of the extreme positions represented by France and the Netherlands.[52] Moreover, the general desire to overcome the stagnation besetting the Community proved so strong that it was actually possible to draft a working program for the coming years that offered all participants something and thus restored a general balance of interests. Under pressure from France, it was decided that the transitional period of the Common Agricultural Market would definitely end at the close of 1969. The Six agreed "to stop the clock" to come to a financial arrangement that would allow the transition to the final phase of the Common Market according to the schedule foreseen by the EEC Treaty.[53] In marathon negotiating sessions in December 1969 and February 1970, the Council of Ministers agreed on the terms for the completion of the Common Agricultural Market. The EC's budget was to be financed in the future from its own resources – from border levies on agricultural products imported into the Community and from the common external tariff.[54] Because these revenues were expected to fall as a result of reductions in international tariffs under the auspices of the General Agreement on Tariffs and Trade (GATT), it was also decided at the Hague that 1 percent of each member state's value-added tax would be transferred to the Community as well.

---

50 "Unsere fünf Partner sowie England und die Gipfelkonferenz, Aufzeichnung 20.11.1969," Politisches Archiv des Auswärtigen Amtes [hereafter PAAA], B 20, 1428.
51 Marie-Thérèse Bitsch, "Le sommet de La Haye. La mise en route de la relance de 1969," in Loth, *Crises and Compromises*, 539–66, at 550–1. See also N. Piers Ludlow, "An Opportunity or a Threat? The European Commission and the Hague Council of December 1969," *JEIH* 9, no. 2 (2003): 27–40.
52 See Hiepel, "In Search of the Greatest Common Denominator."
53 Kommuniqué der Konferenz der Staats- bzw. Regierungschefs in Den Haag am 1. und 2. Dezember 1969, paragraph 5, BaK, B 102, Bundeswirtschaftsministerium, 93456. For the further proceedings, see Fernschreiben aus Brüssel von Ständigem Vertreter Sachs, 9.2.1970, betr.: 102. Tagung des Rates der europäischen Gemeinschaften am 5./6./7. Februar 1970, Archiv der sozialen Demokratie, Depositum Katharina Focke, 199.
54 Fernschreiben aus Brüssel von Ständigem Vertreter Sachs, 9.2.1970.

France was largely successful in advancing its interests in the Hague and obtained preferential treatment for its agricultural products. West Germany and Italy, in contrast, had to reckon with disproportionately high contributions. Italy did, though, succeed in its demand that wine and tobacco be included in the CAP. The member states vigorously pursued their own national interests in the negotiations, but they were also under tremendous pressure to come to terms because France had made an agreement on agriculture the precondition for taking up negotiations on enlargement. Agreement on enlargement was facilitated by the expectation that the candidates for membership – Britain, Denmark, Ireland, and Norway – accept the *acquis communautaire*, the body of Community treaties and regulations. For France, it was crucial that Britain not be allowed to call the fundamental agreements on the Common Agricultural Market into question.

The official communiqué issued at the close of the Hague summit did not name a date for the start of negotiations on enlargement. This silence was important for Pompidou. He was still under pressure at home from the guardians of the Gaullist legacy who saw any concession on British entry as a sacrilege. But, as Brandt later recounted, Pompidou did finally give his word of honor during a dinner in the course of the summit that the negotiations could begin in the summer of 1970.[55]

A quid pro quo thus cleared two fundamental obstacles on the road to further integration. Possibilities for extending integration to new areas were also considered.[56] As for deepening, the summit participants agreed in principle to take up the challenge of establishing a common economic and monetary policy in the course of 1970, and they enlisted Prime Minister Pierre Werner of Luxembourg to draft a plan for economic and monetary union.[57] With a call for a "community of stability and growth," West Germany was able to push through its ideas on harmonizing economic and monetary policy.[58]

On Brandt's suggestion, the summit adopted a declaration on political cooperation and agreed that a committee under the supervision of the

---

55 Willy Brandt, *Begegnungen und Einsichten. Die Jahre 1960–1975* (Hamburg, 1976), 312ff.

56 PAAA, B 20, 1440, Wesentliche Ergebnisse der Gipfelkonferenz in Den Haag am 1. und 2. Dezember 1969, Aufzeichnung vom 4.12.1969.

57 Paragraph 8 of the communiqué. On the basis of the memorandum from Commissioner Raymond Barre of February 1969. The continued international and European currency fluctuations – devaluation of the franc, revaluation of the D-mark – threatened the system guaranteed prices for agricultural products expressed in units of account based on the dollar (green dollar) and required complicated compensatory measures (subsidies or tariffs).

58 BaK, B 102, 93456, Aufzeichnung Everling, 3.12.1969, Betr. Gipfelkonferenz. The fundamental conflict between monetarists (France and Belgium) and economists (Germany, the Netherlands) was thereby only bracketed off but by no means eliminated.

foreign ministers would prepare a plan on political cooperation by July 1970, the date Pompidou informally accepted for the beginning of negotiations with Britain. For the first time since the failure of the Fouchet Plan, the EC members agreed to put cooperation on foreign policy back on the agenda. The green light for European Political Cooperation (EPC) is all the more remarkable as it did not play a part during the presummit discussions and consultations. Unexpectedly, it was mentioned toward the end of the final document, following sections on cooperation in industrial research, the European Atomic Energy Community, the creation of a European university, social policy, and relations with the European Free Trade Association (EFTA) and coming just before a declaration of intent to motivate the youth of Europe to support the integration process (paragraph 16). The placement of the paragraph on political cooperation and a European foreign policy did not correspond with its actual significance. The Community's foreign policy tasks were couched in solemn but vague references to the European contribution to détente and understanding, to its "responsibility in the world of tomorrow" and to the political finality of the Community.[59]

The report on a common foreign policy that the committee led by Belgian diplomat Étienne Davignon presented in July 1970 was very cautious and oriented toward the lowest common denominator. The Davignon Report recommended only increased coordination of foreign policy by means of biannual meetings of the member states' foreign ministers. The proposal suited French interests as, first, it amounted to the creation of a purely intergovernmental coordinating body outside of the institutions and mechanisms of the Community, and, second, the envisioned body would not be able to make binding decisions.[60] Its range of action on foreign policy matters would be limited; moreover, the crucial area of defense was completely left out of consideration. The foreign ministers' consultations were nonetheless a starting point and opened the possibility for the Europe to become an actor in international politics. The first meeting of the foreign ministers under the auspices of EPC took place in Munich on November 19, 1970; the Middle East conflict and the negations on the Conference on Security and Cooperation in Europe were discussed as possible areas of coordinated action.[61]

---

59 Quoted from the preamble of the official communiqué: Kommuniqué der Konferenz der Staats- bzw. Regierungschefs in Den Haag am 1. und 2. Dezember 1969.
60 See Pierre Gerbet, "Georges Pompidou et les institutions européennes," in *Pompidou et l'Europe*, 55–84.
61 See "Runderlass des Ministerialdirektors von Staden, betr. Europäische politische Einigung," *AAPD* 1970, doc. 564.

The Hague summit sent a clear signal that the EEC was not in the throes of disintegration. To the contrary, the summit was a turning point. The member states resolved several long-standing problems and demonstrated unanimous will to advance the process of European integration. They did not adopt the more ambitious plans for intensifying cooperation in a variety of areas, though some had been prepared to go further.[62] However, the orientation toward the most common denominator often prevailed over the Community's decision-making process, and this was not well suited to going beyond the completion of long-postponed tasks. All further projects were destined for incremental realization in accordance with the Community's own dynamism and had to be developed "in a process of continual creation."[63]

GREAT BRITAIN AND THE COMMUNITY

In a conversation with Kiesinger, Pompidou compared the so-called English affair with Alphonse Daudet's *L'Arlésienne*, a play that revolves around a woman who never appears. "In regard to Great Britain, he wanted to express that he had had enough of such stories. The woman must make an appearance now or never."[64] The Hague summit had prepared the way for the United Kingdom to make its stage debut before the Community on June 30, 1970, with the official opening of accession negotiations.[65] The British government was forced to put its cards on the table – precisely as Pompidou had insisted – and to make clear just how seriously it wanted to join the Community. For Britain, the main problem was the CAP. Because of Britain's preferential trade relations with the Commonwealth, there were problems with duties on Caribbean sugar imports and New Zealand dairy products. The decision in the Hague to give the Community its own financial resources, above all by means of levies and tariffs, made the situation more difficult for Britain than it had been in 1967, the year it applied for membership. Britain faced the prospect of contributing a disproportionately high amount to the Community's budget on account of its heavy reliance on

---

62 According to the plan of the German commissioner Hans von der Groeben: "Programm für Europa, vom 23. Juni 1969," excerpt in *EA* 24 (1969): D 412ff.

63 According to Belgian Foreign Minister Pierre Harmel on the occasion of the first Council of Ministers with delegates of the applicant states, June 30, 1970. See *AAPD* 1970, doc. 289.

64 Conversation of September 9, 1969, quoted from the German minutes of the meeting: *AAPD* 1969, doc. 282. There, the opera by Georges Bizet was mentioned, but the original play is from Daudet. See AN, 5 AG 2, 1010, Entretien en tête à tête entre le Chancelier Kiesinger et le Président Pompidou, 9.9.1969.

65 *AAPD* 1970, doc. 289.

food imports from the Commonwealth. The British government therefore regarded a longer transition period as justified and necessary.[66] France was not receptive to Britain's arguments.

Monetary and political cooperation were further sticking points. Pompidou was worried about the role of the sterling as a reserve currency and what that role meant for the currency balance within the Community and plans for monetary cooperation.[67] In the negotiations on political cooperation, France took a hard line. Britain had pressed from the outset to be allowed to participate in EPC early on – even before its entry into the Community.[68] Brandt supported the British position, but Pompidou blocked it from the start. Although the other member states also advocated a closer link with Britain, Paris made the British accession to the Community a precondition for participation in EPC.[69] There was an "obligatory correlation" between the economic Europe and the political in French eyes, and France wanted to prevent the possibility of British participation in political cooperation even if the negotiations on its EEC entry ended in failure.[70] There seemed to be suspicion in Paris that the British government might willfully provoke collapse of the economic integration process while pursuing political leadership in Europe, with the goal of transforming the Community into a free trade area.[71]

In the light of the numerous problems, one must ask why Britain, regardless of which party held power, so adamantly pressed to enter the Community between 1967 and 1970. Its motives were, in fact, purely political, which explains why, for example, it rejected alternatives such as the trade arrangement proposed by the West Germans and the French.[72] The prevailing view in the Foreign Office was that membership in the European

---

66 See the British commentary in the membership application: *AAPD* 1970, doc. 289, p. 1065.
67 In a conversation with Willy Brandt, July 3, 1970. AN, 5 AG 2, 104.
68 "Aufzeichnung des Ministerialdirektors Frank, Betr.: Großbritannien, die Europäischen Gemeinschaften und die politische Zusammenarbeit," *AAPD* 1970, doc. 131.
69 According to the minutes of the first foreign ministers' meeting to implement the EPC, Mar. 6, 1970, *AAPD* 1970, doc. 101.
70 "Runderlass des Ministerialdirektors Frank, Betr.: Deutsch-französische Aussenministerkonsultation am 25. Mai in Paris," *AAPD* 1970, doc. 237.
71 This is how the British delegation perceived the French attitude. See Gabriele Clemens, "Der Beitritt Grossbritanniens zu den Europäischen Gemeinschaften," in Knipping and Schönwald, *Aufbruch zum Europa*, 306–28, at 323. Indeed, Pompidou was to some extent paranoid in his perception of British goals for entry by assuming that the British, having failed to destroy the Community from the outside, now aimed on destroying it from the inside. See Projet de Compte Rendu du Conseil sur les Affaires Européennes du Mardi 21 Octobre 1969, AN, 5 AG 2, 52.
72 Melissa Pine, "Perseverance in the Face of Rejection: Towards British Membership of the European Communities, November 1967–June 1970," in Knipping and Schönwald, *Aufbruch zum Europa*, 287–305, at 297.

Communities offered the sole possibility of preventing Britain's slide into political impotence. Faced with a gradual loosening of the special relationship with the United States, London could envision Britain sinking into political insignificance between the two superpowers and a Franco-German continental bloc.[73] In its commentary on the application for entry, the British government emphasized the political aspect of European unification, which would have to extend into the field of defense. Europe, it argued, would have to be prepared to take on "a larger share of responsibility for its own defense."[74] Pompidou's suspicion that Britain was trying to compensate for the loss of its role as a world power was certainly justified. British wishful thinking is illustrated by the revealingly blunt remark by Foreign Secretary George Brown to Foreign Minister Willy Brandt in December 1967: "Willy, you must get us in, so we can take the lead."[75]

Brandt worked hard to achieve an agreement with both allies, but, when in doubt, he gave priority to the "crucial alliance" with France.[76] He thus sided with Paris on the question of the entry candidates' participation in EPC during a December 1970 discussion of the Davignon Report between the six member states and the four states seeking membership.[77]

Britain expected that any economic advantages it might derive from EEC membership would only come in the long term, if ever. In the short term, it faced the prospect of the previously noted disadvantages arising from the CAP and import tariffs, which prompted fears of price increases and inflation. The Labour government under Harold Wilson hoped, above all, that membership would provide a boost to Britain's industrial sector in the intermediate and long terms; his hope was grounded on the example of West Germany's experience in the Community.[78] The advantages of membership, Wilson believed, would gradually offset and eventually outweigh the disadvantages.[79]

---

73 See Clemens, "Der Beitritt Grossbritanniens."
74 See *supra* note 65, at 1064. In the discussions on burden sharing within the NATO Eurogroup, Britain then showed little willingness to take on a greater role for itself. See, e.g., "Botschafter von Hase an das Auswärtige Amt, 16.11.1970, Betr. Gespräch mit Premierminister Heath," *AAPD* 1970, doc. 555.
75 Brandt, *Begegnungen und Einsichten*, 201–2.
76 On Franco-German relations in Europe, see Claudia Hiepel, "Willy Brandt, Georges Pompidou und Europa. Das deutsch-französische Tandem in den Jahren 1969–1974," in Knipping and Schönwald, *Aufbruch zum Europa*, 28–46.
77 *AAPD* 1970, 2184–5.
78 Alan S. Milward, "The Hague Conference of 1969 and the United Kingdom's Accession to the European Economic Community,"*JEIH* 9, no. 2 (2003): 117–26, at 119.
79 Clemens, "Der Beitritt Großbritanniens," 309. Clemens draws on the British government's white paper of February 10, 1970, which analyzed the effects of the entry on the United Kingdom's economy.

Britain realized that coming to an understanding with France would be the key to success in the membership negotiations. A new entente cordiale could strengthen Western Europe, opening the way for it to influence the policies of the superpowers, and would serve as a check on West Germany's growing power within Europe. Britain's interests here may well have been in fundamental agreement with those of France.

The decision to let Britain join the EC was made easier for Pompidou by the cautious rapprochement with the United States, initiated by de Gaulle in the wake of the franc crisis. Pompidou then carried it further with his accession to the new system of drawing rights in the International Monetary Fund (IMF).[80] French fears of Britain as an American Trojan horse in the Community subsided as relations with Washington improved. Pompidou began to value Britain, as he told Nixon, because it could serve as a counterpoise to an economically strengthened West Germany, whose *Ostpolitik* was at the point of competing with the French claim of exclusivity in détente policy.[81] In general, however, France's position was highly ambiguous. Paris remained hard on the terms of entry and regarded the negotiations as a test of Britain's seriousness about joining the Community.[82] The fact that the West German position was moving closer to French increased Britain's willingness to compromise.[83] Hence, Britain's assurances to the United States that, in the event it joined the EEC, it would advocate less protectionist and more liberal trade policies within the EEC were not realistic.[84] Given its political goals and its economic weakness, Britain could hardly be expected to transform the Community from within to make its policies more acceptable to the United States. It could be neither a political nor an economic Trojan horse.

FROM DWARF TO AN ACTOR IN TRANSATLANTIC RELATIONS?

The Hague summit and plans for enlargement adopted there firmly established the EC as an "international political reality."[85] Nevertheless, it was still a "shackled giant" that did not know what to do with its power and potential.[86] The expanded Community would have a total population larger

---

80 Theo M. Loch, "Ausgangsposition für die europäische Gipfelkonferenz in Den Haag," *EA* 24 (1969): 707–16, at 708.
81 As Pompidou said to Nixon in Feb. 1970, according to Kissinger, *Memoiren*, 455.
82 Pompidou to Kiesinger, Sept. 8, 1969: *AAPD* 1969, doc. 279.
83 Clemens, "Der Beitritt Grossbritanniens," 323.
84 Ibid., 318.
85 Malmgren, "Europa, die Vereinigten Staaten und die Weltwirtschaft."
86 So German Commissioner for Foreign Relations Ralf Dahrendorf, "Möglichkeiten und Grenzen einer Aussenpolitik der Europäischen Gemeinschaften," *EA* 26 (1971): 117–30, at 121.

than that of the United States. The volume of its external trade would also be larger than America's, and its gross domestic product would be nearly as large. It would clearly play a leading role in the world economy, and from that role it would have both the ability and the right to shape international economic relations.[87] Economically, Europe would not be confined to the six founding EEC members and the four candidates for membership. The EEC had preferential trade agreements with the six EFTA member states and twenty-one African states through the Yaoundé (1963/1971), Arusha (1969), and Lomé (1975) agreements.[88] Britain's entry would add eight Anglophone states to Europe's preferred trading partners. Seven Mediterranean states were linked to the Community through preferential agreements, and there was the possibility of similar agreements with another six. The EEC, in sum, stood at the center of a potential trade bloc of fifty-eight states extending from the Arctic Circle to the northern border of South Africa.

By the time of the Hague summit, Europe had become an economic giant that Washington increasingly saw as a threat. The CAP was an obstacle to the American goal of liberalized trade in agricultural products. European farm subsidies encouraged production, threatened American exports, and forced U.S. farmers to compete with subsidized European agricultural goods on the world market.[89] In Kissinger's view, the United States had laid the foundation for problems in transatlantic relations by having initially supported European agricultural integration. In contrast to the ever-growing number of skeptics in the United States, however, he did not harbor doubts about the EEC and did not consider European economic integration a threat to American interests.[90] Nixon's view was similar, and he used the occasion of a conversation with Brandt to stress his support for Europe's political unification.[91] In urging the EEC to accept Britain as a member, Nixon and Kissinger were holding to a long-established goal of American

---

87 According to Malmgren, "Europa, die Vereinigten Staaten und die Weltwirtschaft," 117.

88 On January 1, 1971, two agreements signed in 1969 went into effect: one on the renewal of the association agreements between the EEC and the associated African states (at Yaoundé in Cameroon) and another on the establishment of an association between the EEC and three more African states at Arusha, Tanzania. See Kurt Düwell, "Die Entwicklungspolitik der Europäischen Gemeinschaft zwischen Jaunde und Lomé (1963–84)," in Knipping and Schönwald, *Aufbruch zum Europa*, 187–200.

89 This was the Americans' position. See William Diebold Jr., "Europa und die Vereinigten Staaten. Perspektiven der wirtschaftlichen Beziehungen," *EA* 25 (1970): 597–608, at 601. The American critique conveniently ingonred that fact that the United States, too, had implemented protectionist measures.

90 Kissinger, *Memoiren*, 461.

91 "Aufzeichnung des Bundeskanzlers Brandt, 11.4.1970. Betr. Gespräche mit Nixon in Washington am 10. und 11. April 1970," *AAPD* 1970, doc. 153.

foreign policy. Nixon's declaration that the United States was willing to accept the economic disadvantages that might come with European integration nonetheless drew strong protests from the government agencies affected, above all the Departments of Commerce and Agriculture. They called for measures to help offset anticipated losses in U.S. agricultural and industrial export sales, and a number of influential lobbies took up their call.[92]

Nixon and Kissinger received little support from Europe in their efforts to counter protectionist and isolationist forces at home. Part of the reason was institutional. The EC was busy with its own problems, above all the negotiations on enlargement, and was clearly not in a position to be active on two fronts at the same time. Moreover, there was no European body with the authority to develop autonomous political initiatives. The authority of the Commission was limited, and the Council of Ministers was an unwieldy forum for decision making. The Committee of the Permanent Representatives existed to carry out directives issued by the individual member states. It was precisely on account of these institutional weaknesses that Richard Schaetzel, the U.S. representative to the Community, had welcomed the decisions and guidelines approved at the Hague.[93]

Another problem was the substance of transatlantic relations. The EC's foreign relations were still primarily viewed as trade relations. There was, however, more to transatlantic relations than trade, and economic issues could not be separated entirely from security and defense policy. Transatlantic dialogue did take place on a variety of levels, of course. For example, NATO served as a forum for addressing the divisive question of burden sharing. There, Europe was represented by the Eurogroup – but without France! Monetary issues were dealt with by the IMF's Group of Ten, and trade questions under the auspices of GATT. There was, however, no single European conversation partner with which Washington could address the overarching questions of transatlantic relations. It remained to be seen what would develop from EPC.

West Germany tried early on to create a firm institutional structure for transatlantic dialogue. In 1970, Brandt proposed the creation of a "contact committee" for ad hoc EC-U.S. discussion on trade issues. It would address clashes of European and American interests before they developed into full-blown conflicts. Brandt emphasized that he was not empowered to speak

---

92 Kissinger, *Memoiren*, 459.
93 J. Robert Schaetzel, "Die neuen Dimensionen der Beziehungen zwischen einer erweiterten Europäischen Gemeinschaft und den Vereinigten Staaten," *EA* 26 (1971): 859–70, at 865.

for the EC, and, always acting with an eye to France, he was very cautious in formulating the proposal.[94]

Informal talks between the EC and the United States began in October 1970, the former represented by Commissioner for Foreign Relations Ralf Dahrendorf and the latter by Under Secretary of State for European Affairs Nathaniel Samuels.[95] The talks were followed by casual meetings every six months between EEC and American officials. But as early as November 1970, Nixon indicated that he was increasingly inclined to think that such talks were disadvantageous for the United States. There was mounting pressure from Congress.[96] Then, in the middle of 1971, the administration reversed its position and took the infamous unilateral measures that shattered the economic and monetary foundations of the Atlantic partnership: it imposed import tariffs and eliminated the convertibility of the dollar into gold.

The years 1969–70 can be understood as the beginning of a period of change in transatlantic relations. The U.S. government was deeply divided over its commitments in Europe, and there were hardly any signals from the Community that it would take up the new Atlantic partnership. Some Europeans thought that the American question would be resolved automatically when Britain finally entered the Community. Others postponed potential initiatives to a later date. Thus, in the middle of 1970, the planning staff at the West German Foreign Office began considering whether it would be sensible to develop a longer-term European initiative that would, of necessity, address the links between integration, defense policy, and the envisaged Economic and Monetary Union.[97] Yet Europe was still unable to agree on a coherent vision, or even to realize it, and so the United States eventually launched another initiative for a new transatlantic partnership in 1973.

---

94 "Aufzeichnung des Bundeskanzlers Brandt, 11.4.1970."
95 Dahrendorf reported about these informal contacts on the Council of Ministers session, Oct. 26–7, 1970, which largely dealt with trade politics (*EA* 25, Z 237). See also Schaetzel, *Unhinged Alliance*, 146ff.
96 Kissinger, *Memoiren*, 462.
97 PAAA, B 1 (Ministerbüro), 472, Leiter des Planungsstabes, Aug. 10, 1970.

6

Unraveling the Ties That Really Bind

The Dissolution of the Transatlantic Monetary Order and the European Monetary Cooperation, 1965–1973

HUBERT ZIMMERMANN

One of the less conspicuous elements that held the Cold War transatlantic alliance of Western Europe, the United States, and Canada together was the monetary system created at the Bretton Woods conference of 1944.[1] Its defining feature was not the often-cited link of the U.S. dollar to gold at a fixed price but rather institutionalized transatlantic cooperation in managing international financial relations, balance of payments crises, and fixed exchange rates. Comprehensive capital controls gave governments autonomy in implementing their domestic economic strategies, which were often geared toward promoting social stability. Since the Cold War was also to a large extent an economic contest, monetary stability became an essential underpinning of the transatlantic security relationship. Thus, when transatlantic cooperation in this field collapsed in the late 1960s and early 1970s, the implications for the Atlantic community were enormous. This chapter discusses how this happened and identifies one of the most significant long-term consequences: the evolution of a European monetary order that eventually was to replace transatlantic monetary cooperation. Drawing on archival sources from the United States and Europe, it analyzes the crucial

---

1 The actual blueprint devised during the conference was never fully implemented. Even after the return to convertibility from 1958 to 1971, a period that is often referred to as the heyday of the Bretton Woods system, the working of the system deviated in important aspects from what had been proposed at Bretton Woods. In this chapter, the author uses the phrase "Bretton Woods system" in the way it is conventionally used in most of the literature, that is, with reference to the framework for international monetary relations in the Western world during the postwar period until 1971–1973. On the development of the system, see Harold James, *International Monetary Cooperation since Bretton Woods* (Washington, D.C., 1996).

decade from 1965 to 1975, during which this important transformation occurred.

International monetary diplomacy rarely makes the headlines; usually, foreign exchange movements, which are as crucial to international trade and investment as the operating system is to a computer, occur without much noise and government involvement. Many textbooks present the monetary system as a neutral mechanism, chosen rationally to enhance the efficient working of the economy. However, like operating systems, owning a dominant currency conveys power: the structural power to shape the environment in which others have to operate.[2] Smaller monetary powers are often forced to pursue policies against their underlying preferences to accommodate external pressures.[3] Thus, to an important degree, the way in which international monetary relations are organized gives structure to international relations. Yet we still possess only a rather vague understanding of the international political impact of monetary relations. The years under scrutiny here provide an excellent case study on the relationship between power, the international monetary environment, and international relations.

The early 1970s was a period of intense conflict between the United States and most of the Western European states in monetary matters. It is generally asserted that President Richard Nixon's decision to decouple the dollar from gold signaled the end of Bretton Woods and paved the way for the new neoliberal world of flexible exchange rates.[4] It is also well known that the Europeans regarded Nixon's decision as a blatantly unilateral act and that it triggered angry comments from European governments and the press. Those years also saw the first – failed – attempt at European monetary integration. Some accounts of this attempt, based on archival materials, have been published and largely confirm the well-known reasons previously brought forward to account for the failure, particularly the different monetary philosophies of France and West Germany, and the economic turmoil of the early 1970s.[5] However, the connections between American policy and the renewed push for a European Monetary identity are still rather unclear.

---

2 Susan Strange, *States and Markets* (London, 1988), 26.
3 David Andrews, "Cooperation, Coercion, and Asymmetric Adaptation" (Paper presented at the 2nd Pan-European Conference on EU Politics, Bologna, June 24–26, 2004).
4 See Wolfram E. Hanrieder, *Germany, America, Europe: Forty Years of German Foreign Policy* (New Haven, CT, 1989), 291; Henry R. Nau, *The Myth of America's Decline* (New York, 1990), 158–67.
5 See Wilkens Andreas, "Der Werner-Plan. Währung, Politik und Europa, 1968–71," in *Aufbruch zum Europa der zweiten Generation. Die Europäische Einigung 1969–1984*, eds. Franz Knipping and Matthias Schönwald (Trier, 2004), 217–45; Hubert Zimmermann, "The Fall of Bretton Woods and the First Attempt to Construct a European Monetary Order," in *From the Werner Plan to the EMU: A European Political Economy in Historical Light*, eds. Lars Magnusson and Bo Stråth (Brussels, 2001), 49–72.

This chapter sheds light on this question and discusses the significance of the European-American rift on monetary policy.

TRANSATLANTIC COOPERATION IN MONETARY POLICY

Chaos in monetary markets and the beggar-thy-neighbor policies of the interwar period were among the most important causes behind the rise of Nazism: that was a core conviction of the Anglo-American officials who planned a new international order for the postwar world. One of their most important conclusions was that international capital movements had to be kept under the tight supervision of states.[6] Only under such a regime would states be free to pursue domestic economic policies to integrate frustrated social groups, on the Left and the Right, without being undermined by currency speculation.[7] This system of embedded liberalism was the essence of the postwar monetary order known as the Bretton Woods system.[8] Centered on the dollar as the core currency, which was linked to gold at a fixed price of $35 an ounce, and strongly biased toward fixed exchange rates, the system required institutionalized cooperation among the Western economic powers. New organizations such as the International Monetary Fund (IMF), the Organisation for European Economic Cooperation (OEEC), the European Payments Union (EPU), and the Bank for International Settlements (BIS) were created to aid states in the supervision of markets. Initially, this framework seemed to be an obvious success. During the 1950s and 1960s, Western Europe experienced an economic miracle driven by export-led growth. Beyond the economic benefits it offered, the system served the geopolitical aims of the participants by facilitating the unprecedented expansion of U.S. commitments in Western Europe. This spared the Western Europeans exorbitant and potentially inflationary military expenditures and allowed them to concentrate on economic growth and social stability. However, as important and welcome as American support for the reconstruction and integration of European economies was, there was always a certain uneasiness in Western Europe, even outside

---

6 On this point, see Eric Helleiner, *States and the Reemergence of Global Finance* (Ithaca, NY, 1994). Helleiner also shows that the move toward convertibility in 1958 was limited to current account transactions by nonresidents and that a real liberalization of capital movements was achieved only in the 1980s.

7 Ibid., 49–50. See also Ronald I. McKinnon, "The Rules of the Game: International Money in Historical Perspective," *Journal of Economic Literature* 31 (March 1993): 1–44.

8 G. John Ruggie, "International Regimes, Transactions, and Change: Embedded Liberalism in the Postwar Economic Order," *International Organization* 36 (1982): 379–415.

leftist and nationalist circles, over American economic and military support.[9]

The United States also profited enormously from the Bretton Woods system. The role of the dollar as the linchpin of the system absolved it from the necessity to pursue potentially costly adjustment policies. This is one of the main benefits of monetary power.[10] As lender of last resort, the United States also cast the decisive vote in the emerging postwar monetary governance structure. Finally, the United States reaped the benefits of seigniorage and profited from the fact that trade in currencies and major international commodities was conducted in dollars.[11] In addition, the monetary system tied the Cold War alliance together in an economically integrated zone of prosperity. Monetary policy thus became an integral part of transatlantic relations.

It soon became clear, however, that the dollar-gold link was the Achilles' heel of the transatlantic system. American balance of payments deficits from 1958 onward signaled that the dollar might be overvalued. This suggested to dollar holders that they should trade dollars for gold, at the guaranteed price, instead of running the risk of a dollar devaluation. As a result, U.S. gold reserves shrank rapidly.[12] The elimination of deficits became a major preoccupation of presidents, starting with Dwight D. Eisenhower. Washington called on its allies for support. The result was an intensification of transatlantic cooperation. Countries experiencing balance-of-payments problems were bailed out by coordinated action; new credit facilities were created; and transatlantic monetary policy institutions multiplied.[13] This strategy initially alleviated the situation, but by the mid-1960s, its limitations were evident. Monetary crises had become regular events, pushing

---

9 See Christopher Gehrz and Marc Trachtenberg, "America, Europe, and German Rearmament, August–September 1950: A Critique of a Myth", in *Between Empire and Alliance: America and Europe during the Cold War*, ed. Marc Trachtenberg (Lanham, MD, 2003), 1–31.

10 Jonathan Kirshner, "Money Is Politics," *Review of International Political Economy* 10 (November 2003): 645–60; Benjamin J. Cohen, "The Revolution in Atlantic Economic Relations: A Bargain Comes Unstuck," in Wolfgang F. Hanrieder, ed., *The United States and Western Europe: Political, Economic and Strategic Perspectives* (Cambridge, MA, 1974), 406–37.

11 Seigniorage entailed (1) the holding of non-interest-bearing dollar currency by other countries (in 1998, this was estimated to amount to 50–60 percent of the total U.S. money stock, and (2) financing external deficits by borrowing its own currency with the benefit of a liquidity discount equivalent to $5 billion to $10 billion annually. See Roy Portes and Helene Rey, "The Emergence of the Euro as International Currency," *Economic Policy* 26 (1998): 309–10.

12 The reserves declined from $22.86 billion in 1957 to $17.80 billion in 1960. See Hubert Zimmermann, *Money and Security: Troops and Monetary Policy in Germany's Relations to the United States and the United Kingdom, 1950–1971* (Cambridge, 2002), 247. On the monetary crises stemming from American payments deficits, see James, *International Monetary Relations*, 154–61.

13 Paul Volcker and Gyohten Toyoo, *Changing Fortunes: The World's Money and the Threat to American Leadership* (New York, 1992).

currency matters to the headlines. The expansion of multinational enterprises and the creation of a huge Eurodollar market permitted increasing speculation against currencies deemed to be over- or undervalued.[14] In late 1967, the British pound was devalued, signaling a decisive defeat for Prime Minister Harold Wilson's government in its desperate struggle since 1964 to preserve the value of sterling vis-à-vis other major currencies.[15] In March 1968, a two-tier market for gold was introduced, preventing private market participants from converting their dollar holdings to gold.[16] In May 1968, student and worker unrest in France caused capital flight and recurring pressures on the value of the franc, which the French government was able to withstand only by using very tough capital controls. Vietnam-related government expenditures and Lyndon B. Johnson's Great Society programs caused inflation and led to repeated crises of confidence in the dollar.[17] And in November 1968, May 1969, and October 1969, there was pressure to revalue the D-mark upward.

Faced with monetary turmoil on an unprecedented scale as well as the possible collapse of the Bretton Woods system, the United States and the European states were confronted with three basic choices for a monetary operating system: transatlantic cooperation, national autonomy, or European integration. There was much uncertainty about and conflict over these alternatives, which presupposed very different policies, in the period from 1965 to 1978.[18] The first option was the retention of (or return to) the transatlantic management of monetary relations. This required the close alignment of Western monetary policies to trends in the dollar exchange rate to avoid excessive imbalances; cooperation, preferably institutionalized, among transatlantic monetary authorities; and acceptance of the leading role of the dollar. The second was the option of "benign neglect" of external imbalances, which entailed flexible exchange rates, liberated capital markets, and monetary policy set according to purely domestic objectives. At the core of this option lay the idea of national autonomy, that is, the conduct of monetary policy with disregard to external considerations. The third option was a new, regionally managed European monetary order in

---

14 Helleiner, *States and the Reemergence of Global Finance*, 81–95.
15 Hubert Zimmermann, "The Sour Fruits of Victory: Sterling and Security in Anglo-German Relations during the 1950s and 1960s," *Contemporary European History* 9 (2000): 225–44.
16 Robert M. Collins, "The Economic Crisis of 1968 and the Waning of the 'American Century,'" *American Historical Review* 101, no. 2 (1996): 396–422.
17 Hubert Zimmermann, "Who Paid for America's War? Vietnam and the International Monetary System, 1960–75," in *America, the Vietnam War, and the World: Comparative and International Perspectives*, eds. Lloyd C. Gardner, Andreas Daum, and Wilfried Mausbach (Cambridge, 2003), 151–74.
18 On the options open to the United States and Europe, see Zimmermann, "The Fall of Bretton Woods."

which monetary relations were closely coordinated among the participating governments; simultaneously, the regional monetary zone as a whole appreciated (or depreciated) against the dollar. For the Western Europeans, this option meant in essence monetary integration. At the end of the 1970s, most members of the European Community (EC) settled for this third option, monetary integration in a European framework. Although the decision for monetary integration remained controversial and the creation of a working European monetary order was beset by numerous international and domestic conflicts, the European option prevailed in the end.

In the early 1960s, however, transatlantic cooperation was still supported by almost all important countries and institutions. The rival option of unilateralism always figured in the debates of those years because it was pursued in a very outspoken way by one country: France. As soon as Charles de Gaulle assumed the presidency in 1958, he embarked on a mission to regain French national autonomy. In the mid-1960s, he directed his attention to monetary policy. He considered autonomy in the pursuit of monetary policy as one of the essential attributes of state power. To the Gaullists, the Bretton Woods system symbolized a "monetary Yalta" imposed by the two Anglo-Saxon powers.[19] The Gaullist critique of the monetary system centered on two points: first, the overvaluation of the dollar with respect to gold helped U.S. companies to buy up European industries with cheap money; second, the key currency role of the dollar allowed Washington to finance its expansive foreign policies by printing money.[20] In February 1965, the French president threw down the gauntlet: he announced that France would henceforth exchange every dollar it earned immediately for gold in order to force the United States to agree to a radical change in the monetary system. De Gaulle's action occurred without consultation and was a flagrant unilateral act that violated the norms of the transatlantic order. It did not bring Bretton Woods down because none of the other European states supported the move. Even in France, opinion was divided.

Struck by de Gaulle's challenge to Bretton Woods, historians often overlook the fact that French monetary thinking was not monopolized by

---

19 Testimony of Jean-Yves Haberer, Chef du Cabinet of French Foreign Minister M. Debré, in *De Gaulle en son Siècle*, ed. Institut de Gaulle (Paris, 1992), 3:55–6. The phrase Haberer used was "Yalta monetaire fait à deux."

20 "There is nothing that escapes American imperialism. It takes many forms, but the most insidious is the dollar," Charles de Gaulle declared on Feb. 27, 1963: quoted in Alain Peyrefitte, *C'était de Gaulle* (Paris, 1997), 74. On French monetary policy in this period, see Michael D. Bordo, Dominique Simard, and Eugene N. White, "France and the Bretton Woods International Monetary System 1960 to 1968," in *International Monetary Systems in Historical Perspective*, ed. Jaime Reis (New York, 1995), 153–80.

Gaullist ideas. In 1964–65, Finance Minister Valéry Giscard d'Estaing advocated European integration in the monetary field to create a regional bloc that might insulate Europe from the impact of the dollar.[21] Neither the West Germans nor Giscard's own government were ready yet for this idea, however, and Giscard subsequently left the government. His thinking, however, reflected the uneasy coexistence of two schools of thought on international and European policy in France. As Stanley Hoffmann argued in a landmark article in 1966, the French establishment was divided between those who wanted to achieve French greatness – *grandeur* – through a policy of national autonomy, using European integration only selectively, and those who wanted to use Europe systematically to enhance the French leverage in world politics.[22] As long as de Gaulle ruled, the former would prevail. France, therefore, concentrated on achieving a reform of the system through negotiation and conflict with the United States on a worldwide level.[23]

As for the West Germans, they strongly favored continued transatlantic cooperation. This choice rested on the security-money link: the paramount importance of the transatlantic alliance conditioned Bonn's monetary policy.[24] In the so-called offset negotiations that began in 1961, the German government agreed to support the dollar to an unprecedented degree by buying weapons and treasury bonds from the United States. In 1965–66, the offset system came under heavy strain. Chancellor Ludwig Erhard had promised the United States the fulfillment of all obligations deriving from the offset agreement but could not live up to his pledge. His famous trip to Washington to ask Johnson for a payments moratorium ended in complete disaster.[25] As a consequence of domestic economic troubles and the disintegration of its political authority, the Erhard government collapsed soon afterward and bequeathed the offset problem to its successor. The heavy-handed tactics of the Americans caused deep resentment within the West German government, even though Erhard's political fate had already been sealed before the trip.

The new government of Chancellor Kurt Georg Kiesinger was able to instrumentalize the argument of stabilizing the alliance with the United States to persuade the Bundesbank to help. That help came in the form of the so-called Blessing letter, a pledge by Bundesbank president Karl Blessing

---

21 Politisches Archiv des Auswärtigen Amtes, Berlin (hereafter PA-AA), Dept. III A 1, 176, Botschaft Paris to AA, Jan. 19, 1965.
22 Stanley Hoffmann, "Obstinate or Obsolete? The Fate of the Nation State and the Case of Western Europe," *Daedalus* 95 (1966): 862–912.
23 David Howarth, *The French Road to EMU* (London, 2001), 30–4.
24 On this link, see Zimmermann, *Money and Security*, passim.
25 Ibid., 171–208.

to refrain from converting dollars into gold.[26] It constituted a sizable loss of autonomy, as it forced the Bundesbank to retain the dollars in its reserves at potentially high risk. Not surprisingly, Blessing later regretted the letter and admitted that he had signed it only because the government had argued that the alliance with the United States would be thrown into disarray if he did not.[27] The Blessing letter in effect condemned the Bundesbank to neutralize the dollars streaming into the D-mark and flowing into the Federal Republic by various means without being able to exchange them for gold directly. The restrictive policies required by this situation often conflicted with the perceived necessities of West German domestic macroeconomic policy. Caught between its allegiance to the Bretton Woods system, domestic economic requirements, and pressures from its own government, the Bundesbank struggled in the following years to regain its domestic autonomy. Increasingly, that meant trying to escape international – that is, Atlantic and European – constraints and advocating floating exchange rates.

At the same time, the West German government began to have strong doubts about the existing transatlantic order. The American policy of brinkmanship on monetary issues and the offset problem had led to considerable resentment. In the wake of the Vietnam War, the United States was less supportive of the fundamental goals of West German foreign policy, which in turn reduced Bonn's readiness to back the dollar. In a letter to Kiesinger, Economics Minister Karl Schiller went so far as to recommend that the German government follow de Gaulle's example in undermining the dollar-gold link.[28] This would have toppled the transatlantic system immediately. However, as long as the monetary crisis did not interfere too strongly with economic growth, German exports, and the stability of the European Community, the geopolitical imperative of preserving the transatlantic alliance remained paramount for the government.

The inherent contradictions in the West German position soon multiplied. The Bonn monetary conference of November 1968, which reunited the ten leading Western economic powers, was the key event. The conference had been preceded by speculation against the French franc, the

---

26 Text of the letter in *Hearings before the Combined Subcommittee of Foreign Relations and Armed Services Committees on the Subject of United States Forces in Europe*, United States, 90th Congress, 1st sess., May 3, 1967 (Washington, D.C., 1967), 81ff. This commitment was a result of the acrimonious negotiations among the United States, Britain, and West Germany on the costs of stationing American and British troops in Germany and the possibilities for Bonn to offset those costs.

27 He called the letter a "damn thing" and said that, instead of signing it, he should have simply converted dollars into gold until the transatlantic order came down; see the quotation in Leo Brawand, *Wohin steuert die deutsche Wirtschaft?* (Munich, 1971), 62.

28 PA-AA, IIIA1, vol. 180, Schiller to Kiesinger, Jan. 12, 1967.

British pound, and indirectly, the U.S. dollar. London, Paris, and Washington exerted concerted pressure on West Germany to revalue the D-mark. Bonn, however, refused to participate in a multilateral realignment of exchange rates. For the first time, it pursued a policy of national autonomy without regard to the problems of its partners. This decision was based on the conviction that the strength of the D-mark proved the soundness of its policies and on the perceived necessity of sustained growth and exports, which might have been damaged by an appreciation of the D-mark.[29] The international response to the conference, however, showed that the Kiesinger government's strategy of sticking exclusively to its domestic preferences damaged its relations with its major allies. In a summary memorandum on the meeting, the Foreign Ministry, citing the press, warned of diplomatic isolation.[30] The Bonn conference clearly exposed the problem that the pursuit of a monetary diplomacy based on purely domestic objectives had the potential to undermine the government's geopolitical goals. In addition, it also revealed a dilemma with respect to Bonn's European policy. The Chancellery outlined the situation in January 1969:

Germany is confronted with two options – according its stability policy priority over European policy (i.e. the preservation and further development of the Community). A stability policy resulting from this option and shielded from external influences will inevitably set in motion tendencies for a dissolution of the EEC; – or, instead, according its European policy a certain priority over stability policy and accepting higher inflation than hitherto, be it through a renunciation of certain external economic preferences or within a common growth and economic policy.[31]

The same view was expressed in the Foreign Ministry.[32]

In 1969, this conflict gradually moved to the forefront of debates within the West German government. New speculation put the D-mark repeatedly under increasing pressure, setting in motion a prolonged public argument about the value of the mark. The Bundesbank saw no other option than revaluation to neutralize excess liquidity. However, the government refused – mainly out of concern for the interests of exporters.[33] As a result, Franco-German relations dipped to a postwar low, as the franc was again in the center of speculation. Infuriated by their costly yet ineffective efforts to

29 Otmar Emminger, *D-Mark Dollar Währungskrisen. Erinnerungen eines ehemaligen Bundesbankpräsidenten* (Stuttgart, 1986), 143–4.
30 PA-AA, IA2, vol. 1553, Memorandum of Dept. III: Bonn monetary conference, Nov. 25, 1968.
31 Bundesarchiv (BA) Koblenz, B 136/3332, Dept. III/1 (Meyer) to Chancellor Kiesinger, Jan. 8, 1969.
32 PA-AA, I A 2, 1553, Memorandum by State Secretary Lahr, Jan. 7, 1969.
33 Susan Strange, *International Economic Relations of the Western World, 1959–71.* Vol. 2, *International Monetary Relations* (London, 1976), 325.

stem the speculative flows and by the havoc created by the monetary crisis in the European Community's Common Agricultural Policy (CAP), the French repeatedly protested at the highest levels against Bonn's nationalist monetary policy.[34] Once again, monetary policy exposed the incompatibility of the West German government's anti-inflationary domestic monetary policy and its interest in strengthening European cooperation. Finally, in October 1969, after a change of government, the Federal Republic revalued the D-mark. It also began to take the European option more seriously.

This shift became obvious very soon. One of the most surprising results of the Hague summit of the EC in December 1969 was the agreement to establish the European Economic and Monetary Union (EMU). The proposal had been put forward by Chancellor Willy Brandt, and it reflected Bonn's growing dissatisfaction with the working of the transatlantic system. The French enthusiastically embraced the idea of EMU because it offered the possibility of institutionalized cooperation with the West Germans in the event of troubles for the franc. It was precisely this aspect of EMU – a commitment to intervene that went beyond the obligations imposed by the Bretton Woods system – that led the Germans to proceed very cautiously in the ensuing negotiations.[35] As always in times of change, several competing options arose simultaneously. Many policy makers and experts still hoped for a reform of the Bretton Woods system. In their eyes, the idea of EMU seemed utopian. Moreover, German and French authorities were not yet convinced that a policy of national autonomy would be infeasible. For these reasons, the monetary union plan that resulted from the negotiations chaired by Prime Minister Pierre Werner of Luxembourg came to naught. Ultimately, however, American policies prompted a revival of interest in EMU and made a return to the transatlantic option impossible.

THE SLOW DEMISE OF BRETTON WOODS

In monetary policy, Nixon proved to be the true successor of de Gaulle. During his administration, the idea that the transatlantic monetary system was a burden on the United States and that the United States should pursue a policy of monetary autonomy became official policy. The coolness of the Western Europeans with regard to the U.S. war effort in Vietnam, the widening American trade deficit, and the Republicans' distrust of

---

34 *Akten zur Auswärtigen Politik der Bundesrepublik Deutschland* (hereafter *AAPD*) 1969, vol. 1, doc. 147, Conversation of Chancellor Kiesinger with French Ambassador Seydoux, May 7, 1969, 559–62.
35 See the chapter by William Gray in this volume.

multilateralism combined to produce a rather abrupt change in America's basic monetary strategy.

The option of pursuing a unilateral monetary policy was discussed during the first weeks of the Nixon administration. At issue was the relaxation of controls on American investment abroad that had been imposed by the Johnson administration. Nixon had criticized the controls during the presidential campaign, and many of his advisers were now recommending that he simply abolish them.[36] However, the State Department and National Security Adviser Henry Kissinger warned that such a step might trigger currency speculation and damage relations with the Europeans, who would have to cope with the effects. "The main effect of this reaction would be a setback to our efforts to improve the monetary system through cooperative steps with the Europeans," Kissinger wrote in a memorandum to the president. He added that a "unilateral suspension of gold convertibility – essentially adoption of a floating exchange rate for the dollar – would represent a massive display of U.S. power and rupture our efforts to forge a new partnership with Europe on the basis of greater equality."[37] During Nixon's first year in office, the administration held vaguely to the idea of attempting a multilateral approach to the monetary problem.[38] However, because Nixon himself was not interested in pursuing the issue and monetary markets were relatively calm, no specific initiatives were taken. As he stated in a summary of his priorities in early 1970, "I do not want to be bothered with international monetary matters."[39] Because the administration was pursuing a relatively restrictive financial policy to bring the inflation caused by Johnson's expansion of government spending under control, international markets regained confidence in the dollar.

Speculation against the dollar resumed, however, when the Federal Reserve lowered interest rates in 1971 and hopes for a quick termination of the Vietnam War faded. The Nixon administration soon abandoned its reservations toward unilateral remedies for this predicament. The frustration about the dollar problem and perceived European unhelpfulness in this area was reinforced by an increasingly suspicious view of European integration. In the economic sphere, Europe came to be seen as rival, not as partner.

---

36 *Foreign Relations of the United States* (hereafter *FRUS*) 1969–76, vol. 3, Action Memorandum from R. Cooper and F. Bergsten of the NSC Staff to Kissinger, Jan. 28, 1969, 5–6.
37 *FRUS* 1969–76, vol. 3, Memorandum from Kissinger to Nixon, Mar. 17, 1969, 30.
38 Joanne Gowa, *Closing the Gold Window: Domestic Politics and the End of Bretton Woods* (Ithaca, NY, 1983), 79.
39 *FRUS* 1969–76, vol. 3, Memorandum by President Nixon to Kissinger, Haldeman, and Ehrlichman, Mar. 2, 1970, 95.

Nixon's secretary of the treasury, John Connally, gave voice to this new perspective:

I believe we must realize there is a strong element of thinking within Europe that would take advantage of weakness or clumsiness on our part to promote the Common Market not as a partner but as a rival economic bloc, competing vigorously with the dollar and reducing or shutting out, as best as it can, U.S. economic influence from a considerable portion of the world.[40]

Nixon's basic attitude was similar:

Nationalism in Europe is stronger than nationalism in the U.S. and it is damned strong here. They enjoy kicking the U.S. around. Eighty-eight percent of all the European media is violently anti-U.S. They will cut their own throats economically to take us on politically.... European leaders want to "screw" us and we want to "screw" them in the economic area.[41]

Another ominous sign for the transatlantic monetary system was the realist perspective on international relations prevalent within the Nixon administration and the strong disdain for international institutions it engendered. As Connally explained to Italian Prime Minister Emilio Colombo, "We are strongly concerned that the existence of various international entities such as the IMF, the OECD, the EEC, and the GATT are not always coordinated and tend to impede the solution of problems. In a fast moving age, when problems arise we cannot afford to be bogged down by hide-bound institutional arrangements."[42]

The increasing criticism directed toward the Common Market reflected the Nixon administration's strong preoccupation with European policies in the fields of trade and agriculture, especially the accelerated conclusion of preferential trade agreements with third-world countries and the price subsidies for European agricultural exports. In part, the administration was echoing congressional complaints. Meeting with a West German delegation, the American special envoy Peter Petersen bluntly summed up the mood in Congress: "For 25 years we have helped these European bastards getting back on their feet and now they take us for a ride."[43] A White House extremely concerned about reelection could not be expected to be unreceptive to such opinions. When the EC was about to raise its grain import levies, for example, Secretary of Agriculture Clifford M. Hardin recommended using "all U.S. Government resources to reverse Germany on this

40 Declassified Documents Reference System (hereafter DDRS) 1999, doc. 385, Connally to President Nixon, June 8, 1971.
41 *FRUS* 1969–76, vol. 3, Memorandum of Conversation, Sept. 11, 1972, 262, 264.
42 Ibid., Editorial Note on Nov. 30, 1971 meeting, 579.
43 *AAPD* 1973, vol. 1, doc. 52, Frank-Petersen talk, Feb. 16, 1973, 246.

question, even at the risk of interfering with the UK–EC negotiations or of creating difficulties for Brandt. Otherwise, the Administration will have serious political problems in Indiana, Illinois, Ohio and Missouri."[44] In the margins of this memorandum, Nixon scribbled, "But the emphasis must be on U.S. interests. We cannot continue to sell out U.S. interests for [the Department of] State's 'foreign policy consideration.'"[45] Nixon had been very hawkish on U.S. trade policy toward Europe from the outset.[46] The State Department, which noted "a deep seated and widespread hostility towards the Community in several agencies of the Executive branch,"[47] was in a hopeless position when it tried to argue that European integration was generally advantageous for the United States.

The Bretton Woods system fell victim to the doubts about Europe prevailing in Washington. In August 1971, faced with official European demands for dollar–gold conversions, Nixon, without consulting the Europeans, decided to close the gold window and imposed a 10 percent surtax on all imports to the United States. The objective behind these decisions, as the records of the debates within the government show, was not to create a new monetary system or to impose a dollar standard on the world but to reverse the terms of trade by forcing the Europeans to revalue their currencies.[48] In essence, the decision to end dollar convertibility was, therefore, a response to the ongoing integration of Western Europe (and the rise of Japan) and not to monetary problems. The Americans made it clear that they contemplated no change in the price of gold or in the dollar exchange rate. Instead, they demanded the revaluation of European and Japanese currencies so as to produce a payment swing of $13 billion – a mind-boggling figure – in favor of the United States.

The real Nixon shock was not the closing of the gold window. That did not cost the Europeans much and was probably inevitable. There was already a de facto ban on gold conversions, and Washington had made clear that it would not tolerate a further decline in its gold stock. The shock to the Europeans came, rather, from the radical challenge to European trade interests posed by Nixon's blunt act of brinksmanship. The structural power inherent in the dollar's reserve currency role became obvious. The burden of adjustment was shifted abroad, and America's autonomy regarding its

---

44 *FRUS* 1969–76, vol. 4, Memorandum from Kissinger to Nixon, Jan. 2, 1971, 640.
45 Ibid., 641.
46 *FRUS* 1969–76, vol. 3, Information Memorandum Bergsten to Kissinger, Apr. 14, 1969, 49.
47 Ibid., Memorandum from Deputy Undersecretary of Economic Affairs Samuels to Kissinger, Aug. 20, 1970, 110.
48 The American trade balance was negative in 1971, for the first time since 1946. See Embassy of the U.S., "London: Trade," http://www.usembassy.org.uk/trade18.html.

domestic policies and the size of its external commitments was preserved. The Europeans, however, were left with two unpleasant options for dealing with the resulting dollar glut: revalue their currencies against the dollar (and damage their exports) or try to neutralize the capital inflow by restrictive measures in their domestic economies.

In the following months, Washington did not propose any solution apart from repeatedly stating that it needed a massive improvement in its trade account. The United States stopped supporting the exchange rate of the dollar. Consequentially, the dollar rapidly slid against other major currencies despite desperate attempts by Europe and Japan to control the movements.[49] The chaos ended only when, in December 1971, Nixon and French president Georges Pompidou met in the Azores and cobbled together a memo of understanding outlining a new monetary order. It envisioned allowing most of the major currencies to appreciate against the dollar to help the U.S. trade balance, lifting the 10 percent surtax, raising the dollar price of gold, and establishing more flexible margins for exchange rates.[50]

The Smithsonian Agreement, as the plan was dubbed, was hailed as a new founding treaty for the international monetary system. It soon began to unravel, however. Low American interest rates, which should have boosted the American economy during the election year, led U.S. investors to search for better returns abroad, pushing dollars to Europe and Japan. Pompidou immediately complained that the United States was not defending the new agreement.[51] When the sudden floating of the pound in June 1972 ended a period of relative calm on monetary markets, most Europeans could not but agree.[52] The new West German finance minister, Helmut Schmidt, made this point very clearly to U.S. Ambassador Martin Hillenbrand in early August 1972. "He could not understand the passivity of the U[nited] S[tates] in the international monetary field during recent months," Hillenbrand reported to Washington. "This had made it extremely difficult for our European friends to believe that the U.S. really wanted to adhere to the Smithsonian Agreement."[53] Speculation against the dollar continued unabated. In the late summer of 1972, the Federal Reserve finally intervened on a small scale – with surprising success. Further interventions

49 Gilbert Milton, with Peter Oppenheimer and Michael Dealtry, *Quest for World Monetary Order: The Gold-Dollar System and Its Aftermath* (New York, 1980), 186–9.
50 *FRUS* 1969–76, vol. 3, Paper agreed by President Nixon and President Pompidou, n.d., 597–9.
51 Ibid., Letter from President Pompidou to President Nixon, Feb. 4, 1972, 604–6.
52 Ibid., Secretary of Treasury Shultz to Nixon, July 1972, 631.
53 Ibid., Embassy Bonn to Department of State, Aug. 1, 1972, 649. Charles Coombs, who was responsible at the time for the foreign exchange operations of the Federal Reserve, complains about "the total absence of any commitment by the U.S. to help defend [the Smithsonian Agreement]." See Charles Coombs, *The Arena of International Finance* (New York, 1976), 225.

were, however, later vetoed by the Treasury.[54] Washington, finding itself in a defensive position, agreed only to a very limited extent of international cooperation, abandoning even that whenever opportune. It also resisted European calls for renewed enforcement control of capital movements.[55] In February 1973, Secretary of the Treasury George Shultz publicly remarked that "American policy for interest rates and domestic liquidity will only be determined in accordance with the needs of the United States economy, excluding other international concerns."[56]

American monetary policy between 1971 and 1973, in sum, was not based on a master plan to destroy Bretton Woods. The Nixon administration's aversion to time-consuming international coordination and to state-administered capital controls led, however, to the system's progressive disintegration. The emergence of monetarist thinking served to justify the U.S. attitude. The target of American monetary measures was the emerging trade power of Europe and Japan. The West European reaction to this attitude evolved from disbelief to an increasing determination to pursue the European option.

THE EUROPEAN RESPONSE

The Western European frustration with American monetary policy under the Johnson administration gave way to increasing resentment as the Nixon administration exerted mounting pressure on the Europeans to hold dollars and thereby underwrite policies they could no longer support. Although most Western European political leaders were still hopeful after the Hague summit that some kind of transatlantic solution could be found, European governmental officials and central bankers became less and less willing to make sacrifices for the sake of transatlantic cooperation and opted increasingly to coordinate their monetary policies. The negotiations on monetary union thus went ahead after the Werner plan was presented despite insurmountable differences of opinion among the governments. Often, it seemed as if the project was about to end in utter failure.

Such a moment came in May 1971. During this month, West Germany was confronted with an enormous influx of foreign currencies, especially dollars, which forced it to close the foreign exchange markets. The Bundesbank had tried in vain to counter the dollar glut with its traditional

---

54 Ibid., 226–7.
55 Helleiner, *States and the Reemergence of Global Finance*, 116.
56 Quoted in Loukas Tsoukalis, *The Politics and Economics of European Monetary Integration* (London, 1977), 127.

instruments. In its monthly report for May 1971, it noted that the "reduction in the discount rate on March 31, 1971 was motivated solely by external considerations; it was no longer in conformity with domestic conditions."[57] The defense of the dollar–D-mark exchange rate made the simultaneous pursuit of anti-inflationary policies and an autonomous macroeconomic policy at home impossible. The bank's governing council was split over whether the Federal Republic should give up intervention altogether and float the D-mark or try to hold on to the Bretton Woods system with capital controls and a temporary float. Bundesbank's vice president Otmar Emminger and others advocated a permanent float, arguing that it would allow the Bundesbank to concentrate on domestic stability and the fight against inflation.[58] The Brandt government and Bundesbank president Karl Klasen, however, warned against such a course for political reasons. The Foreign Ministry summarized the arguments for and against floating the D-mark and noted that flexible exchange rates would in fact enhance the Bundesbank's autonomy over domestic economic policy. It would, however, have severe consequences for the EC, especially for CAP and the planned monetary union. "A unilateral German monetary action without prior consultation would throw the EC into a crisis and give rise to doubts about Germany's adherence to the treaties."[59] In the end, the government tried to square the circle by temporarily floating the D-mark and attempting to get the other Europeans on board for a joint float against the dollar, thereby creating a common bloc against the dollar. Bonn promised to extend monetary support to other European currencies so that they could stay in line with the D-mark. However, France and Italy refused to go along with a float out of fear that their economies would lose competitiveness vis-à-vis the United States; instead, they urged Germany to impose strict capital controls.[60] That was anathema to the German Ministry of Economics, and the D-mark floated unilaterally in May 1971, effectively putting an end to any prospect of achieving European monetary union in the near future. After the German decision to float, the French were furious and suspected the Germans of intentionally torpedoing the CAP as well as slavishly following Washington.[61] The dilemma for the Brandt government, which

---

57 *Monatsbericht der Deutschen Bundesbank*, May 1971, 7.
58 Dorothee Heisenberg, *The Mark of the Bundesbank: Germany's Role in European Monetary Cooperation* (Boulder, CO, 1999), 31.
59 PA-AA, IIIA1, vol. 585, Memorandum by von Bismarck-Osten, May 6, 1971.
60 Otmar Emminger, "Deutsche Geld- und Währungspolitik im Spannungsfeld zwischen innerem und äußerem Gleichgewicht, 1948–75," in *Währung und Wirtschaft in Deutschland, 1876–1975*, ed. Deutsche Bundesbank (Frankfurt, 1976), 181
61 PA-AA, IIIA1, vol. 585, Ambassador Ruete, Paris, to Foreign Office, May 13, 1971.

was torn between the transatlantic option, European integration, and the politically risky option of a unilateral D-mark policy, persisted.

The floating dollar created wild fluctuations among European currencies, caused incessant political conflict among the EC members, and damaged the fabric of European integration. The French press expressed extreme irritation with West Germany's refusal to side with France in actively resisting the American attempt to force the Europeans to let their currencies appreciate against the dollar.[62] Paris insisted on a return to fixed exchange rates and used extensive capital controls to avoid a revaluation of the franc, which it saw as a threat to the CAP and its strategy for keeping French high-tech industries competitive in global markets.[63] It therefore refused to join a common EC float. Ironically, France now became the last defender of the Bretton Woods system.

The continuing American disinterest in negotiating a new transatlantic order practically forced the European option first on West Germany and, in the end, on France as well. In September 1971, a group of Social Democratic Bundestag representatives left a meeting at the Treasury in Washington "in shock" after having been informed that objective of American policy was a "capitulation" of the rest of the world in monetary affairs.[64] German decision makers repeatedly warned their American interlocutors that the continued failure of transatlantic cooperation would lead Bonn to pursue the European option. Reporting the attitude of German officials regarding monetary reform, the U.S. embassy in Bonn wrote in November 1971: "The alternative to an early world-wide solution is, according to the Germans, an interim European solution."[65] Bundesbank vice president Emminger stressed the same point in talks with American officials. He argued that "in absence of a general settlement . . . it would be impossible to resist a 'European solution' now."[66] Brandt also made this point very clear to a visiting American delegation in October 1971: "If no agreement with the U.S. can be found by the end of the year, pressure will rise in Europe to take measures to avoid a collapse of the EC. We would be forced to look for a common base with France even if that places us at a disadvantage."[67] In fact, two months later, in a meeting with Pompidou, Brandt said, "Now

62 *AAPD* 1971, II, doc. 282, Blomeyer-Bartenstein, Paris, to Foreign Office, Aug. 25, 1971, 284–5, esp. n. 4.
63 PA-AA, III A 1, vol. 610, Feit (Embassy Paris) to Foreign Office, Aug. 19, 1971.
64 Ibid., Bundespresseamt, Nr. 9696, Sept. 18, 1971.
65 *FRUS* 1969–76, vol. 3, Telegram from Embassy in Germany to Department of State, Nov. 24, 1971, 571.
66 Ibid., Telegram from Embassy in Germany to Department of State, Nov. 17, 1971, 568.
67 *AAPD* 1971, vol. 3, doc. 338: Brandt-Irwin talk, Oct. 7, 1971, 1503.

a point has been reached from which one knows that the issue is not the German-American relationship but a policy from a European point of view, not against the U.S., but towards the U.S."[68]

For the West German government, the Bretton Woods compromise of embedded liberalism had seen its day. In July 1972, Schmidt informed Schultz that the Federal Republic would not continue to sacrifice its essential interests for the sake of the dollar exchange rate.[69] France, likewise disillusioned with the American response and realizing that it could not pursue an autonomous policy any longer, resigned itself to a common European revaluation against the dollar. The result was the "snake," an attempt to keep the fluctuations of European currencies against one another and against the U.S. dollar within narrow bands. The agreement, which took effect in April 1972, soon ran into difficulties when Britain decided to float the pound. Nevertheless, the EC heads of government once again affirmed their determination to achieve monetary union at the Paris summit of October 1972.

The final blow to this option of transatlantic monetary cooperation came in the spring of 1973. Once again, huge sums of speculative capital moved to Germany. Faced with the prospect of yet another revaluation, the government was determined to resist being "brought to its knees again."[70] The Germans suspected that the United States was trying to use the situation once more to improve its trade and currency position.[71] Brandt issued an urgent appeal to Nixon for the American authorities to support the German efforts and for negotiations for a new monetary system to start immediately.[72] In addition, the Germans tried to coordinate another joint float. The French were at first intransigent. Pompidou told the German ambassador that a common European float would be a concession to the United States that would bring nothing for the Europeans in return.[73] Finally, the Europeans and Americans met on February 13, 1973, and agreed on a concerted transatlantic realignment that included a devaluation of the dollar by 10 percent.[74]

This attempt at transatlantic cooperation – the last, as it turned out – survived for only about a month. When a new wave of speculation hit

68 Ibid., doc 427, Brandt-Pompidou meeting, Dec. 3, 1971, 1877.
69 *AAPD* 1972, vol. 2, doc. 205, Botschafter Pauls, Washington, an das Auswärtige Amt, July 21, 1972, 939–42.
70 *AAPD* 1973, vol. 1, doc. 38, Chancellor Brandt's Meeting with Belgian Prime Minister Leburton, Feb. 7, 1973, 191.
71 Ibid, doc. 41, Memorandum by VLR Jelonek, Feb. 9, 1973, 206.
72 Ibid., doc. 44, Brandt to Nixon, Feb. 9, 1973, 218–20.
73 Ibid., doc. 46, Freiherr von Braun to AA, Feb. 10, 1973, 223–5.
74 Ibid., doc. 50, Memorandum by VLR I Dohms, Feb. 13, 1973, 239–41.

currency markets and the Americans told the Europeans that they would not undertake any new efforts in monetary policy before trade and agricultural issues were resolved, Germany stopped intervening to support the dollar–D-mark exchange rate.[75] French efforts toward a new bilateral Franco-American understanding failed. In an emergency meeting on March 11, 1973, the EC members (excluding Italy) decided on a joint float and on the termination of their buying dollars; Norway and Sweden later joined in as well.

As a result of the float, the dollar plunged to unheard-of levels. Inflation was rampant, and the commodity markets were in chaos well before the oil shock began in late 1973. Despite these problems, the debate was over: the Europeans had embarked on the road to monetary integration, and the United States would go its own way on monetary policy. In a Bundestag debate on March 15, 1973, Brandt announced that "nobody should be under any illusions. Today, stability policy cannot be defined against Europe, but for all practical purposes only with Europe."[76] In this sense, 1973 was indeed the Year of Europe.

CONCLUSION

The Bretton Woods system was dead. Did the events analyzed in this chapter matter, and if so, what was their impact on transatlantic relations? I argue that they mattered a great deal and decisively shaped the last third of the twentieth century. Placing the world on a dollar standard allowed the United States to continue its huge current account deficits, freeing Nixon's successors from the obligation to adjust their policies. This implied the availability of almost unlimited funds for venture capital in the emerging knowledge-based economy. When the oil-producing countries looked for places to profitably reinvest the enormous profits the increase in oil prices had generated, the U.S. market was the preferred venue because of both its size and the fact that the dollar remained the only real international currency. Thus, the United States profited from the end of Bretton Woods. However, with respect to its core monetary objective between 1971 and 1973 – namely keeping Western Europe open to American trade interests – the Nixon administration failed. More than thirty years and several rounds of world trade talks later, the American government still continues to fight against EU trade preferences.

---

75 Ibid., doc. 80, Memorandum by VLR Vogel, Mar. 11, 1973, 376; Emminger, "Deutsches Geld und Währungspolitik," 532.
76 Bundestag, *Stenographische Berichte*, 82, 98–9. His words were probably directed against the Bundesbank.

The Europeans' attempts to coordinate their monetary policies began very inauspiciously. In April 1973, a European reserve fund was established that required regular contacts of European monetary decision makers to coordinate policies. The attempt to keep European currencies within narrow bands of the snake was, however, not very successful. Nonetheless, the issue of improved monetary cooperation was now pursued energetically by European leaders, especially by the former finance ministers Helmut Schmidt and Valéry Giscard d'Estaing after they ascended, respectively, to the chancellorship and the presidency. The final product of these efforts was the creation of the European Monetary System in 1978, which in turn became the nucleus of the monetary union launched in 1999.

7

Toward a "Community of Stability"?

The Deutsche Mark between European and Atlantic Priorities, 1968–1973

WILLIAM G. GRAY

Whatever happened to Gaullists and Atlanticists? As scholars of international history have reminded us in the past few years, West German elites fought viciously in the mid-1960s over geopolitical priorities. Was the Bonn Republic to align with the West in a narrow sense, meaning Western Europe under French leadership, or did its allegiance belong to the broader transatlantic community?[1] The debate subsided in the late 1960s, in part because Christian Democratic leaders regained tighter control over their party, but more importantly, also because Charles de Gaulle's uncooperative attitude toward NATO and European integration managed to progressively alienate most West German political elites. Despite the famous Élysée Treaty of January 1963, which instituted routine Franco-German consultations on political, economic, cultural, and military affairs, de Gaulle failed to win over the Federal Republic to a preferential partnership.[2]

By the early 1970s, new battle lines had been drawn in West German politics. Historians are most familiar with the partisan fight over *Ostpolitik*, which tested the constitution to its limits when the Christian Democrats attempted to unseat Chancellor Willy Brandt.[3] Within the

---

1 This theme is explored convincingly in Ronald J. Granieri, *The Ambivalent Alliance: Konrad Adenauer, the CDU/CSU, and the West, 1949–1966* (New York, 2003). See also the early chapters of *The Strategic Triangle: France, Germany, and the United States in the Shaping of the New Europe*, eds. Helga Haftendorn, Georges-Henri Soutou, Stephen F. Szabo, and Samuel F. Wells Jr. (Baltimore, 2006).

2 For an overview, see Reiner Marcowitz, *Option für Paris? Unionsparteien, SPD und Charles de Gaulle 1958–1969* (Munich, 1996).

3 The most vivid account is still Arnulf Baring, *Machtwechsel. Die Ära Brandt-Scheel* (Stuttgart, 1982). For a detailed study of the CDU/CSU's policies, see Andreas Grau, *Gegen den Strom. Die Reaktion der CDU/CSU-Opposition auf die Ost- und Deutschlandpolitik der sozialliberalien Koalition 1969–1973* (Düsseldorf, 2005).

Brandt government, however, a more philosophical feud raged over economic and monetary policy. Once again, Bonn appeared to face a choice between European and transatlantic solutions; it was a familiar dilemma that resembled the Gaullist-Atlanticist debate in many respects. With Paris and Washington advocating radically different models of international monetary relations, Bonn could scarcely cooperate with one side without angering the other. This time, though, the outcome favored France. West German leaders came to assign their European identity higher priority; more remarkably, perhaps, they came to stress cooperation with Paris as the driving force of European integration.[4]

Scholars long accustomed to this Franco–German motor may not appreciate just what a startling turnaround it represented. Throughout the 1960s, the Social Democrats had resisted Gaullist temptations; one observes little emotional connection between Willy Brandt and de Gaulle in this period, and his adviser Egon Bahr could be downright suspicious.[5] When the Brandt government came to power in 1969, it paid the usual deference to European unity, but – as this chapter argues – it envisioned a relatively open Europe in harmony with liberal economic principles. The Social Democrats' leading voice on economic questions, Karl Schiller, often sounded like a more Keynesian stepchild of Ludwig Erhard. Ironically, it was the tumultuous character of the international monetary environment that drew Bonn into deeper commitments to European integration – specifically, a plan to achieve economic and monetary union (EMU) within ten years. Karl Schiller's efforts to shape EMU in accord with German priorities, as a "community of stability and growth," aroused hostility in Paris and Brussels and found only inconsistent support in Bonn. Meanwhile, Schiller's devotion to the Atlantic monetary order, the classic Bretton Woods system, came to seem anachronistic in light of the Nixon administration's highly autarkic behavior. More politically savvy members of Brandt's cabinet, such as Helmut Schmidt, learned in the early 1970s that a measured accommodation of French views would prove the only reliable means for West Germany to avoid diplomatic isolation.

---

4 Essentially, I argue that this period is essential for understanding the choice for Europe, illuminated on the basis of other case studies in Andrew Moravscik, *The Choice for Europe: Social Purpose and State Power from Messina to Maastricht* (Ithaca, NY, 1998).

5 See, e.g., a note by Bahr expressing his doubts about French defense policy, Sept. 30, 1968: Archiv der Sozialen Demokratie – Bonn [AdsD], Depositum Bahr, Bd. 399, Mappe 1. For an overview of Brandt's interactions with de Gaulle in this period, see Maurice Vaïsse, "De Gaulle et Willy Brandt: deux non-conformistes au pouvoir," in *Willy Brandt und Frankreich*, eds. Horst Möller and Maurice Vaïsse (Munich, 2005), 103–14.

SCHILLER, BRANDT, AND THE "COMMUNITY OF STABILITY AND GROWTH"

It would be difficult to exaggerate the significance of the concept of stability for West Germany in the decades after 1945. This entailed, above all, the avoidance of inflation – a difficult feat in a time of phenomenal growth. The Bundesbank's success in delivering price stability had, indeed, helped to lend the institution a semimythical aura as protector of the German mark.[6] But what did stability mean in an international context? As one crisis after another wracked the pound sterling, German economists spoke about the need to secure West Germany's open flank. The Federal Republic was, after all, a trading nation par excellence, reliant upon imports just as much as exports to balance out its manufacturing-heavy economic profile. Rising prices in France, Britain, and the United States kindled fears of imported inflation – the prospect that West Germany could not long stay immune from international price trends.[7]

Almost instinctively, West German economists and politicians sought safety in numbers. In December 1966, the grand coalition led by Kurt Georg Kiesinger expressed its interest in creating a hard-currency bloc with other stability-conscious states. Collectively, such a bloc would function as a community of stability, a European zone that might remain insulated from the harsher international climate.[8] But the six members of the European Community were hardly ideal candidates as partners in a hard-currency bloc; outside currencies such as the Swiss franc showed greater compatibility with the D-mark. Whenever vague proposals surfaced about the monetary unification of the Common Market, German officials expressed caution. "A currency union is desirable in the long run as the crowning achievement of integration," remarked State Secretary Rolf Lahr of the Foreign Ministry to a French colleague, "but the time for this is not yet ripe. Without common budgetary and capital market policies it's inconceivable."[9] The travails of

---

6 For a readable overview, see David Marsh, *The Most Powerful Bank: Inside Germany's Bundesbank* (New York, 1993). The British edition featured a more potboiling title, *The Bank That Rules Europe*.
7 Such concerns were expressed often in the annual reports by the Economic Advisory Council [Sachverständigenrat], a body of five economists called into being in 1963 as a means of offering independent expert advice to the government.
8 Chancellor Kurt Georg Kiesinger spoke of creating a "hard currency bloc" in his inaugural government declaration of Dec. 13, 1966. For efforts by the Economics Ministry [BMWi] to sketch out detailed proposals, see BMWi (Fünfgelt), Vermerk, Dec. 16, 1966: Bundesarchiv Koblenz [BAK], B 136 [= Bundeskanzleramt], Bd. 3322.
9 Ref. I A 2 (Poensgen), Aufz., Aug. 2, 1968: Politisches Archiv des Auswärtigen Amts – Berlin [PA/AA], B 52, Bd. 596.

the French franc seemed to justify their skepticism. In the wake of the May events in 1968, de Gaulle's administration was dogged by constant rumors of devaluation. By the late fall, speculators, bank savers, and even tourists were rushing to convert their francs into marks, triggering a spectacular flow of currency into West Germany.[10]

The embarrassing strength of the D-mark, revealed in full force in the winter of 1968–69, generated contradictory political pressures. One result was a new round of proposals for tighter monetary cooperation among the Six, such as the Barre Plan introduced by the European Commission in Brussels in February 1969.[11] This arrangement would have created a "monetary assistance mechanism" within the European Community (EC), a kind of emergency fund for member states facing short-term difficulties. German officials examined the proposal conscientiously but without much enthusiasm. A token gesture of Community solidarity was one thing, but they did not want to end up bailing out European partners for the consequences of their own profligacy.[12] German orthodoxy stressed the need for fiscal restraint and stiff resistance to the unions' demands for exorbitant pay hikes. In the absence of discipline by governments, central banks, and employers, the purchasing power of a currency was bound to wane. Linking the D-mark to the fate of the French franc or the Italian lira would only make sense if the guardians of those currencies would submit to wideranging forms of economic coordination on a Community level – common targets for inflation and budget deficits, for example. Tighter consultation was, indeed, one component of the Barre Plan, and it was this facet of the program that was embraced by Chancellor Kurt Georg Kiesinger and other West German officials. In July 1969, Bonn's representatives voted with their European partners to endorse the general principles of the Barre Plan.[13] But consistent and timely communication would not come naturally to Europe's

10 William Glenn Gray, "'Number One in Europe': The Startling Emergence of the Deutsche Mark, 1968–1969," *Central European History* 39, no. 1 (March 2006): 56–78.
11 Emmanuel Apel, *European Monetary Integation 1958–2002* (London: Routledge, 2002), 29–30. For an early critical reaction, see Otmar Emminger, "Betr.: Monetärer Mechanismus," Mar. 1, 1969: Historisches Archiv der Deutschen Bundesbank – Frankfurt [HA BBk], B 330, Bd. 480/1.
12 Reactions by the AA and BMWi to the Barre Plan are documented extensively in PA/AA, B 52, Bd. 600. See, e.g., Ref. III A 1 (Rombach), Vermerk, Ressortbesprechung der Abteilung E des BMWi, Mar. 24, 1969; and State Secretary Harkort's note of Apr. 5, 1969.
13 For a detailed account of the relevant meeting of the Council of Finance Ministers, see DG Brussels (Sachs) 1696, July 18, 1969: PA/AA, B 52, Bd. 589. For Kiesinger's support, see his letter to Schiller, Apr. 25, 1969: PA/AA, B 52, Bd. 600. It is still not clear that tenuous German endorsement of the Barre Plan constituted an "ideological shift," as Hubert Zimmermann argues; see "Der unschlüssige Hegemon. Deutschland und die Anfänge der europäischen Währungsintegration," in *Aufbruch zum Europa der zweiten Generation. Die europäische Einigung 1969–1984*, eds. Franz Knipping and Matthias Schönwald (Trier, 2004), 203–16, at 213.

finance ministries. Just one month later, the French government surprised everyone with a sudden (though not unwelcome) move to devalue the franc by 11 percent.[14]

To Karl Schiller, Bonn's powerful Social Democratic minister of economics, this was just further evidence that the Federal Republic must retain the freedom to act independently for the sake of preserving stability. With intense speculative crises rocking the international monetary system several times a year, West Germany needed sound insulation against imported inflation. One solution was to render the system as a whole less crisis prone; thus, Schiller eagerly assisted the Nixon administration's efforts in 1969 to revise the statute of the International Monetary Fund (IMF) and introduce more flexibility to relations among world currencies.[15] Closer to home, Schiller advocated an adjustment in the parity of the D-mark, which he judged to be undervalued vis-à-vis the dollar, the franc, and other major currencies. Revaluing the D-mark upward would, he insisted, help to neutralize imported inflation by lowering the prices Germans paid for imported goods. It would also help to restore equilibrium to the international monetary system, thus quelling the all-too-frequent rushes on the D-mark.[16] In Schiller's view, the Barre Plan and other programs for European monetary integration were not so much unwelcome as irrelevant for addressing the major economic challenges confronting the Federal Republic. The Atlantic community remained Schiller's principal frame of reference.

Here, and on most other economic issues, he clashed sharply with Kiesinger throughout the spring and summer of 1969. Kiesinger and influential business supporters of the Christian Democrats balked at the prospect of a more valuable D-mark, fearing that it would unfairly strike at the competitiveness of German exports.[17] The issue essentially tore apart the coalition government in Bonn. During the election campaign that followed, Schiller won the upper hand, thanks in no small part to the emphatic support of nearly every economist in Germany. It was easy to demonstrate that consumers could expect to benefit from a more valuable D-mark.[18] Willy Brandt may have been the chancellor candidate of the Social Democrats,

---

14 See DG Paris (Limbourg) 1949 and 1950, Aug. 9, 1969: PA/AA, B 52, Bd. 608; and many further telegrams in the same volume.
15 For a summary of Schiller conversations with Treasury Secretary David M. Kennedy, see DepSta (Rogers) to US Bonn 89501, June 3, 1969, confidential: NARA, RG 59, ANF, Box 857 (FN 10).
16 Although outvoted in the cabinet, Schiller expressed his views with startling frankness to the Bundestag; see Deutscher Bundestag, 5. WP, 235. Sitzung (May 14, 1969): *Sten. Ber.*, 12962.
17 See Kiesinger's lengthy comments to the CDU-Fraktion, May 13, 1969, pp. 6–24: Archiv für Christlich-Demokratische Politik – St. Augustin (ACDP), VIII-001-1019/1.
18 Gray, "'Number One in Europe,'" 74–6.

but Schiller's technocratic expertise proved invaluable in reassuring voters about the SPD's competence in core economic issues. There was no question that Schiller would occupy a prominent place in the new social-liberal coalition of Social Democrats and Free Democrats forged by Brandt in the fall of 1969.[19]

Even before it had been constituted, Brandt's government fell afoul of the European Commission. Anxious to get control over another rush of speculative capital – the third such onslaught in less than a year – the Bundesbank had put forward an unorthodox procedure in September 1969: allowing the D-mark to float with respect to other world currencies, at least temporarily. The outgoing Kiesinger cabinet endorsed this measure, finding it preferable to an outright revaluation of the D-mark.[20] From Brussels's perspective, however, the floating D-mark was an affront to the principles of the Common Market. How could the Common Agricultural Policy (CAP) possibly function when the value of the German currency shifted on a daily basis? Jean Rey, president of the European Commission, proposed a drastic remedy – a ban on West German imports of EC farm products. Rey went on to lecture Bonn about how it should have addressed the latest rush of speculative capital, namely by introducing a system of capital controls to limit inflows and outflows of currency.[21] Karl Schiller was incensed: he and most other German financial officials considered capital controls a bureaucratic, dirigiste policy at odds with the unfolding of a free market economy. He swiftly brought suit before the European Court of Justice to stave off implementation of the Commission's import ban.[22] Tempers cooled – and legal action was suspended – when West German officials persuaded the Commission that the float would be temporary. And indeed, virtually the first official act of the Brandt cabinet in late October was to fix the D-mark at a new, higher parity against the dollar and other world currencies. For a brief time, at least, West Germany would experience a respite from financial panics.

Brandt now faced pressure to prove his good intentions toward the European Community. His inaugural statement, delivered on October 28, 1969, had little to say about European integration; it was obvious that the new

---

19 Even those scholars most engaged in Brandt scholarship acknowledge that Schiller was the dominant personality of the 1969 election. Daniela Münkler, *Bemerkungen zu Brandt* (Berlin, 2005), 126.

20 For summaries of the cabinet meeting of Sept. 29, 1969, see remarks by Brandt and Schiller to the SPD-Parteirat, Sept. 30, 1969: AdsD, records of the SPD-Parteivorstand.

21 Thus an official proclamation by the Commission of Oct. 2, 1969; see also DG Brussels (Sachs) 2127, Oct. 1, pp. 4–5: both in PA/AA, B 52, Bd. 587.

22 Schiller to Rey, Oct. 2, 1969: PA/AA, B 52, Bd. 587.

chancellor had not developed any specific agenda in this area.[23] But the Christian Democratic opposition prodded Brandt to show greater initiative at the upcoming European summit conference at the Hague. Most insistent on this point was Walter Hallstein, former president of the European Commission. He urged Brandt to assuage concerns about Germany in East and West by underscoring the Federal Republic's "honest and unflinching incorporation into a European community." In Hallstein's view, Bonn should help to push integration forward into its next stage, EMU.[24] A similar message reached the chancellor from another old hand: Jean Monnet, the father of most postwar schemes for European integration. Now that de Gaulle had finally retired from the political scene, Monnet saw an opportunity for constructive German leadership: suppose Brandt were to propose the founding of a European Reserve Fund – and place at Europe's disposal a portion of the Federal Republic's considerable currency reserves?[25]

This was a red flag for German financial experts, who balked at the notion of simply handing over the Bundesbank's reserves to the EC. Schiller's ministry raised its usual objections, noting that it was hopelessly premature to take concrete steps toward monetary integration so long as economic fundamentals were so divergent across the European Community.[26] Officials at the Foreign Ministry agreed that economic convergence – the harmonization of growth rates and inflation – must precede the definitive linking of Europe's currencies.[27] But Brandt recognized the political value of an active *Westpolitik* to balance out his ambitious plans for Ostpolitik. Governing as he did with a precarious majority, it made sense to score points on issues such as European unity that commanded "tripartisan" support in the Bundestag. The challenge, then, was to craft an approach toward Europe that would encourage tangible progress toward integration without jeopardizing Germany's own economic stability.

The solution adopted by Brandt's cabinet was to articulate ambitious long-term goals while emphasizing their gradual, discrete realization. At the

---

23 It is true, however, that Brandt had recently appointed a state secretary to the chancellor's office with a mandate to help coordinate policy toward European integration: Katharina Focke, formerly a kind of pro-European lobbyist. Claudia Hiepel, "In Search of the Greatest Common Denominator: Germany and the Hague Summit Conference 1969," *Journal of European Integration History* 9 (2003): 63–81, esp. 71.

24 Deutscher Bundestag, 6. Sitzung (Oct. 29, 1969): *Sten. Ber.*, 6. WP, 96–7. For background on how the CDU repositioned itself in 1969 as the most unreserved proponent of European integration, see Henning Türk, *Die Europapolitik der Großen Koalition 1966–1969* (Munich, 2006), 209–22.

25 Monnet to Brandt, Oct. 31, 1969: WBA, Bundeskanzler, Bd. 14. See also Brandt's conversation with Monnet, Nov. 7, 1969: PA/AA, B 1, Bd. 499.

26 Schiller to Brandt, Nov. 6, 1969: BAK, B 102, Bd. 93468.

27 Herbst, Aufz., Betr.: EG-Gipfelkonferenz: Entwurf des Bundeskanzleramtes für eine Eingangserklärung des Herrn Bundeskanzlers (Stand: 25. 11. 1969), Nov. 26, 1969: PA/AA, B 52, Bd. 603.

Hague summit on December 1, 1969, Brandt struck this balance masterfully, announcing: "My government is prepared to take the path toward economic and monetary union, soberly and realistically, step by step." Brandt explained that the increasing interdependence of the European economies made tighter coordination unavoidable:

> Economic imbalances between [Community members] today have a direct impact, with little delay, upon the overall development of the Community. Inflationary tendencies in one country rapidly threaten stability in others and the equilibrium within the Community. This leads to distortions and limitations in the traffic of goods, services, and capital; the Common Agricultural Market is endangered. The Community as a whole suffers. This danger can only be averted if we move more quickly on the path toward becoming a community of growth and stability.[28]

The terms "stability" and "growth" were instantly recognizable as the watchwords of Schiller's economic policy. To speak of the future Europe as a community of growth and stability was, metaphorically, to anticipate the spread of German conditions to the wider European Community. Brandt did not underplay the difficulties: "Structural differences between our states and remaining divergences in economic goals and behavior are realities that can only be changed through persistent common effort." But he attempted to soften the political controversy by characterizing EMU – and the accompanying drive for convergence – as a functional necessity of European integration.

Brandt's position at the Hague marked the culmination of intensive deliberations in Bonn. While pledging German support to the goal of European monetary union – perhaps within a decade – Brandt inserted enough cautionary notes to safeguard German economic interests in the meantime. He endorsed Monnet's call for a "European Reserve Fund" but referred obliquely to "necessary prerequisites" that must precede its creation.[29] More importantly, he insisted that the nascent community of stability in Europe must remain "open to the world" (*weltoffen*): "We surely all agree that our Community is not intended as a new bloc, but rather as an exemplary order." Neither Brandt nor his Social Democratic colleagues embraced the model of an exclusive European Community operating independently of, or even in rivalry with, the wider Atlantic world. But the following years would severely upset the balance in German policy, as Bonn's partners forced the

---

28 The full text of Brandt's statement of Dec. 1, 1969 is available online through the European Navigator at http://www.ena.lu. The accompanying English translation obscures much of the meaning, rendering "eine Gemeinschaft des Wachstums und der Stabilität" as "a stable, expanding Community."
29 Andreas Wilkens, "Werner-Plan. Währung, Politik und Europa 1968–1971," in Knipping and Schönwald, *Aufbruch*, 217–44, at 222–6.

Federal Republic to make difficult choices among the competing demands of European solidarity, Atlantic responsibility, and domestic stability.

A MONETARY STRAITJACKET?

On the face of it, West Germany had scored an important diplomatic victory at The Hague. Bonn's monetary proposals made their way into the final communiqué almost verbatim. The six leaders affirmed that EMU was a viable long-term goal and that European integration "should result in a community of stability and growth."[30] Brandt's determination to expand the European community in other ways – by pressing for British entry, for example, and by instituting channels for political cooperation – contrasted favorably with the more anemic perspectives offered by French president Georges Pompidou.[31] If the Hague summit signaled the starting point for a "second generation" of European integration, as some historians now argue, it was in large part due to German leadership.[32]

However, in the ensuing months, the Brandt government lost control of the process. In early 1970, the EC Council of Ministers entrusted the development of a concrete step-by-step plan to a committee of financial experts under the direction of Pierre Werner, prime minister of Luxembourg.[33] Work in the so-called Werner Group remained sharply divided along national lines, with French, Belgian, and Luxembourg representatives all insisting upon the need for early steps toward monetary cooperation, while German and Dutch experts still emphasized the priority of economic convergence.[34] Under the circumstances, the obvious compromise was to embrace the principle of parallel movement: at each progressive stage in the plan, both economic and monetary coordination would intensify. This unnerved officials in Bonn's Ministry of Economics and at the Bundesbank in Frankfurt; they feared that acceding to French and Belgian demands in the first stage would disastrously weaken the D-mark. Pooling currency

---

30 A. G. Harryvan and J. van der Harst, eds., *Documents on European Union* (New York, 1997), 168–9. For an earlier German draft, see von Staden, Aufzeichnung, Nov. 26, 1969: PA/AA, B 52, Bd. 603.

31 The French press drew unflattering assessments of Pompidou's performance; see DG Paris (Blomeyer) 1300, Dec. 2, 1969: PA/AA, B 52, Bd. 603. For a more charitable view, see Katrin Rücker, "Willy Brandt, Georges Pompidou et la sommet de La Haye en 1969," in Möller and Vaïsse, *Willy Brandt und Frankreich*, 181–97.

32 Knipping and Schönwald, *Aufbruch*; also Franz Knipping, *Rom, 25. März 1957. Die Einigung Europas* (Munich, 2004), 156–61. Knipping credits the success to French initiatives.

33 Werner was known as a proponent of rapid European monetary integration; for this reason, his selection aroused suspicion in Bonn's Ministry of Economics. BMWi (Everling) for Rohwedder and Schiller, Mar. 3, 1970: BAK, B 102, Bd. 93457.

34 For a detailed account of the Werner Plan negotiations, Wilkins, "Werner-Plan," 226–35.

reserves, creating a distinct European monetary fund, and locking in present exchange rates in Europe or at least drastically narrowing the margins of flexibility among them – all seemed hazardous to Germans determined to uphold the stability of their currency.[35]

A more political issue divided the Werner Group as well: the relationship between the nascent European monetary personality and the wider international system. French and Belgian representatives stated openly that they sought European cooperation to diminish their reliance upon the dollar.[36] Although this was, indeed, inherent in the logic of European monetary union, German officials eschewed any language that suggested animus toward American economic power. They also fretted about a seeming disconnect between European plans and broader trends in the international monetary system. At the very moment when France was trying to narrow the margins among European currencies, the United States was prodding the IMF to introduce *more* flexibility into the international monetary system. These were, in essence, two contrasting models for making the system less crisis prone. Paris sought to create ironclad exchange rates that speculators would not dare to attack; Washington hoped that loosening the margins among exchange rates would help to absorb shocks more readily. Schiller and the Bundesbank both favored flexibility over rigidity, expressing interest in American proposals for a "crawling peg" adjustment system that might allow exchange rates to glide up and down periodically.[37] At the same time, they recognized that France's positions within the Werner Group were, in part, designed to mobilize the European Community against American-led reform efforts.[38] It was little wonder that German experts often seemed ambivalent about the EMU agenda they had helped to launch. The consolidation of Europe appeared all too likely to tip over into an anti-American project.

Within the Brandt government, however, came pressure for a more conciliatory attitude toward Paris. Katharina Focke, a parliamentary state secretary in the Chancellery, complained that the Ministry of Economics was "too perfectionist" in its approach; she pleaded for greater German

35 See the panicky letter from Johannes Schöllhorn, Bonn's top representative in the Werner group, to Bundesbank president Karl Klasen, Apr. 3, 1970: HA BBk, N 2, Bd. 155.
36 Eyskens to Brandt, May 15, 1970: PA/AA, B 1, Bd. 361. It should be noted that the French and Belgian positions were not identical; the latter placed greatest emphasis on the creation of a European monetary fund while the French showed greater interest in a narrowing of margins.
37 See, e.g., Schiller's comments to Kennedy as reported in DepSta 89501 to Bonn, June 3, 1969, confidential, priority: NARA, RG 59, ANF 67–69, Box 857 (FN 10). On the preference of Otmar Emminger, vice president of the Bundesbank, for a "discretionary crawling peg," see his letter to Milton Friedman, July 16, 1969: HA BBk, N 2, Bd. 76.
38 Emminger to Schöllhorn, May 12, 1970: BAK, B 102, Bd. 93470.

sensitivity to French and Belgian perspectives.[39] Brandt himself instructed Schiller to seek out a "bearable" compromise, lest Pompidou accuse him of backing away from his commitments at the Hague. He also wrote to Karl Klasen, the Bundesbank president, expressing his hope that "all sides" would show readiness to overcome their differences of opinion. Within the cabinet, Brandt pleaded for fresh evidence of German commitment to the European cause.[40] The political background was obvious: the chancellor hoped to defang Christian Democratic attacks against his foreign policy, which had developed a venomous intensity by the summer of 1970. Brandt needed to balance the unpopularity of his negotiations with Moscow by reaffirming his government's good citizenship in Western Europe.[41] The chancellor was not oblivious to concerns about safeguarding Germany's currency; he explicitly favored putting "our stamp" on European monetary policy, so that "our economic conceptions can be brought to bear at the Community level." But he was working against a deadline. Brandt very much hoped to achieve formal agreement on EMU in the second half of 1970, while West Germany held the rotating chair of the Council of Ministers. The controversial Moscow and Warsaw treaties were to be balanced out with a far-reaching European agreement on par with the original Treaty of Rome.[42]

Under the circumstances, it is remarkable that the German and Dutch position held together just long enough to prove decisive within the Werner group. (Support from Italian financial experts helped, though it came at the price of promising German backing for a European regional aid program.) The Werner Report, published in mid-October 1970, retained essential elements of West Germany's original proposals. It presented a step-by-step plan for achieving economic and currency union by the end of the decade. Beginning January 1, 1971, the Community would proceed through three basic phases, with economic convergence and monetary cooperation running in parallel. Two items that Germans considered premature – the

---

39 Focke to Detlev Karsten Rohwedder, Aug. 21, 1970, p. 3: PA/AA, B 52, Bd. 591.
40 Brandt to Schiller, May 27, 1970: BAK, B 102, Bd. 93462; Brandt to Klasen, June 18, 1970: HA BBk, N 2, Bd. 156. Brandt's reasoning in the second letter is implicitly tautological: "Because the committee of central bank presidents is taking part in this effort, there is certainty that adequate account will be taken of currency policy considerations." For Brandt's remarks to the cabinet on June 25, 1970, see BMWi (Everling), July 2, 1970: BAK, B 102, Bd. 120349.
41 On these political considerations, see Focke's letter of Aug. 21, 1970, cited previously.
42 Brandt to Schiller, Oct. 21, 1970: PA/AA, B 52, Bd. 592. Much of the scholarly conversation has revolved around whether Brandt bought French goodwill on Ostpolitik through concessions on problems of European integration; Andreas Wilkens argues that there is little evidence of this in "Willy Brandt, die deutsch-französischen Beziehungen und die Europapolitik (1969–1974)," in Möller and Vaïsse, *Willy Brandt und Frankreich*, 199–214, at 203–4. But the Focke and Brandt letters cited in this paragraph show domestic pressures in Bonn having the same effect.

creation of a European monetary fund and "the progressive elimination
of exchange rate fluctuations between Community currencies" – would
not be mandatory until the second stage, though Europe's central banks
were "invited" to narrow the bands between their currencies right away
"on an experimental basis."[43] Whether the Community would actually
make it to the second stage was, of course, anyone's guess. Much would
depend on whether some degree of convergence could be attained in the
interim. This evident caution during the early phases was counterbalanced
by a fairly detailed exposition of the kind of institutions that would necessarily result from successful economic and monetary union: a European central
bank (modeled, implicitly, on the Bundesbank) and centralized economic
decision making by the EC.

To Schiller, the Werner Plan marked "the very limits of what can be
accepted responsibly from the standpoint of economic stability."[44] But from
the French perspective, the plan offered too little of substance early on and
an alarming degree of supranationalism in its later phases.[45] Pompidou's
government thus acted to minimize the significance of the Werner Report,
dismissing it as a nonbinding expert opinion.[46] The European Commission
assisted in this gambit, producing a draft resolution on monetary integration
in late October that directly contradicted the spirit of the Werner Plan. It
made few references to goals such as stability, dropped the stated parallelism
between economic convergence and monetary measures, and called for
a formal narrowing of margins among the European currencies as soon
as possible.[47] Given the magnitude of disagreements on display, it proved
impossible to hold to Brandt's time line. The final Council of Ministers
meeting in 1970, chaired by Karl Schiller, dragged on into the early morning
hours of December 15 without yielding a breakthrough.[48]

In the weeks that followed, Pompidou's paramount objections became
clear. The French president refused to sign on to EMU in a form that
would limit French sovereignty in the foreseeable future. "The chancellor is a good German; I am a good Frenchman," Pompidou remarked.
"We've got to build a Europe where our nationalities are at home."[49] Paris

---

43 For lengthy excerpts from the Werner Plan, see Harryvan and van der Harst, *Documents on European Union*, 169–72.
44 Schiller to Brandt, Oct. 14, 1970: BAK, B 102, Bd. 93463.
45 US Paris (Culley) 14528, Oct. 22, 1970: NARA, RG 59, ANF, Box 819 (FN EEC).
46 See remarks by Maurice Schumann, the French foreign minister, at a Council of Ministers meeting in Luxembourg: DG Luxembourg 208 (Sachs), Oct. 27, 1970: *Akten zur Auswärtigen Politik der Bundesrepublik Deutschland [AAPD]* 1970, eds. Ilse Dorothee Pautsch et al. (Munich, 2001), 1853–5.
47 For this analysis, see BMWi (Tietmeyer), Aufz., Nov. 3, 1970: PA/AA, B 52, Bd. 592.
48 DG Brussels (Sachs) 3821, Dec. 15, 1970: *AAPD* 1970, 2279–85.
49 Remarks to the German ambassador at a New Year's reception, cited in AA (Ref. III A 1) to BMWi, BMF, and Bundesbank, Jan. 8, 1971: PA/AA, B 52, Bd. 593. See also Andreas Wilkins,

sought economic cooperation without political limitations; yet Bonn would not commit its economic and financial strength without requisite political controls at the community level. The impasse was finally broken by a sloppy compromise brokered during bilateral Franco-German consultations: the Council of Ministers resolution would get an escape clause (*clause de prudence*) affirming that, if the first stage of economic and monetary union proved unsatisfactory, Community members would have the right to abandon the project.[50] In the meantime, the first stage would commence, with an experimental narrowing of margins among Europe's currencies to begin within a matter of months.

The final version of Europe's step-by-step plan, approved by the Council of Ministers on March 21, 1971, represented a significant departure from Brandt's original proposal at the Hague. Whereas German experts had once demanded economic convergence prior to serious monetary measures, the Werner Plan called for parallel development between the two tracks; and even that stipulation had given way to a lopsided emphasis on currency measures. The arrangements of March 1971 afforded the stability-conscious countries little leverage for nudging their partners toward less inflationary social and budgetary policies. Pompidou's government had played the situation cleverly, using influence within the Commission, an excellent understanding of EC procedure, and bilateral pressure on Bonn. Brandt's government was susceptible to this pressure mainly because of its hunger for landmark achievements in Westpolitik. Neither the chancellor nor the members of his cabinet intended for this commitment to EMU to have immediate and negative consequences for Atlantic cooperation; but the finer points of the European step-by-step plan worked at cross-purposes with developments in the international monetary system. The EC's commitment to monetary integration would prove hopelessly premature.

THE CLOSING OF THE ATLANTIC OPTION

For the fourth time in four years, West Germany's open flank invited a torrent of speculation in the spring of 1971. Initially, it was an interest rate gap that had drawn capital to Germany; with interest rates running

"Willy Brandt," 210 (citing Pompidou's remarks at various cabinet meetings); on French policy more generally, see Eric Bussière, "France, European Monetary Cooperation, and the International Monetary System Crisis, 1968–1973," in Haftendorn, *Strategic Triangle*, 171–87.

50 See the Franco-German consultations of Jan. 25, 1971: *AAPD* 1971, eds. Martin Koopmann, Matthias Peter, and Daniela Taschler (Munich, 2002), 129. The escape clause aroused concern among ardent Europeanists in Italy, who worried about the prospect of a reversal of integration measures – something the EEC had not yet experienced, at least formally. Colombo to Brandt, Feb. 4, 1971: WBA, Bundeskanzler, Bd. 54, Bl. 47–9.

some 2–3 percent higher than in the United States, a considerable inflow could be registered by the end of 1970.[51] But the pace accelerated in March and April, thanks in part to an unfortunate tendency of German financial officials to think out loud about delicate questions of international monetary reform. On April 22, 1971, Schiller told an audience at the Hanover Trade Fair that the Bretton Woods system required more elasticity. "Currency mechanisms that provide a greater capacity for adjustment will give each country more freedom to pursue its own economic goals, without impinging upon the freedom of other countries either directly or indirectly." He insisted that this did not contradict the spirit of Europe's course toward EMU: the Community could simply adopt a strategy of "inward stability, outward elasticity."[52] In effect, Schiller was calling for a joint float of European currencies vis-à-vis the dollar. It was little wonder that currency speculation swelled tremendously in the days that followed. Investors rushed to buy D-marks at the official, fixed parity, anticipating that the mark would soon float upward and provide a handsome return on their investment, just as in 1969.

In late April, Schiller advanced the joint-float proposal in a restricted session of European finance ministers meeting in Hamburg. He tried to sell it as a major, if unanticipated, leap forward in European monetary cooperation; after all, Europe's central banks would have to communicate on a daily basis to move their currencies in tandem against the dollar. Absent this pragmatic solution, Schiller maintained, the only obvious course was a realignment of European exchange rates.[53] His French counterpart, Valéry Giscard d'Estaing, would have none of this, remarking that France would rather endure inflation than weaken the competitiveness of its exports by letting the franc rise against world currencies. If the main problem was the dollar's weakness, perhaps the obvious solution was to devalue the dollar?[54] The Hamburg contretemps signaled the beginning of a long feud between Bonn and Paris over who should bear the adjustment costs of international currency realignment, Europe or the United States.

Inevitably, details of the Hamburg meeting leaked out, which only further accelerated the rush into the D-mark. On May 2, 1971, the Council of Economic Advisors, Germany's most prestigious board of academic economists,

---

51 *Monthly Report of the Deutsche Bundesbank* 23, 2 (Feb. 1971): 41–6.
52 Schiller, Rede zur Eröffnung der Hannover-Messe, Apr. 22, 1971, p. 9: AdsD, SPD-Parteivorstand, Feb.–May 1971.
53 US Bonn (Rush) 5156, Apr. 30, 1971, confidential: NARA, RG 59, ANF, Box 826 (FN 10).
54 Specifically, Giscard advocated a rise in the price of gold, which was tantamount to a devaluation of the dollar. Aside from the previously cited telegram, see "Währung. Man muß was machen," *Der Spiegel*, May 3, 1971, 21–2.

recommended a return to the 1969 model: a temporary, isolated float of the D-mark until the markets could establish a proper exchange rate.[55] Schiller carried this plan with him to a crucial meeting of the Bundesbank's Central Bank Council on May 5. There he encountered unexpected resistance from Bundesbank president Karl Klasen, who refused to countenance a break with the European plan for EMU. For Klasen and a majority on the council, administrative barriers to the inflow of capital represented the lesser evil in dampening currency speculation. Article 23 of the Foreign Economic Law already granted the Bonn government sufficient legal authority to impose capital controls; Klasen urged Schiller to make use of it.[56]

The final decision lay in Brandt's hands. The cabinet had long been split over budgetary issues, with the ministers of economics and finance pressing for fiscal restraint even as the ministers of defense, transportation, and technology ached to introduce expensive new programs. The latter grouping showed less of an allergy toward inflation; and they certainly could not fathom Schiller's willingness to alienate the other European community members for the sake of an isolated float that would probably serve to make German exports less competitive. They pleaded for the use of capital controls in line with Article 23 – a move that would, incidentally, bring German practice more closely in line with that of France and Belgium.[57] Yet Schiller's tactics won over the chancellor. Brandt decided that Germany should press its European partners for cooperation in a joint float; this could, after all, result in a "decisive step on the path toward European monetary union." Absent a consensus in Brussels, Brandt conceded, the D-mark would have to float on its own.[58] "We can't always be the nice boys," the chancellor observed.[59]

Predictably enough, the community's finance ministers failed to reach agreement during a hastily summoned gathering on May 8, 1971. Giscard remained "cool and distant" during the marathon twenty-one-hour session,

55 Details of Schiller's plan made their way into the *Handelsblatt* with startling accuracy; most likely the minister deliberately leaked them. On media coverage and the Council of Economic Advisors, see assorted telegrams from US Bonn in this period in FN 10.

56 The basic course of this meeting is well known; see Dorothee Heisenberg, *The Mark of the Bundesbank: Germany's Role in European Monetary Cooperation* (Boulder, CO, 1999), chap. 2. For the official minutes of the meeting, see BAK, B 136, Bd. 3331.

57 "Kampf gegen die Dollar-Invasion," *Der Spiegel*, May 10, 1971, 19–23. Although this magazine was notorious for spinning news, its reports on internal cabinet debates were usually not far off the mark.

58 Brandt to Scheel, May 7, 1971: *AAPD* 1971, 727–9.

59 US Bonn (Rush) 5773, May 13, 1971: NARA, RG 59, ANF, Box 834 (FN 17); see also Giscard's remarks to Connally, May 20, 1971: *Foreign Relations of the United States* [*FRUS*] 1969–72, vol. 3 (Washington, D.C., 2001), doc. 156.

recognizing that Schiller had prepared a fait accompli. There was, indeed, nothing that France could have said to dissuade the Federal Republic from floating the D-mark – with or without the others' participation. Schiller and the West German foreign minister, Walter Scheel, put their best European faces forward; they indicated their willingness to cooperate in erecting Community-wide barriers against unwanted capital flows.[60] But Giscard remained dead opposed to the prospect of a joint European float or even a widening of the margins between European currencies and the dollar. The final communiqué, issued May 9, averred that, "under normal circumstances," floating rates were incompatible with the functioning of a common market. Bonn's move came without European sanction – though the Dutch opted to follow the German example and float the gulden, which created some political cover.[61]

In the ensuing months, Bonn and Paris each blamed the other for blocking the realization of a "European" solution to the currency crisis. Pompidou was furious at Germany's casual readiness to abandon the step-by-step plan toward EMU.[62] With the D-mark floating, the narrowing of margins among European currencies would have to be postponed indefinitely. Compounding this sin was Schiller's coy evasion of any timetable for ending the temporary float.[63] Most grievous of all, however, was Pompidou's belief that the German move had eased the pressure on the dollar. If the United States had a problem with its balance of payments, why should Europeans go out of their way to remedy the situation? Pompidou complained to Brandt in early July that by floating, Bonn had sided with America against Europe: "It's a question of community spirit."[64]

From a West German perspective, the real problem was French intransigence. After all, if there was any hope of insulating Europe from the consequences of American inflation, it surely lay in a slackening of margins

---

60 On the atmospherics of the meeting and the main points of dispute, see DG Brussels (Sachs) 1382, May 9, 1971: PA/AA, B 52, Bd. 585.

61 To brush over the deep differences, the European ministers did state in the closing communiqué that, "in certain cases the countries in question may for a limited period extend the margins of fluctuation of the exchange rates of their currencies as compared with the present par values." *Monthly Report of the Deutsche Bundesbank* 23, no. 5 (May 1971), 10. But this fell remarkably short of an endorsement of the German and Dutch floats; only in August, after the Nixon shock, did Bonn and the Hague obtain this.

62 For a trenchant analysis of French reactions, see DG Paris (Ruete) 1406, May 13, 1971: PA/AA, B 52, Bd. 585. Immediately after the German decision, Pompidou demonstratively pushed forward a planned meeting with the British prime minister – a standard French method of expressing displeasure with Bonn.

63 Privately, French experts anticipated (with startling accuracy) that the float would last through the end of 1971. US Paris (Watson) 12175, July 17, 1971: NARA, RG 59, ANF, Box 884 (FN 10 Ger W).

64 Conversation Brandt/Pompidou, July 5, 1971: *AAPD* 1971, 1064.

between European currencies and the dollar.[65] The Ministry of Economics acknowledged that some precautions would have to be taken before returning the mark to a fixed parity, to prevent yet another run into the D-mark. As before, though, Schiller and his lieutenants balked at dirigiste measures (such as the notorious Article 23) that would ban the flow of capital by administrative fiat. In their search for market-compatible options, they staked their hopes on a cash deposit law. Corporations drawing funds from outside Germany would be required to place a certain proportion of that sum, up to 50 percent, on deposit in a special account at the Bundesbank.[66] The Bundesbank itself was lukewarm to the proposal; Klasen judged it almost as difficult to administer as direct capital controls.[67] But the resignation of Bonn's finance minister in the early summer augmented the power of Klasen's rival, Schiller. The minister of economics now took over the finance portfolio as well, turning him into a genuine "super minister" with two giant bureaucracies at his disposal. Backed by this formidable *Hausmacht*, Schiller pressed his European colleagues to accept Germany's cash deposit law as a serious contribution to the community's collective battle against unwanted capital flows.

For much of the summer, Schiller's approach had the upper hand in European circles and within Brandt's government. Floating the D-mark had done wonders for monetary stability; the dollar crisis in July and August passed Germany by. Speculators poured their money into the yen instead – and into the franc.[68] Even the so-called Nixon shock of August 1971 did not immediately work to discredit Schiller's Atlanticist orientation. To be sure, European ministers were appalled at Nixon's decision to end the dollar's convertibility into gold; and the uniform 10 percent import surcharge at America's borders was a stinging blow. But when the community members failed to reach a common line in reaction to Washington's affront, it was France that stood out as the noncooperative party. Five of the Six now favored a limited European float against the dollar. Giscard steadfastly refused, insisting on the retention of fixed parities and a restoration of

---

65 BKA (IV/1, Weinstock) for Brandt, July 2, 1971, p. 4: BAK, B 136, Bd. 3323.

66 Schöllhorn, Kabinettsvorlage: "Maßnahmen zur Entmutigung übermäßiger Geld- und Kapitalzuflüsse aus dem Ausland," July 14, 1971: PA/AA, B 52, Bd. 581. The ministry of economics did, at least, make a show of considering options favored in other European capitals; see the extensive drafts in BAK, B 136, Bd. 3323.

67 For an especially clear expression of Klasen's skepticism, see pp. 2–3 of transcriptions from the stenographic record of the Bundesbank Council meeting of Nov. 10, 1971: HA BBk, B 330, Bd. 6165/2.

68 The Bank of France took in some U.S. $1 billion in July 1971, though it disguised this figure through swap arrangements with regional French banks. US Paris (Watson) 13070, July 30, 1971: NARA, RG 59, ANF, Box 827 (FN 10).

dollar convertibility.[69] Paris had, indeed, indulged in a fait accompli of its own, opting to introduce a divided currency market without consulting its partners first.[70]

As the monetary crisis dragged on into the late fall, however, Brandt grew ever more uncomfortable with the deep fissure between Bonn and Paris. The Nixon administration deliberately prolonged the crisis, hoping that other countries would step forward to assume the burdens of adjustment. Schiller's efforts to elicit concessions from his American counterpart, Treasury Secretary John Connally, went nowhere; for several months, Connally would not even spell out America's asking price for restoring dollar convertibility and removing the hated surcharge.[71] Brandt warned visiting American dignitaries in early October that Germany could not wait "until the European community broke apart." Sooner or later the Federal Republic would have to reach common ground with France, "even if this formula does not completely correspond with our interests."[72] The following week, Brandt's cabinet directed Schiller to show more flexibility in European negotiations. Whereas the economics minister had been hoping to use wider international bodies such as the Group of Ten (G-10) to force Paris to relent, the cabinet felt that consensus at the European level should *precede* efforts to resolve the monetary crisis on a transatlantic basis.[73] This wish would remain unfulfilled; the Federal Republic and France entered the final rounds of negotiation within the G-10 without reaching a common position.

To Schiller's political foes – in industry, in banking circles, and within the cabinet – the ongoing float of the D-mark looked increasingly reckless. Whatever advantage the Federal Republic enjoyed in warding off capital flows seemed to be outweighed by the inexorable rise in the mark's value against all its major competitors.[74] By October 1971, the D-mark stood

69　BKA (IV/1, Weinstock) for Brandt, Aug. 20, 1971: BAK, B 136, Bd. 3332; also DG Brussels (Bömcke) 2507, Aug. 20, 1971: *AAPD* 1971, 1250–6.

70　Specifically, on Aug. 18, the French cabinet introduced a distinction between a commercial franc – to be used for cross-border trade – and a financial franc, which could be bought and sold freely at fluctuating market values. It was a system that Germans had always thought unworkable, given the difficulty of properly insulating the financial and commercial markets from each other.

71　Conversation Connally/Schiller, Sept. 25, 1971: *FRUS* 1969–72, III: doc. 181. An earlier document in this volume, a Treasury contingency plan from May 8, 1971, spells out clearly the advantages of a passive-aggressive strategy in which the United States let a currency crisis develop and then waiting for some time before stating American preferences.

72　[Ulrich] Sahm, Vermerk, "Besuch des amerikanischen Unterstaatssekretärs Irwin," Oct. 7, 1971: BAK, B 136, Bd. 3332.

73　"Wir müssen im Konzert bleiben," *Der Spiegel*, Oct. 18, 1971: clipped in Willy-Brandt-Archiv [WBA], Bundeskanzler, Bd. 17.

74　US Bonn (Rush) 13220, Oct. 22, 1971: NARA, RG 59, ANF, Box 884 (FN 10 Ger W).

some 10 percent above its value before the float in May – a level that German exporters found all too risky. Brandt began to speak out against the danger to the country's competitiveness; and Schiller did all he could to talk the exchange markets down.[75] But the problem only intensified in the late fall, as more and more world currencies turned to floating. The Japanese yen, the Canadian dollar, and the Benelux currencies were all unpegged by the end of September. Unlike their counterparts at the Bundesbank, however, the guardians of these currencies took pains to ensure that their exchange rates did not fluctuate too dramatically.[76] The D–mark was in a very exposed position, raising the possibility that the pending international realignment would lock in the German parity at a highly uncompetitive rate.

The arrangement finally worked out at the G–10 conferences in Rome and Washington – the famous Smithsonian Agreement – owed as much to Giscard's confrontational tactics as to Schiller's accommodation of American interests. The West German "super minister" had long supported Washington's line, arguing that it was not essential to devalue the dollar; he even tried to block European statements demanding this of Washington.[77] Schiller later struck a more balanced tone, insisting that all sides contribute to a currency realignment, but he remained marked with a philo–American scent. So far as public image was concerned, it was the Azores summit between Pompidou and Nixon that finally brokered the substance of the Smithsonian Agreement. And the bargain appeared to vindicate many long–held French views. It called for a return to fixed exchange rates – albeit with a much wider margin than Paris would have liked, 2.25 percent in either direction. It also decreed a devaluation of the dollar against gold while allowing the franc to remain at par, thus honoring France's stubborn refusal to adjust its currency to address American balance of payment problems.[78] American diplomacy rewarded France for defiance while paying scant respect to its obsequious German ally.

The crisis of 1971 left Brandt and his cabinet feeling isolated and determined to give first priority to cooperation with Paris. At a Franco–German summit in February 1972, Pompidou hinted strongly at one means of overcoming the rift: Brandt should distance himself from Schiller's exaggerated liberalism. "Total liberalism means the triumph of the strongest in each

75 See Brandt's comments to the SPD-Parteirat, Oct. 18, 1971: AdsD, SPD-PV, Sept.-Oct. 1971.
76 Conversation Connally/Schiller, Sept. 25, 1971, cited previously.
77 US Bonn (Rush) 11421, Sept. 14, 1971: NARA, RG 59, ANF, Box 827 (FN 10).
78 Interestingly, German experts (Tietmeyer and Emminger) had been quietly pushing this solution, so flattering to Paris, since the end of October.

case," he remarked during a private session. Germany had an advantage over France, but Japan had the edge on Germany. What was the point of "dying" for the sake of preserving "the surface appearance of liberalism"? The French president asked Brandt to consider a stricter regimen of capital controls – perhaps a quota system for barring banks from excessive capital imports.[79] Brandt acknowledged that it was "surely a bit confusing that people who are called socialists are seen here in a liberal light." Schiller, who joined the conversation shortly thereafter, stuck to his usual line. Capital movements were, out of principle, to be welcomed; European integration must not consist merely in "establishing a series of controls." As before, the trick was to combine near-term monetary measures with a serious commitment to economic convergence among the Community members.[80]

Convergence remained an elusive goal, however – at least when it came to deliberately coordinating European budgets, unemployment rates, and business cycles. On a less official plane, the Federal Republic *did* appear to be drawing closer to its Western neighbors: erratic growth and inflation upwards of 5 percent now characterized the German scene.[81] The European common market was further than ever from the "community of stability" that Schiller had once promoted. Other aspects of the minister's program, such as his trademark "global steering" of the economy, were also coming unhinged.[82] Just a few years earlier, German unions had gladly tied wage packages to demonstrable increases in productivity – a program known as "concerted action." However, by the early 1970s, the union leadership, threatened from below, held out for dramatic pay hikes that were guaranteed to drive inflation forward. It was enough to make West Germany's most ardent apostles of stability, the Bundesbank directors, throw up their hands in despair.[83]

From an economic standpoint, then, the spring of 1972 was hardly a propitious moment to relaunch plans for EMU. But Community members, and even more so the European Commission, felt a pressing need to establish Europe's "independent monetary personality" vis-à-vis the United States.

---

79 Conversation Brandt/Pompidou, Feb. 10, 1972: *AAPD* 1972, eds. Mechthild Lindemann, Daniela Taschler, and Fabian Hilfrich (Munich, 2003), 129–31. The French president stopped short of calling for Schiller's resignation; but for a head of state to single out and criticize a minister of another government was a clear mark of disapproval.
80 Ibid., 133 (Brandt) and 137 (Schiller).
81 Figure 4.4c in Eric Owen Smith, *The German Economy* (New York, 1994), 159.
82 For a sample of Schiller's growing hysteria on budgetary matters, see his letter to Brandt, Feb. 29, 1972: WBA, Bundeskanzler, Bd. 17.
83 On Jan. 18, 1973, the Central Bank Council held an all-day theoretical debate on whether monetary policy could have any substantive impact on the economy. The tenor was quite pessimistic. See HA BBk, B 330, Bd. 6701/2.

As early as January 12, 1972, the Commission introduced a fresh proposal for narrowing margins among member currencies. The Smithsonian arrangements created a kind of international "tunnel" measuring 4.5 percent in width (taking into account margins of 2.25 percent in either direction). In March 1972, European Community members agreed to halve that distance, accepting a maximum deviation of 2.25 percent internally. The affected central bankers hastened to devise the technical rules for maneuvering a currency "snake" within the Smithsonian tunnel. On April 24, 1972, the grand experiment began. By European standards, this was all racing forward at remarkable speed.

It derailed within two months. In late June, speculators attacked the position of the pound sterling, which British leaders had chosen – perhaps unwisely – to align with the undulations of the European snake. The Italian currency was next in line for a drubbing; only a special exemption from the rules allowed the lira to retain its position within the snake.[84] Yet it was American behavior, not European weakness, that produced the greatest irritation in both Bonn and Paris. Officials in both capitals attributed the market's unrest to American unwillingness to defend the Smithsonian exchange rates. The Federal Reserve had, indeed, all but ceased intervening in the currency markets in New York, thereby placing the onus of maintaining exchange rates entirely on other central banks.[85] Meanwhile, the low interest rates in the United States – a product of Nixon's reelection strategy – stimulated renewed capital flows in Europe's direction. This had not yet culminated in a serious run into the D-mark, but that moment was close at hand.

Even now, Schiller balked at the prospect of implementing new capital controls in accord with Article 23 of Germany's Foreign Economy Law. But he had lost his last supporters within the cabinet. Karl Klasen achieved a belated revenge for his defeat in May 1971, when Schiller had persuaded Brandt to ignore the Bundesbank's advice. This time Klasen put in a personal appearance at the cabinet meeting on June 28, 1972. Schiller, who was not informed in advance, spoke later of an "ambush."[86] He presented his usual impassioned defense of free market mechanisms and excoriated the

---

84 Specifically, the compromise reached in Luxembourg on June 26, 1972, absolved Rome of having to export gold to settle its short-term balance-of-payments deficits. This amounted to a kind of blank check, precisely the scenario German economists had long feared. US Rome (Martin) 3754, June 28, 1972: NARA, RG 59, ANF, Box 828 (FN 10).
85 As early as January, French leaders – including Pompidou himself – were admonishing the United States to defend the Smithsonian bargain. US Paris (Watson) 1250, Jan. 20, 1972: Box 828, cited previously.
86 Schiller to Brandt, July 2, 1972, persönlich: WBA, Bundeskanzler, Bd. 67.

dirigiste methods preferred across the Rhine – methods that Bonn would be imitating by accepting administrative controls à la Article 23. But Schiller overshot the mark with his dramatic rhetoric and his demonstrative absence from later sessions of the two-day cabinet meeting. Brandt's cabinet voted unanimously to approve Klasen's petition and introduce a handful of minor capital controls. It then awaited the inevitable: Schiller's resignation.[87]

It was, in the end, a less-than-heroic end to Schiller's five and a half years at the Ministry of Economics. The cabinet was rejecting the minister's person as much as his policies; the vain, overbearing professor had completely exasperated his colleagues, particularly after he took on the finance portfolio. In a fit of wounded pride, Schiller followed up his humiliating departure from the cabinet by siding with the opposition Christian Democrats in the fall 1972 elections. It is little wonder that Schiller's legacy is scarcely celebrated today within Social Democratic circles.

All the same, it would be a mistake to overlook the broader change signaled by Schiller's departure from the Brandt government. This becomes evident through a comparison with his successor as super minister, Helmut Schmidt. Where Schiller touted economic goals such as stability and growth, Schmidt accorded higher priority to political objectives. On several occasions, he reminded the Central Bank Council that economic policy was merely one component of foreign policy. Diplomatic and political considerations would ultimately determine Bonn's positions on trade and monetary relations.[88] At the same time, Schmidt downplayed West Germany's independent significance in international affairs; only in conjunction with European partners could the Federal Republic hope to have an impact. If this meant occasionally pandering to French vanity – allowing Paris to "save Europe again," as Schmidt once put it – then Bonn would play along.[89] It was more important to fashion Franco-German consensus than to impress German economic priorities on the European Community. (Later, as chancellor, Schmidt would show less restraint in touting German virtues to European partners, particularly Italy and the United Kingdom.)

Schmidt's policies at the Finance Ministry did not result in a complete rupture of cordial relations between German and American officials on the economic front. Schmidt developed an excellent rapport with Connally's

---

87 See Wolfgang Jäger's account in *Geschichte der Bundesrepublik Deutschland. Die Ära Brandt 1969–1974* (Stuttgart, 1986), 50–2.
88 See, e.g., Schmidt's blunt remarks to the Central Bank Council on Feb. 15, 1973: "The Federal Republic cannot permit the Bundesbank to pursue an autonomous credit policy that undermines the integration efforts of the EEC. Currency policy is today a significant component of foreign policy." HA BBk, B 330, Bd. 6703/1.
89 BKA (Strehlke) for Brandt, Feb. 8, 1973: WBA, Bundeskanzler, Bd. 60, Bl. 162–3.

successor at the Treasury, George Shultz.[90] But the continuing weakness of the U.S. dollar rendered the Bretton Woods system inoperable. Ironically, just nine months after Schiller's stormy departure, Schmidt, Giscard, and even the European Commission found themselves adopting Schiller's old remedy: a joint float of European currencies against the dollar. This step, taken in March 1973, marked the final blow to the worldwide system of fixed exchange rates and, correspondingly, a significant further step in the autonomous development of the European currency snake. In the years to come, many landmarks in Western economic relations – the Rambouillet summit of 1975, the ensuing creation of the G-7, and the introduction of a new European monetary system in 1979 – would result primarily from joint Franco-German initiatives.

In retrospect, it is striking how much more successful Schiller's basic ideas were in the hands of other politicians. While repeatedly accommodating American positions, the super minister had consistently chosen confrontational tactics and faits accomplis in an effort to balance against French influence in the European Community. Schmidt enjoyed greater success by seeking agreement with Paris in advance of major decisions. Under these circumstances, French leaders – above all Giscard – came around to many of the views long advocated by the overly combative Schiller. For much of the 1970s, fighting inflation and preserving stability served as watchwords on both sides of the Rhine. Even two decades later, the language of Bonn's Ministry of Economics still echoed in negotiations leading up to European monetary unification. Prospective euro members had to fulfill convergence criteria to ensure that employment patterns, economic growth, and other indicators fell within a relatively narrow range; and to encourage strict budgetary discipline, the EU countries passed a "stability and growth pact" (which has, unfortunately, proved rather toothless). For all the economic weakness still in evidence inside the euro zone, the common currency promotes precisely the free flow of labor, capital, and goods that the liberal Social Democrat Karl Schiller had once envisioned as a "community of stability and growth."

---

90 Helmut Schmidt, *Men and Powers: A Political Retrospective*, trans. Ruth Hein (New York, 1989), 152–64.

8

The Politics of Planes and Engines

Anglo-American Relations during the Rolls-Royce–Lockheed Crisis, 1970–1971

RAJ ROY

It had not been the most auspicious of beginnings for the Earl of Cromer. Within a matter of days of his arrival in Washington as the new British ambassador to the United States in early February 1971, he had been the recipient of a barrage of complaints about the actions of the government he represented. The unexpected announcement by the British minister of aviation that Britain's most celebrated aero-engine manufacturer, Rolls-Royce, would no longer be able to honor an existing contract to supply the RB-211 engine for the Lockheed Corporation's latest airplane, the L-1011 TriStar jet, had caused outrage in American commercial circles and the highest levels of the U.S. government. By his own admission "under fire,"[1] Rowley Cromer advised his colleagues at the Foreign Office after a series of uncomfortable meetings with the forthright and blunt-speaking U.S. secretary of the treasury, John Connally, that he was left in no doubt as to the "grave consequences for the [U.S.] economy as a whole and for Anglo-American relations in the widest sense" if the engines were not supplied to the Lockheed Corporation as originally agreed.[2]

The first experience of the new British ambassador in Washington appears to be compelling evidence of the gloomy picture of Anglo-American relations during the 1970s so often depicted by historians and former diplomats. Responsibility for the drift and unease that characterized

1 Cromer to Foreign and Commonwealth Office (FCO), Feb. 12, 1971, FV 14/43, Public Records Office (PRO), Kew, UK.
2 Cromer to FCO, Feb. 13, 1971, PREM 15/230, PRO.

The author wishes to thank Professor Thomas A. Schwartz for his invaluable comments and acknowledges the helpful suggestions of the external readers. The author is also indebted to Alison, Saty, and Archana Roy for their encouragement during the research and writing of this article.

169

transatlantic relations during this time has typically been attributed to the British prime minister in the early 1970s, Edward Heath. Heath's most recent biographer has highlighted his "determination" to avoid close ties with the U.S. government or its president, Richard Nixon,[3] while other commentators have noted Heath's conspicuous failure to use the term "special relationship" during his time in office.[4] A passionate believer in the concept of European unity, Heath eschewed all opportunities to forge a close working relationship with the Nixon administration, which had openly welcomed his accession to power in 1970,[5] instead preferring to devote all his energies to achieving his objective of securing British entry to the European Economic Community (EEC).[6] Heath's determination to demonstrate his European credentials evidently came at the expense of harmonious Anglo-American relations. Studies of U.S.-UK relations during this period have noted how, in numerous areas of policy, long-standing Anglo-American cooperation and dialogue had given way to disagreements and acrimony. In international monetary affairs, British foreign economic policy became, in the words of one observer, "plus français que les français" as Britain prepared for membership of the EEC.[7] Nor did the two countries appear to share the same global vision of international security any longer, most notably over the decision of the British government to resume sales of arms to South Africa and the Nixon administration's handling of the Middle East crisis of 1973.[8] By 1973, relations between the two countries, in the view of one analysis, "were becoming distinctly ordinary."[9]

---

3 John Campbell, *Edward Heath: A Biography* (London, 1993), 341.

4 John Dickie, *Special No More: Anglo-American Relations. Rhetoric and Reality* (London, 1994), 144–5. Heath's press secretary, a diplomat seconded from the Foreign Office, Donald Maitland, would admit subsequently that the term was not part of the prime minister's diplomatic vocabulary. See evidence of Sir Donald Maitland, ICBH Seminar, "The Heath Government," *Contemporary Record* 9, no. 1 (1995): 208.

5 After Heath's fall from power in 1974, the president's national security adviser, Henry Kissinger, would tell British politicians and diplomats, "if there was one foreign leader for whom President Nixon had very high regard, it was Ted Heath" and recall how Nixon had telephoned him four times on the night of Heath's election victory to express his delight at the return of a Conservative government in Britain. Kissinger himself declared at the same meeting that he considered Heath "one of the ablest men in British politics." Record of conversation between Kissinger, Harold Lever and Peter Ramsbotham 15/11/76, Kissinger Transcripts, Item KT 02129, Digital National Security Archive (original location: Records of Henry A Kissinger 1973–1977, Box 19, Nodis Memcons, Record Group 59, Department of State, National Archives, College Park, MD).

6 Henry Kissinger, *Years of Renewal* (New York, 1999), 602–3; Dickie, *Special No More*, 144; Raymond Seitz, *Over Here* (London, 1998), 316–17; David Reynolds, *Britannia Overruled: British Policy and World Power in the Twentieth Century* (London, 1991), 241.

7 Henry Brandon, *The Retreat of American Power: Nixon and Kissinger's Foreign Policy and Its Effects* (London, 1972), 240.

8 Andrew Roth, *Heath and the Heathmen* (London, 1972), 214; Robert Hathaway, *Anglo-American Relations since 1945* (New York, 1990), 101–2; Christopher Bartlett, *The Politics of the Anglo-American Special Relationship 1945–1992* (London, 1992), 132–3.

9 David Sanders, *Losing an Empire, Finding a Role: British Foreign Policy since 1945* (London, 1990), 177.

The Heath government's apparent indifference to the needs and the interests of the U.S. government during this period raises important questions about the position and status of the United States in the 1970s. It appears to represent persuasive evidence of the thesis of diplomatic historians that, during the 1970s, the ability of the United States to shape and influence the policies of its European partners was severely diminished. By the early 1970s, America appeared to be entering into a period of protracted economic decline that suggested that it no longer possessed the leverage to influence "the fiscal and commercial policies of emerging capitalist competitors like Japan and the EEC."[10] Accordingly, the period was notable for the growing economic power of the EEC, in particular that of West Germany.[11] In the case of Britain, the Heath government's independent approach to the conduct of foreign policy appears to confirm the argument of those scholars of Anglo-American relations who have concluded that the inability of the United States to shape British decision making had already been exposed by the late 1960s.[12]

Although the aforementioned analyses both of the state of Anglo-American relations and of American power in the late 1960s and early 1970s appear at first blush to be convincing, such views may be rather superficial. More recent research on U.S.-European relations and Anglo-American relations in the 1960s has already cast doubt on the negative prognoses of earlier historians about this period.[13] Previous research by this author on Anglo-American economic relations in the 1960s questioned the significance of a personal rapport at the highest levels in the totality of the relationship, instead revealing that the mutuality of interest together with long-standing institutional relationships ensured that the two nations continued to enjoy an extremely close relationship.[14] Furthermore, recent studies of U.S. foreign policy have demonstrated that, by the 1960s, Washington had come to use different methods to wield influence in the internal politics of its allies. In this context, transnational links between actors and agencies were particularly significant in enabling U.S. officials to shape the internal debates of the British government.[15]

10 Thomas McCormick, *America's Half-Century: United States Foreign Policy in the Cold War and After* (Baltimore, 1995), 162.
11 McCormick, *America's Half Century*, 164.
12 Alan Dobson, "The USA, Britain and the Question of Hegemony," in *No End to Alliance: The United States and Western Europe: Past Present and Future*, ed. Geir Lundestad (New York, 1998), 150.
13 See, e.g., Thomas A. Schwartz, *In the Shadow of Vietnam: Lyndon Johnson and Europe* (Cambridge, MA, 2003); Raj Roy, "The Battle of the Pound: The Political Economy of Anglo-American Relations 1964–1968" (Ph.D. diss., London School of Economics, 2000).
14 Roy, "The Battle of the Pound," 324–5.
15 Raj Roy, "No Secrets between Special Friends: America's Involvement in Britain's Economic Policy October 1964–April 1965," *History* 89, no. 295 (July 2004): 399–423.

This chapter, through an examination of the Rolls–Royce and Lock-heed crisis of 1970–71, argues with reference to the most recently released government documentation that while differences may indeed have existed between Britain and the United States in this period resulting from the British government's efforts to demonstrate to its European partners its commitment to European unity, the mutuality of interest and the unique institutional relationships ensured, as in the 1960s, that the two coun-tries would continue to work closely together when necessary. Moreover, through an examination of the British decision-making process over the Rolls–Royce crisis, it suggests that the position and influence of the United States were still sufficient to enable it to affect the internal policies of an ally such as Britain.

THE HEATH GOVERNMENT AND THE COLLAPSE OF ROLLS–ROYCE

The bankruptcy of Rolls–Royce in early 1971 had stemmed directly from the ambitions of the company and the British government in the 1960s, led by Heath's predecessor, Harold Wilson. Finding the domestic market rela-tively undeveloped for its increasingly sophisticated product range, Rolls–Royce had been eager to break into the lucrative American civil aviation market. Encouraged with promises of assistance from a Labour government eager to boost Britain's flagging export performance and the development of Britain's technological industry,[16] Rolls–Royce vigorously marketed its new technologically superior engine in a fierce battle with its main competitors General Electric and Pratt & Whitney to supply the Lockheed Corporation with engines for its new plane, the L-1011 or the TriStar. An extremely competitive price for the engine eventually enabled the company to out-maneuver its rivals and secure the contract.[17] Unfortunately, the cost of research and development of this technologically advanced engine spiraled out of control as technical difficulties emerged, with damaging effects for the company's financial position.[18] In May 1970, the company approached

16 Note by Jamieson of FCO Export Promotions Department, May 1, 1969, FCO 70/17, PRO. The Labour government ultimately committed itself to providing 70 percent of the launch cost of the RB-211, considerably more than the standard 50 percent, on the ground that "an aero engine industry was a vital national interest"; Geoffrey Owen, *From Empire to Europe: The Decline and Revival of British Industry since the Second World War* (London, 1998), 315.

17 Arthur Reed, *Britain's Aircraft Industry: What Went Right? What Went Wrong?* (London, 1973), 128. The price offered by Rolls–Royce was just under £200,000, some £40,000 less than that offered by General Electric.

18 In tests, the revolutionary hyfil blades in the engine that Rolls–Royce devoted considerable resources to developing had been proved inadequate.

the statutory body responsible for the development and expansion of British industry, the Industrial Re-organisation Corporation (IRC), for financial assistance worth £10 million.[19]

Yet the promise of this loan was not sufficient to enable Rolls-Royce to overcome its difficulties. By November 1970, the new Conservative government of Edward Heath had pledged £42 million of a new £60 million short-term rescue package.[20] Even this more substantial package proved the most temporary of palliatives, for, by late January 1971, officials at the Ministry of Defence were being advised that the directors of the company were considering declaring the company's bankruptcy.[21] For Lockheed, the crisis at Rolls-Royce had very serious ramifications. Going into the 1970s, Lockheed was considered by U.S. government officials to be on the brink of financial collapse.[22] The failure of Rolls-Royce to provide it with the RB-211 could have delayed or even prevented the delivery of the L-1011 to the airlines, an event that would have sent one of the biggest U.S. defense contractors into the financial abyss.

Previous portraits of the British government's handling of the crisis have portrayed the episode as yet another sorry chapter in the story of an Anglo-American relationship in decline. As events unfolded in early 1971, some elements of the press incredulously asked if the British government was seriously committed to the funding of the development of the RB-211.[23] Subsequent analyses appeared to share the view of the media. A more recent and detailed examination of this episode questioned whether any government would have allowed "the crisis to carry Rolls Royce over the edge" as the Heath government had done and concluded that the prime minister had left the resolution of the crisis to the U.S. government.[24] Such a line of argument would appear to further reinforce the thesis of previous studies that in the arena of civil aviation Anglo-American relations in the postwar period were characterized by conflict and competition.[25]

19 Reed, *Britain's Aircraft Industry*, 132.
20 Reed, *Britain's Aircraft Industry*, 134. The remaining £18 million was provided by the Bank of England and a number of private banks.
21 Chronology of Receivership of Rolls-Royce, , Apr. 30, 1971, FCO 14/854, PRO.
22 Record of telephone conversation between Kissinger and Ehrlichman, Dec. 18, 1970, HAK Telcons, Chron Files, Box 8, Nixon Presidential Materials Papers (NPMP), National Archive (NA), College Park, MD.
23 "Does Ted Want to Save the RB-211?" *Economist*, Mar. 13, 1971.
24 John Newhouse, *The Sporty Game* (New York, 1982), 183–4.
25 For an overview of Anglo-American aviation relations in the immediate post-war period see Jeffrey Engel, *Cold War at 30,000 Feet: The Anglo-American Fight for Aviation Supremacy* (Cambridge, MA, 2007). Engel reveals how British policy makers' commercial objectives to secure access to markets in Communist China for the British aviation industry clashed with the political and security objective of the U.S. government to isolate China economically.

This depiction of the British government's indifference toward the continued development of the RB-211 appears to be a credible one, especially in light of the economic and industrial policy of the Conservative Party in the early 1970s. For Heath and his colleagues, who were deeply concerned by Britain's persistent economic malaise in the 1960s, the economic renewal of Britain would be achieved in part through British entry to the EEC, where stiffer competition would shake British industry out of its lethargy. In addition, reduced interference by the state in economic affairs, through the reduction in public expenditure and the tax burden coupled with a thorough overhaul of the legal framework in which the country's trade unions were to operate, would create an environment in the country that was more conducive to economic growth.[26] In Heath's more efficient and competitive Britain, there would be considerably less sympathy from the government for failing businesses than there had been from its more interventionist Labour predecessor.[27]

Nor would supporting the continued development of the RB-211 fit with the prime minister's vision for the role that more technologically advanced British industries would play in the development of a more economically independent and unified Europe. As leader of the opposition in the 1960s, Heath had argued that the development of stronger European industries supported by a more advanced technological base lay not through the creation of an institutional technological community but in greater cooperation and collaboration among businesses in the private sector.[28] Illustrating his point, the Conservative leader had singled out the aircraft industry, where through greater collaboration among the aviation industries in Britain, France, and West Germany, a range of aircraft would be produced to meet the needs of national airlines, thus enabling "development in Europe [to] keep pace with that in America."[29] For a passionate pro-European such as Heath, there was no other option to increasing

---

26 Brendon Sewill, "In Place of Strikes," in *British Economic Policy 1970–1974*, eds. Ralph Harris and Brendon Sewill (London, 1975), 30. A paper prepared by the Conservative Industry spokesman argued that if Conservative economic reforms were implemented, then "the pressures towards efficiency at home and overseas [would] achieve far more than the [Labour] government is, damagingly, seeking to do by intervention." Paper by Keith Joseph on Government Intervention in Industry, 28/02/69 Leader's Consultative Committee (LCC) Files 1/2/15 (69) 221, Conservative Party Archive (CPA), Bodleian Library, Oxford, U.K.

27 Heath, *The Course of My Life* (London, 1998), 330.

28 Heath, *Old World, New Horizons: Britain, the Common Market, and the Atlantic Alliance* (London, 1970), 42–3. The monograph contains a series of lectures that Heath had given at Harvard University in 1967, known as the Godkin Lectures.

29 Heath, *Old World*, 44.

cross-border collaboration because no European member state alone possessed the resources to compete with powerful American industries.[30]

At the outset of the crisis in early 1971, it was certainly logical to conclude that the prospect of assistance from the British government for the funding of the RB-211 was highly unlikely. In late 1970, the government chose to allow the Mersey Docks and Harbour Board to go into liquidation after a period of protracted financial difficulty rather than provide government assistance.[31] Nor did it appear that the government was any more sympathetic to established blue-chip companies. Even as it became increasingly clear in the latter half of 1970 that an element of government assistance was an essential ingredient of any short-term rescue package for Rolls-Royce, the prime minister appeared deeply hostile, declaring that "it was wrong that. . . firms [in financial difficulties] should have any Government money. It should not be the tax payer but the shareholders and the bankers who had allowed these companies to be so badly managed who should take the consequences."[32] In the event, because of "special considerations," the government had reluctantly agreed to provide further temporary short-term assistance in November 1970, but only "the minimum needed to salvage Rolls Royce in the national interest."[33]

At first blush, the newly released government documentation on this topic appears to bear out the views articulated in previous accounts of the British government's attitude toward this industrial crisis. When the cabinet committee established by the prime minister in late January 1971 to consider the government's response to the failure of Rolls-Royce met, the prime minister and his senior advisers concluded that they would not prevent the company from being declared bankrupt.[34] Those parts of the company that were engaged in military projects were to be nationalized. As for the RB-211, Minister of Aviation Frederick Corfield stated that the engine was "significantly behind its competitors"[35] and announced in the House of Commons that the government would have no liability for the contract between Rolls-Royce and Lockheed. The most that the government could

---

30 Heath, *Old World* , 44.
31 Jock Bruce-Gardyne, *Whatever Happened to the Quiet Revolution? The Story of a Brave Experiment in Government* (London, 1974), 29–30.
32 Note of a meeting between PM and senior ministers 02/10/70, PREM 15/002, PRO.
33 Ibid.
34 Records of meeting of Rolls-Royce Cabinet Committee, 29/01/71 and 01/02/71, CAB 130/3446, PRO.
35 Philip Whitehead, *The Writing on the Wall: Britain in the Seventies* (London, 1985), 57.

offer was a willingness to explore the future of the RB-211 with the receiver of the company.[36]

In terms of external considerations, the British government, in line with its commitment to secure British entry to the EEC, seemed more interested in the concerns of its European partners about the ramifications of the collapse of Rolls-Royce. In its first briefing on the subject for the foreign secretary, Alec Douglas-Home, the Foreign Office was in no doubt that "everything should be done to minimise risk of damage to European industrial partners, especially in view of... the importance attached to British technology as a factor in getting into Europe."[37] The prime minister's preoccupation also appeared to lie in Europe. British officials noted that he had expressed his wish that the British ambassador in Paris, Christopher Soames, should pay a personal visit to Chaban Dalmas, the French prime minister, to assure him that the collaborative ventures involving French companies and Rolls-Royce would be safe.[38]

Nor did there appear to be any supporters of the RB-211 within the British government. The Treasury, with its perpetually vigilant eye on the levels of public expenditure, weighed in against any further funding for the development of the engine, describing as it "indefensible."[39] The Central Policy Review Staff (the "Think Tank"), the body established by Heath on his accession to power to advise the prime minister on long-term problems and issues, was similarly hostile to the continuation of the RB-211.[40] The former chief scientific adviser to the government, Sir Solly Zuckerman, who continued to serve as a consultant to Downing Street, had no doubts that the RB-211 was not a viable project, arguing that the RB-211 was distracting Rolls-Royce from participating more fully in European collaborative ventures.[41]

Yet a closer scrutiny of the documents suggests that the British government was far from indifferent to the position of Lockheed or to the concerns of the Nixon administration. On hearing of the impending meltdown of Rolls-Royce, Corfield expressed his concern that the collapse of the aero-engine manufacturer "could produce serious political repercussions" in terms of U.S.-UK relations.[42] Even in those departments where sentiment appeared to be hostile to the future of the RB-211, there were

36 Reed, *Britain's Aircraft Industry*, 136.
37 Briefing paper from Cromartie to Foreign Secretary, Jan. 29, 1971, FCO 14/838, PRO.
38 Note from Armstrong to Graham, Feb. 4, 1971, CAB 164/999, PRO.
39 Note from Barrett to Ryrie, Jan. 1, 1971, T 225/3558, PRO.
40 Memo from CPRS to Heath, Mar. 3, 1971, T 340/66, PRO.
41 Note from Zuckerman to Heath, Feb. 24, 1971, PREM 15/230, PRO.
42 Note of a meeting between Corfield and Cole, Jan. 31, 1971, FV 14/42, PRO.

still many senior officials who were attuned to the broader issues at stake in this crisis. At the Treasury, Sir Samuel Goldman, the mandarin at the center of Anglo-American economic collaboration in the 1960s, noted that the predicament of Rolls-Royce generated "issues of Anglo-American relations . . . which [would] need delicate handling."[43]

Indeed, the record reveals that even though Rolls-Royce was technically insolvent, the government still sought to allow Washington to voice its opinion. Even after learning from Nixon administration officials and Lockheed itself that there appeared to be no immediate funds available for the financing of the development of the RB-211,[44] the prime minister still suggested that a message be conveyed to the board of Rolls-Royce that he would speak directly with Richard Nixon in the hope that it might persuade the board to defer their declaration of the company's bankruptcy until the president's views were known.[45] In the event, with Rolls-Royce insolvent and no sources of further funding available from across the Atlantic, the cabinet finally heeded the warnings of its counsel that, under English company law, the directors of Rolls-Royce would be personally liable for allowing the company to trade while insolvent and any further assistance from the government to Rolls-Royce would expose to it all of the liabilities of the company.[46] Faced with no realistic alternatives, the cabinet formally agreed that Rolls-Royce should declare itself insolvent.[47]

Even on the part of the pro-European prime minister, there appeared to be genuine appreciation of the effect of the collapse of Rolls-Royce in the United States. Far from seeking to avoid discussing the matter with the Nixon administration, he had made early use of the transatlantic telephone line to reassure a concerned Nixon administration about his willingness to work closely with the U.S. government in this crisis. After acknowledging to National Security Adviser Henry Kissinger that he "fully realise[d] the very serious ramifications for you [the Nixon administration] as far as Lockheeds [sic] [was] concerned,"[48] Heath assured Nixon that it would be feasible for the new nationalized company to continue to produce the RB-211, provided that the contract could be renegotiated.[49] While the prime minister had not formally committed his government to the continued development

43 Note of a meeting with Henry Benson by Goldman, Jan. 26, 1971, T 225/3558, PRO.
44 Note of a meeting between Haughton, Corfield, and Davies, Feb. 2, 1971, PREM 15/229, PRO.
45 Note of meeting of Rolls-Royce Cabinet Committee, Feb. 3, 1971, CAB 130/504, PRO.
46 Record of cabinet meeting, Feb. 2, 1971, CAB 128/49, PRO.
47 Record of cabinet meeting, Feb. 3, 1971, CAB 128/49, PRO.
48 Record of telephone conversation between Heath and Kissinger, Feb. 1, 1971, PREM 15/229, PRO.
49 Record of telephone conversation between Heath and Nixon, Feb. 3, 1971, PREM 15/229, PRO.

of the RB–211, the internal deliberations of the government and the telephone conversations between the two leaders had shown that the British government could not and would not readily dismiss the concerns of the Nixon administration.

The crisis at Rolls-Royce was another unwelcome addition to the existing troubles of Lockheed and the Nixon administration. By 1971, it had become clear that in a fierce competition in the late 1960s to supply the Department of Defense with a specialist transport plane (the C-5A), Lockheed had seriously underbid to secure the award of the contract.[50] Costs had escalated wildly out of control and a subsequent settlement with the Nixon administration concluded at the beginning of February 1971, in which the company would be required to absorb $200 million of the cost of the overrun for the C-5A, had left the company in a position where its cash liabilities now exceeded its assets.[51] Although a $600 million credit had been negotiated with a syndicate of banks to finance the building of the L-1011, without the delivery of the RB-211, Lockheed faced the real prospect of being unable to supply the L-1011 to the airlines that had already placed orders and of defaulting on its loans.

The ripple effect of a collapse of Lockheed appeared endless. In the competitive world of aviation, the three major U.S. domestic airlines that had agreed to purchase the Lockheed L-1011 could ill afford not to add the new plane to their fleets. The largest name of them all, Trans World Airlines (TWA), had declared losses of $100 million in its accounts for the previous financial year, and the financial positions of Eastern Airlines and Delta Airlines were similarly precarious.[52] One of the possible ramifications of the collapse of Lockheed was the bankruptcy of America's leading airlines and Lockheed's subcontractors, a deeply worrying prospect to the president, who told his advisers, "[If] Lockheed may go down... then TWA is in serious trouble, but more than that... there's $750 million dollars of subcontracts alone all riding on this thing."[53]

The crisis that now faced the Nixon administration had broken out at a time when the aviation industry was experiencing a severe downturn in its

50 Newhouse, *Sporty Game*, 113; Cable from Armstrong to FCO recording conversation between Heath and Robert Lovatt, Oct. 21, 1970, PREM 15/003, PRO.
51 "It's Just Too Dear," *Economist*, Feb. 13, 1971; "In Lockheed's Shoes," *Economist*, Feb. 20, 1971.
52 "Rolls-Royce: Worse to Come?" *Economist*, Feb. 27, 1971.
53 Recording of a conversation between Nixon and advisers, Feb. 19, 1971, 452–4, White House Tape Recordings, NPMP, NA.

fortunes. With the profits of airlines having fallen dramatically, major airframe manufacturers in the United States faced an uncertain future. Boeing had been forced to lay off eighty thousand employees at its plant in Seattle in a desperate bid to stave off financial oblivion,[54] while the future of one of America's prestige projects, the supersonic transport (SST) plane, which had been enthusiastically supported by the president, also lay in the balance after the Senate had voted to cut federal funding for the development and testing of the plane in December 1970.[55] With two hundred thousand jobs already at stake in the battle for the SST, the closure of Lockheed's plant in Burbank, California, and the possible collapse of some of the subcontractors that it had employed to work on the L-1011 would have created a serious crisis in the aviation industry.

Moreover, the crisis had occurred when business confidence in the American economy generally appeared to be highly fragile. In April 1970, when it appeared that the highly leveraged Pennsylvania New York Central Transportation Company (Penn Central), the seventh-largest corporation in the United States, was on the edge of bankruptcy, panic had set in Wall Street as investors had refused to consent to its credit being rolled over. The Nixon administration had faced the prospect that the Penn Central crisis could trigger a domino effect in the commercial paper market as nervous creditors called in loans in droves. On that occasion, the Federal Reserve had averted a serious liquidity crisis on the financial markets by injecting funds into the market.[56] With the U.S. economy only just beginning to show signs of recovery in early 1971, Nixon and his advisers were accordingly "scared to death to let L[ockheed] go into receivership."[57]

The potential collapse of Lockheed, its subcontractors, and a number of airlines in combination with the suspension of the SST project therefore raised the specter of a sharp rise in the unemployment figures in an industry already beset with troubles and a wider market collapse on the scale of Penn Central. Nixon was acutely aware of the ramifications of higher unemployment figures,[58] considering them to have "far more powerful implications politically than inflation."[59] The political implications included his hopes

---

54 "It's Just Too Dear," *Economist*, Feb. 13, 1971.
55 "SST Still in the Air," *Economist*, Mar. 20, 1971.
56 Allen J. Matsuow, *Nixon's Economy: Booms, Busts, Dollars and Votes* (Lawrence, KS, 1998), 75.
57 Note of a meeting Nixon and advisers, Feb. 10, 1971, Ehrlichman Notes, White House Special Files (WHSF), Staff Member Office Files (SMOF), Notes of meetings with the President, Box 4, NPMP, NA.
58 H. R. Haldeman, *The Haldeman Diaries: Inside the Nixon White House* (New York, 1994), 313–14; Matsuow, *Nixon's Economy*, 97.
59 Memo by McCracken, Feb. 9, 1971, President's Office Files, Memos for the President, Box 84, NPMP, NA.

of electoral victory in 1972, which, as Nixon himself recognized at the time, was by no means assured.[60] The results of the congressional elections in November 1970 had been far very far from an endorsement of the Republican Party or Nixon, in spite of his active role in the campaign,[61] an outcome that had caused him considerable concern.[62] Writing in his diary at the time, White House Chief of Staff H. R. "Bob" Haldeman recorded Nixon's fear of "screwing up [his reelection in] 1972."[63] Against this background, the threat posed to Nixon's electoral hopes by the fallout from the potential collapse of Lockheed was not being dismissed lightly by those close to the president. One business associate of Nixon's, Frank Gard Jameson, informed British officials that if the Lockheed plant were to close in the president's home state of California, where "the political situation was very important and personal to [Nixon]" then "he would almost certainly lose California."[64]

The prospect of the collapse of Lockheed also struck a blow at the heart of the president's longer-term political strategy. Eager to forge a new electoral coalition for the Republican Party, Nixon's objective had been to make inroads into the electoral constituency of the "Silent Majority,": especially blue-collar workers.[65] The president's persistent courtship throughout 1970 and 1971 of AFL-CIO leader George Meany, a longtime Democrat, was a critical element of this strategy.[66] Nixon had begun to make tentative progress in his bridge building with the AFL-CIO by 1970, most notably when Meany and construction workers had publicly rallied to his side during the U.S. bombing of Cambodia in the spring of 1970.[67] However, Meany had already demonstrated that his union was taking a close interest in the fortunes of the aviation industry through his staunch support for the SST. If Lockheed were to be declared bankrupt, Richard Nixon's hopes of building a new electoral coalition with the help of the unions would be dealt a very severe blow.

The president's political fears, possibly exacerbated by a warning from the U.S. embassy in London that noted the British government's "disinclination

---

60 Richard Nixon, *The Memoirs of Richard Nixon* (London, 1978), 497.
61 Stephen Ambrose, *Nixon: The Triumph of a Politician 1962–1972* (New York, 1989), 390–7.
62 Haldeman, *Haldeman Diaries*, 207–10. According to Haldeman, Nixon went "on and on about analysis of campaign."
63 Haldeman, *Haldeman Diaries*, 211.
64 Note of a conversation with Frank Gard Jameson to Heath 15/03/71, PREM 15/231, PRO.
65 Haldeman, *Haldeman Diaries*, 117–18; Matsuow, *Nixon's Economy*, 1–2.
66 An excerpt of a memo for Nixon from 1971 in advance of a meeting with Meany noted that one of the purposes of the White House was "to be sure that . . . [Meany] has the feeling of access to the President." Memo to Nixon, May 7, 1971, White House Central Files, CM 37, Confidential File, Box 4, NPMP, NA.
67 Matsuow, *Nixon's Economy*, 71.

to pay any significant price to keep alive the RB-211 engine contract,"[68] caused him to increase the pressure upon the British government. Acting on Nixon's instructions,[69] John Connally summoned Rowley Cromer to the Treasury Department, where he spared the British ambassador no details of the nature of the consequences for the American economy if Lockheed were unable to receive the RB-211 engines.[70] In the short time that he had been in Washington, Cromer could see that the new secretary of the treasury spoke with "unmistakeable authority" and concluded that the president had specifically selected Connally to deliver the views of the administration to emphasize the damage that might be inflicted on Anglo-American relations if Rolls-Royce failed to supply the RB-211.[71]

The combination of the forceful Connally and wave upon wave of negative press publicity had caused Cromer to be deeply worried as to the future for the Anglo-American relationship and Britain's commercial reputation in the United States. Reflecting on the crisis in a direct personal message to Edward Heath, he warned that a collapse of Lockheed would inflict considerable damage on the president's expansionary economic policy. Yet the British ambassador knew that there was a broader concern that was as significant as the political difficulties that would be created should Lockheed fail. Drawing on his knowledge and experience as a former governor of the Bank of England, he sensed that the markets could well collapse following the failure of Lockheed, and he was in no doubt as to where the responsibility for such an event would be attributed in the United States: "For Creditanstalt read Rolls Royce: in 1931 Britain went off the Gold Standard, in 1971 Britain caused major sectors of American industry to fail." The ambassador concluded that such hostile sentiment would adversely affect the attitude of the United States not just toward Rolls-Royce but also to British aviation manufacturers in general in the United States.[72] Britain's "national integrity as a commercial nation [is] at stake," concluded a concerned British ambassador.[73]

Cromer's fears about Britain's commercial standing in the United States were already being realized. Charles Tillinghast, chairman of TWA, whose fortunes were now inextricably linked to those of Lockheed, had already very publicly pointed to a "lack of confidence which this act has engendered

---

68 Memo from Annenberg to Rogers, Feb. 12, 1971, RG 59 State Department Central Files 1963–1973, FN 6–1 UK, NA.
69 Memo for President's Files, Feb. 10, 1971, President's Office Files, Memos for the President, Box 84, NPMP, NA.
70 Cable Cromer to FCO, Feb. 10, 1971, PREM 15/230, PRO.
71 Ibid.
72 Ibid.
73 Cable Cromer to Heath, Feb. 14, 1971, PREM 15/230, PRO.

with regard to any future undertakings by Rolls Royce *or other British aviation companies*" [emphasis added].[74] In mid-February, the chairman of the U.S. Civil Aeronautics Board, Secor Browne, met with British Defence Secretary Peter Carrington, who had been charged with the responsibility of resolving the crisis, and warned him that the default of Rolls-Royce on its obligations could seriously affect sales of the Concorde in the United States and cause the U.S. Navy to become "prejudiced" against the Harrier aircraft that it had planned to buy.[75]

The American government and leading businesspeople were not content to convey the threat that the bankruptcy of Rolls-Royce posed to the export potential of the British aviation industry in the United States simply via diplomatic channels or public statements. British industrialists and business leaders traveling throughout the United States soon came away from their meetings with their American counterparts fully aware that Britain's long-term trading prospects were at risk if Rolls-Royce should fail to fulfill its contractual obligations.[76] A delegation from the Confederation of British Industry informed the British trade and industry secretary, John Davies, that a visit to the United States had confirmed that prospects for the Concorde in the United States and participation by British companies in collaborative projects in the United States would be jeopardized if the RB-211 were not to be continued.[77] The adverse reaction of the aviation industry to the crisis began to extend to other sectors of American industry. In California, the Los Angeles chamber of commerce cabled the chairman of the USA Committee of the London chamber of commerce, Martin Redmayne, warning that the previous record of "profitable" trade between Southern California and the United Kingdom would be "seriously damaged" by the bankruptcy of Rolls-Royce.[78]

THE HEATH GOVERNMENT'S U-TURN

The various forms of pressure being exerted by the Nixon administration and American industry had begun to make a significant impression on the British decision-making process. British officials noted that Cromer's frequent and concerned cables reporting the Nixon's administration's views

---

74 "Lockheed's Search for Survival," *Business Week*, Feb. 13, 1971.
75 Record of conversation between Carrington and Secor Browne, Feb. 16, 1971, FCO 14/841, PRO.
76 Record of a telephone conversation between Armstrong and Keith, Feb. 12, 1971, PREM 15/229, PRO.
77 Letter Davies to Carrington, Feb. 16, 1971, FCO 14/841, PRO.
78 Cable LA Chamber of Commerce to London Chamber of Commerce, Feb. 18, 1971, FCO 14/842, PRO.

had "injected a much needed sense of urgency into the series of enquiries [being carried out into the future of the RB-211]."[79] The prime minister himself asked Cromer to assure Connally that the British government was neither "negative nor defeatist" in its approach to the resolution of the crisis.[80] And even though the British government had commissioned two reports on the costs of estimates of the funding for the RB-211, it was aware well before the publication of the reports that, because the RB-211 was likely to be "a lossmaker on commercial terms," the question facing the government was the extent of the loss it was willing to accept to prevent British economic interests and Anglo–American relations from being damaged.[81] The warnings about future British economic interests were already clearly troubling members of the ministerial committee for the minutes revealed their desire to correct the American perception of the government's handling of the crisis to prevent harm from being inflicted on the "major promotional effort planned for California" in 1971.[82] These two significant considerations would ensure that the government's negotiating position in respect of the main features of the new contract for the production of the RB-211 would be substantially altered.

The British government had initially proposed to set up a joint venture company with the Lockheed Corporation to share the risks and costs of the development of the RB-211. Included in its opening bid was a request that the price of each engine be increased and that a warranty be provided as to Lockheed's financial position, thus enabling the British government to complete the RB-211.[83] When Lockheed chairman Dan Haughton rejected this offer, the British government abandoned the concept of a joint venture with Lockheed, instead suggesting that Lockheed simply pay an increase in the engine price while providing a warranty. Yet even Heath had his doubts as to whether the Nixon administration would be in a position to provide any warranty.[84]

However, by the end of March 1971, the Heath government was in no position to withdraw from their tentative commitment to fund the RB-211, even though the price offered for the engines was considerably short of the £97 million originally demanded. In Washington, Connally had responded positively to the request of Rowley Cromer for assistance in the form of a U.S. government warranty, informing him that he would recommend to the

---

79 Letter Hanbury-Tennison to Tebbit, 16/02/71, FCO 14/841, PRO.
80 Cable Heath to Cromer, Feb. 17, 1971, FCO 14/842, PRO.
81 Record of Rolls-Royce Ministerial Group Meeting, Feb. 16, 1971, CAB 134/3449, PRO.
82 Ibid.
83 Record of Rolls-Royce Ministerial Group Meeting, Feb. 23, 1971, CAB 134/3449, PRO.
84 Record of Rolls-Royce Ministerial Group Meeting, Mar. 17, 1971, CAB 134/3449, PRO.

president that the administration approach Congress to ask for a warranty. Such was his confidence in himself and his influence over the president that Connally had assured the British ambassador that he expected the president to implement his recommendation.[85] Faced with this level of cooperation from the Nixon administration, the British government understood that it could ill afford the tensions that would be created if should rebuff American assistance.[86]

The British attitude toward the engine price and the nature of the warranty being provided by the U.S. government continued to soften further still. At the outset, Heath and his colleagues were agreed that any U.S. government guarantee for Lockheed must be a "water-tight contractual agreement."[87] However, following an intervention by Cromer to the effect that it would be a mistake to look for a cast-iron guarantee from the Nixon administration,[88] members of the British government abandoned this particular requirement, declaring that there could not be any justification to withdraw from the RB–211 project given the cooperation of the United States.[89] Nor did the commitment of the British government waver even through three long months in the summer of 1971 when it was far from certain that Congress would approve the guarantee for a loan to Lockheed.[90] In the event, intensive lobbying on the part of John Connally did prove sufficient to secure the approval of a skeptical Congress by the narrowest of margins at the beginning of August 1971, thus ensuring the immediate future of the RB–211 and the production of the TriStar. With financial backing secured, Lockheed would go on to manufacture and supply the TriStar to its customers, powered with Rolls-Royce engines as originally envisaged.

CONCLUSION

Although the bankruptcy of Rolls-Royce had created considerable and protracted concern on both sides of the Atlantic, the two governments cooperated far more closely than has previously been thought to be the case. In Washington, the Nixon administration, recognizing that the British

---

85 Record of Rolls-Royce Ministerial Group Meeting, Mar. 22, 1971, CAB 134/3449, PRO.
86 Ibid.
87 Ibid.
88 Cable Cromer to FCO, undated, PREM 15/231, PRO.
89 Record of Rolls-Royce Ministerial Group Meeting, Mar. 22, 1971, CAB 134/3449, PRO. Instead, members of the ministerial group suggested that other means could be found for the U.S. government to reimburse the British government should the TriStar not ultimately be produced.
90 Record of meeting of Economic Policy Committee, July 27, 1971, CAB 134/3377; Memo by Corfield, July 27, 1971, CAB 134/3380, PRO.

government would need assistance to ensure that the crisis was resolved and considering the British prime minister a "great guy – comp[ared] to [Heath's predecessor Harold] Wilson"[91] and Britain to be America's "only reliable major ally,"[92] had undertaken the difficult task of seeking a congressional guarantee for U.S. government loans provided to Lockheed. It was a considerable achievement for the Nixon administration to secure this guarantee, given the strong opposition to government assistance for Lockheed it had faced.[93] Yet, understanding that the needs of the British and American governments were now intertwined, the secretary of the treasury had relentlessly pressed Congress to provide the guarantee that would assure the future of the L-1011, eventually overcoming both personal and ideological opposition within Congress and Lockheed's major competitors.[94]

Across the Atlantic, the British government had been equally active. Far from seeking to disengage his government from the Rolls-Royce debacle, the prime minister had recognized early on that it was a matter that was of considerable importance to both governments. Moreover, the position of the British government in respect of the new price for the engines,[95] and the nature of the warranty offered by the U.S. government had altered substantially as it became aware through diplomatic and commercial channels of the threat that the crisis posed both to Richard Nixon's domestic position a year before a presidential election and to Britain's trading reputation abroad. It was a fact recognized by Connally, who advised the president that "the British have come a long way,"[96] and by some members of the British cabinet, who complained about the constant shifting in the government's negotiating position and queried whether "this would be the end of our retreat."[97]

91 Record of meeting, Dec. 17, 1970, Haldeman Notes, July–December 1970, WHSF, SMOF, Box 42, NPMP, NA.

92 Record of a meeting between Nixon and his advisers 09/02/71, Ehrlichman Notes, WHSF, SMOF, Notes of meetings with the president, Box 4, NPMP, NA.

93 John Connally with Mickey Herskowitz, *In History's Shadow: An American Odyssey* (New York, 1993), 250. The same senators who had opposed further funding for the SST were similarly opposed to government assistance for Lockheed. Lockheed's major competitor, General Electric, had also expressed opposition to government aid for Lockheed; letter from Peterson to Connally describing General Electric's opposition, Apr. 23, 1971, White House Central Files, CM 37, Confidential File, Box 4, NPMP, NA.

94 Charles Ashman, *Connally: The Adventures of Big Bad John* (New York, 1974), 190. The chairman of the powerful Banking and Currency Committee in the House of Representatives, Wright Patman, was reputed to heartily dislike Connally.

95 The British government accepted a price that was £47 million less than its original estimate of £97 million.

96 Recording of a meeting between Nixon and Connally, Apr. 22, 1971, 486–3, White House Tape Recordings, NPMP, NA.

97 Record of cabinet meeting, Mar. 29, 1971, CAB 128/71, PRO.

The true extent of the British government's willingness to accede to the demands and concerns of the American government can be fully appreciated when considered in the wider context of the prime minister's objectives in industrial policy and his longer-term vision of securing British entry to the EEC. From its accession to power, the Heath government had been determined both to bring public expenditure firmly under control and to change the environment in which business operated in Britain. The leitmotif of the government's economic policy was subsequently captured in the simple but emphatic statement of Christopher Chataway, the minister for telecommunications in the Heath government that "intervention was taboo."[98] As the crisis broke, the American ambassador in London, Walter Annenberg, doubted whether the prime minister could "fashion a solution meeting our [American] requirements" because the issue posed "philosophical and financial problems" for the Conservative government.[99] Indeed, for some members of the British government, the continuation of the RB–211 was the antithesis of the government's belief that "industry must not look to be bailed out of loss-making ventures."[100] Moreover, accepting a lower engine price would mean that the costs borne by the British government would increase significantly, a prospect that was deeply unpalatable to some members of the ministerial committee who considered that the extra cost would represent a "serious strain on the economy."[101]

The continued commitment of the British government to fund the development of the RB–211 was also harmful to its longer-term objective of securing entry to the EEC. It was not lost on British officials in the early 1970s that the argument for British membership of the EEC was still to be won, particularly in France, where mistrust of British motives remained unchanged at the highest levels of the French government. The British diplomat entrusted with task of bringing about an improvement in Anglo-French relations, Christopher Soames, later recalled that "the belief in France . . . was [that] we had . . . sold out to the Americans because our deterrent was American manufactured."[102] Heath himself had appreciated that the French president, Georges Pompidou, continued to share the suspicion of his predecessor, Charles de Gaulle, that Britain remained "too closely attached to the United States" and he still had doubts as

98 Transcript of interview with Christopher Chataway, Seventies Collection, Box 002/9, Archive of the London School of Economics and Political Science (LSE Archive), U.K.
99 Memorandum from Rogers to Nixon, Mar. 3, 1971, RG 59 State Department Central Files 1963–1973, POL 1 UK, NA.
100 Record of Rolls-Royce Ministerial Group Meeting, Mar. 3, 1971, CAB 134/3449, PRO.
101 Record of Rolls-Royce Ministerial Group Meeting, Mar. 26, 1971, CAB 134/3449, PRO.
102 Transcript of interview with Christopher Soames, Seventies Collection, Box 002/5, LSE Archive.

to "whether the [United Kingdom] would be prepared to defend European interests in the face of likely economic and political onslaughts from outside."[103] At a time when the Heath government was entering into negotiations to secure British membership in the EEC, its actions in the aviation sector were therefore being viewed by EEC member states, in particular France, in a highly political light. At a meeting with officials in early March 1971, the prime minister learned that Solly Zuckerman had discovered from his French contacts that "President Pompidou was continuing to take a close interest in this matter [the RB-211] and had expressed the view that continuation with the RB-211 would distract Rolls-Royce from [E]uropeanisation."[104] The well-connected adviser further warned Heath that his sources in the French government had informed him that "the reaction [of the Europeans to the development of the RB-211] would be bound to affect our EEC application."[105]

The decision to proceed with the RB-211 was even less propitious as it came at a time when the British government had not displayed any marked enthusiasm for collaboration in the European aviation industry. In December 1970, the Heath government had rejected an offer to rejoin a European consortium for the construction of the Airbus A300 on the grounds that European governments would be unable to require national airlines to alter their procurement policy to purchase the A300 with Rolls-Royce engines.[106] While Christopher Soames concluded that a decision not to rejoin the Airbus A300 consortium would not cause the British government "to lose much political credit in terms of commitment to Europe,"[107] a commitment to the pan-European project by the British government would, as a cabinet paper noted, constitute proof of Britain's wish to be "good Europeans."[108]

---

103 Heath, *Course of My Life*, 364.
104 Record of meeting between Heath, Carrington, and British officials, Mar. 2, 1971, PREM 15/230, PRO.
105 Memo from Zuckerman to Heath, May 5, 1971, PREM 15/232, PRO.
106 Record of cabinet meeting, Dec. 1, 1970, CAB 128/47, PRO. Indeed, the decision did not appear surprising given that, in opposition, the Conservative Party leadership seemed far from convinced about the merits of participation by British companies in the consortium. A paper prepared for the Shadow Cabinet by Frederick Corfield commenting on the prospects for the Airbus noted, "No aircraft can succeed on the basis of the sort of delay that appears to be inseparable from these political consortia." Paper by Corfield on Airbus, Mar. 7, 1969, LCC 1/2/16 (69) 226, CPA, Bodleian Library.
107 Cable Soames to FCO, Sept. 24, 1970, CAB 168/163. The British government may have defused any resentment by simultaneously announcing that it would not give any financial support to the development of the BAC-311, a national aircraft that would have been in direct competition with the European Airbus had it been built.
108 Memorandum for cabinet by officials on Airbuses, Oct. 8, 1970, CAB 129/152, PRO.

That the prime minister was willing to accept a serious setback to his industrial strategy and potentially weaken his European policy in accommodating American concerns and committing his government to the development of the RB-211 suggests that the British government under Heath's direction still attached enormous importance to its relationship with the United States. Reflecting on the crisis more than a decade later, Frederick Corfield recalled, "There was very considerable Foreign Office interest... [the Foreign Secretary] Alec Douglas-Home was very concerned that we should not let down Lockheed."[109] And Heath himself would acknowledge in his memoirs that one of the primary motivations in this crisis had been his concern that "the knock-on effect on Lockheed of allowing the new engine to be cancelled would badly sour relations with the Americans."[110]

Such a view may seem surprising given the many historical works that have been devoted to Heath's passionate commitment to European unity. However, while the British leader may not have displayed any sentimental attachment for the United States, he appeared eager to maintain a close relationship with the U.S. government on a political level.[111] Even before Heath's accession to power, the American ambassador to Britain in the 1960s, David Bruce, would record in his diary, "[Heath] has been a staunch supporter of [American] policy in Vietnam and of the politicians here, has been one of the most friendly to the Americans."[112] Heath's recognition and acceptance of the significance of Britain's relationship with the United States was revealed by his statement to his colleagues and advisers shortly after assuming power that there was "no other power whose modes of thought were so close to their own [the United States] or with whom they found it so easy to work."[113] From the outset of his premiership, he had sought to preserve the long-standing close dialogue between the two countries. Heath's dispatch of Rowley Cromer, a former governor of the Bank of England and a close personal friend, as Britain's top envoy to the United States indicated that he intended, as he told the president, to ensure

---

109 Transcript of interview with Frederick Corfield, Seventies Collection, Box 006/6, LSE Archive.
110 Heath, *Course of My Life*, 340.
111 Heath did not appear naturally enthusiastic about the country or its people. In a revealing note written by his principal private secretary, Robert Armstrong, the prime minister had apparently expressed his irritation with the demand of the U.S. government that the president travel to Chequers in a motorcade on his visit to the United Kingdom in October 1970, commenting that it was "just the sort of saturation... that earns the Americans a bad name wherever they go." Note from Armstrong, Sept. 26, 1970, PREM 15/714, PRO.
112 Diaries of David K. E. Bruce, Diary Entry, Feb. 16, 1966, Virginia Historical Society, Richmond, VA.
113 Record of meeting, Heath, Douglas-Home and officials, Sept. 30, 1970, PREM 15/714, PRO.

that "the link between us was as good it could be."[114] Even though Henry Kissinger recognized as early as October 1970 that Heath would inevitably distance himself from the United States as he sought to secure British entry to the EEC, he still believed that "relations with the UK [would] undoubtedly retain a special quality of intimacy and informality,"[115] a view to which he continued to subscribe nearly three years later.[116]

This essay also raises the possibility of an alternative conclusion in respect of the state of American power and influence in the world during the 1970s. The willingness of the prime minister to take American concerns into account when formulating his response to the Rolls-Royce bankruptcy was also, in part, recognition of the status and position that the United States enjoyed in the domestic politics of its allies. As the *Economist* noted on the occasion of Edward Heath's first visit to Washington as prime minister in December 1970, any head of government still welcomed the opportunity to have an audience with the American president "to be able to remind [the] electorate back at home that he is the Briton – or German, or Italian, or whoever – who currently has first claim on the presidential ear."[117] It was a fact not lost on the prime minister himself, who, shortly before his visit to Washington in December 1970, had inquired personally into the possibility of the president receiving him at Camp David after their initial talks at the White House to "demonstrate the special relationship between [the] two governments."[118]

While it is easy to conclude that American economic power had declined dramatically in light of the international financial crises and military difficulties it had faced in Southeast Asia in the 1960s and the early 1970s, this argument is perhaps overstated. As has been seen in this examination of the Rolls-Royce–Lockheed crisis, the explicit warnings made both by Nixon administration officials and U.S. business to the British government about the threat to future British trade flows with the United States that would follow on from the failure of Rolls-Royce to deliver the RB-211 engine to Lockheed had clearly held considerable sway over the British government. One paper prepared for the cabinet at the outset of the crisis suggested that the overall loss to Britain's exports could amount to as much

---

114 Cable from Heath to Nixon, undated, PREM 15/211, PRO.
115 Memo from Kissinger to Nixon, Oct. 3, 1970, NSC, President's Trip Files, Visit to the UK, Box 470, NPMP, NA.
116 Memo from Kissinger to Nixon, Jan. 31, 1973, NSC, VIP Visits, Box 942, NPMP, NA.
117 "Don't Expect Too Much," *Economist*, Dec. 19, 1970.
118 Memo from Kissinger to Nixon, Nov. 9, 1970, White House Central Files (WHCF), Countries Files, United Kingdom, Box 80, NPMP, NA; Memo Chapin to Haldeman, Nov. 13, 1970, WHCF, Countries Files, United Kingdom, Box 80, NPMP, NA.

as £3,000 million.[119] For a nation such as Britain, which had repeatedly endured balance-of-payments difficulties in the 1950s and 1960s, the loss of export earnings of this magnitude was simply not palatable.

However, the influence of the United States in the British decision-making process could not be explained simply by its ability to exploit its economic muscle to achieve its objectives or by an acknowledgment on the part of the prime minister of the importance of Britain's relationship with the United States. More subtle forces were at work that enabled the Nixon administration to shape the internal policy debate of the Heath government. Since 1945, the United States had actively sought to build a more open and interdependent economic and security system, through organizations and agreements such as Bretton Woods, the General Agreement on Tariffs and Trade (GATT), the International Monetary Fund (IMF), and the North Atlantic Treaty Organization (NATO). To some theorists, such as Karl Deutsch, this type of system might be characterized as a "pluralistic security community" in which international institutions are created with processes of timely consultation and decision-making procedures.[120] Other theorists contend that such a system creates the opportunity for the development of informal cross-border coalitions and networks between government agencies and actors, which, as this author has found in previous research, may contribute to the outcome of the policy debates of governments.[121] Such networks and alliances, described by Keohane and Nye as "transgovernmental coalitions," help to explain the means by which the Nixon administration was able to influence the policy debate of the British government during the Rolls-Royce–Lockheed crisis. In this case, the long-standing pattern of communication and dialogue between the U.S. government and the British embassy in Washington, in particular with the British ambassador,[122] enabled the Nixon administration to ensure that its

---

119 Memorandum for the Cabinet by Rolls-Royce Official Group, Feb. 24, 1971, CAB 164/999, PRO.

120 Karl Deutsch, *Political Community and the North Atlantic Area: International Organization in the Light of Historical Experience* (Princeton, NJ, 1957).

121 Robert Keohane and Joseph Nye, "Transgovernmental Relations and International Organizations," *World Politics* 27 (October 1974): 47–51; Thomas Risse-Kappen, *Co-operation among Democracies: The European Influence on U.S. Foreign Policy* (Princeton, NJ, 1995), 208; Roy, "Battle of the Pound," 335.

122 The close relationship between the British embassy and the White House was revealed by a letter from Rowley Cromer to Foreign Secretary Alec Home in 1972, when he noted that "all doors" were "most cordially open to him." The ambassador was of the view that he would "expect this [accessibility] to apply to any emissary of the British government." Letter from Cromer to Home, Apr. 4, 1972, FCO 73/138, PRO. The extent to which the British embassy had secured unprecedented access to the innermost deliberations of successive United States governments can be revealed by an insightful witness seminar on the position of the British embassy in Washington. See Gillian Staerck and Michael Kandiah, eds., *The Role of HM Embassy in Washington* (London, 2002).

concerns and representations would be heard during the deliberations of the British government. The Americans had quite deliberately built on this existing close relationship with the British embassy and consciously exploited Cromer's unique access to the prime minister to achieve their objectives.[123] From the perspective of the Nixon administration, Cromer's actions in this crisis had turned him into an effective advocate of American concerns.

But it was not just at the official level where such alliances and links worked to the advantage of the United States. In the academic debate surrounding the significance of these informal cross-border relationships, attention is increasingly being paid to the role of networks between non-state actors, such as social and labor movements and multinational corporations.[124] Even in the somewhat brief episode described in this chapter, it is clear that such transnational networks between British and American business made a vital contribution to the British decision-making process. In this instance, American commercial leaders were determined to ensure that the British government not trigger a major crisis in the American economy, while British industry wished to ensure that a lucrative export market, particularly that of California, should not be foreclosed to British business. That Britain's commercial reputation abroad and the need to improve public perceptions in the United States were recurrent themes in the cabinet debates about the RB-211 is testament to the significance of these informal alliances in determining the outcome of this issue.

Above all, the eight-month crisis had shown that even though the British government, led by a passionate believer in the concept of European unity, was seeking to find a new role in the EEC, it had not chosen to break from its close relationship with the United States, and indeed continued to recognize its significance in both foreign and domestic policy. Britain in time would succeed in its mission to enter the EEC and face the challenge of developing a more European focused economic and industrial policy that might be reconciled with its long-standing politico-economic ties across the Atlantic. However, even though Edward Heath had very publicly emphasized the importance of pan-European industrial collaboration, as the withdrawal of the Conservative government from the European Airbus project in 1970 had

---

123 Letter from Cromer to Greenhill, 17/02/71, FCO 14/842, PRO. Cromer noted how Kissinger understood that his link to the prime minister "provide[d] a means of interchanging ideas . . . separately from official channels."

124 Thomas A. Schwartz, "The United States and Germany after 1945: Alliances, Transnational Relations, and the Legacy of the Cold War," *Diplomatic History* 19 (1995): 567–8; Thomas Risse-Kappen, ed., *Bringing Transnational Relations Back In: Non-State Actors, Domestic Structures and International Institutions* (New York, 1995).

already revealed, it was not axiomatic that Britain's membership of the EEC would result in ever-greater participation by British industry in European markets and ventures. Indeed, even before Heath had succeeded in securing Britain's entry to the EEC, an assessment of the British aircraft industry prepared for the pro-European Conservative Party leader had expressed concern at the recommendation of a committee (the Plowden Committee) that the future of Britain's aircraft industry lay in increased cooperation in Europe. Instead, Heath's closest advisers had argued that "European cooperation should not be exclusive. There may well be opportunities for collaboration with the United States to a much greater extent than the Plowden Report seems to recognise."[125] The reaction of British business to the potential impact of the Rolls-Royce–Lockheed crisis on continuing access to American markets had borne out this line of thinking, demonstrating that British business leaders would continue to think globally in terms of their growth and development, an approach that would only serve to reinforce the existing close politico-economic ties between Washington and London. In an increasingly global and interdependent economy, it appeared that the unique relationship between Britain and the United States was likely to survive any challenges that lay ahead.

125 Paper by Robert Carr on the Plowden Report for Parliamentary Debate on Feb. 1, 1966, 28/01/66 LCC 1/2/4 (66) 77, CPA, Bodleian Library.

PART THREE

Reasserting U.S. Leadership?

Kissinger's Year of Europe and Beyond

9

Asserting Europe's Distinct Identity

The EC Nine and Kissinger's Year of Europe

DANIEL MÖCKLI

On April 23, 1973, National Security Adviser Henry Kissinger launched a transatlantic initiative that was to mark and bedevil European-U.S. relations for more than a year. Addressing the editors of the Associated Press at the Waldorf-Astoria hotel in New York, Kissinger labeled 1973 the "Year of Europe" because "the era that was shaped by decisions of a generation ago is ending" and the "dramatic transformation of the psychological climate in the West" required a "new era of creativity."[1] Given the nuclear parity between the superpowers, the relaxation of East-West tensions, and the onset of interbloc negotiations, on the one hand, and, on the other, increasing transatlantic economic competition, Kissinger suggested that the Atlantic relationship be redefined and that a "new Atlantic Charter" with a "clear set of common objectives" be jointly drafted and ready for President Richard Nixon to sign during a trip to Europe toward the end of the year.

Kissinger urged that the endless controversies within the alliance on defense and détente should give way to a new consensus on security. A more rational defense posture ought to be found. As fear no longer sufficed to unite the West, the allies should now identify common interests, purposes, and values beyond security and extend their cooperation to the political and economic realms. The United States, for its part, would make further concessions for the sake of European unity, provided that there was a spirit of reciprocity. And domestic pressure notwithstanding, the U.S. government pledged not to withdraw its forces unilaterally from the old continent if the allies agreed to a fairer distribution of the defense burden.[2]

---

1 The speech is reproduced in Gerhard Mally, ed., *The New Europe and the United States: Partners or Rivals* (Lexington, MA, 1974), 29–37.
2 Ibid.

What Kissinger thought would have an effect similar to that of the announcement of the Marshall Plan a quarter century earlier brought about some of the most acrimonious transatlantic debates in the post–World War II period. The proposed charter never saw the light of day, and the failure of the exercise could be only thinly disguised by a face-saving declaration signed at the Brussels NATO summit in June 1974.

In this chapter, I trace the course of the turbulent Year of Europe from a European perspective. Focusing on France, West Germany, and Britain as the three major European powers, I argue that the U.S. initiative, instead of strengthening the Atlantic cohesion, inadvertently became a catalyst for European political unity and turned into another round in the conflict over Europe's role in the world and within the West. Contrary to previous struggles, however, the rift this time occurred primarily between the United States and Europe, and not among the three big European countries.

The rift between Europe and the United States was caused mainly by the differing conclusions that the two sides of the Atlantic reached about structural changes in the international system. While Washington seemed to regard détente as a potential threat to Western unity – a threat that required the consolidation of U.S. leadership and an expansion of the Atlantic security community to the political and economic realms – the Europeans saw in the reduction of bipolar confrontation both the opportunity and need to define and defend their own interests and to become a distinct entity in international politics. Similarly, while the United States viewed the enlargement of the European Community (EC) in 1973 and Europe's growing economic power as potential threats to Western stability, to the EC Nine, these developments meant, above all, the long-awaited chance to advance European unification.

The unique constellation of personalities leading Europe between 1970 and 1974 further accounts for the fact that the Nine came to exploit Kissinger's proposal to move Europe closer to becoming a distinct actor in international affairs. British Prime Minister Edward Heath was an ardent supporter of a European foreign policy; West German Chancellor Willy Brandt was more willing than any of his predecessors to defend German and European interests; and French President Georges Pompidou and Foreign Minister Michel Jobert represented a distinctly European variation of Gaullism. Thus, key members of the Nine were, for once, governed by leaders with at least partly compatible visions of Europe's future. A French policy change in June–July 1973 in favor of a "political Europe," a shared disdain for Kissinger's diplomatic methods, and the erosion of U.S. moral authority in the wake of Watergate contributed to the Nine's joint – and unexpected – answer to Kissinger's initiative: a European-American draft declaration that made the case for a new bilateralism between the Nine and the United States and asked Washington to acknowledge Europe as a second decision-making center in the West, and a separate declaration on European identity.

European political unity was short lived, however. Kissinger challenged Europe's efforts to speak with one voice as soon as the efforts were directed at the United States or seemed incompatible with American interests. Much of the Year of Europe negotiations, therefore, dealt with the procedural question of U.S. involvement in European decision making. While several factors account for the diminished effectiveness of European political co-operation by spring 1974, Kissinger's lack of understanding of the concept of European integration and his failure to support the political identity of the Nine was, from the perspective of the three major European powers, the most important one.

THE U.S. CHALLENGE AS A CATALYST FOR EUROPEAN UNITY

Kissinger's initiative did not come as a complete surprise to the Europeans. Beginning with a press conference in September 1972, he had publicly announced several times that the Atlantic relationship was the cornerstone of his "structure of peace" and should be adapted to the new international circumstances as soon as peace was established in Vietnam. He had also aired some of his ideas before his speech in confidential exchanges with European leaders, including Pompidou, Heath, and Egon Bahr, the architect of Brandt's *Ostpolitik*. At Kissinger's request, the British had even started a secret dialogue on a new "general framework" for institutionalizing the Atlantic relationship, and in March 1973, the French had accepted a U.S. proposal for bilateral talks with a view toward redefining U.S.-European relations, putting an end to the "German ambiguity" (*l'ambiguité allemande*) and placing Ostpolitik in a more solid Atlantic frame.[3]

Yet the Europeans were nonetheless caught off guard when Kissinger proclaimed the Year of Europe. They had not expected such far-ranging proposals in a speech about which they had been informed at short notice (and with the request that it receive strong public backing), and they felt that

---

3 French embassy Washington (Jacques Kosciusko-Morizet), "Dejeuner en tête à tête avec M. Kissinger," Mar. 16, 1973, Archives Nationales (hereafter AN), Kosciusko-Morizet Papers (582AP), 37; British Cabinet Secretary Burke Trend to Heath, "Discussion with Dr. Kissinger," Apr. 24, 1973, Prime Minister's Office (PREM) 15/1359; Henry Kissinger, *Years of Upheaval* (London, 2000), 130–43.

they had not been consulted adequately. Moreover, Kissinger's suggestions, from a European point of view, came at an awkward time. The EC had just completed its first round of enlargement with the accession of Britain, Ireland, and Denmark on January 1, 1973. Pompidou's lifting of the French veto on accession negotiations at the 1969 Hague summit had also opened the way for two ambitious projects: economic and monetary union (EMU) and European political cooperation (EPC). The EPC project was set up as an intergovernmental mechanism outside EC structures, and it aimed at harmonizing national foreign policies on specific issues. The first practical results had been mixed. However, at their first summit in Paris in October 1972, the Nine declared their intention of converting their relationship into a European Union by 1980 and of making the "New Europe" – as the enlarged EC was now often referred to – a powerful actor in international politics.[4]

The Europeans were thus preoccupied with their own affairs at the time of Kissinger's appeal. And they were puzzled about U.S. intentions: Was Kissinger encouraging European unity and suggesting an Atlantic partnership like the partnership of two equals that John F. Kennedy had envisioned? Or did he have in mind a multipolar Atlantic community, under strong U.S. leadership, in which Atlantic cooperation would necessarily have to grow at the expense of European cooperation? The fact that Kissinger's Year of Europe speech had identified European unity only as a function of Atlantic strength, attributed to Europe regional rather than global interests, and suggested including Japan in the Atlantic exercise led the Europeans to believe that the Nixon administration built its design not so much on European unity as on the principle of U.S. preponderance in the West.

While the French expressed such fears more strongly than the British and West Germans, the three governments agreed on some central points. Given the fragile state of European unity, they considered Kissinger's initiative premature; accordingly, they regarded the time frame for executing his proposal as unrealistic. They rejected Kissinger's call for issue linkage in the negotiations, fearing that the United States would take advantage of European dependence on the American nuclear deterrent and the American forces in Europe to extract economic and monetary concessions. They were also worried that the Nixon administration intended to bring Europe's distinct conception of détente into line with U.S. policies, and they suspected that

---

4 Daniel Möckli, *European Foreign Policy during the Cold War: Health, Brandt, Pompidou and the Dream of Political Unity* (London, 2009).

this spectacular U.S. initiative was meant in part to distract the American public from the unfolding Watergate crisis.[5]

STRUGGLING FOR A COMMON ANSWER

How should the Europeans respond? The West Germans were forced to produce the first response, as Brandt was scheduled to visit Nixon only a few days after the speech. Some members of Brandt's Social Democratic Party were hostile to Kissinger's initiative. Herbert Wehner, the influential leader of the party's Bundestag caucus, publicly described the initiative as "monstrous" and privately warned Brandt that it reflected the "wishful thinking of a great power" (*Grossmachtwunschdenken*).[6] Brandt, while he also had doubts, was willing to seek a compromise. Although his Ostpolitik required national flexibility and alliance policies that were not too restrictive, it could not be pursued without the support of West Germany's key ally.

Bonn also saw opportunities in Kissinger's initiative. Brandt hoped that the proposed talks with the United States would result in the institutional link between the EC and Washington that he had long been advocating. Further, the Federal Republic saw an opportunity to advance European political unity and to demonstrate that Europe could speak with one voice. Many in the Foreign Ministry believed this. In particular, Walter Scheel, West Germany's foreign minister and leader of the Free Democratic Party, was convinced that by 1980 the Nine would have a common foreign policy and, further, that he would be the ideal choice as Europe's first foreign minister.[7]

During their May 1973 summit, Brandt was astonished that Nixon seemed to view Europe as merely a network of bilateral relations. Brandt emphasized that he had come to Washington as Europe's spokesperson. He asked Nixon to treat the Nine as if their political unity had already been accomplished. He convinced Nixon to drop the label "new Atlantic Charter" and suggested that he visit not only NATO but also the European

---

5 Note Foreign and Commonwealth Office (FCO), "The Year of Europe: The Impact on Transatlantic and Anglo-American Relations: An Analytical Account – February–July 1973," Oct. 1973, PREM 15/2089; circular by Geoffroy de Courcel, Secretary-General at the French Ministère des Affaires Etrangère (MAE), Apr. 28, 1973, MAE États-Unis 1137; FRG embassy Washington (Berndt von Staden) to Auswärtiges Amt (AA), Apr. 26, 1973, *Akten zur Auswärtigen Politik der Bundesrepublik Deutschland* (hereafter *AAPD*) 1973, doc. 118.

6 Klaus Harpprecht, *Im Kanzleramt: Tagebuch der Jahre mit Willy Brandt* (Reinbek, 2000), 101; letter Wehner to Brandt, Apr. 27, 1973, Archiv der sozialen Demokratie (AdsD), Willy Brandt Archive (WBA), Bundeskanzler (BK) 21.

7 See Scheel's remarks at the EPC meeting of June 5, 1973, draft record AA, B21/747; Egon Bahr, *Zu meiner Zeit* (Munich, 1996), 94.

Community during his next trip to Europe. Brandt rejected a global
approach to Atlantic negotiations, and he succeeded in having references to
Europe's "global responsibilities" and to the need for a balanced partnership
between Western Europe and the United States in the joint communiqué
issued at the close of the summit.[8]

Both the British and the French governments were astonished at the
briskness with which Brandt appeared to have confronted the U.S. administration. But London and Paris reacted differently when an enthusiastic
West German delegation reported that it had made the international role
of the Nine the focus of the Year of Europe. Whereas the British favored a
positive response to Kissinger's initiative and a common European position
in the negotiations with Washington, the French had serious doubts about
both.

The British did not like the Year of Europe initiative. The Foreign and
Commonwealth Office (FCO) called it "PR-oriented" and maintained
that Kissinger's criticism of NATO was "exaggerated" and aimed primarily at subordinating Europe's economic interests to Washington's political
exigencies.[9] Heath, who saw every year of his term as a year of Europe,
was furious about the whole concept: "For Henry Kissinger to announce
a Year of Europe without consulting any of us was rather like my standing between the lions in Trafalgar Square and announcing that we were
embarking on a year to save America!"[10] But though Foreign Secretary
Alec Douglas-Home occasionally had to ask Heath to limit his public criticism, Heath acknowledged that Nixon needed support to contain U.S.
domestic pressure to reduce the U.S. defense commitment to Europe. As
did Brandt, Heath also recognized the advantages of using the Atlantic
initiative to boost the unification of Europe – his foreign policy priority.
More than any other British prime minister, Heath stood for a strong political Europe. Since taking office in June 1970, he had advocated a common
European foreign policy, which, from his point of view, was essential to
renew British influence in world affairs and to provide a political structure for the EC to pursue its external relations. Heath also ordered the
FCO to investigate the possibility of a European defense. He had initiated
a secret dialogue with Pompidou on the feasibility of a European nuclear
deterrent; and he generally seemed prepared to forfeit Britain's "special

8 Letter von Staden to State Secretary Paul Frank, May 12, 1973, *AAPD* 1973, doc. 139; Willy Brandt,
  Begegnungen und Einsichten: Die Jahre 1960–1975 (Munich, 1978), 412.
9 Trend to Heath, May 2, 1973, PREM 15/1541; note FCO, "US Policy towards Europe," May 9,
  1973, FCO 82/284.
10 Edward Heath, *The Course of My Life: My Autobiography* (London, 1998), 493.

relationship" with the United States for the sake of a leading British role in Europe.[11]

If Heath initially refused to take the lead in formulating a unified European response to Kissinger's proposal, it was for fear of a negative turn in Anglo-French relations, the cornerstone of his foreign policy concept. It had taken him too long to convince Pompidou that Britain was no longer a U.S. Trojan horse in the EC to risk the restored Anglo-French entente over the Year of Europe. When Kissinger visited Britain on May 10, 1973, Whitehall thus made some vague procedural suggestions about Kissinger's initiative but remained noncommittal about the content of any possible declaration.[12]

FRENCH FEARS AND BRITISH OVERTURES

Heath, like Brandt, was aware that the key to progress lay in France, but when he suggested in Paris that Pompidou should put forward his own draft declaration, the French president "indicated dissent with a deprecating smile" and rejected a collective European response.[13] Pompidou feared that if the Europeans dealt with such a wide range of political and economic issues, the still-fragile intergovernmental EPC would succumb to the much stronger EC machinery, thus giving the European Commission a de facto role in foreign affairs – which Pompidou rejected. Further, he was convinced that Europe was not ready to define a common position toward the United States. Pompidou was more supportive of European integration than de Gaulle had been, but he was skeptical about EPC and believed that political unity could better be achieved through EMU. With monetary cooperation in disarray, Heath being the only genuine European he could spot in Britain, and West Germany increasingly leaning toward the East and pursuing its long-term goal of reunification, how could a European foreign policy be feasible? This perceived lack of European cohesion also led him to reject a meeting of the Nine with the U.S. president; in Pompidou's view, such a meeting could amount only to a "ballet of the Nine before Nixon" comparable to a meeting of Roman vassals with Caesar.[14]

---

11 Working Group on Europe, "European Political Unification: Note by the Foreign and Commonwealth Office," Oct. 26, 1971, FCO 30/842; Cabinet minutes of a meeting on "European Defence Co-Operation," Mar. 8, 1971, Cabinet Office Records (CAB) 130/517; conversation between Heath and Pompidou at Chequers, Mar. 19, 1972, PREM 15/904. See also Edward Heath, *Old World, New Horizons: Britain, the Common Market and the Atlantic Alliance* (London, 1970).

12 Conversation between Trend and Kissinger, May 10, 1973, PREM 15/1541.

13 Conversation between Heath and Pompidou, May 21, 1973, PREM 15/1541.

14 Conversation between Pompidou and Brandt in Paris, June 21, 1973, AN, President Pompidou Papers (5AG2), 106.

The French internal assessment of Kissinger's speech was devastating. The initiative was regarded as an "imperious text" aimed at subordinating Europe and challenging French leadership in the EC; at sharing burdens but not responsibility; and at reintegrating France's nuclear weapons and its détente policies into NATO.[15] Pompidou, eager to maintain the good relations he had built with the Nixon administration, had constructive discussions with Kissinger on transatlantic problems. He remained intransigent, however, about the Year of Europe even though Kissinger acknowledged Gaullist France as his principal partner in Europe and said he would leave France a free hand in organizing Europe, and even though he promised to intensify the secret dialogue on nuclear cooperation with France that had been initiated in 1971. Pompidou also warned against reopening the discussion on alliance reform. Given the authoritarian regimes in Greece and Portugal, talk about common NATO values was hypocritical, and some member states, such as the Netherlands and Denmark, would continue to neglect their defense obligations regardless of what NATO might decide. At the Reykjavik summit in late May 1973, Pompidou rejected Nixon's warning that the United States could disengage from Europe, pointing out that Europe would then most certainly be reduced to a regional role – under Soviet influence. Pompidou also rejected a bilateral agreement on procedures, a timetable for drawing up the principles of a transatlantic declaration, and Kissinger's proposal of a confidential steering group of the four or three (without West Germany) major Atlantic powers, and conceded merely to receive Kissinger secretly for further talks in Paris.[16]

Inflexible as the French appeared at the end of May, their position developed remarkably in the two months that followed, resulting in a hesitant backing of a common European answer. When Michel Jobert, Pompidou's confidant and former general secretary, took over the Quai d'Orsay as foreign minister in April 1973, he sought to redirect French policies toward a *Europe européenne* based on Franco-British leadership, and he saw the Year of Europe as a test of the Nine's readiness to formulate genuinely European solutions.[17] Jobert was encouraged in his policy reassessment when Heath confidentially proposed on July 2 to draft two declarations, one on the alliance and one on European relations with the United States, as well as a third, internal document on Europe's distinct identity. The French

15 Jean-Bernard Raimond, Technical Councilor of the President, to Pompidou, May 3, 1973, AN 5AG2 1021.
16 Conversation between Pompidou and Nixon and Kissinger in Reykjavik, May 31, 1973, AN 5AG2 1023; conversation between Pompidou and Kissinger in Paris, May 18, 1973, AN 5AG2 1022.
17 Note MAE, June 19, 1973, AN 5AG2 1035. On Jobert, see Mary Weed, *L'image publique d'un homme secret: Michel Jobert et la Diplomatie Française* (Paris, 1988).

realized that a two-declaration approach would circumvent global negotiations and the thematic expansion of Atlantic cooperation. And British
backing for a distinct European identity independent of Washington was
almost a Gaullist dream come true.[18]

French foreign policy deliberations were decisively influenced by the
bilateral "Agreement on the Prevention of Nuclear War" that Washington
and Moscow signed on June 22, 1973. Pompidou and Jobert saw in the
agreement a potential denuclearization of European security. They were
shocked at the new superpower consultative machinery, which in their eyes
meant a blow to French-Soviet relations, allied defense, the UN Security Council, and Western Europe's autonomy. Convinced that the Year
of Europe was intended to serve what amounted to a superpower condominium, the French eventually accepted that the Nine needed to join forces
and defend their own interests.[19]

THE NINE UNITE

While Jobert continued to reassure an impatient Kissinger that Paris's stub-
bornness had more to do with the Gaullist need for public drama than
with real resistance,[20] the Nine finally began to work out a common European position within EPC in July. Bonn and London had become fed up
with Kissinger's unusual style of diplomacy and had decided to escape from
the procedural morass created by the American insistence on bilateral talks
among the four great powers. Kissinger's obsession with secrecy and clandestine consultation had caused much misapprehension and confusion in
Europe. It also contradicted the EPC information practices that the Nine
generally followed after bilateral talks with third powers and prompted other
EC members, like Italy, to seek talks with the United States, too.[21]

Support for a European counterposition increased as the Europeans came
to the conclusion that the two draft declarations on transatlantic relations
Kissinger had sent to Bonn, London, and Paris served American interests
alone. After a last round of bilateral discussions with Kissinger and Nixon
on July 12, 1973, Bonn informed Paris and London that Kissinger now
seemed willing to underwrite "virtually any definition" of the European

18 Robert Armstrong (Private Office), "Note for the record," July 3, 1973, PREM 15/1542; note
   FCO, "Meeting of Political Directors Helsinki 5/6 July: Europe/US Relations (Item 2)," July 4,
   1973, FCO 30/1736.
19 Michel Jobert, *Mémoires d'avenir* (Paris, 1974), 232.
20 Conversation between Jobert and Kissinger in Paris, June 8, 1973, AN 5AG2 1023.
21 Speaking notes for a British delegation meeting Kissinger in Washington, "President Nixon's
   message of July 26 to the Prime Minister," July 27, 1973, PREM 15/1543.

personality. The West German Foreign Ministry was thus in agreement with its British counterpart that the best way forward was to ignore the Kissinger drafts, take advantage of Washington's desperate desire for a declaration, and start work on Europe's own drafts.[22]

EUROPEAN AMBITION AND TRANSATLANTIC DISCORD

On July 23, 1973, one week after the Watergate scandal took a new turn with the discovery of the White House taping system, the Nine officially decided at an extraordinary meeting of the EC foreign ministers to work out a joint answer to the Year of Europe. The French were still reluctant. They kept rejecting the participation of the European Commission and even insisted that the EPC meeting take place in Copenhagen, the capital of the acting Danish presidency, rather than in Brussels, where the same ministers were to hold their EC Council meeting in the afternoon.

But Jobert finally helped find a compromise by giving priority to the identity paper proposed by Heath. He argued that Europe should "affirm its identity in all directions, on all issues, and for herself."[23] Work on a European-U.S. declaration and preparations for Nixon's visit should be postponed until the end of 1974, he argued, when the enlarged European entity would be more stable (and France would be presiding over the EC). According to Jobert, the Nixon administration, seemingly worried about the changing balance between superpower détente and its alliance policies, was behaving like a "pyromaniac fireman" and should not be allowed to dictate the speed of Europe's response to Kissinger.[24]

Given, however, that the other eight EC members insisted that discussions on the relations of the Nine with Washington should progress simultaneously, Jobert agreed that the Nine in EPC should also prepare a report on potential elements of a "constructive dialog" for the ministerial meeting in September 1973. There were also agreements to exchange information on bilateral dealings with the United States, to coordinate the position of the Eight (the Nine excluding Ireland) on a declaration on the alliance, and, *ad referendum*, to meet Nixon jointly during his visit in a form to be determined.[25]

---

22 Conversation between Douglas-Home and Guido Brunner, head of the West German Planning Staff, July 18, 1973, FCO 30/1737. On the Scheel talks in Washington and the outline of a West German draft declaration, see *AAPD* 1973, no. 222.
23 Circular by de Courcel, July 24, 1973, MAE Europe Généralités 3810.
24 Jobert quoted in circular AA, July 23, 1973, *AAPD* 1973, no. 229.
25 Ibid.; circulars (no. 1528–31) by Douglas-Home, July 24, 1973, PREM 15/1543.

The Americans reacted harshly to these decisions. Nixon, in a letter to Brandt, expressed "in all candor" his surprise at the approach of the Nine, who now appeared unwilling to discuss the Year of Europe with the United States until September. He flatly refused to travel to Europe unless the heads of government were willing to sign a substantial Atlantic declaration. After Brandt replied that Washington should not feel excluded when the Nine moved toward the long-term U.S. goal of having Europe speak with one voice, the president wrote in a second letter that it was "inconceivable that our allies will no longer be engaged in a joint Atlantic process but in a negotiation between the United States, on the one hand, and the EC Nine on the other."[26] The British also received a strongly worded letter, and during a meeting with British Cabinet Secretary Burke Trend, an emotional Kissinger made clear that British-American relations had reached a low point. Kissinger warned that Europe would have to accept "very painful" consequences if an "adversary relationship" were to develop between it and the United States. He made it clear that he had never "intended to use this initiative to build Europe" and was critical of the Nine's procedure of showing their drafts to him only after these had been discussed "with Norway [*sic*], Luxembourg and even Ireland" and of then sending the Nine's acting president, the Danish foreign minister, whose name he did not even know, as a "messenger boy" without authority to negotiate. The Year of Europe, he said, was over, and it was now up to the Europeans to convince the United States that they could come up with something more than a "statement of banalities."[27]

ANGLO–FRENCH LEADERSHIP, WEST GERMAN UNEASE

Although the West German leaders had become frustrated with Kissinger, who had famously asked whom he should call to talk to Europe, but now seemed to oppose Europe's move toward unity, they took the U.S. threat seriously. The Foreign Ministry urged its European partners that a substantial European–U.S. communiqué be signed during Nixon's visit that would take into account U.S. needs and would mark the beginning of what would become an institutionalized Atlantic dialogue. If failure of the Nine to deliver such a communiqué led to U.S. troop reductions in West Germany, Bonn warned, the West German public might well demand that

---

26 Letters from Nixon to Brandt, July 30 and Aug. 11, 1973; letter from Brandt to Nixon, Aug. 4, 1973, AdsD, Egon Bahr Papers (EB), 332. For the letters of Brandt and Scheel to Nixon and Kissinger informing them about the EPC meeting, see *AAPD* 1973, nos. 232 and 230.
27 Conversation between Trend and Kissinger in Washington, July 30, 1973, FCO 82/311.

the country's security be ensured through a bilateral arrangement with the East rather than through deeper integration in the West.[28]

The Heath government, too, was now eager to quickly present the United States with a comprehensive European proposal and began to lobby the Nine at all levels. But London was unimpressed by Kissinger's threats and urged its partners to stand together and not allow Washington to play the Europeans off against one another. The FCO confidentially approached the French in August with draft papers on a European–U.S. declaration and the European identity. The content of these papers caused surprise in Paris because the British had obviously taken French reservations into account. The declaration was written in constructive but vague language. It reaffirmed what had already been agreed on in earlier communiqués without breaking new ground. While it requested that the United States recognize Europe's political role in the world, it offered no substantive concessions to any U.S. demands. The French thought the identity paper also "very well drafted," particularly because it insisted that the Europeans define their own goals rather than seek to placate the United States.[29]

EUROPE BECOMES A DIPLOMATIC ACTOR

When a British and a West German top diplomat went to Paris for parallel but separate talks with Jobert on the Nine's next steps on August 29, 1973, the French finally took the reigns into their own hands. Jobert, who had privately discussed how to proceed with his old friend Heath a few days earlier while on vacation in England, now indicated to FCO diplomat Thomas Brimelow that France would support the British draft in EPC, provided that Douglas-Home did not let it be "massacred" – a condition Whitehall accepted.[30] Meanwhile, the French also succeeded in breaking West German resistance to the British drafts, which Bonn could hardly believe had been written by the FCO on account of their seemingly Gaullist content. West German State Secretary Paul Frank was bombarded with wild accusations that the Federal Republic, by behaving like an American satellite, was blocking the unification of Europe and that it had betrayed France, which had loyally supported Ostpolitik only to see Bonn relapse

---

28 U.K. embassy Bonn (Nicholas Henderson) to FCO, Aug. 3, 1973, on a conversation with Frank, PREM 15/1544; FRG embassy Paris (Horst Blomeyer-Bartenstein) to Frank, Aug. 30, 1973, *AAPD* 1973, doc. 265.
29 Political Director François Puaux to Jobert, "Entretien avec M. Ewart-Biggs – Relations Europe – États-Unis," Aug. 9, 1973, MAE Europe Généralités 3810.
30 Conversation between Heath and Jobert at Knoll Farm, Aldington, Ashford, Aug. 26, 1973; conversation between Brimelow and Jobert, Aug. 29, 1973, both PREM 15/1546.

to the *Westpolitik* of Ludwig Erhard. So great was French pressure that Frank suggested to his government that West Germany no longer expose itself to the controversies over European–U.S. relations, but let the French and British have their way and simply inform its European partners and Kissinger that it would have preferred a more substantial declaration.[31]

Internal EPC preparations now went smoothly. When the ministerial meeting finally took place on September 10, 1973, it was an overwhelming success. The Nine agreed on ten subjects to be discussed with Nixon. In particular, they approved the part of the declaration that dealt with foreign policy matters and proposed a new European-American bilateralism. They also established a procedure for the European Commission to participate in those parts of the declaration that dealt with issues that were within the competence of the Community, and they proposed that negotiations with the United States take place in ad hoc meetings between the political directors of the Nine and their U.S. counterpart. Finally, they agreed to accelerate work on a European identity. Douglas-Home talked of a turning point in EC history and the beginning of a "new diplomacy." Jobert began to hope that 1973 could still become the Year of Europe, though in a different way than Kissinger had intended. Even the West Germans were relieved that the Europeans were at least able to present Kissinger with a jointly written document.[32]

Kissinger, now secretary of state, received the European draft a few days later. Unsurprisingly, he expressed his disappointment at the "feeble" document that, in his eyes, would amount to little more than a U.S. endorsement of what the Europeans had decided at their summit in 1972. But he seemed less bitter than the Europeans had feared. He agreed to negotiate on the document and implicitly approved the two-declaration approach. To the relief of the Federal Republic in particular, Kissinger even publicly called this attempt by Europe to speak with one voice on a transatlantic matter "an event of the greatest significance" that might come to be seen as one of the decisive moments of the postwar period.[33]

The key to this moderate response was what Jobert called his "idea of maneuver" ("idée de manoeuvre"). The French speculated that Kissinger would tolerate a disadvantageous declaration with the Nine if the United States were compensated by a substantial declaration of the Fifteen in

---

31 Frank, "Meine Gespräche in Paris am 29. August 1973," Aug. 31, 1973, *AAPD* 1973, doc. 267.

32 Douglas-Home (from Copenhagen) to FCO, Sept. 11, 1973, FCO 30/1740; Michel Jobert, *L'autre regard* (Paris: Grasset, 1976), 329–30; circular AA, Sept. 12, 1973, *AAPD* 1973, doc. 280.

33 FRG embassy Washington (von Staden), "Gespräch zwischen dem Herrn Bundeskanzler und Aussenminister Kissinger am 26.9. von 17.30–18.10 Uhr," Sept. 26, 1973, *AAPD* 1973, doc. 297; Kissinger, *Upheaval*, 703–4.

NATO. Accordingly, in early September, Jobert asked François de Rose, the French permanent representative at NATO, to secretly prepare a draft on transatlantic security that would take into account U.S. concerns. The resulting French text included references to issues that were important to Paris, such as the specificity of European defense, the relevance of nuclear deterrence, and the role of British and French nuclear forces. But in emphasizing the indivisibility of allied security and in identifying common defense as a precondition of détente, the French text included remarkable concessions to Washington.[34] Kissinger was obviously surprised and later referred to the document as the "most constructive gesture of any European minister in the Atlantic dialogue." While he criticized the fact that the document failed to identify a political role for NATO, he accepted the French draft as a basis for negotiations.[35] After months of French and U.S. intransigence toward British, West German, Turkish, Canadian, and Dutch draft proposals, NATO, too, was able to launch substantial negotiations on the Year of Europe by early October.

COMPETING MODELS OF WESTERN UNITY

Jobert's plan to offer a substantial transatlantic declaration in exchange for U.S. recognition of an independent political role for the EC might have succeeded had it not been for the Arab–Israeli October War of 1973. In the wake of that conflict, the deepest rift since the Suez crisis opened within the Western alliance and the polarization between Europe and the United States increased.

The October War accentuated the transatlantic conflict because all of the controversial issues of the Year of Europe that had hitherto been negotiated on only an abstract level came into the realm of practical politics. The Arab–Israeli conflict revealed the stark differences in European and U.S. perceptions and interests, the mutual lack of consultation and trust, and the desire of the Nine to make their own voice heard in international politics. The Europeans had long warned the Nixon administration in vain about the danger of war in the Middle East, and they now partly blamed U.S. indifference for the severe economic crisis they faced as a result of the "oil weapon" – the production cutbacks, embargo measures, and massive price increases – that Arab governments used to force a pro-Arab peace settlement.

---

34 De Rose, "Origine et mise au point du Papier Français de déclaration sur les relations Atlantiques," handwritten note (twenty-five pages), undated, autumn 1973, in the author's possession; Jobert, *regard*, 333; for the draft of Oct. 3, 1973, see FCO 41/1189.
35 Kissinger, *Upheaval*, 705.

The Nine viewed the conflict much less in terms of East-West relations than did the United States. Therefore, they rejected collective alliance measures to protest against Soviet military supplies being sent to the Arabs. Some of them also denied the U.S. permission to ship Israel supplies from their territory. Furthermore, the Nine were shocked to learn that Washington, without informing them, had put its troops on worldwide alert. In their declaration on peace in the Middle East (November 6, 1973), the Western Europeans for the first time publicly formulated an independent position on a foreign policy issue and defended positions that the United States saw as contrary to its own objectives and interests. Kissinger and Nixon reacted with irritation, public threats, and a new series of sharply worded letters. A particularly ugly row took place between the Heath government and the Nixon administration, the latter accusing the former of "decayed Gaullism" and of appeasing the French in their attempt to build Europe on an anti-American basis.[36]

The negotiations on the two declarations could not progress in such a heated atmosphere. Debates on the NATO declaration were temporarily suspended at the insistence of the French, and the negotiations between the Nine and U.S. representatives Walter Stoessel and Helmut Sonnenfeldt on the European-American declaration stagnated. Washington rejected a preamble to the declaration that posited the Europeans "on the one hand" and the United States "on the other hand," and it demanded, among other things, that the declaration include mention of the concepts of interdependence, partnership, and advance consultation.[37] Of the Nine, the French were evidently the most opposed to such Atlanticist jargon. But to France's surprise, all of the Nine were prepared to defend their original position. They also stressed the priority of European unity and rejected any substantial concessions to U.S. demands. The result was much transatlantic to-and-fro over commas and wordings. A new clash also arose over how to deal with Japan and Canada. The Nine offered bilateral declarations with each, whereas Kissinger proposed one common Atlantic declaration for all.[38] As both sides realized, the Year of Europe was gradually turning into

---

36 "Declaration on Middle East," Nov. 6, 1973, reproduced in Christopher Hill and Karen E. Smith, eds., *European Foreign Policy: Key Documents* (London, 2000), 300–1; Ministry of Defence, "Note for the record: Discussion between the Defence Secretary and the U.S. Secretary of Defense (Mr. Schlesinger) Held over Luncheon at HM Ambassador's House in The Hague on Wednesday, November 7, 1973," Nov. 9, 1973, FCO 41/1154; despatch by the UK ambassador to Washington, Lord Cromer, "The Middle East and US/UK Relations," Jan. 9, 1974, FCO 82/304.

37 For the three negotiation rounds between the Nine and the United States on Sept. 29, Oct. 18, and Nov. 14, 1973, see the circulars by Puaux of Oct. 1 and 20, and Nov. 15, 1973, MAE États-Unis 1137.

38 Note AA, "Einbeziehung Japans in Grundsatzerklärung EG-US," Nov. 29, 1973, AA B21/751.

a far-reaching struggle over competing models of how to reorganize the West.

ADVANCING "L'EUROPE EUROPÉENNE"

The French, appalled that Europe had been "treated like a 'non-person' and humiliated in its inexistence" during the October War,[39] were now firmly in the lead in politically organizing the Nine. Pompidou, persuaded by Jobert to prioritize the development of political cooperation, proposed to his eight counterparts on October 31, 1973, that the European heads of state or government become involved in EPC and have regular, intimate summits on foreign policy issues. Pompidou suggested that the first such summit be held in Copenhagen at the end of the year to deal with the Middle East. At the same time, Jobert argued publicly for European defense cooperation.[40]

Paris also made sure that the work of the Nine on the European identity was accelerated. The resulting paper was a comprehensive manifesto outlining Europe's ambition to play an active role in world affairs. Naturally, it was the product of a compromise. In their draft, the British had wanted to define the European identity in comparison to the United States only; they also wanted to keep the document confidential and wanted to add other papers on the Soviet Union, China, and other countries at later stages. The French draft did not refer to the process of integration at all but more generally identified the constitutive elements of a European identity and sketched the principles of relations with individual third parties. There was also an Irish draft, which primarily assessed the progress of EC institutions.[41]

The final version, issued as the Declaration on European Identity at the Copenhagen summit of the Nine on December 14, 1973, was a fusion of all three drafts, inspired mainly by the French approach. After it had been decided to make the paper public and work out confidential country annexes later, the Federal Republic argued for a general description of the distinct European personality rather than a narrow focus on European-U.S. relations. Thus, the first part of the declaration, "The Unity of the Nine Member Countries of the Community," broadly identified the defining features of the European identity; it also referred to existing institutions

---

39 Jobert addressing the Assemblé Nationale on Nov. 12, 1973, quoted in Jobert, *regard*, 344.
40 For Pompidou's letter to the Eight, see MAE Europe Généralités 3789. For Jobert's speech of Nov. 21, 1973, see Assembly of Western European Union, Proceedings, 19th Ordinary Session, Second Part, IV (Nov. 1973), 124–8.
41 The British draft papers can be found in FCO 30/1738 and PREM 15/1544. For versions of the French paper, see AN 5AG2 1035 and FCO 30/1750.

and policies as an essential part of the identity and defined the Nine as a "community of values" that would be open "to other European nations who share the same ideals and objectives." It then argued that "international developments and the growing concentration of power and responsibility in the hands of a very small number of great powers mean that Europe must unite and speak increasingly with one voice if it wants to make itself heard and play its proper rôle in the world." It also included a vague compromise on European defense.[42]

The second part, "European Identity in Relation to the World," opened at West Germany's insistence with the assurance that European unification was not inspired by a desire for power but served as an "element of equilibrium" and a "basis for cooperation." It then listed the objectives of political cooperation and outlined the principles of relations to individual third countries or country groups, including the United States. The declaration ended with a reminder about the dynamic nature of the European construction and with the indication that the Nine would progressively define their identity in comparison to third parties more closely, with a view to the "framing of a genuinely European foreign policy."[43]

U.S. COUNTERPROPOSALS

The fact that the year 1973 ended with a declaration on the identity of the Nine rather than with an Atlantic charter must have appeared provocative to the Nixon administration. Kissinger, in a heart-to-heart discussion with the British in late November, called the French assumption that the United States would not "retaliate" against such designs "the worst decision since the Greek city states confronted Alexander." Too serious, he said, was the breakdown of U.S.-British-German leadership in NATO, too negative the dissolution of the "special relationship," too unreliable the Brandt government, on whose conversations with Moscow the United States had "hair-raising intelligence."[44]

Kissinger put forward his counterproposals in December 1973. During his first appearance at the NATO ministerial meeting in Brussels, he made clear in three frank exchanges with European foreign ministers that, in view of the October War experience, Washington would now insist on new forms of transatlantic consultation. At the traditional Quadripartite Dinner on the

---

42 The declaration is reproduced in Hill and Smith, *European Foreign Policy*, 93–7.
43 Ibid.
44 U.K. embassy Washington (Cromer) to FCO, Nov. 24, 1973, on a conversation with Kissinger, FCO 82/309.

eve of the NATO meeting, Kissinger argued that he had lost interest in the European–U.S. declaration but wanted to integrate consultation procedures between the United States and the Nine into the existing NATO machinery. After an unusually sharp dispute with Jobert during the actual NATO meeting, he specified that the political directors of the allies should subsequently meet at regular intervals in the NATO Council to discuss political issues inside and outside the alliance area. Finally, during an extraordinary meeting with the Nine, Kissinger said that the European–U.S. declaration should, at least, be made shorter and more political, and he insisted that a procedure be worked out to give the United States a say in the formative period of European decision making. "[W]e had expected fireworks," the British noted on Douglas-Home's return from Brussels, adding that these "duly took place."[45] Washington, in fact, confronted the Europeans with a triple challenge: regarding the relevance of EPC, regarding the view held by several governments that NATO should not expand its functions into the political and economic realm, and regarding the assumption that NATO should not deal with out-of-area issues.

Kissinger raised the stakes further, when, in his address to the Pilgrims Society of London on December 12, 1973, he publicly argued that "Europe's unity must not be at the expense of Atlantic community." He offered the Nine a "special relationship," proposed new Atlantic cooperation in the field of energy, and warned that Europe and the United States had only two choices left: "creativity together or irrelevance apart."[46] Neither the substance nor the timing of his speech was accidental. The ongoing oil crisis was the single most important issue for all industrial democracies at the end of 1973, and a common energy policy and the question of how to deal with the oil-producing Arab countries was the most pressing item on the agenda of the summit of the Nine in Copenhagen that was to take place only two days later.

STALEMATE AT THE COPENHAGEN SUMMIT

If the Eight were increasingly confronted with polarizing French and U.S. views about Atlantic cooperation, the European summit in Copenhagen failed to set a course for Europe's relations with the United States. Preoccupied with short-term economic crisis management, the Nine found

---

45 FCO brief for Douglas-Home, "Cabinet: NATO Ministerial Meeting," Dec. 12, 1973, FCO 41/1143. On the meetings in Brussels, see the telegrams of the West German delegation, *AAPD* 1973, doc. 410, 413, 414.
46 The speech is reproduced in Mally, *New Europe*, 39–46.

little time for pursuing the planned strategic debate on EPC. They did stress their determination to pursue their own policies by confirming their distinct approach to the Middle East, contrary to U.S. wishes. They also received a delegation of Arab ministers and indicated their wish for dialogue with the oil-producing countries. But they were unable to agree on how to deal with the energy crisis. Nor could they establish a European energy policy or come up with a joint answer to Kissinger's proposals. Most Europeans were worried that the suggested Atlantic energy action group might bring about confrontation with the oil-producing countries. But while France was hostile to the idea of Atlantic energy cooperation in principle, most of its partners did not want to dismiss the proposal out of hand.[47]

The debates among the Nine revealed frictions in the common front that did not augur well for European unity. The Heath government – faced with a massive economic crisis and domestic protests, and under attack for its pro-European policies – could no longer afford to emphasize EC solidarity at all costs, and it was growing tired of French rigidity in defending a distinct European personality. France, by seeking more than any other country to secure its energy supplies in bilateral deals with Arab countries, also violated the principle of economic solidarity. On the political level, France grew suspicious of Bonn and London giving in to institutionalizing the Atlantic dialogue. The West Germans became increasingly unwilling to pump money into the Common Market without evidence of further advancement of European integration.[48] As it would soon turn out, the political identity of the Nine was not strong enough to weather the double challenge of eroding economic solidarity and transatlantic confrontation.

1974: EUROPEAN DISINTEGRATION

In his memoirs, Kissinger abruptly states that the Year of Europe was "over" at the end of 1973.[49] However, as far as the substance of his initiative is concerned, the first six months of 1974 saw both the peak of confrontation between Europe and the United States and the working out of compromises. While the negotiations on the transatlantic declaration were resumed and the Nine began to revise their draft on European-U.S. relations, Atlantic

---

47 Three circulars by Puaux of Dec. 18, 1973, MAE Europe Généralités 3789.
48 Paper FCO Planning Staff, "British Foreign Policy: The Scope for Chance," Feb. 12, 1974, FCO 30/2457; U.K. embassy Paris (Edward Tomkins) to Brimelow, "Transatlantic Relations," Nov. 30, 1973, FCO 82/289; West German Parliamentary State Secretary Hans Apel in an oral history interview (INT639) on Aug. 17, 1998, "Voices on Europe," European University Institute, Florence, http://www.arc.iue.it/oh/OralHistory.html.
49 Kissinger, *Upheaval*, 729.

consultation was at the forefront of the debate. It was relatively easy for the Nine to agree to transform the U.S. proposal for periodic NATO consultations among the political directors into occasional meetings that dealt with only a specific issue, that were summoned by consensus, and that were attended by officials of levels to be individually decided by national governments.[50] The real challenge was the answer to the U.S. offer of energy cooperation, which had become a symbol for much that the Year of Europe was about.

Faced with European ambivalence toward his energy proposals, Kissinger decided to bring matters to a head by summoning a conference of consumer nations to define common energy policies and principles; West German Federal Minister of Finance Helmut Schmidt had confidentially suggested the idea to him in November 1973. This move at first seemed to consolidate the European front. Despite the warning in Nixon's invitation letter that the Europeans must now decide whether Europe and the United States would work together or go their separate ways, the foreign ministers of the Nine on February 5, 1974, formulated a common position for the conference that was inspired by France: they would accept no permanent consumer organization but would assign follow-up work to existing institutions. Skeptical about Kissinger's confrontational strategy to meet the Arab challenge, they would not attempt to find solutions to energy problems without the producer nations, and they would preserve their right to hold their own dialogue and negotiations with the Arab countries.[51]

This consensus was fragile, however, and emerged only after Jobert had blackmailed his colleagues by giving the choice of either supporting the French position or attending the Washington conference without France. Jobert had effectively asked the Eight to choose between *l'Europe européenne* and Atlantic cooperation. The choice for the Eight became even more difficult when the United States, in confidential bilateral preparatory talks, asked for support for the Atlantic proposal and warned of "political consequences" in the event of noncompliance.[52] Unsurprisingly, European unity disintegrated during the Washington conference of February 11–13, 1974. All the EC member states except France ended up backing the U.S. proposals and no longer resisted an institutionalized follow-up in energy cooperation. Helmut Schmidt, as West Germany's representative, went farthest in his

---

50 Gabriel Robin, Technical Councillor of the President, to Pompidou, Feb. 11, 1974, AN 5AG2 1054.

51 Jobert, *Mémoires*, 286; letter from Nixon to Brandt, Jan. 9, 1974, WBA BK 60.

52 Kissinger, *Upheaval*, 906; Jobert, *L'antre regard*, 367–73; conversation between Scheel and Kissinger in Washington, Feb. 10, 1974, *AAPD* 1974, no 42.

support of Kissinger and left no doubt that, if forced to choose between Europe and the United States, he would opt for the latter. What followed was an ugly dispute between Jobert and Schmidt and endless intra-European consultations. The result was a deep split of the Nine, with France refusing to sign most of the operational parts of the final communiqué, which envisioned the eventual creation of an international energy agency.[53]

A FINAL CLASH: THE EURO-ARAB DIALOGUE AND THE ISSUE OF CONSULTATION

The Washington conference was a blow to European political aspirations, but the blow was not fatal. To the surprise of the Nixon administration, the Nine in their EPC reunion in Brussels on March 4, 1974, agreed to initiate a "Euro-Arab dialogue" that might culminate in a joint meeting of European and Arab foreign ministers. They did so despite previous U.S. warnings that such a meeting might sabotage Kissinger's peace efforts in the Middle East and result in a serious crisis in the alliance. The decision in favor of a European policy of engagement was made on the basis of a report by Scheel that Kissinger had indicated in a conversation only hours before the EPC meeting that he would no longer obstruct the initiative. Yet the West Germans were obviously mistaken. Kissinger, who happened to be in Brussels for a visit to NATO on the same day, reacted very harshly when Scheel briefed him on the decision, and he blamed the Europeans publicly for failing to consult the United States on an initiative that he regarded as a threat to U.S. interests.[54]

The Nine were puzzled. They regarded the accusation that their consultations had been insufficient as unfounded – the Belgian political director, Étienne Davignon, even called it the "act of intellectual dishonesty of the century."[55] But they soon became aware that Kissinger's anger was directed less toward the dialogue than toward the continuing procedural exclusion of the United States from European political decision making. Nixon complained in two chilly letters to Brandt about the "competitive position"

---

53 For the reports of the West German delegation of Feb. 12–13, 1974, and the speech of Schmidt, see Bundesarchiv Koblenz, Carl Carstens Papers (N1337) 63. For the British and French accounts, see Douglas-Home (Washington) to FCO, Feb. 12, 1974, PREM 15/2179, and Jobert, *regard*, 378–82.

54 Note MAE, "Résultats de la réunion ministérielle de la coopération politique du 4 mars," Mar. 5, 1974, MAE Europe Généralités 3792. See also note AA, "Gespräch des Herrn Bundesministers mit Aussenminister Kissinger am 3. März 1974"; conversation between Brandt and Kissinger in Bonn, Mar. 4, 1974; and conversation between Scheel and Kissinger in Brussels, Mar. 4, 1974, all in *AAPD* 1974, docs. 67–9.

55 Claude Arnaud, Deputy Political Director, "Comité Politique des 18 et 19 avril," Apr. 18, 1974, MAE Europe Généralités 3811; Kissinger, *Upheaval*, 925–34.

of Europe toward Washington in the Middle East and demanded "more organic consultative arrangements." He informed the chancellor that he would suspend work on the two declarations until such arrangements had been found and would postpone his trip to Europe to sign them. In a speech in Chicago, he went even further when he questioned the U.S. security guarantee to Europe, arguing that "the Europeans cannot have it both ways: They cannot have the United States' participation and cooperation on the security front and then proceed to have confrontation and even hostility on the economic and political front."[56]

The American threats of withdrawal were clearly directed at the West Germans, who had the least room to maneuver on account of their security dependence. But it was Franco-American relations that now dropped to a new low point, marked by anti-American and anti-French campaigns in the respective media and frustration at the political level. Did Kissinger want "partners or servants" in Europe, Jobert asked James Reston in an interview with the *New York Times* and thanked the journalist for having visited a "provincial politician."[57] Why the systematic French opposition to U.S. policies, if the Nixon administration sought to make Paris its privileged partner and to group Europe around France? Kissinger replied in a conversation with the French ambassador in Washington. Why do they spread fear of a superpower condominium? Why this hostility?[58]

LEADERSHIP CHANGE AND ATLANTIC SOLUTIONS

We can only speculate about how the Year of Europe might have ended if Heath, Pompidou, and Brandt had not left office in spring 1974. What is clear is that when the new governments of Harold Wilson, Valéry Giscard d'Estaing, and Helmut Schmidt came into power, the U.S. demands were quickly met, and designs for a more distinct political identity for Europe were shelved.

The most important change of government, in terms of its effect on Europe's political aspirations, took place in Britain in March 1974. The incoming Labour government declared itself much more Atlanticist in its outlook than Heath. It was critical of the Common Market, demanded

---

56 Letter from Nixon to Brandt, Mar. 6, 1974, reproduced in circular by de Courcel, Mar. 14, 1974, MAE Etats-Unis 1138; letter from Nixon to Brandt, Mar. 15, 1974, AdsD EB 440. On the Chicago speech, see FRG embassy Washington (von Staden) to Scheel, Mar. 17, 1974, *AAPD* 1974, doc. 97.

57 "A Visit with Jobert," *New York Times*, Mar. 10, 1974.

58 French embassy Washington (Kosciuzko-Morizet) to MAE, Mar. 22, 1974, on a conversation with Kissinger, AN 5AG2 117.

a renegotiation of Britain's EC entry terms, and rejected EMU and the vision of a European Union.[59] The new Foreign Secretary James Callaghan pointedly informed his new colleagues that he was "sick and tired of the word 'European Identity,'"[60] that he would no longer accept the adversarial treatment of Washington by the Nine, that he would consult with Kissinger on anything at any time, and that he would block the French-inspired European-Arab dialogue until a satisfactory formula of consultation with the United States had been found.[61]

Jobert's resistance to consultations between the Nine and Washington in the process of European decision making weakened in the course of the spring. Pompidou's death on April 2 and the prospect of a presidential election was one factor. A renewed Anglo-American front opposing the notion of a Gaullist Europe also served to diminish French interest in the EPC. The search for a consultative procedure resulted in the Gymnich formula, a gentlemen's agreement made between the EPC foreign ministers during an informal meeting at Schloss Gymnich, near Bonn, on April 20–21, 1974. Without creating a formal procedure, the Nine agreed that consultations with the United States would take place via the presidency on a pragmatic case-by-case basis at the request of any member and by consensus of all.[62]

As a practical arrangement, the formula was stillborn, because Labour's comprehensive bilateralism with the United States undermined the role of the EPC presidency in U.S.-European consultations right from the beginning.[63] On the conceptual level, however, the Gymnich formula, unspectacular as it appears, was of great significance. As Scheel observed, the formula implied that failure of the Nine to reach consensus on consulting with the United States on any particular issue would result in the removal of this issue from the EPC agenda.[64] Given that the question of consultation would come up mainly in cases where the United States potentially disagreed with European views, and given the likelihood that at least

---

59 Cabinet minutes of a meeting of the "Ministerial Committee on European Community Strategy," Mar. 13, 1974, FCO 30/2388; "Statement by the Secretary of State for Foreign and Commonwealth Affairs in the Council of Ministers of the European Communities in Luxembourg on April 1, 1974," FCO 30/2101.

60 Conversation between Scheel and Callaghan in Bonn, Mar. 21, 1974, *AAPD* 1974, doc. 100.

61 Note MAE, "Réunion ministérielle de la coopération politique," Apr. 1, 1974, MAE Europe Généralités 3792.

62 The Gymnich formula was formally agreed at the EPC ministerial meeting in Bonn on June 10, 1974. See circular AA, June 12, 1974, *AAPD* 1974, doc. 168.

63 Note FCO, "Political Cooperation: The Role of the Presidency in Washington," May 28, 1974, FCO 82/425; "A Stitch in Time?" *Economist*, June 29, 1974.

64 Conversation between Scheel and Callaghan in Bonn, Mar. 21, 1974, *AAPD* 1974, doc. 100.

one EC member in such cases would insist on U.S. involvement in shaping the decision, it was likely that the Nine would be able to pursue common polices only on issues on which they, by and large, agreed with Washington anyway. But, as the French in particular argued,[65] what then was the point of a distinct European foreign policy?

The Gymnich formula could hardly conceal the subordination of European interests to U.S. leadership. The shelving of Europe's political ambitions also became manifest when the Nine complied with Kissinger's request not to deal with the Arab-Israeli conflict and the oil crisis in the Euro-Arab dialogue, and to focus instead on an economic-technical role for Europe in the Middle East.[66] Finally, there was the decision to no longer attempt to formulate a common European policy vis-à-vis the United States and to drop the European-U.S. declaration, which more than anything else symbolized the quasi paralysis of EPC by spring 1974. The Nine had originally agreed at Gymnich that work on both declarations should be completed and that some key passages of the transatlantic draft should be borrowed for a special communiqué for the upcoming twenty-fifth anniversary celebrations of NATO in Ottawa. But in May 1974, the Wilson government unexpectedly presented a complete, revised transatlantic declaration, which it had secretly worked out with Kissinger, and made the case for ending the whole process in Ottawa with this one Atlantic paper.[67] Schmidt, once he had replaced Brandt as chancellor following the Guillaume spy affair, accepted the proposal, as did Giscard after his electoral victory over the Gaullists. The priority of both new leaders was to meet the challenge of economic crisis and mounting inflation, which from their perspective was not feasible without transatlantic cooperation.

The resulting Ottawa Declaration, which the NATO foreign ministers approved on June 19, 1974, and the heads of government signed in Brussels a week later, in some ways represented what Kissinger had proposed more than a year earlier. It was a single declaration that reaffirmed the indivisibility of allied defense, referred to the U.S. engagement in Europe as "indispensable," confirmed the resolution to "strengthen the practice of frank and timely consultations," and subordinated economic differences to the "essential" security relationship. Still, the declaration could not live up

65 Puaux to Jobert, Mar. 14, 1974, AN 582AP 43.
66 Note AA, "Ergebnisprotokoll über das Gespräch des Herrn Bundesministers Genscher mit Aussenminister Dr. Kissinger am 11. Juni 1974 in Bad Reichenhall," June 14, 1974, *AAPD* 1974, doc. 171; Callaghan (Ottawa) to FCO, no. 425, June 19, 1974, FCO 41/1418.
67 FCO steering brief, "Prime Minister's Visit to Brussels: 25/26 June," undated, PREM 16/11; despatch by the UK permanent representative to NATO, Edward Peck, "Atlantic Relations," July 11, 1974, FCO 82/426.

to the expectations that both the United States and the Nine had professed with the Year of Europe. Nor did it provide the alliance with the morale boost and revised defense policy that Kissinger had hoped for. Further, it did not refer to any specific political role for EC countries in international affairs. While it did contain some specific European security concerns and recognized the deterrent value of French and British nuclear forces, there was hardly a trace left of the political vision Europe had pursued in the negotiations. The Ottawa Declaration was as much a symbol of the Nine's relapse into political fragmentation as it was an unspectacular acknowledgment of the need to close ranks at the transatlantic level.[68]

CONCLUSION: OF PHILOSOPHERS AND PRINCES

Various factors account for the fact that the Nine's high political aspirations collapsed again in 1974. Along with the triple change of leadership, structural changes also played an important role. European economies were hit much harder by the oil crisis than was the U.S. economy. That turn of events increased Europe's dependence on the United States once again and meant that the severe economic crisis that unfolded in 1973–74 required transatlantic solutions. Also, whereas the United States had been preoccupied with Vietnam and the restructuring of its relations with Moscow and China in the early 1970s, it became more willing to exert leadership in the West again once superpower détente was on the wane in 1974. However, as far as Jobert, Heath, and Brandt were concerned, the most important factor in Europe's failure to create a political identity was the lack of U.S. benevolence toward and support for EPC.

Jobert, Heath, and Brandt all complained that Kissinger may have been familiar with the balance-of-power Europe of the nineteenth century but that he had little idea of how the EC worked or of how complex and bureaucratic an endeavor it was to reach a common position in the absence of hegemonic leadership.[69] Given Kissinger's repeated threats of U.S. withdrawal from Western Europe should the Nine fail to involve Washington in their decision making, they were also convinced that Kissinger did not really favor European political unity, despite his rhetoric, and that he regarded EPC as a threat to U.S. interests. In his memoirs, Kissinger calls such an interpretation "breathtakingly cynical," but Heath and Jobert would have agreed with Brandt's assessment that the secretary of state saw the Europeans as

---

68 The text of the declaration can be found at http://www.nato.int/docu/basictxt/b740619a.htm.
69 Douglas-Home to Heath, "The Year of Europe," Oct. 17, 1973, FCO 30/1743; Willy Brandt, *Erinnerungen: mit den 'Notizen zum Fall G'*, (Berlin, 1994), 190; Jobert, *Mémoires*, 191–3.

mere pawns in the great chess game between the superpowers. Rather than appreciate their unity as a stabilizing factor in world politics, Brandt maintained, Kissinger enjoyed juggling Paris, London, and Bonn and playing them off against one another.[70]

From a European point of view, Kissinger's attitude was all the more ironic, as he himself, in a scholarly analysis of transatlantic relations published in 1966, had foreseen the troublesome independence of Europe, had accused the United States of being paternalistic toward Europe and impatient of criticism, and had called for "wisdom and delicacy in handling the transition from tutelage to equality." He wrote:

In short, a united Europe is likely to insist on a specifically European view of world affairs – which is another way of saying that it will challenge American hegemony in Atlantic policy. This may well be a price worth paying for European unity; but American policy has suffered from an unwillingness to recognize that there is a price to be paid.

And further: "[S]ome autonomy in political decisions for Europe is psychologically important for the cohesion of the Alliance. Though this proposition will be granted by most American policymakers in the abstract, they tend to resist independence when it takes the form of challenging our judgments."[71] As Foreign Office officials in London noted after reading Kissinger's 1966 paper during the transatlantic crisis of 1973–74, "wisdom is difficult even when the philosophers become princes."[72]

---

70 Kissinger, *Upheaval*, 926; Brandt, *Begegnungen*, 370; Brandt, *Erinnerungen*, 190–2.
71 Henry A. Kissinger, *The Troubled Partnership: A Re-appraisal of the Atlantic Alliance* (New York, 1966), 232, 40.
72 Note FCO Planning Staff, "Too True to Be Good, or Dr Kissinger Then and Now," Oct. 31, 1973, PREM 15/1546.

10

Kissinger's Year of Europe, Britain's Year of Choice

ALASTAIR NOBLE

Henry Kissinger baptized 1973 the Year of Europe: for Britain, it was a year of choice. Already engaged in the détente process with the Soviet Union and the triangular diplomacy that followed President Richard Nixon's visit to China, and fresh from negotiating America's withdrawal from Vietnam, Kissinger sought to combat domestic isolationists and to reassure allies abroad by appealing for the creation of a new framework for the conduct of transatlantic relations – a new Atlantic Charter. This was of great significance for the British, as in January 1973 they had finally joined the European Community (EC). Indeed, Sir Alec Douglas-Home, the secretary of state for foreign and commonwealth affairs, noted later in the year that Britain "must necessarily try to get the best of both worlds: to combine our European policy with the preservation of a fruitful Anglo-American and transatlantic relationship."[1]

Precisely when the British were anxious to demonstrate their European credentials, and when the institutions of European integration were still evolving, Kissinger looked to London for a constructive and enthusiastic response to his initiative. The Nixon administration's implicit objective was indeed ambitious: Britain in its new capacity was to "deliver" Europe.

---

1 The National Archives, Kew (TNA), PREM 15/2089. This file contains a copy of the paper *The Year of Europe: The Impact of Transatlantic and Anglo-American Relations; An Analytical Account-February – July 1973*. This analytical paper on the lessons to learn from negotiations with Kissinger was drafted by the FCO's planning staff.

This study was prepared when the author was a historian with the Foreign and Commonwealth Office (FCO). The views and opinions expressed in this chapter are the author's own and do not reflect those of FCO. Particular thanks for assistance in the preparation of this chapter is owed to Dr. Keith Hamilton, senior editor of the *Year of Europe* volume in the Foreign and Commonwealth Office's official history series Documents on British Policy Overseas. I also thank my colleagues in FCO Historians, Ms. Gill Bennett (retired chief historian), Professor Patrick Salmon (chief historian), and Dr. Christopher Baxter, for their advice and comments.

Britain was after all "America's staunchest and most dependable ally," and Nixon was apparently relieved that Britain had joined the Community with Conservative Prime Minister Edward Heath at the helm. Lord Cromer, the British ambassador in Washington, accurately prophesized that the president's trust sowed the seed for disillusion in the future when Community policy, embracing British policy, contradicted American views.[2] Indeed, the Year of Europe would be characterized by transatlantic disputes, exacerbated by the outbreak of war in the Middle East on October 6, 1973. Meanwhile, France, the Community's most influential member, aimed for a "European Europe," and Paris harbored suspicions that Britain was merely Washington's willing Trojan horse.[3]

This chapter views the events of a pivotal year from a British perspective. Sources emanate from British government records included in the Foreign and Commonwealth Office (FCO) Historians pioneering electronic volume *The Year of Europe: America, Europe and the Energy Crisis, 1972–1974* (2006) as part of the series Documents on British Policy Overseas. The published documents include papers from the Prime Minister's Office, Cabinet Office, and FCO as well as material from the private papers of Douglas-Home and Sir Thomas Brimelow, the deputy and later permanent undersecretary of state at the FCO during this period.

It all started so well. The Republican administration in Washington was delighted at the surprise victory of Heath's Conservatives in the 1970 general election. Kissinger recalled that Nixon was exuberant over an open telephone line in Mexico City, particularly as he had predicted Heath's success.[4] The exuberance soon evaporated. A testy relationship developed. Kissinger later dubbed Heath "the only British leader I encountered who not only failed to cultivate the 'special relationship' with the United States but actively sought to downgrade it and to give Europe pride of place in British policy."[5] In his memoirs, published twenty-five years later, Heath lambasted the Year of Europe: "For Henry Kissinger to announce a Year of Europe without consulting any of us was rather like my standing between the lions in Trafalgar Square and announcing that we were embarking on a year to save America!"[6]

---

2 Keith Hamilton and Patrick Salmon, eds., *Documents on British Policy Overseas.* Series 3, vol. 4, *The Year of Europe: America, Europe and the Energy Crisis, 1972–1974* (hereafter *DBPO* 3:4) (London, 2006), documents 25, 29.

3 TNA, FCO 30/2456, folio 15, Annual Review: France 1973, Jan. 25, 1974.

4 Henry Kissinger, *Years of Renewal* (New York, 1999), 602.

5 Ibid., 602–3.

6 Edward Heath, *The Course of My Life: My Autobiography* (London, 1998), 493.

On October 30, 1972, ten days after the conclusion of the Paris summit of the six present and three would-be members of the EC, Heath wrote to Nixon. He stressed that the long-term relationship between the EC and the United States should be built to reflect the "real interest in maintaining the closest possible ties."[7] British officials still forecast a tough year ahead. Sir Robert Armstrong, Heath's principal private secretary, observed the prime minister's view that Europe should deal with the United States as a Community, especially on trade and monetary matters, to ensure a basis of equality. Heath dismissed French objections to the creation of administrative arrangements to discuss transatlantic problems. The Americans would, without such machinery, find it "too easy to 'divide and rule' the Community."[8]

The Community spoke with one voice on trade issues through the Common Commercial Policy. Monetary questions were a different matter, and the Nine were even further from arriving at a common position on security questions.[9] Both EU foreign ministers and the political directors in Brussels sought to resist the American tendency toward linkage and agreed that negotiations should be kept separate and in their separate institutions.[10] On January 19, Lord Cromer[11] reflected that the Americans were "understandably schizophrenic on whether they want[ed] to see Europe speaking with one voice or to conduct bilateral discussions with capitals." Kissinger would, Cromer stressed, treat relations with Europe as "one ball of wax," a "global" approach stressing the linkage between monetary, trade, and defense issues and seeking greater burden sharing in the Atlantic alliance.[12]

On January 31, Nixon announced at a White House press conference that Europe's problems would "be put on the front burner."[13] When Heath and Douglas-Home, visited Washington and Camp David at the beginning of

---

7 Sir Alec Douglas-Home Private Office Papers, memorandum from Heath to Nixon, Oct. 30, 1972.
8 *DBPO* 3:4, document 4.   9 Ibid.
10 This line had been agreed by Schumann and Scheel, respectively the French and West German foreign ministers, when they dined with Douglas-Home in Brussels on Jan. 15. They had observed the American tendency toward linkage but underlined that this should be resisted if possible. See *DBPO* 3:4, document 11. Although the EC had still to develop common procedures and positions in dealings with the United States, at their meeting on Jan. 16, the EC political directors agreed that negotiations in trade, monetary, and security areas should be kept separate and discussed in their separate institutions. See *DBPO* 3:4, document 12.
11 Lord Cromer was the career banker Rowley Baring, governor of the Bank of England from 1961 to 1966. Between 1959 and 1961, he was financial adviser, minister (economic), and head of the U.K. Treasury and supply delegation in Washington. He was ambassador from January 1971 to January 1974. Thereafter, he returned to business. He died in 1991 at the age of seventy-two.
12 *DBPO* 3:4, document 14.
13 *Public Papers of the Presidents of the United States: Richard Nixon, 1973* (Washington, D.C., 1975), 57. Following his talks with Heath in London, Kissinger had raised the expectation at a press conference on Sept. 16, 1972, that Nixon, if reelected, would launch a new initiative toward Europe, probably taking the form of a tour of European capitals. The phrase "Year of Europe" became current in White House circles from early November 1972. See TNA, PREM 15/2089.

February 1973, the president stated the stark choice on the horizon of constructive competition or bitter, hurtful economic confrontation.[14] Heath
advised that Britain would take account of U.S. views in its contribution to
the foreign relations of the Nine but emphasized that it would be bound by
the Community line.[15] Nevertheless, Nixon's comment that Britain and the
United States must "do some really hard thinking together – without necessarily telling the rest of the Alliance at any particular stage" indicated that
the administration paid little heed to Britain's new circumstances. Indeed,
Britain was already party to the negotiation of a U.S.-Soviet agreement on
the prevention of nuclear war, eventually signed in Washington on June 22,
1973.

This Soviet initiative was revealed by Kissinger to Sir Burke Trend, the
cabinet secretary, in July 1972. Britain was uneasy about proposals that at a
stroke removed the main nuclear threat to Moscow, raised the potential for
Soviet actions against China, threatened to weaken NATO, and created a
difficult political climate for Britain to further develop its own deterrent.
Sir Thomas Brimelow was asked by Kissinger to help draft a revised text.
Knowledge of what became known in London as "Operation Hullabaloo"
was restricted to a small coterie of officials within the White House and
in Whitehall. Cromer was "struck by the astonishing anomaly of the most
powerful nation in the world invoking the aid of a foreign government
to do its drafting for it, while totally excluding its own Ministry for Foreign Affairs." Brimelow effectively became Kissinger's desk officer but his
drafting role helped ensure that the agreement left the U.S. commitment to
its NATO allies largely unimpaired. British participation was not without
potential pitfalls. Cromer stressed "the highly devious nature of Kissinger's
intellectual make-up" and worried that Britain was vulnerable to criticism
from its European partners if Brimelow's role became known.[16]

Similar clandestine negotiations characterized the drafting of a "conceptual framework" titled "The Next Ten Years in East-West and Trans-Atlantic
Relations." This document originated in Kissinger's proposal to outline
common views on political content, military doctrine, and the economic

---

14 *DBPO* 3:4, document 19. In the areas of commercial and monetary policy, the United States dropped
strong hints about what it expected from Britain in its new role in Europe. Treasury Secretary, George
Shultz, said that the United States would look to Britain to give a new direction to the European
approach on questions such as compensation under Article 24(6) of GATT. Likewise, Nixon also
apportioned blame over America's trade deficit – mostly directed at Japan, but not sparing Canada
and Europe. While Nixon maintained that he did not expect Britain to fight America's commercial
battle in Europe, he pointedly warned: "Nevertheless, the British Government must realise that
protectionist and isolationist sentiment in the United States was growing."
15 *DBPO* 3:4, document 19.   16 *DBPO* 3:4, document 44.

aspects of the Atlantic alliance in dealings with the Soviet Union. Meeting British officials led by Trend, in Washington on April 19, Kissinger criticized the paper's lack of dynamism and dubbed it "mildly fatalistic." Kissinger wanted to make the transatlantic relationship "an 'emotional necessity' to American public opinion." In what his British visitors viewed as a "dress rehearsal," Kissinger gave a sneak preview of the imminent Year of Europe speech. He claimed that the speech was "prompted by the President's conviction that, unless the essential basis of Atlantic unity could be reconstituted, everything would go wrong."[17] The Year of Europe speech, delivered by Kissinger at the Associated Press annual luncheon in New York on April 23, called for the reconstitution of the transatlantic relationship. Kissinger hoped that when Nixon visited Europe later in the year a "new Atlantic Charter setting the goals for the future" would be signed.[18]

Kissinger demanded a prompt and positive British response.[19] Douglas-Home authorized an FCO News Department statement that welcomed Kissinger's vision of a unified Europe working cooperatively with the United States.[20] However, Douglas-Home admitted to Kissinger later in the year that the initiative had "frankly, caught us on the hop" and the Community's machinery for rapid response "simply wasn't there."[21] In the meantime, officials in London questioned the need for a new Atlantic Charter, while U.S. hints at a package solution to settle outstanding defense, trade, and monetary matters received minimal acclaim. Publicly, at Dunblane on April 27, Douglas-Home praised a "speech of real importance" and added that "an economically strong and united Western Europe may create some awkward cases of competition for the United States. But a weak and divided Western Europe would be a dangerous source of instability."[22] Privately, Trend cautioned against U.S. attempts to use Britain as Washington's stalking horse.[23]

---

17 *DBPO* 3:4, documents 69, 73, 74. Kissinger tended to concentrate on strategic matters and only touched on the economic differences between the United States and Europe – although he insisted that these, too, should be addressed by the global approach. British ministers such as the minister for trade and consumer affairs, Sir Geoffrey Howe, had warned his European counterparts of the threat of political repercussions arising from a trade war in the aftermath of EC enlargement. European economic cooperation in the face of pressures on the U.S. dollar in early March had been viewed with suspicion in Washington. Nixon had scolded Heath for suggesting that Anglo-German proposals for addressing the currency crisis should be based on the premise of strengthening European integration. See *DBPO* 3:4, document 38.

18 *DBPO* 3:4, document 70. Visiting the United States on Apr. 29, 1973, Chancellor Brandt asked for the removal of the label "Atlantic Charter" from the document to be issued when Nixon visited Europe, as the first Atlantic charter in 1941 had been aimed against Germany.

19 *DBPO* 3:4, document 71.

20 TNA, FCO 82/283, folio 29, Telegram No. 949 to Washington (from PUS), Apr. 24, 1973.

21 *DBPO* 3:4, document 421.   22 *DBPO* 3:4, document 79.

23 *DBPO* 3:4, document 81.

France viewed Kissinger's utterances as a tactical ploy to put Europe on the defensive and opposed linkage. The new foreign minister, Michel Jobert, told Kissinger on May 17 that negotiations about specific problems should take place in their appropriate forums. Kissinger's comment that the United States had a "world role" in contrast to Europe's "regional responsibilities" also irked Paris.[24] Heath found President Pompidou "preoccupied by the institutional aspect" of handling the U.S. initiative on May 21–22. In French eyes, any EC–U.S. declaration would be limited. Following Nixon and Pompidou's Reykjavik meeting (May 31–June 1),[25] on June 5, Jobert confirmed French participation in a common European response to Kissinger's proposals but rejected fresh multilateral European–American machinery.[26]

A single Declaration of Principles addressing security, monetary, and trade questions was deemed "insuperable" in FCO's eyes. Heath reminded his cabinet on June 20 that the enlarged EC was not ready to make a unified approach to Washington. The rather negative French approach won little cabinet sympathy but Anglo–French cooperation was considered fundamental to the Community's success and confrontation was to be avoided.[27] It was also argued that Britain's main concern lay in continued U.S. commitment to Europe's defense. The FCO produced draft declarations for NATO and EC–U.S. contexts as a transatlantic declaration was valuable to Nixon in selling his European policy to Congress.[28] Meanwhile, frustrated at what he perceived as European procrastination, Kissinger had already resorted to threats. He warned British officials in Washington on June 4 that unless there was a quick response Congress would legislate for the withdrawal of seventy-five thousand to ninety-five thousand U.S. troops from Europe.[29] London was unimpressed. Douglas–Home remarked to officials about "a piece of quasi blackmail" and "an act of gross public indecency."[30]

Meanwhile, ascertaining French thinking remained difficult. Jobert was given two American draft declarations in late June to discuss with the British

---

24 *DBPO* 3:4, documents 75, 96. Kissinger had made this claim in his Year of Europe speech.

25 According to the American account of the discussions, the two presidents agreed that the study and development of the concept of the Year of Europe should be pursued "through both bilateral and multilateral exchanges, carried out simultaneously and at high levels." See *DBPO* 3:4, document 107.

26 *DBPO* 3:4, document 110. The British tried hard to gauge French intentions – Jobert seemed enthusiastic for a joint European position, whereas his political director, Puaux, claimed that the French alone were prepared to resist Washington's demands and was in a "mood of withdrawal" on the issue of a common European foreign policy.

27 *DBPO* 3:4, document 137.

28 *DBPO* 3:4, document 144. It was noted that the cabinet did not desire to "take the lead in trying to pull Dr Kissinger's chestnuts out of the fire."

29 *DBPO* 3:4, document 108.   30 *DBPO* 3:4, document 113.

and Germans. When Heath and Douglas-Home met Jobert on July 2, he suggested that the declaration could comprise two communiqués issued after Nixon's proposed NATO and EC visits. Jobert responded that France was "not at all sure that they wanted a document or documents."[31] Jobert argued that political cooperation was not a matter for the EC Council of Ministers and warned that France would absent itself from any discussions if pushed too far. At the Community foreign ministers' meeting (Copenhagen, July 23), progress was limited. Jobert agreed to work on a European identity paper, a British initiative in an effort to cut through the procedural obstacles, but tried to delay consideration of Nixon's projected visit.[32]

Nixon believed that the Nine were preoccupied with procedure and doubted the wisdom of attending NATO and EC meetings if they did not yield worthwhile results. Kissinger was blunter to British officials on July 30. He was most upset that the U.S. government would receive the draft declaration from the Nine from the Danish foreign minister, the Community representative – whom he dismissed as a "messenger boy." Worse followed. Kissinger detected a fundamental change in Anglo-American relations. Britain was accused of disloyalty for failing to inform the United States on the progress of the draft declaration. Kissinger concluded that Nixon's visit was conditional on procedure and content of the Nine's proposals proving to be acceptable and warned that Nixon would not sign a communiqué with anyone below his rank.[33]

Bonn and Paris were cautious about Heath's August 3 suggestion of a tripartite summit to try to cement a common European line.[34] The British minister in Paris, Christopher Ewart-Biggs, observed that neither Pompidou nor Jobert was "sorry to see the American Year of Europe bogged down,"[35] Meanwhile, discussions on draft EC-U.S. and NATO declarations between the EC political directors and U.S. representatives were conducted in a nonconfrontational atmosphere during the late summer.[36] Jobert appeared

---

31 *DBPO* 3:4, document 146.
32 *DBPO* 3:4, document 171. At this meeting on June 23, Jobert also took Michael Palliser aside to berate him over London's dealings with Washington concerning proposed declarations. Douglas-Home dismissed this accusation as "nonsense."
33 *DBPO* 3:4, document 179.   34 *DBPO* 3:4, document 182.
35 *DBPO* 3:4, document 190.
36 *DBPO* 3:4, document 235. The Americans found the EC draft "thin." They wanted greater emphasis placed on the changing nature of the transatlantic relationship and a more solid commitment to partnership and consultation between Europe and the EC. However, as John Oliver Wright, the British political director, pointed out on Sept. 29, there were encouraging signs. The Americans seemed to have accepted the emerging unity of the Nine and were ready to work on the European draft, and the French seemed to agree that "the exercise must proceed to eventual success." Discussions between the EC political directors and between these and representatives of the EC Commission and the United States continued to proceed without rancour in Copenhagen on

to have mellowed but the French remained stubborn over procedure.[37] Ewart-Biggs noted: "They are pathologically sensitive about any implication that Europe is in any sense subordinate to or dependent upon the United States. It is strangely like a sort of Third World psychosis towards the colonial power."[38]

In the meantime, Heath sought to reassure Nixon about events in Europe. In a personal message on September 4, he explained that British actions were "not in any case to confront [the president] with a fait accompli but to provide the basis of a lasting relationship between the United States and Europe."[39] Kissinger, by now secretary of state as well as national security adviser, repeated his grievances to Douglas-Home on September 24. The European declaration was still a fait accompli; their response to the Year of Europe still irritated him.[40] But the administration's attention was elsewhere. Watergate bubbled along, and Vice President Spiro Agnew resigned on October 10 amid allegations that he had accepted bribes while governor of Maryland. Cromer warned that "logic and calm discussion [were] at something of a discount in Washington."[41] The outbreak of war in the Middle East on October 6 only worsened matters.

London and Washington had differing Middle East perceptions. British policy was anchored in Douglas-Home's Harrogate speech of October 1970, underlining Britain's continued support for UN Resolution 242, which it had sponsored in November 1967, calling for Israel's withdrawal from the Occupied Territories.[42] For Britain, the safeguarding of fuel supplies and a resolution of the Middle East crisis were interlinked. There was no meaningful post-Vietnam U.S. initiative to broker a Middle East settlement. Heath vainly hoped that Nixon would address it at his June 1973 summit with the Soviet leader Leonid Brezhnev. He had appealed to Nixon to persuade the Israelis to change their line "in their ultimate interest as well as

---

Oct. 18 and 19. Indeed, on Oct. 19, Wright described the atmosphere as "easy and friendly" largely because of the American representatives Helmut Sonnenfeldt of the National Security Council and Walter Stoessel, assistant secretary for European affairs at the State Department. They seemed ready to accept the Nine's rejection of both Kissinger's ball-of-wax formula and U.S. attempts to institutionalize the EC/U.S. relationship. Even the French seemed ready to adopt a more conciliatory approach but matters were far from settled, and further discussions were dependent on developments in the EC and the timing of Nixon's European trip. See *DBPO* 3:4, document 307.

37 France was apparently concerned at growing West German independence in its dealings with the superpowers. It seemed that Anglo-French agreement would arise from a common desire "to lock the Federal Republic into the European Community and the developing European entity." See *DBPO* 3:4, document 209 for the Heath-Jobert conversation of Aug. 26, and *DBPO* 3:4, document 212 for the Jobert-Heath meeting of August 29, 1973.

38 *DBPO* 3:4, document 210.   39 *DBPO* 3:4, document 217.

40 *DBPO* 3:4, document 232.   41 *DBPO* 3:4, document 239.

42 Douglas-Home's Harrogate speech was reproduced in his autobiography *The Way the Wind Blows* (London, 1976), Appendix B.

ours."[43] In UN debates, Britain followed a policy similar to France.[44] On July 26, when the United States vetoed a UN Security Council resolution calling on Israel to cooperate with UN peace efforts, British diplomats condemned the performance of the U.S. mission as "remarkably inept" and "designed to create the maximum amount of confusion and ill will." Douglas-Home added pithily, "[They] have handled it all very clumsily" and observed to his minister of state, Julian Amery, that the American administration had not followed British advice to engage in constructive dialogue with the Egyptians.[45]

Anglo-American cracks widened when fighting erupted. As the war raged, diplomatic tensions brewed. Britain argued that Syrian and Egyptian forces were only advancing into their own territories – the Golan Heights and Sinai.[46] Britain wanted to avoid floating fruitless initiatives that would alienate Arab states and threaten oil supplies.[47] Meanwhile, the United States rediscovered the United Nations. After discussions with the Soviets, Kissinger pressed Britain to table a cease-fire in situ motion on October 12. Heath and Douglas-Home were wary of Soviet intentions and viewed Egyptian compliance as unlikely. When President Anwar Sadat spoke to the British ambassador in Cairo, Sir Philip Adams, at 2:30 A.M. on the morning of October 13, he dismissed the initiative as a "Kissinger trick."[48] Cromer cautioned that Kissinger was asking Britain to act as an "American stalking horse with the Arabs" and doubted Soviet motives.[49]

Kissinger tried to brush aside British reservations, and on October 13, in a telephone conversation with Douglas-Home, he really "laid it on the line," according to the British account, and put "extreme pressure" on

---

43 *DBPO* 3:4, document 127. The British embassy in Washington thought that the White House would pay little heed to the prime minister's message, preoccupied as it was with Brezhnev's visit and content to wait until what it deemed a suitable time before making any move on Israel. See *DBPO* 3:4, document 139.

44 In April 1973, Britain and France had sponsored a UN motion that condemned Israeli commando raids into Lebanon.

45 *DBPO* 3:4, document 175. Julian Amery, minister of state at the FCO, asked Douglas-Home if Britain "was not going overboard on the Arab side" following events in New York. See this exchange in *DBPO* 3:4, documents 172, 173.

46 Britain preferred a resolution that would reaffirm 242, call for a cease-fire, and call on the UN secretary-general, Kurt Waldheim, to promote a negotiated settlement. See *DBPO* 3:4, document 259.

47 At the outbreak of the war, Britain had imposed an arms embargo on the protagonists. On accusations that Britain had requested that the United States not use U.K. bases or overfly British air space to resupply Israel, Douglas-Home noted in November: "There has also been criticism that we denied facilities to the US for the supply of Israel during the war. This is untrue. The Americans did not ask us for such facilities either in this country or at any of our overseas bases and we did not therefore deny them any. We were in close and continuous contact with the Americans throughout the crisis, as well as with both parties." See TNA, FCO 93/212, folio 293, minute from Douglas-Home to Heath, Nov. 15, 1973.

48 *DBPO* 3:4, document 274.   49 *DBPO* 3:4, document 278.

the foreign secretary to act as requested.[50] Nevertheless, late that same evening Douglas-Home told Kissinger that the time was not "ripe for this initiative."[51] Kissinger told Cromer that the president "could not recall any crisis in the last three years when the British had been with the Americans when the chips were down." Cromer responded that "Europe would not be content to be without Middle East oil because of American actions."[52] The American emergency supply of arms to Israel in mid-October caused the oil producing states to cut production.[53] Britain had imposed an embargo on the supply of weapons to the belligerents at the beginning of the war and had denied the Americans the use of British bases for their resupply operations, but economic concerns now abounded. Indeed, the situation was particularly precarious for Britain. Arab oil accounted for almost two-thirds of the country's consumption. British stocks and oil in transit would barely cover the following three months.[54]

The Americans were far more concerned at Soviet moves in the region than with Western Europe's oil crisis. A cease-fire was cobbled together by Kissinger in Moscow and subsequently accepted by Egypt and Israel as UN Security Council Resolution 338. However, Kissinger, stopping in London on October 22, conceded that he had "given no thought to machinery for observing the cease-fire." Kissinger envisaged direct Arab-Israeli talks with superpower intervention at key stages. Douglas-Home noted the numerous loose ends and haziness about machinery for peace-making and peacekeeping.[55] Moreover, hostilities continued. Israeli forces established a bridgehead across the Suez Canal, and Moscow's Egyptian client faced humiliating defeat. News that Soviet forces were primed for departure to Sinai to unilaterally impose the cease-fire and to extricate the surrounded Egyptian Third Army, led the Nixon administration to put the American forces in Western Europe on alert. The United States decided not to immediately inform its NATO allies of this step.[56] Somewhat predictably, this U.S. unilateral military action inspired little confidence in Europe. Douglas-Home was also worried about Soviet reactions – he was

---

50 *DBPO* 3:4, document 276. Douglas-Home preferred to make a move at the Security Council, ideally in concert with the French.

51 *DBPO* 3:4, document 281. A draft copy of the record of the meeting earlier that evening at the prime minister's country residence at Chequers attended by Heath, Douglas-Home, Lord Balniel (minister of state at the FCO), the PUS, and other FCO officials can be found at *DBPO* 3:4, document 280. When Heath had telephoned Nixon on October 11, the president, beset by domestic political troubles, was apparently too drunk to answer. See *Guardian*, May 27, 2004.

52 *DBPO* 3:4, document 282.   53 *DBPO* 3:4, document 296.

54 *DBPO* 3:4, document 256.   55 *DBPO* 3:4, document 350.

56 *DBPO* 3:4, document 329. At this stage the United States invoked the largely British-drafted Agreement on the Prevention of Nuclear War to warn the Soviets that their unilateral intervention in Sinai would violate its provisions. See Henry Kissinger, *Years of Upheaval* (London, 1982), 286.

not surprised by Brezhnev's robust line and believed that Moscow would not accept another Arab humiliation. Security Council Resolution 340 (October 25) established a UN emergency force, which the United States insisted was not to include troops from the permanent members.

British ministers and officials were not enthusiastic about Kissinger's peace proposals.[57] Heath argued for rapid implementation of Resolution 242 and, on October 31, warned Nixon that otherwise the situation would "almost certainly go sour." He painted a grim scenario in which the Soviets rebuilt Arab military strength, the Arabs progressively reduced oil supplies, and the Western Europeans suffered a "massive economic decline."[58] Heath wanted direct UN participation in Arab-Israeli talks, but Kissinger disagreed and was further frustrated by renewed disputes over the supply and refueling of U.S. aircraft bound for Israel. Again, Cromer was dragged over the coals – a consequence of Kissinger's belief that Europe was jeopardizing the alliance.[59]

Meanwhile, on November 6, a declaration of EC states called for peace negotiations within the "framework of the United Nations." It called for Israel to end the territorial occupation it had maintained since 1967, appealed to all states in the Middle East to recognize the territorial integrity and independence of their neighbors, and said that any settlement had to take into account the Palestinians' legitimate rights. The Americans were distinctly unimpressed with this European initiative, and some were perturbed at the readiness of the Europeans to "give in to 'Arab oil blackmail.'"[60] There was no united European front on oil, and Arab states allocated supplies conditional on political conduct.[61] Britain's relationship with Europe was now tested.[62] Although prices increased, London and Paris were assured

---

57 *DBPO* 3:4, document 328. Kissinger sought to tackle the Arab states first, get them to end the embargo and then help them build a negotiating strategy to be implemented after the Israeli elections of December 11.

58 *DBPO* 3:4, document 350.   59 *DBPO* 3:4, document 352.

60 *DBPO* 3:4, document 396.

61 While HMG was assured by producers such as Saudi Arabia and Abu Dhabi that they had no wish to damage Britain, the Netherlands, which was publicly pro-Israeli, faced an Arab embargo affecting nearly 60 percent of its imported oil supplies.

62 Assisting their allies and partners exposed Britain to Arab wrath and a possible extension of the embargo. Alternatively, blocking the reexport of oil to friendly states, particularly its new EC partners, created practical problems and could have breached the Treaty of Rome by failing to share resources with less-favored partners. The claims of Anglo-French collusion were exaggerated. The British proposal for a joint EC démarche to Arab governments calling for them to stop cutting oil production and not to discriminate against individual EC states was received warily in Paris. The French recalled that some European partners (Denmark, the Netherlands, and the Republic of Ireland) had voted at the United Nations against French nuclear testing and were not enthusiastic about expending their credit in the Middle East for what they saw as disloyal neighbors. Hence agreement on the proposed démarche was delayed until Nov. 21.

that their political stance would preclude further cutbacks. Britain backed long-term EU solidarity on energy matters but FCO officials argued that the immediate priority was to ensure maximum oil imports. To help ease the situation, the EC eventually produced a collective démarche, which was dispatched to Arab capitals on November 22. This explained the contradictions arising from the Arab desire that Europe contribute to a Middle East settlement and the reality that Arab tactics were detrimental to EC interests and European public opinion.[63]

Douglas–Home stressed that the Nine had interests and views on the Middle East and would not remain silent in the midst of these momentous events.[64] However, Washington did not want international involvement. Secretary of Defense James Schlesinger underlined this to his British counterpart, Lord Carrington, on November 7, in a heated discussion at the Hague. Schlesinger railed against what Washington perceived to be Anglo-French collusion − "British policies were taking on a quality of 'decayed Gaullism.'"[65]

The Middle East war and oil shortages overshadowed the completion of the draft EC–U.S. and NATO declarations and the European identity paper. Britain hoped to mend fences with the Americans and simultaneously advocated a common European foreign policy. Nevertheless, late November saw fresh onslaughts on Britain. Kissinger's antennae scented a European–Japanese declaration that undermined his planned trilateral U.S.-EC-Japanese declaration. On November 24, he claimed that "France had made the cold-blooded assessment that it could drive the U.K. to share in the construction of Europe on the basis of coolness towards America in the belief that the Americans would not retaliate. This was the worst decision since the Greek city states confronted Alexander." Douglas–Home responded with a terse personal message to Kissinger noting that, "Though frustrations abound, there is really nothing in my view which justifies the fear that US/British relations are 'collapsing.'"[66] On October 17, in a covering minute to Heath of an FCO Planning Staff analysis of the first months of the Year of Europe, Douglas–Home placed much of the blame for the confusion and friction on Kissinger. Excluding the Washington "bureaucracy," Kissinger had insisted on running "everything that was crucial in foreign and defence policy of the [United States]" from the White House. His "personal diplomacy was combined with a furtive secrecy that bred

---

63 See *DBPO* 3:4, documents 402, 403.   64 *DBPO* 3:4, document 362.
65 *DBPO* 3:4, document 379.
66 *DBPO* 3:4, document 412. For the very direct British response see *DBPO* 3:4, document 421.

suspicion." The foreign secretary concluded that "Dr[.] Kissinger was thus attempting a great deal with slender resources."[67]

France, meanwhile, opposed any European initiative for talks on a European-American declaration in Brussels. Britain had, apparently, returned to its "old ways" with Washington. Sir Edward Tomkins, British ambassador in Paris, reported broad agreement that there "should be a distinct European personality vis-à-vis the Americans, but we want this personality to have a close and satisfactory dialogue [with Washington], and they want it to behave like a young woman anxious to preserve her virginity from the GIs."[68]

Europe remained divided as the energy crisis deepened.[69] British officials maintained that a public declaration of European solidarity on oil would accentuate difficulties with Arab producers. Jobert told Douglas-Home on December 11 that France would not sign up to a consumer state energy declaration but on December 12 Kissinger proposed an energy action group of senior officials from North America, Europe, and Japan.[70] On January 9, 1974, Kissinger invited the foreign ministers of the industrialized oil-consuming nations to a specially convened conference in Washington to develop a consumer action program. Britain welcomed the American initiatives but worried that the Nine might appear over cautious. Indeed, at the European summit (Copenhagen, December 14–15), later described by the British permanent representative in his annual review as "a shambles from which it is only surprising that as much as did emerge," France disagreed with the Community welcoming Kissinger's Energy Action Group,[71] and was unimpressed at the prospect of a "front of rich consumers."[72] Delays confirmed Kissinger's suspicions that the EC was incapable of functioning as an effective partner.

Oil prices had effectively quadrupled since October.[73] The global economic system was threatened. Britain faced growing domestic difficulties

67 TNA, PREM 15/2089.   68 *DBPO* 3:4, document 426.

69 *DBPO* 3:4, document 434. This Joint Intelligence Committee (JIC) paper speculated on the possibility of U.S. military intervention in the Middle East to secure oil supplies. It also noted that the French would be unwilling to associate themselves with any American initiative aimed at tackling the crisis. Meanwhile, Germany and the Netherlands were critical of the failure of Britain and France to back concrete measures to address the oil embargo.

70 *DBPO* 3:4, document 456.

71 *DBPO* 3:4, document 517. The European identity paper, approved by the foreign ministers of the Nine, was published to mark the occasion of the Copenhagen summit meeting on December 14, 1973.

72 *DBPO* 3:4, document 499.

73 Just before Christmas 1973, the Organization of Petroleum Exporting Countries (OPEC) meeting in Tehran announced a further doubling in oil prices. Douglas-Home told Kissinger: "Our preliminary impression is that this doubling of the price goes beyond the stage where it merely places strains on the balance of payments of individual consumer countries. It begins to cast in doubt the capacity of the world economic system to sustain it." See *DBPO* 3:4, document 487.

arising from uncertain oil supplies and spiraling prices. Douglas-Home was anxious to grasp American cooperation – only the United States could solve the problems, Europe could not act alone.[74] As Kissinger had remarked to the NATO ministers on December 10, "The United States could solve its energy problems only with great difficulty, Europe could not solve them at all."[75] This illustrated the altered transatlantic balance of power. European governments had ignored or rejected much of Kissinger's Year of Europe speech. The United States seemed beset by political and economic woes. By January 1974, Watergate still festered but European economies now shuddered from Arab oil price hikes and the paucity of petroleum. To maintain Europe's welfare and security, European governments had to sustain American interest in multinational cooperation.

French politicians and officials questioned the conference venue and level of representation. They argued that it undercut the United Nations and the Organisation for Economic Co-operation and Development. At the European Council discussions on February 5, the French circulated a "very negative" draft – setting out what the conference was not to do. The eventual EC mandate left open the possibility of establishing a framework of international cooperation.[76] The French believed that Kissinger wanted to reduce the EC to an "American poodle" and had lured the foreign ministers to Washington to exploit their disarray. The conference, held from February 11 to 13, was presented with a program for negotiations by Kissinger. Jobert rudely objected to "continuing consultations." Other Europeans finally tired of French conduct. The issues were "too big and their procedural objections too petty." Individual states cooperated nationally with the United States, Japan, and Canada. Douglas-Home and seven of Britain's Community partners backed the American conference communiqué calling for continued consultations. France, which backed an independent European line, was isolated – betrayed, in French eyes, by partners who had failed to respect the Community mandate.[77]

The conference highlighted Britain's uncomfortable problem. Britain had hoped that EC membership would increase its influence in Washington but always realized that France presented a difficult obstacle. Britain tried to avoid appearing to be Washington's Trojan horse. Paris was paranoid

---

74 *DBPO* 3:4, document 516. 75 *DBPO* 3:4, document 447.

76 *DBPO* 3:4, document 534.

77 DBPO 3:4, document 562. Diplomatic Report No. 192/74, The Washington Energy Conference, Feb. 10–13, 1974, dated Feb. 27, 1974. France abstained from a number of sections in the conference communiqué. The British report admitted that procedural issues dominated the conference and that there had been no attempt to actually tackle energy questions.

about any transatlantic gesture appearing to formalize Western Europe's subordination to the United States. However, the depth of the energy crisis restricted Europe's choice. Hardheaded economic and political factors made American realities preferable to French obstinacy. French exceptionalism only offered competitive bilateral deals with producers, further driving up prices. The United States had global reach and economic clout. French power remained regional. The idea that British interests were best served through the Community was weakened. Heath's pro-European government also perished – after the February 1974 general election. James Callaghan, Euroskeptic and Washington friendly, became foreign secretary. Britain had made some definitive choices during a fraught year.

11

West Germany's Long Year of Europe

Bonn between Europe and the United States

FABIAN HILFRICH

Anticipating Donald Rumsfeld's infamous distinction between a cynical "old" Europe and a vigorous "new" Europe and exploiting the mythical purity of American purpose, Henry Kissinger blamed the transatlantic confrontation over and partial failure of his Year of Europe initiative not only on President Richard Nixon's diminished authority in the wake of Watergate but also on the wily machinations of Old World diplomats. According to Kissinger, the Europeans were unjustified and ungrateful in torpedoing a generous American initiative to rededicate the Atlantic alliance.[1] With new archival material becoming available, a more nuanced view of the crisis is emerging that takes into account the views and actions of Washington's European allies.[2] The Europeans had reason to believe that the Year of Europe was not, as Kissinger would have it, a benevolent grand design. As a result of this belief, and using the opportunities presented by détente and European integration, the Europeans became more self-assured and resisted what they perceived as Washington's efforts to reassert its leadership role in the transatlantic alliance. The ensuing confrontational negotiations with the United States deepened European political integration, which prompted concerns in Washington that Europe might become not only an economic rival but also a political competitor. But Washington's fears were

---

1 Henry A. Kissinger, *Years of Upheaval* (Boston, 1982), 193–4. On this purported contrast between Europe and the United States, see Richard J. Barnet, *The Alliance: America, Europe, Japan – Makers of the Postwar World* (New York, 1983), 320.
2 See Daniel Möckli, "Asserting Europe's Distinct Identity: The EC Nine and Kissinger's 'Year of Europe'" and Alastair Noble, "Kissinger's Year of Europe, Britain's Year of Choice" in this volume. On Anglo-American relations in the early 1970s, see Catherine Hynes, *The Year that Never Was: Heath, the Nixon Administration and the Year of Europe, 1970–1974* (Dublin, 2009). The most useful contemporary account is James Chace and Earl C. Ravenal, eds., *Atlantis Lost: U.S.-European Relations after the Cold War* (New York, 1976). See also Joseph Godson, ed., *Transatlantic Crisis: Europe and America in the 70's* (London, 1974).

exaggerated. When world affairs intruded upon the transatlantic confrontation over the Year of Europe – namely, the Yom Kippur War and the oil crisis – Kissinger quickly regained the upper hand. For a number of reasons – underlying differences within Western Europe, the role of the United States in the defense of Europe, and the structural constraints imposed by world politics – European unity turned out to be shallower than the rhetoric of European statesmen would have suggested.

This chapter analyzes the role played by West Germany during the Year of Europe. Although the transatlantic row was multilateral in character, I argue that West Germany occupied a key position that largely determined the outcome of the power struggle within the Western alliance. Traditionally acting as mediator between the United States and a more independent-minded France, Bonn was initially willing to risk at least temporary alienation from Washington in exchange for more meaningful European integration during the Year of Europe. On account of the extraordinary achievements of *Ostpolitik*, it is frequently forgotten that Brandt actually assigned the project of European integration the highest priority in his inaugural speeches in 1969 and 1973.[3] Yet Bonn emerged not only as a crucial actor but also as the primary target for pressures from both Paris and Washington. This was primarily a result of the conflict between its desire for European integration and its dependency, greater than that of Britain or France, on the American security guarantee. This dilemma ultimately explains how Bonn was able to emerge as a crucial actor within in the Western alliance and play an instrumental role in resolving the acrimonious conflict unleashed by Kissinger's Year of Europe initiative.

THE DISCONTENTS OF DÉTENTE OR THE IMPORTANCE OF PROCEDURE

The Year of Europe unfolded against the background of a plethora of unresolved issues in the transatlantic alliance, including economic competition, monetary policy, the neglect of Europe as a consequence of the Vietnam War, and congressional pressure on the White House to have the Europeans pick up more of the cost of stationing American troops in Europe or to reduce troop levels there.[4] That pressure also accounts for Bonn's readiness

---

3 Werner Link, "Aussen- und Deutschlandpolitik in der Ära Brandt 1969–1974," in *Republik im Wandel 1969–1974: Die Ära Brandt*, eds. Karl Dietrich Bracher, Wolfgang Jäger, and Werner Link (Stuttgart, 1986), 241. On the centrality of European integration in Brandt's thinking, see Frank Fischer's introduction to *Willy Brandt: Ein Volk der guten Nachbarn, Aussen- und Deutschlandpolitik 1966–1974*, vol. 6 of *Willy Brandt: Berliner Ausgabe*, eds. Helga Grebing, Gregor Schöllgen, and Heinrich August Winkler (Bonn, 2005), 22–5.
4 See Möckli, "Asserting Europe's Distinct Identity."

to strengthen European political and defense cooperation.[5] The political atmosphere of the Year of Europe was set by what could be called the discontents of détente. Instead of confirming the course of the alliance, détente not only loosened the ties between the allies by reducing fear of the Soviet threat but also created deep mistrust among them. The source of that mistrust was procedure. Whether in the form of Soviet-American negotiations, West German Ostpolitik, or Paris' channel to the Kremlin, détente had been pursued largely through bilateral dealings.[6] Bloc-to-bloc negotiations – the Conference on Security and Cooperation in Europe (CSCE) and Mutually Balanced Force Reduction (MBFR) talks – were only beginning. Although the Western allies informed one another of the progress they were making in their respective talks with the Soviet Union, suspicions lingered that not all was being divulged or that separate deals might be struck. Bonn's Ostpolitik was subject to particular scrutiny because the NATO allies feared it might lead to the neutralization – the "Finlandization" in the jargon of the time – of the Federal Republic. Toward the end of the Year of Europe, Bonn's NATO partners sternly demanded that they be kept better informed of its dealings with the Eastern bloc.[7]

The Western Europeans were equally suspicious of the negotiations between the superpowers, which they suspected of planning to divide the world between them in condominium. The allies had expressed such fears during the Strategic Arms Limitation Talks (SALT) negotiations, which, as they noted, touched on European security but without European participation. The most severe blow to confidence within the alliance, however, came in the early stages of the Year of Europe, when, in June 1973, Washington and Moscow signed an accord on preventing nuclear war. Although this was a largely symbolic agreement, the Europeans feared that it might compromise NATO's strategy of flexible response, the heart of Western Europe's security guarantee. The agreement made the Europeans more suspicious of the Year of Europe initiative and even led the West Germans to establish a group within the European Political Cooperation (EPC) framework to study the effects of the Soviet-American accord on allied defense.[8]

---

5 See Matthias Schulz, "The Reluctant European: Helmut Schmidt, the European Community, and Transatlantic Relations," in this volume.
6 An important exception was the Four Power talks on the status of Berlin.
7 Krapf, Brussels (NATO), to German Foreign Office, May 2, 1974, *Akten zur Auswärtigen Politik der Bundesrepublik Deutschland* (hereafter *AAPD*) 1974, doc. 141. On the suspicions toward the Federal Republic, compare Barnet, *The Alliance*, 288–98; and Gottfried Niedhart, "Ostpolitik: Phases, Short-Term Objectives and Grand Design," *Bulletin of the German Historical Institute* (2004, suppl. 1): 120–1.
8 On the West German suggestion to found such a group, see Cable by van Well, Jan. 15, 1974, *AAPD* 1974, doc. 8. On the complaints about the June 1973 U.S.-Soviet agreement, compare Memorandum by Citron, Oct. 3, 1973; *AAPD* 1973, doc. 305; and Michel Jobert, *Mémoirs d'avenir* (Paris, 1974), 241.

The mistrust engendered by détente's bilateralism prompted the Europeans and Americans to trade polemical accusations that the other was more willing to negotiate with Moscow than with its NATO partners.[9] Thus, by 1973, European-American relations were hampered by discontent with détentès bilateralism on both sides of the Atlantic as well as by the belief that existing diplomatic procedures did not allow for the exercise of meaningful influence at the transatlantic level. It was against this background that the Year of Europe unfolded.

BONN'S RESPONSE TO KISSINGER'S INITIATIVE

Much as Kissinger may have later claimed that the United States intended only to reinvigorate the alliance and to protect it against the isolationist impulses of Congress,[10] the Year of Europe was actually conceived in a less benign and cooperative spirit. As Daniel Möckli notes in his contribution to this volume, European leaders were aware of such an initiative since late 1972, well before Kissinger's April 1973 speech.[11] More importantly, signals from Washington in the first quarter of 1973 indicated that the initiative was confrontational rather than benevolent. In January, Nixon announced that the problems with Europe "will be put on the front burner," ominously adding that the partners on both sides of the Atlantic had a monumental choice to make. They could either be "competitors in a constructive way" or engage "in economic confrontation that could lead to bitterness and which would hurt us both."[12]

The West German government received similar signals through diplomatic channels. In January, Secretary of State William Rogers informed Ambassador Rolf Pauls that Nixon was furious about European criticism of the Christmas bombing in Vietnam.[13] In late February, Pauls reported to Bonn about a briefing by Luxembourg's ambassador in Washington on a meeting between Foreign Minister Gaston Thorn and Kissinger. Kissinger reportedly indicated that the president's anger would influence the upcoming negotiations with the Europeans. Their criticism of the Vietnam War,

---

9 Conversation between Brandt and French President Pompidou on Nov. 26, 1973, *AAPD* 1973, doc. 390; Kissinger in a meeting with Scheel; Memorandum by Brunner, July 16, 1973, *AAPD* 1973, doc. 222; Kissinger, *Years of Upheaval*, 702.

10 Kissinger, *Years of Upheaval*, 193–4.

11 Möckli, "Asserting Europe's Distinct Identity."

12 "The President's News Conference of January 31, 1973," *Public Papers of the Presidents of the United States: Richard Nixon – 1973* (Washington, D.C., 1975), 57.

13 Pauls to Scheel, Jan. 10, 1973, *AAPD* 1973, doc. 9. On Nixon's anger, see also Kissinger, *Years of Upheaval*, 137.

Kissinger stated, "has wrought more damage than any other event in the years since the Second World War. What the president feels for the European allies now, is only a matter of reason." As Pauls observed, Kissinger's irate behavior toward Thorn could probably be taken as the "psychological prelude" to the upcoming negotiations.[14]

Hence, Kissinger's April 23 speech did not take Bonn by complete surprise, but its broad scope was nonetheless unexpected. Crucial elements of the speech attest to Washington's confrontational approach, as Möckli notes, and contradict Kissinger's later claims about Washington's noble motives. His distinction between America's global interests and Europe's merely regional interests no doubt rankled. Other comments, though, had more ominous implications. First, there was his highly qualified support of European integration: "For us, European unity is what it has always been: not an end in itself, but a means to the strengthening of the West. We shall continue to support European unity as a component of a larger Atlantic partnership."[15] In other words, European integration had to remain compatible with and subordinate to the overall interests of the transatlantic alliance. The second disturbing aspect was the comprehensive approach to transatlantic problems that Kissinger outlined. In essence, he and Nixon sought to apply the same linkage strategy in their dealings with the Western allies that had served them so well in their negotiations with the Communist adversaries.

Berndt von Staden, Pauls's newly arrived successor in Washington, was critical in his analysis of Kissinger's speech. While acknowledging that Kissinger's speech represented "an emphatic affirmation of the Atlantic Alliance," Staden recognized that Washington was not fully supportive of further European integration. Kissinger's speech, he reported, expressed "the yearning for the situation of the 1950s and 1960s . . . when the United States possessed undisputed supremacy, when Western Europe did not appear as a competitor, was accordingly dependent and asked for little say in the matter, but instead left the leadership role to the United States without question."[16]

Like most European observers, Staden reserved his strongest criticism for the envisaged linkage strategy, of addressing all transatlantic issues

14 Pauls to German Foreign Office, Feb. 24, 1973, *AAPD* 1973, doc. 64.

15 Kissinger, "The Year of Europe," Address before the Annual Meeting of the Associated Press Editors at New York, Apr. 23, 1973, *Department of State Bulletin* 68 (1973), 595. On the traditionally qualified U.S. support for European integration, see W. H. Roobol, "Enduring Ambivalencies," in *The United States and the European Community: Convergence or Conflict?* ed. H. M. Belien (The Hague, 1989), 17.

16 Staden to German Foreign Office, Apr. 26, 1973, *AAPD* 1973, doc. 118. Retrospectively, Deputy Foreign Minister Paul Frank classified the Year of Europe as a publicity stunt; Frank, *Entschlüsselte Botschaft: ein Diplomat macht Inventur* (Stuttgart, 1981), 148. See also Jobert, *Mémoirs d'avenir*, 231.

simultaneously. He clearly foresaw the danger that Washington would try to exact economic and political concessions in return for a continued defense commitment to Europe. That the Federal Republic was more vulnerable to this form of blackmail than the nuclear club members France and Great Britain, he did not have to point out to his superiors in Bonn.[17] Having the dubious honor of being the first European statesman to visit Washington in the wake of Kissinger's speech, Chancellor Willy Brandt also seized the opportunity to warn that "steps in one area should not adversely influence others."[18] London and Paris also resisted Kissinger's intended approach, dubbed "globalisation" by the French, and most of the EC member states had agreed by early June that they would refuse to negotiate on Kissinger's terms.[19]

PROCEDURE AS SUBSTANCE

Throughout the difficult negotiations that followed, Kissinger impatiently stressed that he was interested in substance rather than procedure.[20] This statement obscures the fact, however, that, in this instance, procedure was substance – as much as it had been in the bilateralism of détente. Kissinger's own suggestion of linkage was both procedural and substantive. The comprehensiveness of Kissinger's proposed agenda cut across the established fora for transatlantic dialogue and raised the question of which Europe Washington wanted to negotiate with. Was it the European Community, which had just grown to nine member states with the inclusion of Great Britain, Denmark and Ireland? Or, as military issues were also to be addressed, was it NATO, from which France had partially withdrawn and of which Ireland was not a member? And what about institutions like the General Agreement on Tariffs and Trade or the International Monetary Fund? Important political issues had not previously been addressed in these fora but rather bilaterally. The fact that the Europeans rejected linkage determined their refusal of the American proposition that the Year of Europe result in *one* solemn declaration signed at *one* summit meeting.[21]

17 Staden to German Foreign Office, Apr. 26, 1973, *AAPD*, 1973, doc. 118.
18 Memorandum by Brandt, May 1, 1973, *AAPD*, 1973, doc. 124.
19 For the term "globalisation," which was soon to be adopted as jargon by the German foreign policy elite as well, see the Memorandum by Frank, Aug. 31, 1973, *AAPD* 1973, doc. 267. On the consensus within the EPC to reject the proposed linkage, see Cable by Schlingensiepen, June 5, 1973, *AAPD* 1973, doc. 178.
20 See, e.g., van Well's account of the meeting of the foreign ministers of France, Germany, Great Britain, and the United States, Dec. 9, 1973, *AAPD* 1973, doc. 410.
21 On the decision-making process, see Möckli, "Asserting Europe's Distinct Identity."

Similarly, the slow evolution of a common European position on procedure has to be attributed to substantive concerns. While Europe's "big three" initially followed Kissinger's preferred approach of secret bilateral negotiations, they realized by July that this approach impeded a unified European response, created distrust, and angered the excluded allies. The bilateral approach was, therefore, a direct challenge to EPC, the body established in 1970 for the purpose of formulating a European foreign policy. Meeting in Copenhagen in late July, the EC foreign ministers decided to reverse course and to negotiate exclusively through EPC. The political directors representing the foreign ministries were instructed to prepare a draft declaration on political and economic matters, while another declaration dealing primarily with military matters was to be drafted within NATO.[22]

This decision was embarrassing for Bonn because Foreign Minister Walter Scheel had just presented two draft declarations in Washington and promised more refined versions shortly. In the wake of the Copenhagen meeting, however, he informed Kissinger that "everything should be avoided that could disturb [the EPC] in forming its opinion and working out a draft. I would therefore prefer not to send you a more precise version of Germany's ideas right now." Noting the harm that a bilateral approach might do, Scheel warned that a further exchange of drafts could lead to "obstructive misunderstandings."[23]

Bonn endured the ensuing wrath of the Nixon administration because strengthening EPC, an organization the Brandt government had fathered, was one of its most important foreign policy objectives. Already in June 1972, during preparations for the October EC summit in Paris, Brandt had emphasized to French President Georges Pompidou that negotiations with the United States would be one area in which EPC could prove itself and through which it would be deepened.[24] After the French consented not only to a transatlantic dialogue through EPC but also to a closer institutional connection between the EC and EPC, which they had long resisted, Bonn clearly gave securing progress on EPC priority over not alienating Washington.[25]

22 Cable by Dohms on the EPC Ministerial Meeting on July 23, 1973, *AAPD* 1973, doc. 229.
23 Scheel to Kissinger, July 25, 1973, *AAPD* 1973, doc. 230.
24 Brandt to Pompidou, June 28, 1972; Minister's Office, vol. 498, Files of the German Foreign Office, Berlin. See also Link, "Aussen- und Deutschlandpolitik in der Ära Brandt 1969–1974," 245.
25 Despite Jobert's retrospective portrayal of France as the lone defender of European independence against U.S. predominance, Paris was driven less by a desire to advance European integration and more by the realization that a pan-European approach to negotiations was the only way to control the partners and to avert concessions to Washington. Staden intimated as much to U.S. Deputy Secretary of State Rush in early September, saying that a convoy could only go as fast as its slowest

The American reaction to the European draft proposal on economic and political cooperation[26] was predictably acerbic when Danish Foreign Minister Knut Børge Andersen, in his function as EPC representative, went to Washington to discuss it in late September. Kissinger dismissed the procedure. It was "not acceptable . . . as something permanent," he argued, because the United States "had not been present during the discussions and was now presented with a position by a spokesman who was not able to negotiate before having again consulted with his eight colleagues."[27] While Kissinger undoubtedly put his finger on the central weakness of European institutions, his impatient response to cumbersome procedures revealed very substantive concerns that European political integration that would exclude the United States. Andersen's presentation of the European draft proposal reinforced Washington's determination to be included in the European decision-making process rather than wait to negotiate with European institutions after the Europeans had decided on a common position. With their resistance to Europe's multilateral approach – evident, too, in their categorical refusal to sign a European-American declaration at a meeting with EC institutions rather than with European heads of state[28] – Kissinger and Nixon not only powerfully underscored their preference for traditional bilateral diplomacy and their conception of international relations as relations between nation-states but also betrayed their opposition to European political integration.

In the first meeting of the political directors after Andersen had presented Kissinger with the EPC draft declaration, Assistant Secretary of State Walter Stoessel and Undersecretary Helmut Sonnenfeldt insisted that the United States be given "the opportunity, through consultations, to make its opinions heard during the phase in which the Europeans formed their own opinion."[29] Kissinger reiterated this demand in talks with European leaders and in his "Pilgrims" speech in December, which he himself had billed as a conciliatory gesture.[30] Despite American claims to the contrary,

---

ship and that France was currently that ship. Compare Jobert, *L'Autre Regard* (Paris, 1976), 298; Staden to Scheel, Sept. 7, 1973, *AAPD* 1973, doc. 277.

26 For a discussion of its contents, see Möckli, "Asserting Europe's Distinct Identity."

27 Memorandum by Andersen, *AAPD* 1973, doc. 296n7. Kissinger's unfavorable comments were leaked to the press, probably by European diplomats; David Binder, "Hard Europe Line Laid to Kissinger," *New York Times*, Sept. 30, 1973. On Kissinger's anger, see also Staden to Scheel, Oct. 1, 1973, VS-Vol. 528 (014); B 150, Copies 1973, Files of the German Foreign Office, Berlin. For Kissinger's contrastingly positive evaluation in public, compare his news conference, Sept. 26, 1973, *Department of State Bulletin* 69 (1973), 476.

28 See, e.g., Memorandum by Brunner, July 16, 1973, *AAPD* 1973, doc. 222. On the genesis of the European proposal, see Cable by Schlingensiepen, June 6, 1973, *AAPD* 1973, doc. 178.

29 Cable by Simon, Oct. 1, 1973, *AAPD* 1973, doc. 301.

30 Kissinger, "The United States and a Unifying Europe," 779.

these requests suggested that Washington was unwilling to accept Europe as a "distinct entity" – the formulation chosen in the Europeans' September draft. A political entity would normally make its decisions first and then enter into negotiations with its partners. It is, therefore, not surprising that the Europeans resisted the American demand.[31]

Procedural questions thus turned out to be crucial because the American initiative almost forced Europe to define itself and its response in opposition to Washington. Nowhere was this more apparent than in the other important decision taken at Copenhagen in July: the EPC would not only prepare a draft for a European-American declaration but also formulate a document on European identity.[32] Procedures came to symbolize the approach both sides were taking toward Europe's pursuit of integration. By means of EPC, most of the EC members were trying to develop and express a European identity that the United States was apparently not yet willing to accept.

PRESSURING BONN: THE ISSUE OF CONSULTATIONS

For the Europeans, the Yom Kippur War threw into stark relief that the procedural question of consultations emerged as the main substantive issue in transatlantic negotiations. All the NATO partners objected to not being consulted about U.S. weapons shipments to Israel, but the Federal Republic was particularly concerned because most of these weapons had been stored on its territory. U.S. Ambassador Martin Hillenbrand did contact Foreign Minister Scheel on October 16, but only to provide information rather than to engage in actual consultation – he admitted that the first flights from U.S. bases in West Germany might already be under way. Contrary to subsequent American complaints about Bonn's uncooperative attitude, Scheel actually consented to the shipments, provided that they were presented as a measure taken purely on American authority.[33] After the armistice was signed in the Middle East on October 22 – and after West Germany had been put under pressure by the Arab states – the Brandt government requested that the shipments be stopped, only to discover that American arms were still being loaded onto Israeli ships in West German harbors – a fact that undermined

---

31 This was the reason why the French rejected the terms "partnership" and "consultation," which the Americans sought to insert in the European draft declaration; Cable by Poensgen, Oct. 12, 1973, *AAPD* 1973, doc. 323. On the European refusal, see also Möckli, "Asserting Europe's Distinct Identity."

32 Cable by Dohms on the EPC Ministerial Meeting at Copenhagen, July 23, 1973, *AAPD* 1973, doc. 229.

33 Conversation between Scheel and Hillenbrand on Oct. 16, 1973, *AAPD* 1973, doc. 322.

Bonn's denial that it had given tacit consent to the shipments.[34] Washington's decision on October 25 to put U.S. troops worldwide on highest alert without consulting the allies deepened the crisis; Kissinger's feeble and condescending explanation that Washington thought it was acting in the best interest of the alliance did nothing to defuse the dispute.[35] In the eyes of the Europeans, Washington's actions during the Yom Kippur War suggested that transatlantic consultations would always be a one-way street: Washington would demand a say in European decisions without allowing Europe a reciprocal influence. American unilateralism during the October War clearly reflected Washington's conviction, so eloquently expressed in Kissinger's Year of Europe speech, that only the United States had global responsibilities.

As if in defiance of this attitude, the Europeans, including an initially reluctant Federal Republic, followed France's lead in devising a Middle East policy of their own, passing a heavily pro-Arab resolution in early November and initiating a "Euro-Arab dialogue."[36] This European incursion into international politics infuriated Kissinger and led to a temporary informal suspension of transatlantic negotiations. In late October, Kissinger told von Staden that he was "so bored" with the negotiations, and he added ominously that Nixon's would be the last administration with an emotional attachment to Europe.[37] Although it was not clear to Bonn whether Kissinger was still seeking some sort of transatlantic declaration, Kissinger left no doubt that the United States would continue to insist on having a say in the European decision-making process.[38] It was not until the NATO summit and Kissinger's meeting with European foreign ministers in December that negotiations were resumed.[39]

34 Compare the conversation between Frank and the American envoy Cash, Oct. 24, 1973, *AAPD* 1973, doc. 335.
35 See Staden to German Foreign Office, Nov. 2, 1973, *AAPD* 1973, doc. 356. On the Yom Kippur War's effect on the transatlantic alliance, compare Barnet, *The Alliance*, 322–6; and James Chace, "Is There a Price to Be Paid?" in Chace and Ravenal, *Atlantis Lost*, 69–74.
36 Jobert suggested such an approach in a speech before the Assembly of the Western European Union on Nov. 21, 1973; *Politique Etrangère* (2e semestre, 1973), 209. In a conversation with Jobert on Nov. 26, West German Foreign Minister Scheel welcomed the idea but insisted that the Middle East had to be stabilized, possibly pacified, before such talks could begin; *AAPD* 1973, doc. 391.
37 Staden to Scheel, Oct. 26, 1973, *AAPD* 1973, doc. 341. To one of the leaders of the German opposition, Franz Josef Strauss, Kissinger complained much more forcefully that the recent events raised doubts about whether the Europeans would be able to take on even regional responsibilities. See Staden to Frank, Oct. 20, 1973, *AAPD* 1973, doc. 332.
38 On the German confusion, see Memorandum by Steffler on the French-German Consultation of the Political Directors, Dec. 18, 1973, *AAPD* 1973, doc. 424.
39 On the resumption of transatlantic consultations in December, the NATO summit, Kissinger's meeting with the European foreign ministers, and his "Pilgrims" speech in London, see Möckli, "Asserting Europe's Distinct Identity."

A more serious crisis for Bonn was still to come. Kissinger had already scored a tactical victory in the transatlantic row with his proposal for a meeting to devise a common response to the oil crisis. With Bonn's support – and despite Paris's bitter resistance – the Washington Energy Conference took place in February 1974. Despite the backing he had received from Bonn for the Washington conference, Kissinger took advantage of the next opportunity to exert pressure on the Brandt government in the hope of resolving the transatlantic confrontation to his satisfaction.[40] Once again, the question of consultations was at issue. On the eve of an EPC ministerial meeting on March 4, 1974, during which the shape of the Euro–Arab dialogue was to be finalized, Kissinger met with Scheel. In his memoirs, Kissinger writes that their conversation was very pleasant and touched on the Euro–Arab dialogue only in passing. He was thus shocked, he recounts, to be "presented publicly and without warning with a fait accompli" in Brussels, namely with the decision for a far-reaching dialogue with the Arab countries. Kissinger then exploded in public, accusing the Europeans of sabotaging the Middle East peace process, and he kept up a steady barrage of scathing criticism after returning to Washington. On March 15, Nixon weighed in with his most serious attack on the European allies to date, charging the Europeans of "ganging up" on the United States, and ominously held out the possibility of reducing the American military presence in Europe.[41]

German archival records suggest, however, that Kissinger staged this crisis to exert maximum pressure on Bonn, to derail the Euro–Arab dialogue, and to achieve a satisfactory procedure for future American-European consultations. According to the German sources, the envisioned talks between the European and Arab states had, in fact, been the main topic of conversation during Kissinger's meeting with Scheel. Scheel had assured him that the dialogue would focus on economic questions and regional development, and that oil and political questions would be kept off the agenda. Although Kissinger reiterated his concerns, he did not express anger or ask that the Europeans suspend their idea.[42] Scheel reported on this rather

---

40 For details, see Möckli, "Asserting Europe's Distinct Identity."
41 Kissinger, *Years of Upheaval*, 927–34. On his criticism in Washington, which was supposedly leaked by the press without permission, see "Goodwill Pledge by Kissinger to Resolve Issues with Allies," *International Herald Tribune*, Mar. 13, 1974. Nixon, "Address to the Executives' Club," Chicago, Mar. 15, 1974, in *Public Papers of the President of the United States. Richard Nixon: January 1 to August 9, 1974* (Washington, D.C., 1975), 276. The public attacks were accompanied by a harsh letter of Nixon to Brandt, Mar. 6, 1974; as quoted in Brandt to Nixon, Mar. 8, 1974, *AAPD 1974*, doc. 81n2. For a more detailed analysis of Nixon's speech and letters, see Möckli, "Asserting Europe's Distinct Identity."
42 Memorandum of Conversation by Simon, Mar. 3, 1974, *AAPD 1974*, doc. 67.

undramatic conversation to the other eight EC foreign ministers; Kissinger might thus have contributed to the passage of the document on the Euro-Arab dialogue.[43] Certainly, his harsh criticism in Brussels the day after his meeting with Scheel came as a surprise to the Europeans, not least of all to the West Germans.[44]

To be sure, Kissinger's worries that the Euro-Arab dialogue might touch on political questions and thereby obstruct his own initiatives in the Middle East were not unfounded.[45] Nonetheless, his claim of not having been consulted was dishonest. This reading of the incident is supported by the fact that the controversy faded away quickly once Kissinger and Nixon had had their opportunity to criticize the Europeans. In a conversation with the German ambassador on March 16, Kissinger apologized for "misunderstanding" Scheel. He even admitted that an unnamed European government had passed the draft resolution on the dialogue to the State Department in advance, but he claimed that it had not reached him before the meeting in Brussels. In light of how incensed Washington was when the idea of a Euro-Arab dialogue was first mooted, it is extremely difficult to believe the State Department would have allowed such a lapse. In fact, Kissinger's concluding assurance that his government was much more upset about France points to the true objective of the staged crisis, namely to divide the European partners and to increase the pressure on Bonn, the most vulnerable of the European allies when questions about American security guarantees were raised, as they had been in Nixon's speech.[46]

By holding Scheel personally responsible and by implying that better consultation mechanisms could have avoided the embarrassing crisis,[47] Kissinger also achieved progress on the issue of transatlantic consultations. In mid-March, German diplomats circulated a formula in Europe that became the basis for a transatlantic agreement: the United States would be consulted

---

43 On the EPC ministerial meeting, see Memorandum by Simon, Mar. 7, 1974, *AAPD* 1974, doc. 77.

44 Conversation between Scheel and Kissinger, Mar. 4, 1974, *AAPD* 1974, doc. 69.

45 The previously mentioned November 1973 EPC declaration on the situation in the Middle East had already been decidedly pro-Arab. More importantly, during his recent trip to the region's Arab countries, Jobert suggested repeatedly that the European-Arab dialogue would compensate for the continent's absence from the Geneva peace conference. This interpretation of the dialogue would actually imply its political significance, even though France had officially consented to keep political questions out of the dialogue. See, e.g., Jobert's address at the dinner given by the Syrian Foreign Minister Khaddam, Jan. 28, 1974, *La Politique Etrangère* (1er semestre 1974): 67.

46 Staden to Scheel, Mar. 16–17, 1974, *AAPD* 1974, docs. 96–97. In a conversation on Mar. 7, Frank already speculated about the fabricated nature of Kissinger's outburst and his "divide et impera" approach to transatlantic relations; *AAPD* 1974, doc. 76.

47 Kissinger's advisers made this point to the German ambassador; Staden to Foreign Office, Mar. 6, 1974, *AAPD* 1974, doc. 97n19.

on initiatives by the Nine *after* their political directors had come to a decision but *before* the decision was finalized by the foreign ministers.[48] While Kissinger's calculated eruption may have moved the West Germans toward compromise on the issue of consultations, other factors certainly contributed to greater European flexibility as well. The oil shock and the energy conference convinced many Europeans that they needed Washington's support to solve their energy problem, and the new British government exhibited a decidedly pro-American bent.[49]

Hence, two of Europe's big three were determined by March 1974 to end the acrimonious squabbling between Europe and the United States, and they needed only to make clear to Paris that it could join in or be left out in the cold.[50] In mid-April, the Nine met with European Commission President François-Xavier Ortoli at Castle Gymnich near Bonn and settled on a gentlemen's agreement for consultations with the United States. The Gymnich formula stipulated that if one member state wanted the EPC to consult with a non-European ally, the Nine would discuss it and direct the current holder of the EPC presidency to initiate such consultations.[51] As Möckli perceptively points out, the negative policy implicit in the formula was also important: if the member states could not agree on consulting the United States on a particular issue, it would, if possible, be removed from the European agenda and moved to the bilateral level. At the same time, each member state was free to consult Washington bilaterally. At Gymnich, the Nine effectively abandoned all pretense of initiating foreign policies anathema to their American partner.

Jobert was able to block adoption of the Gymnich formula, which he considered a capitulation to American demands, until the presidential election in April 1974 following Pompidou's death. In mid-June, however, with new governments in place in London, Paris, and Bonn, the Nine confirmed the Gymnich accord. In a further concession to the United States, introduced by Bonn's new foreign minister, Hans-Dietrich Genscher, they

---

48 See Cable by van Well, *AAPD* 1974, doc. 89. With the exception of the French, all other political directors agreed that this suggestion should be discussed with the Americans.
49 See Möckli, "Asserting Europe's Distinct Identity," and Noble, "Kissinger's Year of Europe, Britain's Year of Choice."
50 Conversation between Scheel and Foreign Minister Callaghan in Bonn, Mar. 21, 1974, AAPD 1974, doc. 100.
51 On the Gymnich Conference, Apr. 20–21, 1974, see Memorandum by van Well, Apr. 22, 1974, *AAPD* 1974, doc. 128. Jobert's rejection of a binding decision was due at least in part to the presence of EC Commission's President Ortoli in Gymnich: the French had traditionally been hesitant about involving the commission in political matters. For the text of the gentlemen's agreement, see Cable by von der Gablentz, May 29, 1974, *AAPD* 1974, doc. 155.

also struck a clause from their political directors' report that held out the possibility of including political issues in the Euro-Arab dialogue.[52]

Kissinger thus prevailed in the end by increasing pressure on Bonn and using tactical maneuvers to regain the upper hand in the competition for power within the Atlantic alliance. The subsequent implementation of the Gymnich formula showed that precise procedures of transatlantic consultations mattered less as long as the Nine tacitly relinquished their ambition to devise a foreign policy independent of Washington. The most important consultations would again take place on the bilateral level. Nevertheless, during the Year of Europe crisis procedures had been important as they embodied Europe's search for an independent foreign policy and signaled Washington's reserves against a political integration of Europe.

EUROPEAN POLITICAL INTEGRATION AND AMERICAN BARGAINING CHIPS

What became of European political integration during the Year of Europe? Initially, the positive impulses from the EC summit in Paris in late 1972 and the confrontational attitude of the United States in 1973, together with European fears of a superpower condominium, provided a boost to political integration. The July 1973 decision by the EC Nine not to be split by separate bilateral negotiations with Washington and to proceed instead through the EPC sent a strong signal to Washington. In short order, the Europeans agreed on a draft transatlantic resolution, embarked on their own Middle East policy, and passed a declaration on European identity.[53] Kissinger strenuously objected to the document on European identity as yet another example of the Nine's confrontational attitude. With its emphasis on the Nine as an "autonomous, unmistakable whole" in world affairs and on Europe's "global responsibilities," it did in fact implicitly raise objections to certain aspects of his Year of Europe address. Furthermore, by reiterating their goal of entering into an independent "constructive dialogue" with Canada and Japan, the Europeans deliberately antagonized Kissinger, who had wanted to include these two countries in a "trilateral" declaration of all Western partners – under American leadership, of course.[54]

---

52 On the decision on transatlantic consultations, see Cable by von der Gablentz, June 12, 1974, *AAPD* 1974, doc. 168. On the European-Arab dialogue, see Memorandum by Redies, June 12, 1974, *AADP* 1974.
53 See Möckli, "Asserting Europe's Distinct Identity."
54 For the "Document on the European Identity," Dec. 14, 1973, *Europa Archiv 1974*, D 50–3. On European approaches to Japan and Canada in November 1973, see Cable by van Well, Nov. 15, 1973, *AAPD* 1973, doc. 377nn9–10.

Despite this extraordinary – by European standards – demonstration of a unified political will, European governments, Bonn in particular, were painfully aware of their deficiencies in the realm of defense and openly admitted their dependence on the United States in the identity document. Throughout the Year of Europe, U.S. forces on the continent were Kissinger's and Nixon's most important bargaining chip. Given the congressional pressure on the White House to reduce the American military commitment in Europe, the Nixon administration's warnings that it could not stave off the isolationist forces forever if the Europeans continued their obstinacy sounded credible.[55] Conscious of the West Germans' fears on this point and afraid that Bonn might cave in to the American linkage strategy, Paris employed several strategies to reassure Bonn. At first, French officials insisted publicly and privately that Nixon's threats of troop reductions were not credible because American national interests required the presence of U.S. troops in Europe.[56] When this strategy proved insufficient, the French initiated talks on closer defense cooperation with the Germans and the British.[57] Given Paris's fierce determination to maintain complete independence in defense up to that point, Bonn and London eagerly seized on this opportunity.[58]

The eagerness with which the Germans pursued the French offer of defense cooperation and their previously mentioned willingness to endure Washington's anger demonstrated a marked, if temporary, change in attitude that historians of Bonn's foreign policy usually overlook. At least for certain periods during the Year of Europe, the Federal Republic under Brandt abandoned the role of dutiful mediator between France and the United States and sought to exploit the transatlantic crisis as an opportunity to extract French concessions on European integration. The importance the Brandt government attached to European integration was reflected in

---

55 For such warnings, see, e.g., Conversation between Brandt and Nixon, Sept. 29, 1973, *AAPD* 1973, doc. 298; Memorandum by Simon, Mar. 3, 1974, *AAPD* 1974, doc. 67.

56 Jobert, Address before the Western European Union, Nov. 21, 1973; *Politique Étrangère* (2e semestre 1973): 210. Jobert reiterated this view in conversations with German diplomats and politicians; see Memorandum by Frank, Aug. 31, 1973, *AAPD* 1973, doc. 267, and Bahr to German Foreign Office, Nov. 20, 1973, *AAPD* 1973, doc. 382.

57 See, e.g., Jobert before the French National Assembly, June 19, 1973, *Politique Étrangère* (1er semestre 1973), 176, and Pompidou at a press conference, Sept. 27, 1973, *Politique Étrangère* (2e semestre 1973): 117–18.

58 The talks on cooperation actually went so far that, in November 1973, Jobert told Scheel that he could imagine a day when French ground forces would defend parts of the Federal Republic's eastern border. Conversation between Scheel and Jobert, Nov. 9, 1973, *AAPD* 1973, doc. 368. Similarly, French Defense Minister Robert Galley told his German colleague Georg Leber that France considered the Federal Republic's eastern border as its own defensive line; Memorandum by Pfeffer, Sept. 6, 1973, *AAPD* 1973, doc. 275.

a Foreign Ministry analysis of the French NATO declaration draft of early October 1973. Although one might expect that the report would focus on the question of how palatable the draft would be to the Washington, it opened with an analysis of the draft's implications for European defense cooperation.[59]

Nevertheless, neither West Germany nor Great Britain assumed that the foundations of Western Europe's security would change over night. A European defense more independent of the United States was a desirable objective, in Scheel's view, but it could be achieved only in the long run. In the meantime, a German Foreign Office policy paper stated unequivocally: "The Atlantic Alliance remains the basis of our security."[60] Moreover, the paper continued, European defense cooperation ought to be embedded within NATO. Accordingly, the Germans and the British sought to draw France into NATO's Eurogroup, but the French, in a thinly veiled attempt to build a structure parallel to NATO, argued for reanimating the Western European Union.[61] These opposing positions were ultimately the rock on which the brief flirtation with a common European defense policy foundered.

Despite progress in the talks on European defense cooperation, differences soon became evident, even in the realm of political cooperation. Already in August 1973, Bonn found itself having to perform a difficult balancing act after having accepted the "Gaullist" British proposal as the basis of the EPC draft declaration under pressure from Paris. The Brandt government was well aware that it provoked American resentment by giving priority to European integration, but it still clung to its belief that European integration and transatlantic unity were compatible. Even as the Nine were presenting a united front to Washington in August and September 1973, the fault lines within Europe were apparent: Paris was willing to confront the Americans head-on, but Bonn, though prepared to risk minor disagreements, did not want to permanently antagonize Washington. The foreign policy dilemma Bonn faced under Brandt is perhaps best explained by describing transatlantic relations as matter of the head and the European

59 Memorandum by van Well, Oct. 8, 1973, *AAPD* 1973, doc. 315.
60 Scheel in conversation with German Defense Minister Leber, Sept. 4, 1973; Memorandum by Pfeffer, Sept. 5, 1973, *AAPD* 1973, doc. 274. For the Guidelines Paper, Nov. 12, 1973, see AAPD 1973, doc. 372. In mid-December, Bahr warned Brandt that Pompidou's forthcoming proposal for a European security council would only amount to an "insecurity council," and he emphasized that West German security was only ensured within NATO. Bahr to Brandt, Dec. 14, 1973, Depositum Bahr, Box 436, Friedrich-Ebert-Stiftung, Bonn.
61 Conversation between Scheel and Prime Minister Heath, Nov. 22, 1973, *AAPD* 1973, doc. 385; Conversation between Scheel and Jobert, Nov. 26, 1973, *AAPD* 1973, doc. 391. On the British position, see also Memorandum by Pfeffer, Feb. 7, 1974, *AAPD* 1974, doc. 38.

project as a matter of the heart. In the late summer of 1973, Bonn was still able to resist the pressure from both Paris and Washington to choose sides but that choice could no longer be avoided toward the end of the long Year of Europe when the head won out over the heart.

In the end, it was the oil crisis and American policies to counter it that undermined European unity. Unable to arrive at a common energy policy at the Copenhagen summit in December 1973, the Europeans had failed to furnish an answer to the most pressing problem of the day.[62] Kissinger's surprise offer of an American-sponsored energy conference succeeded in splitting the Europeans. As Möckli demonstrates, French intransigence led to a major confrontation between Jobert and Helmut Schmidt at the Washington conference, but Bonn had in fact lost patience with Paris before then.[63] When Jobert, on January 18, 1974, sent a letter to the United Nations urgently calling for the convocation of an energy conference under its auspices, West German Deputy Foreign Minister Paul Frank called on the French ambassador and warned that France's absence from Washington would drive Bonn to withdraw its support for Paris's cherished plans for the Euro-Arab dialogue. He added brusquely that France's pro-Arab policies had not yielded any tangible results in the energy sector.[64] The French did participate in the Washington conference but refused to commit to any follow-up measures and organizations. As if to take revenge for the German preconference pressure, Jobert attacked Schmidt for having gone beyond the EC mandate for the conference and publicly accused him of having betrayed the common European cause.[65]

While Kissinger's initiative on energy cooperation brought intra-European problems out into the open in early 1974, some centripetal forces had already been inherent in the initial response to the Year of Europe initiative. National interests had weighed more heavily than European ones in the major European powers' decisions in favor of deepening political cooperation in July 1973. Having fathered EPC in 1970, West Germany regarded a common strategy for negotiating with the United States as an ideal opportunity to express and expand political integration. France, in contrast, seized on the EPC primarily to obstruct negotiations with the

62 Willy Brandt deplored this failure in his memoirs, *Begegnungen und Einsichten* (Hamburg, 1976), 599.
63 Möckli, "Asserting Europe's Distinct Identity."
64 *Politique Étrangère* (1er semestre 1974): 8; von der Gablentz to Foreign Office, Jan. 23, 1974, *AAPD* 1974, doc. 23.
65 On the Washington Energy Conference, see Memorandum by Dannenbring, Feb. 15, 1974, *AAPD* 1974, doc. 49. On Jobert's attacks on Schmidt, see Jobert, *Mémoires d'avenir*, 277; Link, "Aussen- und Deutschlandpolitik," 262. See also Kissinger's account, *Years of Upheaval*, 911–20, and Helmut Schmidt's, *Menschen und Mächte* (Berlin, 1987), 202.

United States and to ensure that its European partners would not give in to American pressure. When EC member states felt that their immediate national interests would best be served by alignment with the United States – as most did on the issue of energy – European unity quickly evaporated.

The commitment to a common foreign policy remained fragile in the wake of the Year of Europe.[66] At the UN General Assembly in the fall of 1974, France and Italy voted in favor of granting the Palestinian Liberation Organization (PLO) observer status even though there had been no decision on this sensitive issue at the European level. Similarly, France was again willing to assent when the Arab nations demanded that the PLO participate in the Euro-Arab dialogue, while most other European countries objected.[67] This disagreement led to a suspension of the project Kissinger had so vigorously criticized.

In NATO, Nixon and Kissinger obtained their declaration, which – as Möckli notes – amounted to a routine reaffirmation of Atlantic unity and made no reference to an independent European foreign policy.[68] As a snub to Washington, France sent Prime Minister Jacques Chirac rather than President Valéry Giscard d'Estaing to the Ottawa NATO summit, and faint echoes of the acrimonious Year of Europe disputes could still be heard in Nixon's and Chirac's public comments on signing the Ottawa Declaration. Whereas Nixon underscored the need for consultation outside the realm of NATO affairs, Chirac stressed the independence of all NATO members, regardless of size, and their status as equals.[69]

CONCLUSION

Did, then, the Year of Europe have any lasting effect on transatlantic relations? Although Kissinger's initiative ended with little more than a ceremonial declaration of transatlantic unity that was quickly forgotten, the controversy it sparked reflected important patterns in transatlantic and in intra-European relations. Hardly a benevolent initiative intended for the common good of the alliance, the Year of Europe was aimed at maintaining American predominance in a new era of détente and European political

---

66 On the relatively successful EPC within the CSCE, see Sarah B. Snyder, "The United States, Western Europe, and the Commission on Security and Cooperation in Europe, 1972–1975," in this volume.
67 See UN Ambassador von Wechmar to Foreign Office, Oct. 14, 1974, *AAPD* 1974, doc. 306n5. On the participation of the PLO in the European-Arab dialogue, see Memorandum by Schirmer, Dec. 18, 1974, *AAPD* 1974, doc. 379.
68 Möckli, "Asserting Europe's Distinct Identity."
69 Krapf to German Foreign Office, June 26, 1974, *AAPD* 1974, doc. 191.

integration. Those developments and the diminished authority of an American president under threat of impeachment emboldened the Europeans not only to resist American pressure but also to express European identity and strengthen European integration. Kissinger may have been outraged that the Europeans sought to define their identity in opposition to the United States, but his heavy-handed assertion that European integration had to remain subordinate to transatlantic interests almost forced the Nine to set off their enterprise from the Atlantic alliance. The very fact that Nixon and Kissinger employed the strategy of linkage, moreover, seemed to indicate to Europeans that Washington would be taking a more adversarial stance in transatlantic relations and would aggressively use the U.S. military presence in Europe to exact political and economic concessions.

The highly qualified character of American support for Western European integration was evident in Kissinger and Nixon's impatience with EPC and their insistence on consultations before the Europeans made any political decisions. By indicating a preference for a bilateral approach and by insisting on being consulted before any European decision, they in effect laid claim to veto rights in European affairs.

If the Year of Europe failed to consolidate American hegemony as Kissinger and Nixon had hoped, it also proved a disappointment to the European governments that had considered it an opportunity to advance European integration. Europe's essentially negative self-identification, defined by resistance to the U.S. initiative, was not a sufficient basis for an integrated foreign policy in the long run. The EC member states made great strides toward political cooperation in the beginning of their Year of Europe deliberations, but only because their individual national interests briefly coincided. Ultimately, the gap between the French and West German positions on transatlantic relations – the French use of the EPC against the United States versus Germany's desire for European political integration but not to the permanent detriment of German-American relations – could not be bridged. Hence, it was only a question of time before events and external pressure would undercut the fragile coalition. The decisive event was, of course, the oil shock, and external pressure came in the form of Kissinger's Washington Energy Conference initiative. In this instance, Kissinger's bilateral approach and his wily cabinet-style diplomatic maneuvering bore fruit. As soon as the Europeans discovered that their interests were no longer identical, the harmony and common will evaporated.

While the changes of government in the big three European countries between March and May of 1974 contributed to the speedy resolution of the transatlantic crisis, the fact that the Brandt government had paved the way for the Gymnich compromise indicates that Europe's dilemma went deeper than personalities or parties. In the end, the EPC turned out to be little more than a platform for institutionalized negotiations between nation-states, much as the skeptical Kissinger had expected. The Middle East crisis made the Nine realize how right Kissinger had been in his assessment of Europe's global weight. If Washington lacked the power to shape a Europe of its own liking, it could nonetheless use its influence to break up a seemingly unified European front. Given West Germany's inherently vulnerable position, it is not surprising that Kissinger focused on Bonn when he escalated the pressure on Europe in March 1974.

The final results of the Year of Europe were thus decidedly mixed. For a time, Europe had stood up to American demands of predominance. The intrusion of world politics into the insulated transatlantic dialogue quickly proved, however, that Europe still lacked the power – and the will – to deal with a global emergency. Because of this deficiency, because of the inherent power of the United States, and because of the divergence of national interests in the Old World, European unification against the United States was not possible – nor will it be any time soon.

12

The United States, Western Europe, and the Conference on Security and Cooperation in Europe, 1972–1975

SARAH B. SNYDER

The Soviet Union, hoping for formal recognition of the post–World War II borders in Central and Eastern Europe, had sought a European security conference (ESC) since 1954, but the North Atlantic Treaty Organization (NATO) allies feared that such a conference would be far more beneficial to the Soviets than to Western Europe. Primary Western European concerns were that a conference could strengthen the Soviet position in Eastern Europe, divide the Western alliance, and expand the influence of Soviet Communism internationally. By the late 1960s, however, widespread public interest in reducing East-West tension, and potential strategic gains from a conference overcame Western resistance. The outcome was a complex, drawn-out period of diplomacy broadly divided into three phases: developing consensus to hold an ESC from 1969 to 1972; the Helsinki consultations in 1972 and 1973 to determine the timing and agenda for the conference; and the crucial negotiations of the Geneva stage from 1973 to 1975. The negotiations culminated in a document, the Helsinki Final Act, that contained principles to govern East-West interactions in Europe. In addition to incorporating an agreement on the inviolability of frontiers, the Helsinki Final Act committed its signatories to respect human rights and facilitate human contacts across East-West borders.[1] Often described

---

1 The Conference on Security and Cooperation in Europe (CSCE) negotiations from 1972 to 1975 and the Helsinki Final Act that resulted were structured around four groupings of issues, which were called "baskets." The first dealt with ten principles guiding relations in Europe, most notably Principle Three, which established the inviolability of frontiers and Principle Six, which mandated nonintervention in internal affairs. The first basket also addressed confidence-building measures such as advanced notification of troop maneuvers, prior notification of military movements, provisions for the exchange of observers, and disarmament. The second basket concentrated on economic, scientific, and technological cooperation between CSCE states. It discussed facilitating business contacts, cooperating with

as the "high point of détente," the Helsinki Final Act would prove a key diplomatic turning point in the Cold War.[2]

Throughout the discussions, the United States strained to balance its commitment to NATO and its bilateral interests with the Soviet Union. The primary American objective ostensibly was to maintain allied unity and support Western European interests. However, its other policy prerogatives, namely Soviet-American détente, eventually led the United States to work closely with the Soviet Union to expedite what became known as the Conference on Security and Cooperation in Europe (CSCE). This behavior, in which the United States could often be categorized as playing a mediating rather than a partisan role, piqued allied suspicions of Soviet-American collusion and at times threatened fissures in the Atlantic alliance. Thus, the CSCE presented the United States with a difficult course to navigate – avoiding disadvantage and fracture to the alliance while preserving a newfound partnership with the Soviet Union.

Opposition among the allies to the Soviets' ESC proposal initially was unanimous. The Western European countries had important reservations because of concerns about the myriad Soviet objectives the conference could facilitate, most significantly the legitimization of the Soviet position in Eastern Europe.[3] The United States, uninvited by the Soviets in many of their early calls for a conference, was particularly opposed to the idea. The shock of the 1968 Soviet invasion of Czechoslovakia only further convinced the NATO allies that they should not consider such an initiative.

Nevertheless, many West European governments were keenly aware of their populations' desire for decreased East-West tension. It was in this climate that a new Warsaw Pact appeal for a conference resurrected the

---

respect to industry, encouraging tourism, and expanding transportation networks. The third basket concentrated on increasing contacts through family meetings and reunifications, binational marriages, and travel. In addition, Basket Three also addressed humanitarian issues such as improved working conditions for journalists, increased cultural exchanges, educational cooperation, and better information flow. The fourth basket outlined a follow-up mechanism.

2 Mike Bowker and Phil Williams, *Superpower Détente: A Reappraisal* (Newbury Park, CA, 1988), 63; Peter Wallensteen, "American Soviet Détente: What Went Wrong?" *Journal of Peace Research* 22, no. 1 (1985): 1; Gregory A. Flynn, "The Content of European Detente," *Orbis* 20 (Summer 1976): 402–3; and William G. Hyland, *Mortal Rivals: Superpower Relations from Nixon to Reagan* (New York, 1987), 10. That current scholars and observers attribute a significant role to the Helsinki Final Act and the CSCE meetings that followed in ending the Cold War can be identified in proposals that the CSCE process be exported to other troubling regions, such as Central Asia and the Middle East. The Helsinki process is now widely regarded as a potential paradigm for addressing human rights abuses and a successful model for far-reaching, peaceful political change.

3 NSSM 83, "Current Issues of European Security," Folder NSSM 83 [1 of 4], Box H-166, Institutional National Security Council (NSC) Files, Nixon Presidential Materials Project, College Park, MD (hereafter NPMP).

issue on March 17, 1969. During a NATO ministerial meeting in Washington the following month, many foreign offices went on the record welcoming the appeal and calling for further discussion of the proposed conference. Western European governments, responsive to domestic politics, could not disregard potential opportunities to defuse tension with the Warsaw Pact. Indeed, Italian Prime Minister Mariano Rumor pointed out to U.S. President Richard Nixon that politically he could not reject such a proposal.[4] Moreover, the United Kingdom and others saw potentially positive implications for Eastern European autonomy and warned against dismissing such initiatives.[5]

In the face of Western European interest, the United States' long-held opposition to the conference began to subside. The Soviets removed a significant obstacle to the conference when they indicated that American participation would be acceptable; they later opened the way for Canadian participation as well.[6] In addition, as Soviet-American relations improved through détente, it became more difficult for Nixon and National Security Adviser Henry Kissinger to ignore Soviet General Secretary Leonid Brezhnev's strong interest, as the Soviets had emphasized that the conference was a "pet project" of senior officials.[7] In the early years of the Nixon administration, the most significant issues on the American foreign policy agenda were the Strategic Arms Limitation Talks (SALT) with the Soviets, the quadripartite negotiations regarding Berlin, and the situation in the Middle East; the proposed ESC was of secondary concern. Despite Washington's expectation that such a conference would be of limited value – Kissinger thought the CSCE offered no benefit to the West and would have no practical impact on international relations – it was not willing to sacrifice its recently cultivated relationship with the Soviet Union, its ties to Europe, or its NATO partnership to avoid participation in the ESC.[8]

In the delicate negotiations that led to the CSCE, NATO's broad goals included limiting Soviet influence in Western Europe, maintaining alliance unity, facilitating peaceful political change in Eastern Europe, reducing

4 Memorandum of Conversation, Apr. 1, 1969, Folder 2, Box 694, NSC Files, NPMP.
5 REU 25, "Current West European Attitudes toward a European Security Conference," Apr. 3, 1969, Folder 1, Box 709, Country Files: Europe, NSC Files, NPMP.
6 Kissinger wrote, "This represents a major change in Soviet policy." Memorandum, Kissinger to Nixon, Apr. 3, 1969, Folder 1: Briefing Book, Box 56, Country Files: Europe, HAK Office Files, NPMP. Canada and the United States were not part of the original 1954 Soviet proposal.
7 John J. Maresca, *To Helsinki: The Conference on Security and Cooperation in Europe, 1973–1975* (Durham, NC, 1985), 10; and Telegram, AmEmbassy Moscow to SecState, Feb. 19, 1970, Folder 1, Box 711, Country Files: Europe, NSC Files, NPMP.
8 Jussi Hanhimäki, "'They Can Write It in Swahili:' Kissinger, The Soviets, and the Helsinki Accords, 1973–1975," *Journal of Transatlantic Studies* 1, no. 1 (2003): 37.

East-West tensions, and extracting Soviet concessions on other issues before agreeing to a conference. Allied positions became more complex, however, in the course of the protracted, often-tense negotiations as the conference progressed. Building and maintaining consensus for allied policy in the CSCE was difficult as many countries balanced individual bilateral relationships with their multilateral alliance. As with the United States, some Western European countries were unwilling to jeopardize détente with the Soviet Union for the sake of humanitarian issues. Over time, the CSCE seemed less a symbol of the strength of détente than an indication of its fragility and therefore increased divisions within the West as to what agenda to pursue.

DEVELOPING NATO CONSENSUS FOR A CONFERENCE

After the United States had put aside its objections to an ESC, the NATO allies entered into discussions about how best to achieve allied objectives in such a conference. They sought to develop substantive conference proposals that would turn the CSCE to the allies' advantage. This transatlantic discussion was overshadowed, however, by Kissinger's disregard for the CSCE and his greater interest in Berlin and mutual and balanced force reductions (MBFR).

By the fall of 1970, statements by French and West German leaders forced recognition among the Western allies that a conference had become inevitable, in part because of the fear that those who openly opposed the conference risked being seen as endangering détente. Therefore, the Western allies began multilateral efforts to secure immediate concessions on Berlin and to seize control of the substance of the proposed conference. Both the United States and the Federal Republic of Germany made their participation in the conference contingent on the conclusion of talks between the four postwar occupying powers: Great Britain, France, the United States, and the Soviet Union.[9] In addition, in ministerial meetings and bilateral talks, the NATO allies moved beyond initial Soviet hopes for a short, narrowly defined conference to envision one that would be as advantageous as possible to Western European goals. They explored including freer movement of people, ideas, and information on the agenda, as well as expanded cooperation within Europe and human rights.[10]

9 Telegram, AmEmbassy Moscow to SecState Washington, July 28, 1971, Folder 1, Box 715; and Telegram, AmEmbassy Bonn to SecState Washington, Oct. 14, 1970, Folder 2, Box 713, Country Files: Europe, NSC Files, NPMP.
10 Final Communiqué, May 26–27, 1970, http://www.nato.int/docu/comm/49–95/c700526a.htm.

The United States and most of the allies supported a tough negotiating position with the East on these issues.[11] To determine how the United States and the allies could best use the conference to advance their interests, clearly formulated allied objectives were necessary. In the words of National Security Council staff member Helmut C. Sonnenfeldt, "The main problem, thus, is that the Soviets have clear purposes . . . but the allies and the United States have no conception of what a Conference would achieve other than atmospherics of détente."[12]

Divergent national interests among the allies, however, complicated the development of a uniform NATO position. For example, the United States had concerns that France and the Federal Republic were prepared to participate in a conference without substance, whereas many American administration officials wanted to put the Soviets "on the tactical defensive" by including force reductions on the agenda and supporting a permanent institution to which East Europeans could appeal if threatened militarily.[13] At the same time, NATO coordination suffered from inattention from U.S. policy makers. Throughout the different stages of the CSCE negotiations, the United States perceived its bilateral negotiations with the Soviet Union on arms control and other matters as more significant than the CSCE. Therefore, it was less focused than its allies on the form and content of the conference, and thus, the European allies led the efforts to protect Western interests in the conference preparations, albeit with mixed results. At times, U.S. disinterest enabled the Western Europeans to press more forcefully on proposals intended to open Eastern Europe to outside influence, which the United States would likely have not supported given Soviet opposition to such measures. Yet American inattention to the negotiations also undermined the allied stance, reducing pressure on the Soviets to compromise.

Although the opportunity to garner Soviet compromises appealed to many in the West, NATO's overall priority was to prevent potential negative consequences from the conference. A NATO steering brief emphasized the alliance's defensive posture and outlined important goals for the consultations stage: sustain Western unity, avoid losing public and legislative

11 Telegram, USMission NATO to SecState, Sept. 10, 1971, Folder NSSM 138 [2 of 2], Box H-187, Institutional NSC Files, NPMP.
12 Memorandum, Sonnenfeldt to Kissinger, Nov. 18, 1971, Folder 1, Box H-63, Institutional NSC Files, NPMP.
13 NSSM 138: A Conference on European Security (Analytical Summary), Oct. 2, 1971; NSSM 138: Conference on European Security: Talking Points, Oct. 2, 1971, Folder 1, Box H-63, Institutional NSC Files, NPMP.

support for defense spending, convince the public to be cautious about the benefits of a CSCE, maintain momentum for Western European integration, disagree with the Soviet interpretation of peaceful coexistence, and assert the equality of states in their freedom from intervention. Although NATO members were in general agreement about defensive goals, they disagreed on the balance between extracting concessions and threatening European détente with confrontational negotiations. Potentially offensive objectives included diminishing divisions within Europe; championing human rights; formulating confidence-building measures (CBMs); and most controversially, increasing the autonomy of the Eastern European states.[14] The United States supported a more aggressive agenda in part to demonstrate that significant differences remained between the East and the West, thus necessitating the continuation of the Atlantic alliance and the presence of American troops in Europe.[15]

Despite the secondary role of the United States in these talks, its position was of particular importance because the Western European allies were concerned about maintaining harmony within the Atlantic alliance. The head of the British Foreign and Commonwealth Office's Western Organizations Department, Crispin Tickell, wrote, "We do indeed want to avoid any European/American row about CSCE, and we agree that the avoidance of such a row is more important than abstract arguments about how a hypothetical conference might be prepared."[16] The U.S. CSCE Inter-Agency Task Force's second interim report warned that the allies were splintering into two sides over the shape of the CSCE conference, with some pressing to strengthen détente and others for more substantive negotiations and agreements.[17] The task force suggested that if the NATO allies could

14 Draft Brief, Nov. 13, 1972, G. Bennett and K. A. Hamilton, eds., *Documents on British Policy Overseas: The Conference on Security and Cooperation in Europe, 1972–1975* (DBPO), series 3, volume 2 (London, 1997).

15 A National Security Study Memorandum supported an assertive approach by identifying potential propaganda victories and Soviet concessions. CSCE Task Force Second Interim Report, May 15, 1972, Folder 7, Box 103, Executive Secretary's Briefing Book, General Records of the Department of State, Record Group 59, National Archives, College Park, MD; and Reply to NSSM 138, Oct. 2, 1971, Folder 1, Box H-063, Institutional NSC Files, NPMP (hereafter RG 59). At the same time, however, others such as the National Security Council's Sonnenfeldt were cautious about the CSCE and believed that confrontational negotiations had limited potential significance. In Sonnenfeldt's view, "some debating points may be scored" but, for example, an agreement on freer movement would not significantly affect Europe. Memorandum, Sonnenfeldt to Kissinger, Aug. 19, 1972, "NATO, the Warsaw Pact and Détente, 1965–1973," Cold War International History Project Conference Volume.

16 Letter, Tickell to Butler, Mar. 27, 1972, *DBPO* 3:2. The WOD was the primary group working on CSCE issues for the British government.

17 CSCE Task Force Second Interim Report, May 15, 1972, Folder 7, Box 103, Executive Secretary's Briefing Book, RG 59.

maintain a uniform position, they could exact concessions as a result of Soviet emphasis on a "successful" conference.[18]

There were differences within the Nixon administration as to the significance of allied unity. Some officials, particularly in the State Department, suggested that Washington should agree to go forward with the conference purely to satisfy the desires of its allies. As they tried to formulate an administration policy on the CSCE, officials even considered deferring completely to what the Europeans wanted: "The [United States] could accept whatever issues the Allies deem desirable – the purpose of such an approach being to maintain unity."[19] Others, including Kissinger most importantly, acknowledged the importance of unity but wanted to preserve American negotiating prerogatives to pursue Soviet-American détente and to secure an agreement on MBFR. Nonetheless, the United States needed to maintain some semblance of harmony to preserve the alliance. To this end, Sonnenfeldt suggested that Kissinger dampen Soviet hopes of American cooperation with respect to the CSCE: "We have probably led the Soviets to believe that we are going to be their partner in fixing this conference in advance. In fact we have little freedom of action, given the keen interest of our Allies. Your main purpose, therefore, may be to introduce a note of sobriety in Soviet expectations, without appearing antagonistic toward their pet project."[20] Later Sonnenfeldt warned Kissinger that the importance of allied unity "means carefully resisting the natural temptation to cook the results of the conference with the Soviet Union, privately behind the backs of our friends."[21] This was particularly significant in light of concern by European allies that the United States already had preempted CSCE negotiations with the 1972 Soviet-American Basic Principles and their ongoing worries that the United States would pursue a bilateral agreement with the Soviets, undermining the role of other states in the CSCE consultations.[22] This anxiety was partly due to a general allied belief, largely accurate, that Kissinger did not view the CSCE as a "serious" matter.[23]

---

18 Attachment to Memorandum, Mar. 20, 1972, Folder NSDM 162, Box H – 233, Institutional NSC Files, NPMP. Well aware of the disunity, the Soviets worked to exploit these rifts as they pursued the conference through bilateral meetings with Western countries. Telegram, AmEmbassy Luxembourg to RUEHC/SecState, July 12, 1972, Folder 1, Box 720, Country Files: Europe, NSC Files, NPMP.
19 Memorandum, Folder 1, Box 667, Country Files: Europe, NSC Files, NPMP.
20 Memorandum, Sonnenfeldt to Kissinger, Aug. 8, 1972, Folder 1, Box 495, President's Trip Files, NSC Files, NPMP.
21 Memorandum, Sonnenfeldt to Kissinger, Aug. 19, 1972, "NATO, the Warsaw Pact and Détente, 1965–1973," Cold War International History Project Conference Volume.
22 HAK Talking Points, Dec. 1, 1971, Folder 6, Box H – 32, Institutional NSC Files, NPMP.
23 Minute, Braithwaite, Mar. 2, 1972, cited in *DBPO* 3:2. This estimation was based on the observations of the British counselor in Washington, Michael Butler.

THE HELSINKI CONSULTATIONS AT DIPOLI

The consultations stage to establish the agenda for the CSCE, also known as the Multilateral Preparatory Talks (MPT), began on November 22, 1972, in Dipoli, Finland, not far from Helsinki. As the agenda would determine the substance of the negotiations and the outline of the final agreement, the MPT was a critical component of the CSCE. Thus, the Dipoli phase presented a significant opportunity for the Western powers to seize control of the agenda. American relations with the NATO allies and the Soviet Union during the MPT were shaped by a number of factors: disinterest at high levels of the U.S. administration in the CSCE; Western emphasis on enhanced substance, such as humanitarian provisions, for the conference; Western European concern about public opinion; and increased Soviet pressure on the United States and others to accommodate their objectives.

The United States' relative disinterest in the CSCE continued in the Dipoli phase. In Italian diplomat Luigi Ferraris's view, the American "attitude of detachment" was "ostentatiously" displayed there. He believed that Kissinger regarded the CSCE "as an exercise, at best significant for public opinion, but certainly not as an essential component of the substantial make-up of the process of détente."[24] Indeed, in conversations with the British, U.S. administration official William Hyland described the CSCE as "not important" to the United States; moreover, he suggested that no senior administration officials were focused on the conference.[25] Furthermore, U.S. CSCE delegate John J. Maresca acknowledged that the United States initially pursued a "low profile" at the negotiations.[26] To Maresca, the speaking order at the Helsinki foreign ministers meeting following the MPT most clearly illustrated the American disinterest. According to him, all the other thirty-four states asked for special placement on the speakers' list, whereas the United States made no such request. This led Secretary of State William Rogers to be listed last, an embarrassment only partially lessened after his arrival in Helsinki when the Finnish hosts switched places with the United States, moving Rogers up to the twenty-first position. The Soviets, who had designated a diplomat to wait outside the Finnish foreign ministry overnight to secure their spot on the roster, spoke first.[27] American apathy, it seems, was a result of skepticism about the conference's impact. Kissinger was particularly doubtful about the value of the European focus

---

24 Luigi Vittorio Ferraris, ed., *Report on a Negotiation: Helsinki-Geneva-Helsinki, 1972–1975*, trans. Marie-Claire Barber (Alphen ann den Rijn, 1979), 66.
25 Letter, Graham to Bullard, Mar. 12, 1973, *DBPO* 3:2.
26 Maresca, *To Helsinki*, 44.   27 Ibid., 39–40.

on humanitarian provisions, remarking, "What is it that suddenly possesses the West to believe that it can affect the domestic structure of the Soviet Union through a treaty signed in Geneva of peripheral significance?"[28] Such disinterest by a key American official raised allied concerns about potential negative consequences for NATO interests.

American inattention troubled its European allies because the NATO allies were apprehensive that an agreement between Eastern and Western states could prompt false euphoria, which might unduly raise public expectations or threaten defense spending. Consequently, the British in particular pushed for a hard line on humanitarian issues to demonstrate how little substance détente with the Soviet Union offered.[29] The British and other allies wanted to appease public desire for reduced tension in Europe, but not through empty declarations.

Across the negotiating table, the Soviets expressed concern about the slow pace of the talks, perhaps due to expectations that their bilateral negotiations with the Americans would speed the discussions.[30] American officials repeatedly countered with entreaties to the Soviets to show more flexibility, as the U.S. ambassador to the Soviet Union, Walter Stoessel, argued that the real drag on the discussions was the Soviet position on issues such as human contacts.[31] Unwilling to make compromises, the Soviets and their allies continued to exert bilateral pressure on the Western and neutral states to hasten the talks. Despite the eventual conclusion of the talks in Dipoli, significant work remained for the CSCE delegates in Geneva.

The Helsinki consultations ended on June 8, 1973 with agreement on the "Final Recommendations" that delineated the timing of the formal conference and the four groups of issues, which were called "baskets" in CSCE terminology, to be discussed in the Geneva phase. By the end of Dipoli, the negotiators had already defined the elements of each of the baskets, indicating that delegates at Geneva would consider proposals on freedom of movement, dissemination of information, and different types of exchanges. In addition, the negotiations had outlined what would be the ten principles of Basket One, including the respect for human rights and fundamental freedoms. Broadening the agenda to include these and other issues such as family reunification and working conditions for journalists, not part of early

---

28 Secretary's Staff Meeting Report, Oct. 29, 1973, National Security Archive Collection, Washington, D.C.
29 Minute, Walden to Tickell, Apr. 16, 1973, *DBPO* 3:2.
30 Memorandum, Dobrynin to Kissinger, Apr. 10, 1973, Folder 2, Box 496, President's Trip Files, NSC Files, NPMP.
31 Memorandum for the Record, Apr. 19, 1973; and Telegram, SecState to US Mission NATO, April 1973, Folder 4, Box 77, Country Files: Europe, HAK Office Files, NPMP.

Soviet proposals, led to positive appraisals in the West.[32] Nevertheless, fundamental disagreements within the NATO alliance and between East and West on Basket One and Basket Three issues remained and would characterize much of the negotiations in Geneva. A five-day foreign minister–level meeting officially launched the CSCE on July 3, 1973.

NEGOTIATING THE HELSINKI FINAL ACT AT GENEVA

The Geneva negotiations deepened the stress on transatlantic relations as a result of divisions among the Western allies over the CSCE agenda. The United States continued to strain the alliance, as Kissinger maintained his disinterest in the Geneva talks while persisting in parallel discussions with the Soviets on CSCE issues; moreover, he often blamed the NATO allies for the slow pace of the conference, raising West European suspicions that he might make a deal with the Soviets behind their backs.

Nine months into the talks, at the June 1974 NATO meeting, ministers expressed anxiety about the second stage of the CSCE negotiations, which they said had "advanced unevenly." Progress lagged on significant issues such as CBMs, principles governing relations between states, increased human contacts, and the free flow of information.[33] Several days later, Kissinger wrote that a "major conflict has developed" between the Soviets and the Western allies over the concessions necessary to agree on a final summit.[34] The Soviets had been expected to make compromises on CBMs and freer movement of people in response to earlier Western agreement on frontier inviolability language; instead, the Soviets maintained their previous positions even as they increased pressure to speed the conclusion of the Geneva phase.[35] Such demands, however, increased allied awareness that the Soviets felt time constraints, giving the West leverage as the allies could slow the pace of the negotiations to gain Soviet concessions.[36]

The United States tried to use its unique role to facilitate compromise. For example, en route to Moscow in June 1974, Kissinger stopped in Western Europe ostensibly to consult with the allies but actually to mediate

---

32 Final Recommendations of the Helsinki Consultations (Helsinki 1973), Ottawa 1985, Organization of Security and Cooperation in Europe Archives, Prague, Czech Republic.
33 Final Communiqué, June 18–19, 1974, http://www.nato.int/docu/comm/49–95/c740618a.htm.
34 Memorandum, Kissinger to Nixon, June 27, 1974, Folder 8, Box 8, Office of the Counselor, Helmut C. Sonnenfeldt, 1955–1977, RG 59 (hereafter Sonnenfeldt Collection).
35 Briefing Paper, CSCE, Folder 2, Box 188, Executive Secretary's Briefing Books, RG 59.
36 Basket 3, Folder 4, Box 77, Country Files: Europe, HAK Office Files, NPMP; and Ljubivoje Acimovic, *Problems of Security and Cooperation in Europe* (Rockville, MD, 1981), 114.

between NATO and the Soviets. In his talks with Western European leaders, Kissinger planned to stress the need not only for Soviet compromises but also for realistic allied expectations. According to his briefing notes, Kissinger planned to encourage the allies to work on minimum acceptable conference results, to think pragmatically about what they could gain, and to pursue more effective negotiations with the Soviets.[37] He also sought to reassure the allies that despite their differences of opinion, the United States would not make a preemptive agreement with the Soviet Union.[38]

American efforts to push the Western allies, such as Kissinger's visit, often bred resentment, however. One attempt spurred a British representative to cable home: "The US statement is astonishingly tactless. It totally disregards the views of the Nine as expressed at Brussels and [Geneva], and shows no understanding at all of the character of the CSCE and the role and susceptibilities of the neutrals."[39] The British seemed to recall fondly Kissinger's earlier policy of benign neglect toward the conference, and they feared his increased interest could lead to greater pressure to compromise with the East. They attributed the breach between Kissinger and the nine members of the European Community to Kissinger's misinterpretation of the significance of CSCE to the West and the differences in their understandings of détente; divergent motivations and hopes for détente colored the allies' view of the value of the CSCE throughout this period. In addition, Tickell believed that Kissinger's respect for Metternich-style diplomacy impeded his ability to see the conference in idealistic terms. Kissinger's views, coupled with his inattention to the negotiations and impatience with their pace, often contributed to the differences of opinion between Kissinger and the European Community on the CSCE.[40] For Kissinger, the CSCE negotiations were only a lever to use in his contacts with the Soviets – to be slowed down or sped up as convenient for U.S. foreign policy.

---

37 Briefing Paper, CSCE, Folder 4, Box 189, Executive Secretary's Briefing Books, RG 59; Memorandum, Hartman to Kissinger, Jan. 10, 1975, Folder CSCE 1975 (1) White House, Box 44, National Security Council Europe, Canada, and Ocean Affairs Staff Files, National Security Adviser, Gerald R. Ford Library, Ann Arbor, MI (hereafter Ford Library); Declaration on Atlantic Relations, June 18–19, 1974, http://www.nato.int/docu/comm/49–95/c740618b.htm; and Telegram, Peck to Callaghan, July 4, 1974, *DBPO* 3:2.
38 Briefing Paper: Netherlands; Luxembourg; Italy; Germany; Denmark; France; Belgium, Folder 5; Department of State Briefing Paper, CSCE, Folder 2; Box 188, Executive Secretary's Briefing Books, RG 59.
39 "The Nine" refers to the nine members of the European Community. Telegram, Hildyard to Callaghan, July 24, 1974, *DBPO* 3:2.
40 Memorandum, Elliott to Callaghan, July 29, 1974, *DBPO* 3:2. Maresca suggests that Kissinger pursued a more assertive policy with the Soviets on CSCE in late 1974 and in 1975 as a result of worsening Soviet-American relations and domestic political challenges. Maresca, *To Helsinki*, 46.

The United States was not the only power struggling to balance its relationship with the Soviets and its Western European allies.[41] For example, Franco-Soviet relations further complicated allied coordination on the CSCE. France had devoted considerable energy to détente with the Soviet Union and did not want it to founder on multilateral disagreements. Therefore, at the end of 1974, in anticipation of their bilateral summit with the Soviets, the French retreated somewhat on divisive issues to speed the second stage of the conference.[42] To this end, the French CSCE ambassador acknowledged to U.S. CSCE Ambassador Albert Sherer that the French public was not particularly invested in the conference negotiations and suggested that France would sign a diluted Basket Three to keep the process of détente moving.[43] The Franco-Soviet summit confirmed the weakening French position, and the ensuing bilateral communiqué, especially the seeming lack of Soviet concessions on Basket Three in exchange for a French shift on the summit finale angered Kissinger, who had been pressed by changing international and domestic circumstances to adopt a tougher approach with the Soviets. It produced an anti-CSCE tirade in which he declared: "I couldn't care less what they do in the European Security Conference. They can write it in Swahili for all I care. . . . I don't give a damn about the conference."[44] An American briefing paper described the results of the talks between Brezhnev and French President Valéry Giscard d'Estaing as a "shock" and expressed frustration that France had not

41 As the Geneva stage wore on, there was "the risk of transforming the CSCE into a permanent inter-European debating forum." Ferraris, Report on a Negotiation 402. To avoid such a fate, some allies, such as France and Britain began to shift their positions. Telegram, US Mission Geneva to SecState, Sept. 25, 1974, Switzerland – SDT-To SecState – EXDIS (1), Box 13, President's Country Files for Europe and Canada, National Security Adviser, Ford Library; Briefing Item, Feb. 5, 1975; and Memorandum from Clift to Scowcroft, Feb. 14, 1975, Folder CSCE, 1975 (1) White House, Box 44, National Security Council Europe, Canada, and Ocean Affairs Staff Files, National Security Adviser, Ford Library.

42 Telegram, US Mission Geneva to SecState, Dec. 5, 1974, Folder Switzerland – State Department Telegrams – To SECSTATE – EXDIS (1), Box 13, President's Country Files for Europe and Canada, National Security Adviser, Ford Library. The change in government in France may also have affected French CSCE policy. Although the United States initially expected the French to continue aggressive negotiations and resist a final summit, the French president Valéry Giscard d'Estaing ultimately proved more amenable to Soviet entreaties. Telegram, AmEmbassy Paris to SecState, June 5, 1974, Folder 1, Box 680, Country Files: Europe, NSC Files, NPMP; and Maresca, *To Helsinki*, 108–9.

43 Feb. 20, 1974, Folder CSCE LOG Washington-Geneva, Box 4, Albert W. Sherer Jr. Papers, Yale University, New Haven, CT (hereafter Sherer Papers). In discussing French policy, Kissinger suggested that Giscard might betray the allied position at his upcoming Franco-Soviet summit if Germany had not done so already during German Chancellor Helmut Schmidt's summit in Moscow. Staff Meeting Transcript, Dec. 5, 1974, HAK Staff Meetings, 1973–1977, Transcript of Secretary of State, RG 59; and Secretary's Staff Meeting, Dec. 9, 1974, National Security Archive, Washington, D.C.

44 Transcript, Secretary's Staff Meeting, Dec. 9, 1974, National Security Archive.

consulted or informed the United States of its position in advance.[45] At issue were differences between American and French understandings of détente and their national interests. For the French, the continuation of détente was of paramount importance, and the drawn-out, confrontational negoti-ations at Geneva had begun to threaten the spirit of détente that the CSCE had once represented. The irony of Kissinger's outburst, of course, is that France faced the same challenge as the United States – to protect its national interests without sacrificing NATO objectives.

American policy officially remained supportive of proposals that were important to the allies and to resist Soviet pressure to acquiesce to a summit as the final phase of the CSCE.[46] American officials were extremely cautious to avoid giving the impression that the United States was siding with the Soviets. This even led the National Security Council to recommend denying clearance to a State Department telegram to the Finns noting how many hotel rooms the United States would need if the conference ended with a summit, arguing that such a telegram would leave the United States out in front of its European allies.[47] Similarly, from January through to mid-July 1975, White House Press Secretary Ron Nessen repeatedly prepared to answer questions about the CSCE in line with the NATO position by declaring that more progress was necessary before the United States would agree to hold a summit.[48]

By early May 1975, Sonnenfeldt reported to Kissinger that there was a "virtually unanimous desire" among those in Geneva to end the conference by swiftly moving to the final stage.[49] Yet tension within the NATO caucus had increased because of frustration with the lack of Soviet movement and allegations that the United States might settle for a weaker Basket

---

45 Telegram, SecState to AmEmbassy Brussels, Dec. 12, 1974, Folder Belgium – State Department Telegrams – From SECSTATE – NODIS (3), Box 1, President's Country Files for Europe and Canada, National Security Adviser, Ford Library. The British did not see Giscard's actions in quite the same light – in their reading of the communiqué, the French had not abandoned the allied position, and they believed that Giscard had gotten some Basket Three concessions from Brezhnev. According to Tickell, the French "have a paper." Telegram, AmEmbassy London to SecState, Dec. 10, 1974, Folder United Kingdom – State Department Telegrams – to SECSTATE – EXDIS (1), Box 16, President's Country Files for Europe and Canada, National Security Adviser, Ford Library.

46 Memorandum, Kissinger to Ford, Jan. 17, 1975, Folder CSCE 1975 (1) White House, Box 44, National Security Council Europe, Canada, and Ocean Affairs Staff Files, National Security Adviser, Ford Library. In this context, Sherer emphasized at the North Atlantic Council in December 1974 that maintaining allied unity was necessary to force Soviet concessions on the issues most important to the West. Statement, Dec. 3, 1974, Folder CSCE Geneva, Box 4, Sherer Papers.

47 Memorandum, Clift to Kissinger, Jan. 21, 1975, Folder CSCE 1975 (1) White House, Box 44, National Security Council Europe, Canada, and Ocean Affairs Staff Files, National Security Adviser, Ford Library.

48 Guidance, Folder CSCE, Box 122, Ron Nessen Papers, Ford Library.

49 Memorandum, Sonnenfeldt to Kissinger, Folder 11, Box 7, Sonnenfeldt Collection.

Three, which threatened allied goals. Sherer reported that his delegation was working hard to soothe disagreements among the allies, but trust between many of the countries had waned.[50] Kissinger had long wanted the NATO states to agree on the minimum threshold at which they would hold a summit, but some allies had feared that Kissinger would leak this information to the Soviets and thus had not articulated a negotiating position. Avoiding such talks, however, prevented the allies from developing a more unified position on Basket Three, reaching a compromise with the Soviets, and concluding the conference.

Further complicating the strains caused by the absence of a unified allied position was the continuing low level of American involvement in the negotiations, which persisted throughout the Geneva phase. Shortly after his appointment to head the U.S. delegation at Geneva, Sherer discovered that the American delegates had never received written instructions from Washington.[51] Sonnenfeldt, who was following the CSCE for Kissinger, confirmed that neither Nixon nor Kissinger had been interested in the conference, but they felt it was necessary to participate to placate U.S. allies. Sonnenfeldt suggested as late as January 1974 that "there would be no tears shed in Washington if the conference failed." Sonnenfeldt's justification for the low American profile at the negotiations was that "the allies got us into this mess and they should take the lead in getting us out of it."[52] A Department of State briefing paper suggests more diplomatic reasons for the low profile, namely as a response to competing pressures from the Soviet Union and the Western allies.[53] From a European perspective, however, the United States' apathy posed significant risks. Swiss Ambassador Edouard Brunner expressed concern that Kissinger's lack of interest in and positions on the CSCE created the possibility for a meaningful breach between the European Community and the United States, as Western European public opinion had certain expectations of which Kissinger did not seem cognizant.[54] Sherer's log reveals Kissinger's disinterest also threatened U.S. negotiating positions in Geneva as Kissinger conceded certain points to Soviet Ambassador to the

---

50 Briefing Item, May 27, 1975, Folder CSCE 1975 (3) White House, Box 44, National Security Council Europe, Canada, and Ocean Affairs Staff Files, National Security Adviser, Ford Library; and Apr. 22, 1975; Apr. 23, 1975, Folder CSCE LOG Washington-Geneva, Box 4, Sherer Papers.
51 Jan. 11, 1974, Folder CSCE LOG Washington-Geneva, Box 4, Sherer Papers.
52 Jan. 28, 1974, Folder CSCE LOG Washington-Geneva, Box 4, Sherer Papers.
53 Briefing Paper, CSCE, Folder 2, Moscow Briefing Book Vol. II, Box 189, Executive Secretary's Briefing Book, RG 59.
54 Feb. 9, 1974, Folder CSCE LOG Washington-Geneva, Box 4, Sherer Papers. In addition, the British worried the overall lack of American interest in the CSCE could prompt a bilateral agreement with the Soviets to expedite the second stage to the disadvantage of Western European goals. Steering Brief, Sept. 13, 1973, *DBPO* 3:2.

United States Anatoly Dobrynin that the American delegation had hoped would be part of a compromise or trade.[55]

Kissinger's continuing indifference can be attributed to the level of significance he ascribed to the CSCE. Briefing President Gerald Ford after Nixon's resignation, Kissinger summarized, "On CSCE, we never wanted it but we went along with the Europeans. . . . The Soviet Union wants it as a substitute for a peace treaty. They more or less have that. The big hang-up is on freedom of movement. It is meaningless – it is just a grandstand play to the left. We are going along."[56] Kissinger was interested in the CSCE only as far as it related to his larger, geopolitical goals and U.S. relationships with the Soviet Union and its allies. The actual substance of the talks was less significant in his view, and thus he focused more on timing than content. In the early stages, Kissinger focused on slowing down the progress of the talks to achieve Soviet concessions.[57] Later in the Geneva stage, he tried to accelerate the talks because he perceived a threat to his other priorities with the Soviets. More recently, Kissinger has suggested that he recognized a "long-term opportunity" in the CSCE, but he still identified that "opportunity" as the possibility for the United States to use its participation in the conference as a tool to restrain Soviet behavior.[58] Kissinger, like many other participants at the time, did not foresee the influential role the CSCE would play in ending the Cold War.[59]

Despite expressed U.S. concern for allied unity, Kissinger was working closely and clandestinely with the Soviets to forge compromises at Geneva. For example, the United States and the Soviet Union reached an agreement on Basket Three language, but to avoid raising Western European suspicions they developed a plan whereby "Country X," later decided to be Finland,

55 There even were those in the State Department who expressed concern to Sherer that Kissinger had made a secret bilateral agreement with the Soviets regarding the CSCE. Jan. 12, 1974, Folder CSCE LOG Washington-Geneva, Box 4, Sherer Papers.

56 Memorandum of Conversation, Aug. 15, 1974, Folder, Aug. 15, 1974 – Ford, Kissinger, Box 5, Memcons, National Security Adviser, Ford Library.

57 Hanhimäki, "'They Can Write It,'" 40.

58 Henry Kissinger, *Diplomacy* (New York, 1994), 758.

59 Kissinger, however, tried to suggest that he deserves some of the glory now linked with the Helsinki Final Act. In a 1990 speech to the Gerald R. Ford Foundation, Kissinger located the origins of the fundamental changes taking place in Eastern Europe with the Helsinki Final Act. Discussing the controversy it engendered at the time, Kissinger said, "People didn't recognize that these agreements laid the basis on which one could appeal could on the subject of human rights in Eastern Europe. . . . [It] gave all the fighters for democracy behind the iron curtain a forum and a rallying ground and I think it may have been the most significant agreement that was signed in the last thirty years." Kissinger went on to say, "[The Helsinki Final Act] was signed against violent opposition, by people who are now embracing it." What Kissinger neglected to add in his comments linking Ford's foreign policy with the end of the cold war was that he was one of those who had belatedly recognized the value of the CSCE. Henry A. Kissinger, "William E. Simon Public Affairs Lecture," Jan. 31, 1990, Ford Library.

would introduce the language. The United States would comment favorably on the "new" language once other countries, including the Soviet Union, had reacted.[60] The United States took further steps to shield its bilateral negotiations in secrecy, limiting discussions with the Soviets to Washington and Moscow as opposed to between the delegations in Geneva.[61]

Despite his bilateral discussions with the Soviets, Kissinger clearly believed that the United States had not abrogated its responsibilities to its allies. Sonnenfeldt similarly asserted that, though many Western European nations engaged in negotiations with the Soviets, the United States had been the most forthcoming in sharing its conversations with the other NATO countries.[62] The British ambassador to the United States supported that position, noting that American officials had been "meticulous" in their consultations with the European allies.[63]

Nonetheless, Kissinger's secret bilateral discussions did complicate allied relations. At a May 1975 meeting, Kissinger and Andrei Gromyko engaged in direct negotiations on the outstanding issues in Geneva, including CBM parameters and the follow-up mechanism. When Kissinger later admitted to Gromyko that he had been negotiating without his allies' knowledge, Gromyko expressed concern that their negotiations would produce a backlash from the Western allies, asking Kissinger, "Are you sure they won't cast reproaches on you for being in some kind of collusion?"[64] Indeed, certain Dobrynin-Kissinger bilateral agreements, such as on CBM parameters, inspired "stupefaction and horror" on the part some Western Europeans and neutrals.[65] Moreover, Maresca suggests that without the immediate disavowal of the agreed Soviet-American parameters, a significant rift could have developed between the United States and its allies.[66]

In addition to negotiating secretly with the Soviets during the Geneva stage, Kissinger repeatedly undermined Western European negotiating

60 Memorandum of Conversation, May 7, 1974, Folder 4, Box 71, HAK Office Files, NPMP; and Memorandum, Stabler to Kissinger, June 6, 1974, Folder 8, Box 8, Sonnenfeldt Collection. As Sherer did not know about these discussions, Kissinger was asked to approve instructions informing Sherer of his role in this charade.
61 Memorandum, Hartman to Kissinger, Feb. 16, 1974, Folder 3, Box 2, Office of the Secretary, Records of Henry Kissinger, 1973–1977, RG 59; and Telegram, AmEmbassy Moscow to SecState, Feb. 28, 1974, Folder 1, Box 723, Country Files: Europe, NSC Files, NPMP.
62 Transcript, Secretary's Staff Meeting, Dec. 9, 1974, National Security Archive Collection; and Telegram, AmEmbassy Paris to ALL CSCE Capitals, Dec. 9 1974, Folder USSR (6), Box 17, President's Country Files for Europe and Canada, National Security Adviser, Ford Library.
63 Ramsbotham to Callaghan, June 21, 1974, Gill Bennett and Keith A. Hamilton, eds., *Documents on British Policy Overseas: Détente in Europe, 1972–1976*, series 3, vol. 3 (London, 2001).
64 Memorandum of Conversation, May 19, 1975, Folder 11, Box 7, Sonnenfeldt Collection.
65 June 9, 1975, Folder CSCE Log Washington-Geneva, Box 4, Sherer Papers.
66 Maresca, *To Helsinki*, 164.

positions, as he had during the talks in Dipoli. In response to Gromyko's frustration at the pace of negotiations in Geneva, Kissinger blamed the slow pace on the Europeans, whom he described as "crazy on the subject of human contacts."[67] Similarly, in June 1974, Nixon said to Brezhnev, "We have had a problem, quite candidly, getting our European allies to agree on the substance."[68] In talks with the Soviets, American officials repeatedly shifted responsibility away from themselves to blame the measured pace of the Geneva talks on the West Europeans. Kissinger deflected Soviet complaints on the slow pace of the talks by saying, "The trouble . . . is with our European allies. Speaking very frankly, every country wants to extract something from the Soviet Union."[69] Kissinger's dismissive attitude toward confrontational Western European proposals on, for example, the freer movement of people likely emboldened the Soviets in their unwillingness to compromise.

The Soviets finally displayed greater flexibility in negotiations at Geneva at the end of May 1975. According to Soviet CSCE Ambassador Anatoly Kovalev, Soviet compromises were intended as a "gesture of good will" to expedite the final discussions.[70] The Soviets were more willing to bargain on Basket Three than on the CBMs at the time, but in Kissinger's words, the concessions were "dribbling out."[71] The shift in the Soviet stance may have been due to increased American interest and tough stance in the talks. In the aftermath of the U.S. withdrawal from Vietnam, Kissinger became less enthusiastic about Soviet-American détente and felt compelled by domestic politics to appear firmer on the Soviets.[72] To that end, the United States eventually pursued Basket Three language that adhered to or exceeded

---

67 Memorandum of Conversation, Dec. 22, 1973, Folder 2, Box 69, "The Road to Helsinki," Cold War International History Project Conference Volume. At times, however, this was a strategy to camouflage American intransigence. For example, when Gromyko advocated ending the Conference before the upcoming American summit in Moscow, Kissinger deferred blame to the Western European allies even though he was privately working against such a timetable. Memorandum of Conversation, Apr. 28, 1974, Folder 4, Box 71, HAK Office Files, NSC Files, NPMP.

68 Memorandum of Conversation, June 29, 1974, Folder 3, Box 77, Country Files: Europe, HAK Office Files, NPMP. Comments like these, however, revived concerns about American-Soviet collusion after they inevitably leaked, such as when the Italians learned the United States had told the Soviets the Italians "were being overly difficult" on Basket Three. Telegram, AmEmbassy Rome to SecState, Jan. 9, 1974, Folder 2, Box 696, Country Files: Europe, NSC Files, NPMP.

69 Memorandum of Conversation, Sept. 20, 1974, Folder Letters to and from World Leaders – USSR exchanges, 8/9/74–11/5/74, Box 1, Presidential Transition File, National Security Adviser, Ford Library.

70 Briefing Memorandum, May 29, 1975, Folder CSCE 1975 (3) White House, Box 44, National Security Council Europe, Canada, and Ocean Affairs Staff Files, National Security Adviser, Ford Library.

71 Memorandum of Conversation, May 31, 1975, Folder Britain 1975, Box 4, Sonnenfeldt Collection.

72 Maresca, *To Helsinki*, 120, 158.

Western European goals, and late American support of allied objectives strengthened the final document to the West's advantage. At the end of the Kissinger-Gromyko meeting in Geneva in mid-July, Kissinger finally was able to announce U.S. support for the Canadian proposal to end the Geneva negotiations and begin the CSCE summit in Helsinki on July 30, 1975.[73]

By the time the Helsinki Final Act was signed on August 1, 1975, the content bore little resemblance to early ESC proposals. Instead, the text included a number of unique elements advocated by Western and neutral and non-aligned states that led to the CSCE's influence on the end of the Cold War. The follow-up mechanism in basket 4, commitment to respect for human rights in Basket One, and provisions for human contacts in Basket Three all fostered the development of a transnational network that was able to shape political and social reform in the late 1980s and fundamentally alter the Cold War division of Europe.

Despite myriad briefing papers and memoranda asserting that the United States' objectives were to maintain allied unity and avoid disadvantage to the West, a careful reading of the record suggests its position was more complicated. The principal aim of American foreign policy with regard to the CSCE as practiced by Henry Kissinger from 1969 to 1975 was to participate in the CSCE negotiations with the NATO allies in such a way as to avoid jeopardizing Soviet-American détente. Throughout the early CSCE negotiations, the United States was less interested in the content of the agreed-on text than in using the negotiations to advance other American foreign policy goals. Therefore, Kissinger chose to utilize U.S. entry into the CSCE talks, and later the pace of compromise and concessions, as a means to influence other areas of the Soviet-American relationship. American interests drove Kissinger's tactics, as the CSCE, NATO goals, and Western European concerns were lower priorities for the Nixon and Ford administrations.

The NATO countries had long feared that agreeing to a European security conference could threaten allied unity, but they discounted those concerns because of overriding policy objectives. Nevertheless, during the CSCE negotiations the United States, like other NATO powers such as France and the Federal Republic, struggled to balance its national interests, bilateral relationships with the Soviet Union, and responsibilities to the alliance. Moreover, Soviet negotiating tactics and American actions, in particular Kissinger's secret bilateral talks, strained the NATO alliance.

---

73 Memorandum, Sonnenfeldt and Hyland to Kissinger, July 8, 1975, Folder 8, Box 7, Sonnenfeldt Collection; and Daily Bulletin, July 11, 1975, Folder Miscellaneous 1974 CSCE, Box 5, Sherer Papers.

Despite the complexity of the negotiations and divergent interests, however, negotiating the Helsinki Final Act tested the NATO alliance but did not fracture it.

The ability of the NATO states to remain united despite internal disagreement over negotiating tactics and objectives proved significant for the long-term influence of the Helsinki Final Act and the CSCE. First, the NATO decision to press firmly for human contacts language in the Geneva negotiations heightened the long-term significance of the agreement. In the years after the signing of the Helsinki Final Act, many Western leaders and Eastern European human rights activists used the Basket Three commitments to highlight violations of the agreement, as it was easy to point to specific terms unfulfilled by Eastern governments; eventually the efforts led to significant progress on Helsinki compliance. The allied success in achieving what would prove meaningful human rights and human contacts language was thus essential to the long-term success of the agreement. Over time, Soviet assent to respect human rights and fundamental freedoms, to adhere to provisions governing East-West contacts, and to review progress toward Helsinki implementation at a subsequent follow-up meeting had far-reaching influence on the transformation of Eastern Europe. In addition, the commitment to NATO unity, albeit a tenuous one, throughout the different stages of the negotiations, set a precedent for future follow-up CSCE meetings, producing an advantage for NATO objectives. Through effective coordination and strong leadership, surprisingly by the United States in subsequent years, the NATO allies maintained pressure on Helsinki signatories to uphold their obligations, which slowly led to increased respect for human rights in Eastern Europe and the Soviet Union. Allied efforts throughout the follow-up CSCE meetings to press for greater adherence to the Helsinki agreement succeeded in contributing to the peaceful end of the Cold War.

PART FOUR

Allied Voices, American Choices

The Demise of Détente and the Search for Consensus

13

The Reluctant European

Helmut Schmidt, the European Community, and Transatlantic Relations

MATTHIAS SCHULZ

When French President Charles de Gaulle tried to curb American influence on West Germany by promoting a close Franco-German entente in 1962–63, the Christian Democratic foreign policy expert Kurt Birrenbach confessed to two American friends, "I am afraid that we cannot afford to choose between your country and France. We are practically condemned to be on the best possible terms with both countries."[1] Whereas partnership with the United States was crucial for West Germany's security, partnership with France was the foundation of European integration and thus of a functioning West European economy. Time and again, the argument in West Germany between Atlanticists, who considered the Atlantic alliance crucial for West Germany's international position, and Gaullists, who were in favor of a closer partnership with France at the helm of Europe, appeared futile. Against this background, it seems surprising that Helmut Schmidt, who had cooperated intimately with British and American officials during his tenure as minister of defense (1969–72) and minister of finance (1972–74), and who was at heart an anglophile and a reluctant European when he became chancellor in May 1974,[2] ended up with a discordant relationship with U.S. President Jimmy Carter, tied West Germany closer to France than

---

1 Kurt Birrenbach to Dean Acheseon, and Birrenbach to John McCloy, both letters dated Jan. 31, 1963, Archiv für Christlich-Demokratische Politik, Birrenbach Papers, I-433–10/1.
2 See Matthias Schulz, "Vom Atlantiker zum Europäer? Helmut Schmidt, deutsche Interessen und die europäische Einigung," in *Die Bundesrepublik und die europäische Einigung 1949–2000: Politische Akteure, gesellschaftliche Kräfte und internationale Erfahrungen*, eds. Mareike König and Matthias Schulz (Stuttgart, 2004), 185–220, 189–90.

I thank Chancellor Helmut Schmidt for granting permission to use his personal papers for this research project (Depositum Bundeskanzler Helmut Schmidt, Archiv für soziale Demokratie, Bad Godesberg). In the following, the archival call number 1/HSAA00 refers to these papers.

even Chancellor Konrad Adenauer had done, became a strong supporter of European integration, and played a crucial role in establishing the European Monetary System. How does that fit in with his avowed Atlanticism?

Inge Schwammel argues that from Schmidt's chancellorship onward, West Germany abused European integration in its attempt to become a "great power" and to defend its national interests.[3] Of course, Schmidt defended what he perceived as national interests. Every government does so. But did the German chancellor really embrace European integration to pursue an elusive great power status in the way Schwammel suggests? Roy Jenkins's account of events certainly suggests not. Writing in the late 1980s, Jenkins, president of the European Commission from 1977 to 1981, observed: "I regarded Schmidt (as indeed I still do) as the most constructive statesman of that period, and the one with whom I had the easiest personal relations. I regarded [the West German] Government as a model of centre-left internationalist good sense, and likely to be my strongest champion in any battles that lay ahead."[4] In the following, I argue, largely on the basis of the Schmidt papers,[5] that Schmidt's growing commitment to European integration was, first, a consequence of the Common Market's exposure to external shocks; second, part of a strategy to make German power more

3 Inge Schwammel, *Deutschlands Aufstieg zur Grossmacht. Die Instrumentalisierung der europäischen Integration 1974–1994* (Frankfurt am Main, 1997).
4 Roy Jenkins, *European Diary, 1977–1981* (London, 1989), 11.
5 Most of the internal government documents of the eight years of Schmidt's chancellorship were closed to the public when I first drafted this article, which is largely based on the Helmut Schmidt papers housed in the Friedrich Ebert Foundation's Achiv für soziale Demokratie in Bad Godesberg. When the volumes of the *Akten zur Auswärtigen Politik der Bundesrepublik Deutschland* (hereafter AAPD) for 1975 and 1976 appeared, I checked them to verify or modify my arguments and to include additional evidence where necessary. Important memoirs and analyses by participants in the events discussed here include: Helmut Schmidt, *Menschen und Mächte* (Berlin, 1987); Schmidt, *Die Deutschen und ihre Nachbarn: Menschen und Mächte II* (Berlin, 1990); Schmidt, *Weggefährten: Erinnerungen und Reflexionen* (Berlin, 1996); Jenkins, *European Diary*; Horst Ungerer, *A Concise History of European Monetary Integration: From EPU to EMU* (Westport, CT, 1997); Margaret Thatcher, *The Downing Street Years* (New York, 1993); Valéry Giscard d'Estaing, *Le pouvoir et la vie* (Paris, 1988); Gerald R. Ford, *A Time to Heal: The Autobiography of Gerald R. Ford* (New York, 1979); Jimmy Carter, *Keeping Faith: Memoirs of a President* (Fayetteville, AR, 1995 [1982]); and Cyrus Vance, *Hard Choices: Critical Years in America's Foreign Policy* (New York, 1983). Hans-Dietrich Genscher's *Erinnerungen* (Berlin, 1999) covers the 1970s only sporadically. For an evaluation of Schmidt's European policies, see Schulz, "Vom 'Atlantiker' zum 'Europäer'?"; see also Gisela Müller-Brandeck-Bocquet et al., *Deutsche Europapolitik von Konrad Adenauer bis Gerhard Schröder* (Opladen, 2002). Schmidt's policy toward the United States has been analyzed by Herbert Dittgen, *Deutsch-amerikanische Sicherheitsbeziehungen in der Ära Helmut Schmidt. Vorgeschichte und Folgen des NATO-Doppelbeschlusses* (Munich, 1991); Barbara Heep, *Helmut Schmidt und Amerika* (Bonn, 1990); and, most recently, Klaus Wiegrefe, *Das Zerwürfnis: Helmut Schmidt, Jimmy Carter und die Krise der deutsch-amerikanischen Beziehungen* (Berlin, 2005). All of these studies focus exclusively on bilateral West German–American relations and overlook the European context. Only Wiegrefe has made wide use of the Schmidt papers. On Western European–American relations, see Ronald E. Powawski, *The Entangling Alliance: The United States and European Security, 1950–1993* (Westport, CT, 1994); Geir Lundestad, *"Empire by Integration": The United States and European Integration, 1945–1997* (Oxford, 1998).

palatable to its neighbors; and third, and decisively, a product of his disappointment with American leadership. Schmidt's support for the European project stemmed ultimately from his realization that the existing framework of transatlantic relations did not always provide the most effective instrument for defending West German and Western European interests.

SCHMIDT "ANTE PORTAS": THE EUROPEAN PROJECT AT RISK

As minister of finance in Willy Brandt's government, Schmidt became aware of the growing incompatibility between U.S. policies and the needs of European integration. President Richard Nixon's suspension of the Bretton Woods system of fixed exchange rates in March 1973 not only undermined the Common Market's cohesion but also wrecked European efforts toward monetary integration for the time being. Schmidt helped to save the European edifice by supporting the proposal, put forward by French Minister of Finance Valéry Giscard d'Estaing, that the European Community (EC) member countries' currencies should float collectively in a narrow band against the dollar and all other currencies to protect the Common Market against external turbulence.[6] Schmidt believed, however, that West Germany did not have sufficient economic power to become the leader of a regional monetary system and hoped that the United States would resume monetary leadership as soon as possible.[7] Largely as a result of his reservations, the European monetary cooperation fund set up on April 1, 1973, to back the new exchange rate mechanism (ERM) was not adequately endowed. The central banks of the weaker currency ERM states had to bear the full costs of keeping their rates within the agreed-on exchange rate band.[8] Consequently, when the oil crisis hit in the fall of 1973, the "snake," as the ERM was also known, effectively collapsed: Britain, France, and Italy left the system. The very existence of the Common Market and the customs union seemed to be at risk when Italy, whose economy had been destabilized by dollar-lira fluctuations, introduced a 50 percent surcharge on all imports for six months.

As roughly two-thirds of all West German imports remained within the Common Market or went to associated countries, the EC was vital to the country's prosperity, as Schmidt was well aware.[9] It was around the time of

6 Schulz, "Vom 'Atlantiker' zum 'Europäer'?" 193.
7 Bino Olivi, *L'Europe difficile: Histoire politique de la Communauté européenne* (Paris, 1998), 184–5.
8 Schulz, "Vom 'Atlantiker' zum 'Europäer'?" 195.
9 Regierungserklärung von Bundeskanzler Schmidt vor dem Deutschen Bundestag, May 17, 1974, in *Aussenpolitik der Bundesrepublik Deutschland. Vom Kalten Krieg zum Frieden in Europa. Dokumente von 1949–1989*, ed. Auswärtiges Amt (Bonn, 1990), 406, 408.

the collapse of the Bretton Woods system in 1973 system that Schmidt, increasingly critical of the White House's policies, declared himself strongly in favor of the European Union project under discussion among European leaders.[10] He used his transatlantic credentials to reassure American audiences during his frequent visits that European unification was not directed against the United States. He warned, though, that Washington must not try to prevent it.[11] It was, in short, primarily concern for West Germany's dependence on the Common Market that prompted Schmidt to become gradually more involved with the European project.

Schmidt's growing support for the European project nonetheless remained subordinate to transatlantic cooperation. It is indicative of his continued Atlanticist convictions that, despite strong French resistance, he considered it necessary to keep Western Europe aligned with the United States on energy policy to extract concessions from OPEC and to ensure that Washington take Europe's dependence on Arab oil into account.[12] He strongly supported the Washington Energy Conference in February 1974 to keep the West as unified as possible in its response to the oil crisis.[13] On defense, Schmidt held on to his Atlanticist course, too. While intensifying Franco-German cooperation in the joint development of military technology,[14] he hoped that France would again take a more active role in NATO and thereby strengthen "Europe's" weight in the alliance.[15]

EUROPEAN UNION AS A WAY TO REBALANCE TRANSATLANTIC PARTNERSHIP?

When Schmidt emphasized in his first address to the Bundestag as chancellor that the "creation of a European Union had become more urgent than ever," his main argument was that union was a necessary precondition

---

10 Helmut Schmidt, "Rede vor dem Schweizerischen Institut für Auslandsforschung, Zürich, May 30, 1973," *Bulletin des Presse- und Informationsamtes der Bundesregierung,* June 2, 1973, 651; Schmidt, *Menschen und Mächte,* 196.

11 Helmut Schmidt, "Lecture at Newberry College, South Carolina, Jan. 11, 1973," *Bulletin des Presse- und Informationsamtes der Bundesregierung,* Jan. 15, 1973, 32.

12 See Christopher Piening, *Global Europe: The European Union in World Affairs* (Boulder, CO, 1997), 74.

13 Compare Schmidt, *Menschen und Mächte,* 203–4, and Hélène Miard-Delacroix, *Partenaires de choix? Le chancelier Helmut Schmidt et la France (1974–1982)* (Bern, 1993), 173.

14 After only one Franco-German defense project was concluded in 1974, ten projects were envisaged for 1975; by 1976, the introduction of several new weapons systems had been agreed on. See Chancellor Schmidt to Federal Minister of Defense Georg Leber (copy), January 1975, Note by Carlo Schmid, Mar. 18, 1976, 1/HSAA009010, and Annual report on Franco-German relations 1974 by Carlo Schmid (n.d.), 1/HSAA009010.

15 Schmidt later succeeded in persuading Giscard d'Estaing that France should join NATO's European Planning Group to strengthen the European component of NATO.

for Europe to become an equal partner of the United States.[16] European union, he elaborated, should not replace the transatlantic relationship but serve, rather, to strengthen Europe's position within the Atlantic alliance and globally. This instrumental vision of European union became the hallmark of Schmidt's initial policy on European integration.

The discussion of European union that had intensified during the transatlantic crisis of 1973 resumed after new governments took office in France, Britain, and West Germany in quick succession during the spring of 1974.[17] Jean Monnet and his Action Committee for the United States of Europe, a group of cross-party parliamentary and union leaders, were particularly active in trying to mobilize the new Schmidt and Giscard governments to give fresh impetus to the European project. As a result of the ensuing discussions, the EC decided at its December 1974 summit in Paris to institutionalize meetings of the heads of state and government in what came to be called the European Council. This gubernative body was to meet three times each year to establish consensus on the general direction of EC policies. Shortly after the EC summit, Schmidt, while paying his first visit to President Gerald Ford, defended the creation of the European Council by pointing out the troubled state of the international economy.[18] From the EC's perspective, however, this measure was a consequence of the debate on European Union and a response to the realization that the EC needed better internal coordination in its relations with Washington. The fact that the European Council meetings were to take place jointly with meetings of the foreign ministers within the European Political Cooperation (EPC) framework pointed to the nexus between institutional reform and Europe's new global aspirations.[19] Although the EC member states by no means always spoke in unison, the European Council and EPC created a new "diplomatic culture" that permitted them gradually to develop common views without being directed by an obvious hegemonic leader, as in NATO.

Another important decision made at the EC's Paris summit with a view to strengthening European institutions was the agreement by the heads of state

---

16 Regierungserklärung von Bundeskanzler Schmidt vor dem Deutschen Bundestag, May 17, 1974, *Aussenpolitik der Bundesrepublik Deutschland*, 406.
17 See Daniel Moeckli, "Asserting Europe's Distinct Identity: The EC Nine and Kissinger's Year of Europe"; Alaistar Noble, "Kissinger's Year of Europe, Britain's Year of Choice"; and Fabian Hilfrich, "West Germany's Long Year of Europe: Bonn between Europe and the United States," in this volume.
18 Compare Miard-Delacroix, *Partenaires de choix?* 174.
19 While the European Council met initially three times a year, the foreign ministers would meet four times under the EPC framework. The reforms agreed on at the summit also included direct elections for the European Parliament as a symbolic counterweight to the strengthened role of governments.

and government to commission Belgian Prime Minister Léo Tindemans to prepare a report on the future architecture of European Union. In the process, Tindemans consulted extensively with government officials and parliamentarians in the member states, as well as with representatives of varied interest groups and EC organs. Washington's input, however, was not particularly welcome: on the contrary, Giscard d'Estaing bluntly told Ford that "the political union of Europe is a problem for the Europeans, who need neither to ask for nor to seek outside support."[20] This was not exclusively a French attitude, and one may understand why. For when Tindemans presented his Report on European Union to the European Council in Rome on December 29, 1975,[21] he argued that the disparity between Europe's economic and political power was no longer acceptable in the age of superpower hegemony. Europe had to take "common action to defend its legitimate interests" and "must again become a master of its own destiny."[22] The first point after the introduction states: "European Union implies that we present a united front to the outside world," including, of course, to the United States.[23] To achieve this objective, Tindemans contended, the EC would have to reform its decision-making processes, particularly in the areas of foreign relations and security policy. Regular meetings of the defense ministers were to harmonize their views and prepare a common security policy and increased cooperation in arms production. "European independence" in armaments and the competitiveness of the respective industries should be enhanced. The report reflects both the fears of an American disengagement, and the strains within the transatlantic relationship experienced during the Year of Europe crisis.

Schmidt's Chancellery initially seemed to agree with the general direction suggested by the Tindemans Report.[24] A draft for a government declaration praised it as "realistic and constructive" and argued that it was

now necessary to expand the common policy of the nine member states pragmatically to all fields which are essential for the political and economic existence

20 *Le Monde*, May 31, 1975, cited in Miard-Delacroix, *Partenaires de choix?* 175.
21 Massion [Auswärtiges Amt, hereafter AA] to Chancellor Schmidt, Summary report, Jan. 6, 1976, on Tindemans Report on European Union, Tindemans Report, file 1, 1/HSAA006623. On Tindemans, see Léo Tindemans, *De memoires: gedreven door een overtuiging* (Lannoo, 2002).
22 "Tindemans-Bericht über die Europäische Union, Dec. 29, 1975," excerpts in *Der Aufbau Europa: Pläne und Dokumente 1945–1980*, ed. Jürgen Schwarz (Bonn, 1980), 529.
23 "European Union: Report by Mr. Tindemans to the European Council," December 1975, excerpts in *Building European Union: A Documentary History and Analysis*, eds. Trevor Salmon and Sir William Nicoll (Manchester, 1997), 42–50, 143. See also the letter by the President of the European Council Gaston Thorn to Chancellor Schmidt, Mar. 11, 1976, 1/HSAA006623.
24 Draft of letter from the Chancellor to the President of the European Council, Luxembourg's Prime Minister Gaston Thorn, Mar. 1976, 1/HSAA006623, signed off by the chief of the chancellery.

of our countries. [The EU] shall foster Europe's role in the world, facilitate the establishment of a European economic area, and give people more security and freedom. The collective authority of the Heads of Government in the European Council has to bring about a breakthrough for this common policy.[25]

In letters to the president of the European Council and the Commission, Schmidt underscored that it was very important for West Germany that the foundations for European Union be laid in 1976, when, he might have added, his governing coalition would be up for reelection.[26]

Schmidt's hopes for an election year breakthrough on European Union were jeopardized, however, by a looming disagreement between Britain and France. Reluctantly, the chancellor took on the role of mediator between London and Paris.[27] In Britain, Harold Wilson's government, which had called for a referendum on continued EC membership, was fundamentally unwilling to pursue deeper integration. Both Giscard and Schmidt were highly displeased when Wilson asked for more time to make direct elections to the European Parliament palatable to British voters.[28] Yet the French government, too, viewed the Tindemans Report with reservations.[29] Although the emphasis on security policy must have appealed to Giscard, who regarded cooperation in this area crucial, he knew that neither his coalition nor the governments of several other EC members – including Britain and West Germany – were ready to activate the Western European Union treaty of 1955 or to build a European defense structure parallel to NATO.[30] Moreover, Giscard, in line with Gaullist principle, insisted on

25 Quoted in "Entwurf einer Erklärung des BK zum Bericht von PM Tindemans über die Europäische Union," n.d. [probably January 1976], Tindemans Report, file 1, 1/HSAA006623; see also Salmon and Nicoll, *Building European Union*, who call the report "relatively unambitious," 142.

26 Draft of a letter from Chancellor Schmidt to the President of the Commission of the EC François Xavier Ortoli, Nov. 10, 1975, 1/HSAA006621, and draft of a letter from the Chancellor to the President of the European Council, Luxembourg's Prime Minister Gaston Thorn, March 1976, 1/HSAA006623.

27 Statement by the EC policy coordinators Trumpf and von der Gablentz to State Minister Wischnewski, Foreign Minister Hans-Dietrich Genscher, and Chancellor Schmidt, Mar. 19, 1976, with a view to the discussion of the Tindemans report on the European Council on Apr. 1–2, 1976; Tindemans to Schmidt, Feb. 6, 1976, asking for chancellor's approval for a meeting with EP on the Tindemans report; letter by Massion, AA, to Chancellor Schmidt, Feb. 20, 1976, reporting that British and possibly others had rejected the proposal. Tindemans Report, file 1, 1/HSAA006623.

28 Aufzeichnung des Bundeskanzlers Schmidt, July 27, 1975, *AAPD* 1975, 2:1041.

29 Compare Massion, AA, to Chancelor Schmidt, Feb. 11, 1976, concerning summit in Nice. Includes translation of an article from *Le Monde*, Feb. 10, 1976, in which Giscard's idea of a directorate is mentioned. Tindemans Report, file 1, 1/HSAA006623.

30 In February 1975, German Foreign Office Ministerial Director van Well had been asked by the parliamentary secretary of state in the Quay d'Orsay, Destremau, who professed to know the French president's opinions on that matter, whether Germany would be willing to revive the "sleeping" WEU. Van Well rejected the overture. Aufzeichnung von Ministerialdirektor van Well, Feb. 4, 1975, *AAPD* 1975, 1:105–7. A secret German Foreign Office paper on step-by-step defense integration

strengthening the decision-making powers of the member states' governments in a future European Union instead of building strong supranational
bodies. The Commission, in his view, had to remain an administrative body
subordinate to the member state governments, and he thought it should be
downsized from thirteen to nine commissioners. On this point, Schmidt
and Wilson were in basic agreement with Giscard.[31] Fearing that the accession of new member states would make it more difficult to find agreement
in the Council, Giscard suggested the establishment of a directorate of a
few large states. He rejected, however, the obvious solution to deadlock in
the Council that Tindemans recommended: the introduction of majority
voting.[32]

When he learned of the skeptical French and British reactions, Foreign
Minister Hans-Dietrich Genscher distanced himself from the Tindemans
Report for tactical reasons. He suggested that the responsibility for following
up on it should not be put into the hands of the heads of government
because they would be blamed in the event of failure. Schmidt, heeding
Genscher's tactical concerns, had a working group of leading figures in the
SPD consider the Tindemans Report from a party-political perspective.[33]
Believing that there was little chance that Tindemans's more progressive
proposals would be adopted in the foreseeable future, Schmidt asked the
working group to consider also how far the German public was willing
to go in supporting the reform of European institutions and to "weigh
further progress on Europe against possible limitations [of the integration
process] from a national or economic point of view."[34] Meanwhile, the
Christian Democratic Union and Christian Social Union (CDU-CSU)
urged the government on February 18, 1976, to do everything to secure an
agreement on the direct election of the European Parliament and to have

circulating in July 1975 did not become official government policy. Ambassador Freiherr von
Braun, Paris, to Ministerialdirektor van Well, July 10, 1975, *AAPD* 1975, 2:914–19; and the analysis
pointing out the numerous problems attached to a European defense policy, Aufzeichnung des
Ministerialdirigenten Redies, August 26, 1975, ibid., 1185–9. On France's governing coalition, see
Ambassador Freiherr von Braun, Paris, to Ministerialdirektor van Well, July 10, 1975, ibid., 915;
on the other governments' positions, see Konferenz der Außenminister der EG-Mitgliedstaaten in
Dublin, Apr. 12/13, 1975," *AAPD* 1975, 1:359–61. Callaghan saw the WEU as a fallback solution,
and NATO and EPC the most adequate forums under the current international constellation.
Botschafter von Hase, London, to AA, May 20, 1975, ibid., 550.

31 Aufzeichnung des Bundeskanzlers Schmidt, July 27, 1975, *AAPD* 1975, 2:1041.

32 On the French resistance, see letter by Genscher to the Chancellor, March 25, 1976,
1/HSAA006623; and on French resistance to majority voting Miard-Delacroix, *Partenaires de choix?*
151.

33 Private letter Schmidt to State Minister in the Auswärtiges Amt, Hans-Jürgen Wischnewski, Jan. 16,
1976, signed, Tindemans Report, file 1, 1/HSAA006623.

34 Ibid.

the Tindemans Report accepted as a package deal by the spring.[35] By raising expectations to the maximum, the Christian Democrats hoped that failure to meet them could be blamed on the Schmidt government and exploited during the campaign for the upcoming election.

Schmidt also came under pressure from Tindemans. At the beginning of February, Tindemans voiced his concern about Giscard's proposal for a directorate. He asked the chancellor to try to persuade Giscard to drop this idea, which he considered harmful to the solidarity of the Nine.[36] Tindemans knew from his discussions with the national governments and EC institutions that there was "a profound hostility" toward the idea of a directorate of the larger member states. As the leader of a small country, he was particularly concerned. If Giscard persisted on his course, Tindemans warned Schmidt, he would "thoroughly disrupt" the reform debate and paralyze the EC at a time when it should be laying the foundations for greater "efficiency."[37] Tindemans was counting on Schmidt, he explained, because he was convinced that the chancellor, too, wanted "pragmatic, but significant progress."[38]

In response to Tindemans's plea, the Foreign Ministry advised Schmidt not to support Giscard's idea of a directorate because the other EC partners were "extraordinarily sensitive" on this issue. More effective cooperation among the larger EC member states could be achieved, the ministry believed, "only by practical means, not through institutionalization."[39] Two weeks later, Schmidt responded to Tindemans that the idea of a directorate had not been on the agenda at the Franco-German summit, implying that Giscard had dropped the idea on his own initiative. But some discussion on the issue had obviously taken place, for Giscard received a copy of the letter.[40]

In the light of the disagreements between France, Britain, and West Germany, Schmidt anticipated that the discussions on European Union would stall. To dampen expectations at home, he suggested to the leaders of the parliamentary caucuses that the Bundestag "adjourn" the CDU-CSU motion calling for a public debate on the Tindemans Report before the

---

35 Motion by the CDU-CSU caucus in the Bundestag concerning "Bericht Tindemans über die Schaffung einer Europäischen Union," Feb. 18, 1976, Drucksache 7/4757 des Deutschen Bundestages, 7. Wahlperiode, Tindemans Report, file 1, 1/HSAA006623.

36 Tindemans to Schmidt, Feb. 11, 1976, Tindemans-Report, file 1, 1/HSAA006623.

37 Ibid.   38 Ibid.

39 Von Loeck, AA, to Schmidt, Feb. 11, 1976, Tindemans-Report, file 1, 1/HSAA006623.

40 Schmidt to Tindemans, Feb. 25, 1976 (draft, signed with Schmidt's initials). Tindemans-Report, file 1, 1/HSAA006623.

meeting of the European Council in Luxembourg on April 1, 1976. Instead, he proposed, the Bundestag's foreign relations should committee hold a confidential discussion of the report.[41] The CDU–CSU caucus leader, Karl Carstens, turned down Schmidt's request, arguing that the European Council should be aware of the Bundestag's opinion. Only parliamentary pressure, Carstens contended, could push European integration forward.[42] Schmidt subsequently used the Bundestag debate on the Tindemans Report to blame the oil crisis and Western Europe's economic troubles for the stalemate he expected at the next European Council meeting.[43] Supporting the main points of the Tindemans Report and the goal of a strengthened Europe within the Atlantic alliance, he emphasized the positive developments that had already occurred as well as those that could realistically be expected in the foreseeable future. Alluding to the concession he had obtained from Giscard, he vowed that direct elections to the European Parliament, a goal particularly important to democrats and federalists, would come soon.[44]

Schmidt and Giscard, then, were held back as much by their disagreement on certain points of Tindemans's plan for European Union as by Britain's objections. As Jenkins explained in retrospect, "Schmidt and Giscard were firmly in control of Europe, but for the moment had no direction in which they wished to take it."[45] In reality, the chancellor leaned more toward Giscard's confederal design than he would admit in public because the Bundestag, including his own party's caucus, and public opinion in West Germany favored federalism.[46]

EUROPEAN UNION SHELVED, TRANSATLANTIC PARTNERSHIP REVIVED

The following European Council meeting in April 1976 treated the European Union project in a dilatory fashion, reporting only that it had "tentatively discussed" the Tindemans Report and that it would "complete the

41 Schmidt to leaders of the SPD and CDU–CSU, Mar. 17, 1976, Tindemans Report, file 1, 1/HSAA006623.
42 Karl Carstens to Schmidt, Mar. 17, 1976, Tindemans Report, file 1, 1/HSAA006623.
43 Speech by Schmidt in the Bundestag, Mar. 18, 1976, draft by von Loeck, Mar. 17, 1976, Tindemans Report, file 1, 1/HSAA006623.
44 An accord on direct elections for the EP was concluded on Sept. 20, 1976, but there was no agreement on the electoral rules and the parliament's powers until the Copenhagen summit of Apr. 7–8, 1978. The first elections took place on June 7–10, 1979.
45 Jenkins, *European Diary*, 22.
46 See the contrast between Aufzeichnung des BK Schmidt, July 27, 1975, *AAPD* 1975, 2:1039, where he strongly backs strengthening the European Council, and the SPD's program for the direct elections to the EP, Dec. 10, 1978, in *45 Jahre Ringen um die europäische Verfassung: Dokumente 1939–1984: Von den Schriften der Widerstandsbewegung bis zum Vertragsentwurf des Europäischen Parlaments*, ed. Walter Lipgens (Bonn, 1986), 647–9.

examination by the end of 1976 at the latest."[47] At its summit at the Hague at the end of November 1976, it endorsed the general direction of the report without, however, approving any concrete steps to put the recommendations into practice. Instead, it embraced the idea of incremental reform and made the Commission and the Council of Foreign Ministers responsible for annual reports on the progress toward European Union. Disaster was thereby averted, and Tindemans's proposals were shelved until the time might be ripe for more substantial reform. The only major institutional reform implemented in the mid-1970s, then, was the establishment of the European Council in 1974.[48]

Why did the Nine's enthusiasm for the project of European Union, so evident in 1973–75, fade so quickly? Disagreements within the EC played an important part, as shown previously, but it is also not insignificant that the postponement of further institutional reform came after a remarkable improvement in transatlantic relations. This brings me back to my main argument, namely that a new structural relationship between transatlantic relations and European integration emerged during the long 1970s. In the immediate postwar years, European integration had generally progressed with U.S. support – with the notable exception of the failed European Defense Community project, where U.S. support had turned out to be rather counterproductive. Since the late 1960s, however, it was increasingly the clash rather than the convergence of European and American interests that gave impetus to closer European integration. Indeed, when Washington was attentive to European interests, European enthusiasm for far-reaching reforms of the EC subsided. That, in brief, is what happened in 1975–76.

Faced with the alternative of seeing Europe become a third, more independent force as a result of transatlantic discord or supporting the idea of a strengthened Europe within the Atlantic partnership, the Ford administration opted for the latter and took a more positive stance toward European integration than its predecessor. Ford and Kissinger not only accepted the EC Nine's efforts to develop common policies on the Conference on Security and Cooperation in Europe (CSCE), monetary policy, and energy issues, but also began to view those efforts as a welcome change from the cacophony of disparate voices that had previously emanated from Europe. Personal chemistry also helped smooth transatlantic relations.

---

47 Quoted in "Conclusions of the sessions of the European Council, Apr. 1–2, 1976, Luxemburg; and Summary of the European Council Meeting," *Bulletin of the European Communities*, no. 4 (1976): 83.
48 On direct elections to the EP, see *supra* note 44. The establishment of the European Fund for Regional Development in 1975 was another important step.

Schmidt and Genscher's meeting with Ford and Kissinger in Washington in December 1974 contributed to the improvement. Schmidt and Kissinger were on increasingly good terms with each other; and Schmidt and Ford trusted each other. Schmidt and Kissinger also shared a high opinion of Giscard, and German–American relations benefited from the improvement in Franco–American relations following Giscard's election as president.[49] A new concert among three of the main Western powers thus developed at the beginning of 1975 and contributed to the decline of both Schmidt's and Giscard's interest in European union.

The new climate in transatlantic relations became evident at a series of meetings that took place in January 1975. Strengthened by an accord reached by the EC finance ministers early in the month, Schmidt succeeded in persuading Federal Reserve Chairman Arthur Burns during the latter's visit to Hamburg to agree to a compromise on monetary policy in advance of the International Monetary Fund's (IMF) council of central bank governors meeting scheduled for January 12–13. Returning from the IMF meeting, West German Minister of Finance Hans Apel enthusiastically described it as "one of the most constructive and successful conferences in recent years." He praised in particular the "well balanced compromise" between European and American interests and the agreement on new tools to deal with balance of payments problems caused by the surge in oil prices. Not only had the anticipated "transatlantic row" between the EC and the United States not taken place, Apel reported, but the United States, France, and West Germany had cooperated very closely and successfully.[50]

One of the most important developments in transatlantic relations during Ford's presidency was the agreement, on Giscard's suggestion, to hold "informal" summit meetings of the heads of state and government of the leading industrial nations to address international economic issues. Schmidt strongly supported the summit proposal when Ford visited Bonn in July 1975.[51] The chancellor was convinced, as was Giscard, that the energy crisis and the weakening of American economic power required regular

---

49 Note the numerous references to the good relations among the actors mentioned in the report by van Well on Kissinger's visit to the chancellor on Feb. 15–16, 1975, Aufzeichnung des Ministerialdirektors van Well, Feb. 17, 1975, *AAPD* 1975, 1:155–6. On Kissinger's display of confidence, see Botschafter von Staden, Washington, to AA, May 7, 1975, ibid., 484; Kissinger's next visit in Bonn took place in May 1975: see "Aufzeichnung van Wells, May 22, 1975," ibid., 579–84.

50 Runderlaß des Vortragenden Legationsrates I. Klasse Dohms, Jan. 20, 1975, *AAPD* 1975, 1:39n8; compare 39–40.

51 "Deutsch-amerikanisches Regierungsgespräch, July 27, 1975," *AAPD* 1975, 2:1035.

meetings of the leaders of the major economic powers.[52] He was particularly concerned that the oil crisis could spur a depression if those nations started pursuing beggar-thy-neighbor policies. Several countries were grappling with economic problems that could have severe ramifications for the international economy. Hardest hit was Britain, which was contending with an inflation rate that exceeded 25 percent.[53] At the same time, it was no coincidence that the summit proposal came at a time when the EC was trying to take on more responsibility in the world and increase Europe's political leverage through new multilateral forums and agreements.[54]

Another motive for the initiative, especially on Giscard's part, was to enhance the role of the nation-state. In fact, the proposal introduced his idea of a directorate of great powers through the back door – on the level of the Western alliance rather than within the EC. Schmidt was less concerned with restoring the nation-state than with giving a psychological boost to markets. It was crucial, he thought, that the industrial states demonstrate solidarity and resoluteness in dealing with the economic difficulties. Ford and Kissinger reacted to the summit proposal cautiously but constructively. They insisted that the summit had to be prepared carefully if it was to have the desired effect. Accepting the proposal, Ford delegated former Secretary

---

52 Bernhard May, "Ein schwieriger Lernprozess: Die Weltwirtschaftsgipfel," in *Die USA und Deutschland im Zeitalter des Kalten Krieges 1945–1990. Ein Handbuch*, ed. Detlef Junker (Stuttgart, 2001), 2:382–9, 383–4.

53 Great Britain was hit by the consequences of problematic fiscal policies and strikes; Japan and Italy were hobbled by their dependence on oil imports; and in the United States, several states and cities, including New York City, were on the verge of bankruptcy. On Schmidt's concerns about Britain, see Deutsch-amerikanisches Regierungsgespräch, July 27, 1975, *AAPD* 1975, 2:1035. On the background to the decision by the leading industrial nations to hold economic summit meetings, see Harold James, *Rambouillet, 15. November 1975: Die Globalisierung der Weltwirtschaft* (Munich 1997), 7–14.

54 Among the most important of these agreements was the Lomé Convention of Feb. 28, 1975, which intensified the EC's commercial and financial relations with forty-six African, Caribbean, and Pacific (ACP) states. Under the Lomé Convention, all industrial and 96 percent of all agricultural exports from the ACP countries could enter the European Community duty free. In addition, a price stabilization program was introduced for twelve major ACP export products. Total EC aid to those countries under the agreements stretching from the Yaoundé Conventions (1963) to the expiration of Lomé IV (1999) amount to ECU 46.5 billion (US$58 billion). In addition to the European-Arab dialogue launched in 1974, comprehensive accords with Israel, the Maghreb, and the Mashriq states were also concluded between 1975 and 1978, and trade talks with China began in 1975 and were finalized in 1978. The EC and the Association of South East Asian Nations (ASEAN) held a summit in Brussels in 1978, and they concluded an agreement on economic and development cooperation and trade in 1980. In July 1977, the EC and the member states of the European Free Trade Association (EFTA) signed a free trade agreement. See Elfriede Regelsberger, "Die EPZ in den achtziger Jahren – ein qualitativer Sprung?" in *Die Europäische Politische Zusammenarbeit in den achtziger Jahren: Eine gemeinsame Aussenpolitik für Europa?*, ed. Alfred Pijpers, Elfriede Regelsberger, Wolfgang Wessels (Bonn, 1989), 21–70, 34; Piening, *Global Europe*, 72–4, 190; Harold James, *International Monetary Cooperation since Bretton Woods* (Washington, D.C., 1996), 314–15.

of the Treasury George Shultz, who knew Schmidt and Giscard from their time as ministers of finance, to serve as his emissary in the preparations.[55]

Schmidt's hopes that the Ford administration would cooperate in the area of monetary policy were not disappointed. In November 1975, the heads of state and government of Britain, France, West Germany, Italy, Japan, and the United States – known thereafter as the G-6 – met in Rambouillet, France. The summit resulted in a new agreement on exchange rate surveillance and enhanced the participants' commitment to consultation and cooperation.[56]

Imbued with new confidence in American leadership, Bonn did not worry much when a "growing gap" between the D-mark and other European currencies led to a new crisis in the ERM in the spring of 1976.[57] Although Bonn and Paris intended to coordinate their economic policies,[58] divergent inflation rates, productivity growth rates, and labor costs put upward pressure on the D-mark and downward pressure on the French franc and the Italian lira.[59] As there was no agreed point at which the Bundesbank and other central banks would intervene to help weaker currencies,[60] France, which had rejoined the ERM on July 10, 1975, withdrew again on March 15, 1976, leaving only the Dutch, Belgian-Luxembourg, and Danish currencies tied to the D-mark.[61] Nevertheless, Bonn remained unfavorable toward improving the exchange rate system,[62] apparently counting on sound U.S. and French policies to stabilize the situation. The state secretary in the Ministry of Finance, Karl-Otto Pöhl , expected that, given the Ford administration's fairly successful anti-inflation measures, the United States' return to a positive balance of payments, and the relative stability of the dollar, further fluctuations among the European currencies would be unlikely. "I

55 May claims that it was Shultz who convinced Ford to accept it: May, "Ein schwieriger Lernprozess," 385. Documents in the German archives suggest, though, that Ford was already fairly positive during his visit in July. See Deutsch-amerikanisches Regierungsgespräch, July 27, 1975, *AAPD* 1975, 2:1035–7.

56 On the Rambouillet summit, see documents 348–50 in *AAPD* 1975, 2:1634–54. James, *International Monetary Cooperation*, 267–73. Canada joined in 1976 what then became known as the G-7.

57 "The Snake Must Be Strict," interview with Karl-Otto Pöhl, *Newsweek*, Apr. 5, 1976, 13.

58 Compare Miard-Delacroix, *Partenaires de choix?* 175, 177.

59 Between 1974 and 1977, growth rates in the EC member states ranged from less than 1 to 10 percent. Cumulated inflation rates ranged from 5 to 100 percent. See Ungerer, *Concise History of European Monetary Integration*, 148.

60 "The Snake Must Be Strict," 13.

61 The Swedish and Norwegian krone had also joined the system, but neither country was a member of the EC. They quit in 1977 and 1978, respectively.

62 French Minister of Finance Jean-Pierre Foucade's proposals for an improvement of the snake in 1974 came to nothing in the face of German criticism that budgetary discipline had to precede any further steps toward monetary union. And the Dutch Minister of Finance Wim Duisenberg's demand for a more effective mechanism for coordinating exchange rates within the EC lacked support in both the Committee of Central Bank Governors and the EC's Monetary Committee. See Ungerer, *Concise History of European Monetary Integration*, 138–9.

think that now we are . . . close to a new equilibrium."[63] Bonn had no desire, and saw no necessity, to lead in Europe or to push forward European monetary integration. On the contrary, it relied strongly on the United States in monetary policy as it did in defense.

Indeed, from a West German perspective, relations between the United States and Western Europe were smoother during Ford's presidency than they had been for years. The irritations of the Year of Europe had been overcome, and both sides had learned to manage pragmatically their rivalries in multilateral and bilateral consultations.[64] And Kissinger flattered the Europeans during a visit to London in the summer of 1976 by saying that the United States benefited from cooperation with a strong and united Europe.[65]

EXPECTATIONS DISAPPOINTED: TRANSATLANTIC DISCORD AND THE CREATION OF THE EUROPEAN MONETARY SYSTEM

When Jimmy Carter took office in January 1977, Schmidt and his government were confident that the old and new multilateral frameworks for transatlantic relations would help them to maintain a strong influence in Washington. The Foreign Ministry considered the alliance the "decisive factor" in European–American relations and was under the impression that U.S. support for NATO had revived under Ford.[66] Carter's address to the NATO Council on December 9, 1976, in which he demanded and in return promised close consultations with the allies, assured Bonn that he was as fully committed to the alliance as Ford had been. A confidential memorandum prepared by the Ministry of Foreign Affairs with a view to British-German consultations that winter argued that the larger European states should emphasize in their first talks with the new administration in Washington that their priority was the "concrete expansion of the Atlantic partnership."[67] Among the developments speaking in favor of such an expansion were the rapidly increasing capital flows between the two continents, the role the

63 "The Snake Must Be Strict," 13.
64 Memorandum "Atlantische Partnerschaft (im Lichte des Amtsantritts Präsident Carters): Zur Gesprächsführung mit PM Callaghan und AM Crosland," Jan. 21, 1977, 1/HSAA006688; cf. Botschafter Krapf, Brüssel (NATO), to AA, Nov. 26, 1975, *AAPD* 1975, 2:1689.
65 Speech held on June 25, 1976, see Memorandum "Atlantische Partnerschaft (im Lichte des Amtsantritts Präsident Carters): Zum Sachstand," Jan. 21, 1977, 1/HSAA006688, 4.
66 Memorandum "Atlantische Partnerschaft (im Lichte des Amtsantritts Präsident Carters): Zum Sachstand," Jan. 21, 1977, 1/HSAA006688, 1.
67 Memorandum "Atlantische Partnerschaft (im Lichte des Amtsantritts Präsident Carters): Zur Gesprächsführung mit Premierminister Callaghan und Aussenminister Crosland," Jan. 21, 1977, 1/HSAA006688, 3.

alliance had to play in helping to foster democratic developments in Portugal and Spain, and the need to counterbalance the new generation of intermediate range nuclear missiles the Soviet Union was deploying in Eastern Europe. The Western European governments were also eager to influence the arms control negotiations and coordinate the second round of CSCE talks with Washington. In addition, the West German Foreign Ministry stressed that the EC Nine and the United States needed to hold multilateral discussions on cooperation to assure the successful conclusion of the Tokyo Round of General Agreement on Tariffs and Trade (GATT) negotiations. Whereas the British and the French governments often preferred to work on a bilateral level with Washington, the Schmidt government saw the intensification of relations between the Nine and the United States as the main task for the coming years.[68] Since the introduction of EPC, the Bonn government had developed a strong preference for multilateral rather than bilateral negotiations with Washington. The Foreign Ministry held the view that the European allies were in a better position to make their views heard if they used multilateral frameworks: "good bilateral relations with the United States are no substitute for the consolidation of our multilateral cooperation networks both in NATO and between the Nine and the United States," a January 1977 memorandum on the Atlantic partnership stressed.[69] Bilateral relations, it went on to argue, should be used mainly to lubricate multilateral talks in NATO and economic relations between the Nine and the United States.[70]

Schmidt's own expectations of Carter were positive. He predicted in his so-called Marbella Paper – a memorandum he drafted while on vacation at the end of 1976[71] – that 1977 would be dominated by the "primacy of economic policy."[72] He thought that his coalition government had won the 1976 Bundestag elections because West Germany had weathered the oil crisis better than other countries, as the country's low unemployment rate

---

68 See memorandum "Europapolitische Schwerpunkte im ersten Halbjahr 1977, hier: EPZ-Fragen," Jan. 11, 1977, 1/HSAA006688.
69 "Atlantische Partnerschaft... Zum Sachstand," Jan. 21, 1977, 1/HSAA006688, 3. In the GATT forum, the EC had already taken over negotiations in the 1960s when the customs union was built, and there were direct negotiations between the Commission and the U.S. Department of Trade.
70 "Atlantische Partnerschaft... Zum Sachstand," Jan. 21, 1977, 1/HSAA006688, 3.
71 The paper was written in Marbella, Spain, where Schmidt had spent a fortnight of vacation at the end of 1976; he polished the paper over the following Easter and sent it to members of the party leadership and confidants on April 22, who discussed its conclusions. See Erwägungen für 1977, Jan. 5, 1977, 1/HSAA009302.
72 Erwägungen für 1977, Jan. 5, 1977, 1/HSAA009302, 1.

and its growing per capita income showed.[73] West Germany's "unheard of richness in currency reserves,"[74] which had been accumulated partly under previous governments of course, and its hard-currency policy made soaring oil prices easier to digest. In short, Schmidt believed in the virtues of the "German model." He even surmised, probably overestimating himself, that his advice to Ford had helped the U.S. economy to perform so well.[75] When, to his surprise, Ford was not reelected, he expected that Carter, like his predecessor, would listen to his counsel.

Schmidt soon found himself engaged in major conflicts with Carter, however. He first became alarmed when he realized that Carter was a Keynesian. Then he was shocked that Carter did not seek his advice at all. As spring arrived, he was disturbed that he had not yet received an invitation to the White House. Carter seemed to take no active interest in West Germany and avoided Schmidt, who had too obviously favored Ford during the campaign. He sent Brandt as special emissary to Washington to pour oil on the troubled water, but that did not help. Despairing, he then turned to the president of the European Commission for advice.[76]

Even before Carter and Schmidt met at the London G-7 Summit in May, the two governments clashed over the export of nuclear power plant technology and enrichment facilities by West German companies. In his memoirs, Schmidt claims that Carter's demand that West Germany renege on a major nuclear technology deal concluded with Brazil in 1975 was caused by the introduction of new U.S. policies on the export of sensitive technology. Contemporary German newspaper coverage also implied a connection between U.S. policies and the competition between U.S. and German suppliers of nuclear technology. However, not only had the previous U.S. and British administrations expressed concern that the deal with Brazil might be an infraction of Bonn's obligations under the 1968 Nonproliferation Treaty,[77] but Ambassador Hellmuth Roth, the Foreign Ministry's senior expert on arms control and nuclear proliferation, had repeatedly warned the Ministry of Foreign Affairs about the incompatibility of the

---

73 Unemployment in West Germany stood at 4.3 percent in 1976, compared to 8.1 percent in the United States. The economic growth rate in the United States dropped to −1.8 percent in 1975 but then rebounded to 6.3 percent in 1976. Memorandum by BMWi/AA, "Weltwirtschaftslage," Jan. 5, 1977, 1/HSAA006688, 5–6.
74 Erwägungen für 1977, Jan. 5, 1977, 1/HSAA009302, 1.
75 Ibid., 3.
76 Jenkins, *European Diary*, entry for Mar. 18, 1977, 69 and 68f.
77 Aufzeichnung des Ministerialdirigenten Lautenschlager, Apr. 16, 1975, *AAPD* 1975, 1:392–6, esp. 396; Ministerialdirektor Hermes to Embassy in Washington, June 12, 1975, ibid., 739–44.

arrangements with German obligations under the treaty. Roth even criticized the manipulation of the press by the government (and the nuclear lobby) to convey the impression that the deal involved no risks. "The idea that we succeeded in bringing the legitimate export interests of the Federal Republic into line with the government's non-proliferation policy in the Brazil treaty," Roth wrote in a memo, "is a self-deception."[78] At least in this transatlantic crisis, the West German government was chiefly responsible. Fortunately for Schmidt, Giscard lent him support both in public – arguing that if Carter wanted the European allies to follow his policies concerning sensitive technologies, he should consult them beforehand rather than give orders after the fact[79] – and during the discussion of the issue at the London economic summit in May 1977.[80] When Schmidt finally met with Carter in Washington in July 1977, the two succeeded in defusing the issue.[81] The chancellor announced that West Germany would not conclude any new nuclear technology export agreements for the time being and proposed the establishment of a new multilateral forum to draft rules for the export of such technologies.[82] Carter, putting great effort into making Schmidt's visit a success, voiced support for that proposal as well as with Schmidt's proposal that the alliance make greater use of multilateral forums.[83] Despite these reciprocal overtures, however, clouds remained on the horizon.

As early as February 1977, Schmidt and French Prime Minister Raymond Barre had realized that Carter's energy, fiscal, and monetary policies were failing to restore confidence on the capital markets.[84] In the lead-up to the London summit, Jenkins, who would be representing the EC for the first time at a G-7 meeting,[85] expressed increasing concern about the effects of

---

78 Note by Ambassador Roth, confidential, Feb. 12, 1975, *AAPD* 1975, 1:140; and by the same, confidential, June 18, 1975, ibid., 772–75, quote 773.
79 See the discussion of the issue in Heep, *Helmut Schmidt und Amerika* 71–86. On Franco-German cooperation, see Miard-Delacroix, *Partenaires de Choix?* 195–200.
80 Weltwirtschaftsgipfel in London, May 7, 1977, *AAPD* 1977, 1:576–9.
81 Deutsch-amerikanisches Regierungsgespräch in Washington, July 13, 1977, *AAPD* 1977, 2:950–9.
82 Speech by Schmidt to the National Press Club, Washington, D.C., sent by German Embassy in D.C. to AA, June 30, 1977, 1/HSAA006699.
83 Ambassador von Staden to Schmidt, July 18, 1977, 1/HSAA006699.
84 Prime Minister Raymond Barre, according to a note by von Loeck, AA, dated Feb. 7, 1978, about conversation between Schmidt and Barre during the French-German consultations on Feb. 6, 1978, 1/HSAA006712.
85 The European Parliament and the EC member states who had been excluded from the first G-6 summit demanded vigorously that the EC, as the world's largest trading group with an internal market as large as that of the United States, be admitted. Despite initial French resistance, a formula was found and Commission President Roy Jenkins participated in the G-7 in 1977. Canada had been admitted in 1976. On Giscard d'Estaing's initial resistance, see translation of a letter of Giscard d'Estaing to Jenkins, n.d., 1/HSAA006690.

the United States' "mounting external oil demand," which, in tandem with surging oil prices, was exerting "the most unbalancing effect upon world trading patterns."[86] The French government maintained that the United States would have to reduce its dependence on oil imports to improve it external balance.[87]

With the Europeans worried about the implications of U.S. policies and stunned by the new phenomenon of stagflation, the London G-7 summit started in a tense atmosphere. Somebody had to take the lead in cleaning up the mess. While Carter humbly stated he had come to "learn," everybody else expected the United States to assume its responsibility as the world's leading economic power. Schmidt, angry about Carter's insistence on raising the nuclear trade issue, squarely attributed the world's economic problems to the growing U.S. balance-of-payments deficit, which spread inflation internationally, the collapse of the Bretton Woods system, and the explosion of oil prices since 1973.[88] Still, he thanked Carter for the U.S. energy program, which was supposed to reduce U.S. dependence on foreign oil (but which Congress would not accept). But, after warning expressly against competitive devaluation policies, known all too well from the Great Depression, Schmidt also put great emphasis on the substantial German contribution toward improving the U.S. external balance. The Federal Republic had accepted an 18 percent increase in the value of the D-mark since early 1976 despite its heavy dependence on exports.[89] However, the thanks Schmidt apparently expected from Carter were not forthcoming. On the contrary, the president responded to the challenge by implying that the West German and Japanese governments were not doing enough to stimulate economic growth. He also blamed them for the current American balance of payments deficit, which he put at US$20 billion, by pointing

86 See Jenkins's Memorandum to the European Council, Copenhagen, Apr. 7–8, 1978, attached to a letter to Chancellor Schmidt dated Apr. 3, 1978, 1/HSAA006713, 4; and memo by Meyer-Sebastian concerning American balance-of-payments problems, June 24, 1977, 1/HSAA006699. From 1973 to 1979, U.S. crude oil imports soared, and the cost of oil imports grew from US$4.6 billion for 1.4 billion barrels in 1973 to more than $15 billion for roughly the same amount of oil in 1974, then from $34 billion for approximately 2.5 billion barrels in 1977 to $46 billion for roughly the same amount in 1979. In other words, the United States was increasing its dependence on foreign oil instead of reducing it after the oil price hike of 1973–1974. See data in U.S. Census Bureau, Foreign Trade Division, http://www.census.gov/foreign-trade/statistics/index.html.
87 See Prime Minister Raymond Barre, according to a note by von Loeck, AA, dated Feb. 7, 1978, about conversation between Schmidt and Barre during the French-German consultations on Feb. 6, 1978, 1/HSAA006712, and report by the coordinator for Franc-German relations, Carlo Schmid, Mar. 1978, 1/HSAA009010.
88 For a summary, see Weltwirtschaftsgipfel in London, May 7, 1977, *AAPD* 1977, 1:562–76; and a secret document of the same date, with the same title, ibid., 576–83.
89 Weltwirtschaftsgipfel in London, May 7, 1977, *AAPD* 1977, 1:568.

to their surpluses.[90] He expected West Germany and Japan to pursue the deficit-expanding fiscal policies he had decided were the best means to kick-start the world economy.[91] West German Minister of Finance Hans Apel, dissenting, pointed out that the German trade surplus had declined substantially since 1974 as a result of growing imports from developing countries.[92]

The accusatory atmosphere and Schmidt's resistance to Carter's pressure made the summit experience very annoying for both. Had Carter invited Schmidt to Washington earlier, the two might have been able to prepare an agreement. To understand Schmidt's rejection of fiscal expansion, it is important to bear in mind the European experience in the 1970s until then. With its modest budget deficits and respectable growth rates, West Germany provided a model of successful anti-inflationary policy. Britain, in contrast, had followed the Keynesian policy of deficit spending, which, under the Labour governments of Harold Wilson and James Callaghan, had produced nothing but high inflation, negative or stagnant growth, mass unemployment, and a discontented, strike-prone workforce.[93] In light of this background, Callaghan's support for Carter's demands carried little weight.[94] Moreover, Carter's lumping West Germany together with Japan was not justified. West Germany had an open economy, whereas Japan's was practically closed to imports other than primary resources.[95] Schmidt had other reasons, too, for rejecting Carter's call for action to spur growth. The Organisation for Economic Co-operation and Development expected the growth rate of the West German economy to slip from 5.5 percent in 1976 to 3.5 percent: there was thus no reason either to panic or to spend

---

90 Ibid., 570. A Foreign Office memorandum for the chancellor's visit to the United States, July 13–15, 1977, projected an American balance-of-payments deficit of US$27 billion by the end of the year: June 24, 1977, 1/HSAA006699; Olivi, *L'Europe difficile*, 234; U.S. Census Bureau, Foreign Trade Statistics, http://www.census.gov/foreign-trade/statistics/index.html.
91 Olivi, *L'Europe difficile*, 236.
92 "Weltwirtschaftsgipfel in London, May 7, 1977," *AAPD* 1977, 1:572.
93 Compare his criticism in the Marbella Paper, Erwägungen für 1977, Jan. 5, 1977, 1/HSAA009302, 18.
94 Callaghan made his demands public in a radio broadcast on Jan. 2, 1977. During the British-German consultations at Chequers on Jan. 23–24, 1977, Schmidt signaled support for certain demand-increasing policies but warned him not to try any more Keynesian experiments. Telegram German Embassy to Auswärtiges Amt, Jan. 28, 1977, 1/HSAA006688. Britain had experienced an inflation rate of 23.2 percent and a real decline in gross domestic product in 1976, but Callaghan expected a substantial improvement of the British balance of payments as a result of North Sea oil exports. Compare memorandum by BMF/AA for British-German consultations in Chequers on Jan. 24, 1977, "Zu TOP 'Internationale Währungsfragen,'" Jan. 12, 1977, 1/HSAA006688, 1; and Memorandum by BMWi/AA, "Weltwirtschaftslage," Jan. 5, 1977, 1/HSAA006688, 14.
95 Only 1.1 percent of West German exports went to Japan in 1976. Memorandum by BMWi/AA, "Weltwirtschaftslage," Jan. 5, 1977, 1/HSAA006688, 7.

generously.[96] Given the Common Market's need for monetary stability, experimenting with larger deficits under the prevailing economic conditions was simply not advisable. Schmidt's hands were also tied domestically.[97] The West German government, he realized, was entering a debt trap: "The state of federal finances imperatively requires the stop of any real growth in current expenditures."[98] Schmidt's instincts and analysis of the situation made it impossible for him to heed Carter's recommendations.[99]

Another, more dramatic conflict erupted in the fall of 1977 as a result of Carter's uncertain and somewhat erratic nuclear arms policies. A prelude of sorts occurred in February of that year when Vice President Walter Mondale spoke, during a visit to Paris, of Carter's wish to reduce nuclear weapons "to zero" if possible. This remark called the American nuclear umbrella into question and caused concern among French officials, who thought such a policy unrealistic. Somewhat condescendingly, Genscher urged his French counterpart that Carter be given a little more time to become acquainted with the complexities of nuclear strategy.[100] Half a year after this mishap, Carter wanted to demonstrate America's reliability to the allies amid growing apprehension in Western Europe about the Soviet deployment of a new generation of intermediate range nuclear missiles, the SS-20s. At a meeting of the permanent representatives to NATO on September 13, an American delegation of experts argued strongly in favor of deploying neutron bombs in Western Europe as a counterweight to the SS-20s.[101] Carter thought he had to make a decision quickly to prevent the anticipated emotionalization of public debate about the new nuclear weapon, which used enhanced radiation to kill people while doing much more limited damage to infrastructure than traditional nuclear weapons. He gave the allies time only until the end of September for consultation – that is, little more than two weeks – while insisting that the final decision as to whether to produce the weapon was his alone. Confronted by a renascent peace movement at home, several

---

96 Both data are for January to November 1976. Memorandum by BMWi/AA, "Weltwirtschaftslage," Jan. 5, 1977, 1/HSAA006688, 3, and passim.
97 The Bonn government planned for the budget deficit to reach up to 4 percent, the maximum Schmidt thought acceptable given the forecasts. But the Bundesrat had vetoed an increase of the value-added tax for 1977, although the government's expenses and functions were expanding. See Erwägungen für 1977, Jan. 5, 1977, 1/HSAA009302, 32.
98 Ibid., 34.   99 Ibid., 20.
100 See Thiele, AA, and [illegible] for Schmidt, concerning conversation between foreign ministers Genscher and Louis de Guiringaud at the Franco-German summit, Feb. 3, 1977, and for Genscher's reaction longer summary of the same conversation by Ambassador Wormser, same date, 1/HSAA006689.
101 See Botschafter Pauls, Brussels, to AA, secret, Sept. 13, 1977, *AAPD* 1977, 2:1187–90; compare the contribution in this volume by Joe Renouard and D. Nathan Vigil, and Wiegrefe, *Das Zerwürfnis*, 180ff.

of the Western European governments, including Bonn, were highly displeased by the pressure Carter was exerting and complained that they had not received adequate information. Meeting in Bonn on September 27, Schmidt told U.S. National Security Adviser Zbigniew Brzezinski that the American public debate on the bomb had stirred up confusion in Europe and that the pressure from Washington was highly counterproductive and might lead to resentment. He suggested giving European decision makers and citizens alike more time to consider the issue, and he also recommended that the neutron bomb be put on the agenda for disarmament talks with the Soviets.[102] Moreover, Schmidt pointed out that the neutron bomb decision consisted, in fact, of three separate decisions that would involve three different groups of decision makers: whether the United States would produce the neutron bomb, whether NATO would add it to its arsenal, and if so, where it would be deployed. These three decisions could not be melded into one, the chancellor insisted, and should not be hurried. Finally, Schmidt made clear that if the deployment of the neutron bomb would make sense only in West Germany, which appeared to be the case, massive public resistance was to be expected. In response, Brzezinski argued that because it would only make sense to deploy the new weapon in Central Europe, the production decision could not be separated from the deployment decision. Congress, he went on to explain, had already allocated funding for production at the administration's request. The president now had to decide within forty-five days whether to decline the funding; if he did not, the allocation funds would become a law.[103] In other words, Washington had already made the initial decision without consulting the allies. Schmidt then told Brzezinski that the Federal Security Council would debate the issue on October 6.[104] Without waiting for the outcome of the West German deliberations, Carter publically declared himself in favor of producing the neutron bomb on October 4.

Grudgingly, Schmidt backed Carter's decision and persuaded his fellow Social Democrats, largely against their will, to accept it. On January 10, 1978, the Federal Security Council agreed to its deployment under certain conditions. But after the Social Democratic Party had given in, drawing much criticism from the media and party rank and file, and NATO had started to work out an agreement, Carter changed his mind and cancelled

102 Conversation Schmidt – Brzezinski, Sept. 27, 1977, *AAPD* 1977, 2:1250–1.
103 This is how Brzezinski explained the time pressure to Schmidt, Conversation Schmidt – Brzezinski, Sept. 27, 1977, *AAPD* 1977, 2:1252.
104 See Bundeskanzler Schmidt to Bundesminister Leber, Sept. 6, 1977, ibid., 1329–32.

production of the neutron bomb on April 7. Schmidt was furious. The neutron bomb fiasco did irreparable damage to the Schmidt–Carter relationship. Schmidt lost whatever confidence he had had in the president.[105]

Thus, relations between the two reached a nadir in late 1977 and early 1978.[106] Yet looking at the chronology of events, the reasons for Schmidt's turn toward a European solution to international monetary problems lay more in the economic realm than in the neutron bomb disaster, which exploded in his face only in April 1978. The latter simply confirmed Schmidt in his view that he could not rely on Carter and had to shoulder new responsibilities in Europe himself. The situation was indeed dire. Despite Carter's attempt to stimulate economic activity, American economic growth declined. The deficit fueled inflation in the United States, and the dollar "overhang" aggravated inflationary trends worldwide.[107] As a consequence, the dollar, which had been valued at DM 4 in the late 1960s under the old system of fixed exchange rates, had fallen to DM 2.36 by October 1977 and continued to fall until hitting DM 1.76 in the autumn of 1978.[108] Some in Europe thought Washington was pursuing a policy of competitive devaluation and thereby making a farce of the Rambouillet declaration. Western European exports were certainly hurt on the world markets, and the Common Market had been manifestly destabilized by the dollar's rapid decline.[109] Especially the Common Agricultural Market began to crumble in the fall of 1977, and by the end of 1978, common prices for foodstuffs scarcely existed anymore.[110] Hence, since late 1977, Schmidt was in despair over his inability to influence American policy effectively. Reform of the international monetary system seemed impossible.[111] In his

105 Giscard d'Estaing, *Le pouvoir et la vie*, 132–5; quotation 135. On Schmidt's complaints about Carter, see Jenkins's diary entry for Feb. 28, 1978: Jenkins, *European Diary* 224–5. See also Dittgen, *Sicherheitsbeziehungen*, 161–76, esp. 171–3.

106 Schmidt, *Menschen und Mächte*, 318–31; Giscard d'Estaing, *Le pouvoir et la vie* 132–5; Jenkins, *European Diary*, 224–5.

107 Olivi, *L'Europe difficile*, 236–7; Andreas Falke, "Zwischen liberalem Multilateralismus, Neoprotektionismus und regionaler Integration: Amerikanische und deutsche Handelspolitik," in Junker, *Die USA und Deutschland*, 345.

108 Ibid., 197.

109 Growth in the EC slowed from an annual average of 2 percent in 1974–1978 to an average of 0.6 percent in the years 1979–1982: see Gerold Ambrosius, *Wirtschaftsraum Europa: Vom Ende der Nationalökonomien* (Frankfurt am Main, 1996), 123. Reduced growth was also a consequence of the second oil crisis, which followed the toppling of the shah of Iran.

110 Schmidt's policy statement before the Bundestag, Dec. 6, 1978, in *Aussenpolitik der Bundesrepublik Deutschland*, 487.

111 See Jenkins's diary entry for Nov. 10, 1977, on his discussion with Schmidt in Bonn; Jenkins, *European Diary*, 169.

view, U.S. policies were irresponsible: "the world economy was without leadership, without coordination."[112]

The leaders of the European Commission in Brussels took a more creative approach to the impasse. Speaking in Florence in late October 1977, Jenkins argued that the Europeans should overcome the monetary crisis collectively by coordinating monetary policies within the Community.[113] The only way to shield the Common Market from the effects of international monetary disorder, he insisted, was to endow the EC with a regional monetary leadership role.[114] He disputed the French argument that monetary union would force budgetary discipline and the German view that budgetary discipline would have to precede monetary union. The internationalization of economic life, he countered, was inevitable and the creation of a common European currency would reap enormous advantages for West European economies in terms of rationalization and competitiveness. A European central bank would be much better poised to fight against inflation than a multitude of national banks. In November, the Commission presented a working paper on the establishment of a European monetary union.[115] Jenkins continued to mobilize European elites and repeated his call for a European monetary arrangement before the European Parliament on January 17, 1978, presenting monetary union as the key to growth, jobs, and economic security. It would reduce the vulnerability of European national currencies to external shocks, he argued, and pave the path to political union.[116]

Schmidt had reportedly fallen asleep when Jenkins presented his initiative at the European Council meeting in December 1977, and when the Council gave a green light to the Commission to prepare proposals for monetary cooperation, it did not mean that this would reap any result.[117] Yet at some point – it is not exactly clear when – Schmidt became convinced that

112 Schmidt, *Die Deutschen*, 138. In his diary entry for Nov. 10, 1977, Jenkins writes, "The world needed a lead, but he [Schmidt] couldn't give it. . . . The United States almost effortlessly could, but Carter shows no signs of doing so": so Schmidt, according to Jenkins, 169, see also diary entry, Feb. 28, Jenkins, 224–5.

113 "Jean Monnet Lecture Delivered by the Right Hon. Roy Jenkins, President of the Commission of the European Communities," Florence, Oct. 1977. See Salmon and Nicoll, *Building European Union*, 154–61; and compare Schulz, "Vom 'Atlantiker,'" 200.

114 The whole initiative was prepared by the staff of the European Commission. See Jenkins, *European Diary*, 23–4.

115 Mitteilung der Kommission der Europäischen Gemeinschaften über die Aussichten der Wirtschafts- und Währungsunion, Nov. 17, 1977, in Schwarz, *Der Aufbau Europas*, 579–86.

116 See Olivi, *L'Europe difficile*, 232.

117 Diary entry for Dec. 5, 1977: Jenkins, *European Diary*, 181. On the European Council meeting of Dec. 5–6, 1977, see Runderlaß des Vortragenden Legationsrates I. Klasse Engels, Dec. 8, 1977, *AAPD* 1977, 2:1722–7.

this was the way to go. During a meeting on February 6, 1978 – that is, two months before Carter reversed his neutron bomb decision – Schmidt and Barre agreed during French-German consultations that they would launch a common initiative on monetary policy after the French elections in April.[118] When Jenkins visited Schmidt on February 28, the chancellor surprised him by announcing that he was thinking about an initiative leading toward monetary integration:

> You may be shocked, you may be surprised at what I intend to do, but as soon as he French elections are over, probably at Copenhagen – assuming the French elections go all right and that there aren't any Communists in the French government – then I shall propose, in response to the dollar problem, a major step towards monetary union; to mobilize and put all our currency reserves into a common pool, if other people will agree to do the same, and to form a European monetary bloc. . . . Do you think it is worthwhile?[119]

By early 1978, the combination of the international economic situation and frustration with Carter had made Schmidt receptive to Jenkins's preparatory efforts and willing to confront the likely resistance of the powerful Bundesbank to his plan. While Schmidt tried to convince Callaghan, who had voiced skepticism about Jenkins's initiative, and consulted with Giscard on strategy,[120] Jenkins worked behind the scenes to convince the heads of state and government of the necessity of finding common solutions to the international economic problems.[121] In a memorandum to the European Council, he pointed out that deficit spending had produced more inflation than growth, that EC trade was slacking, and that the "international monetary system – or lack of system – [was] in chaos."[122] Despite the collapse of the Bretton Woods rules, he observed, the dollar was still the "only effective medium of international exchange." Even in the European financial markets, Eurodollars dominated trade and capital markets. Jenkins found that this predominance was quite out of proportion with the weight of the U.S. economy in Europe: "There is a fundamental asymmetry about the United States having withdrawn from the responsibilities of Bretton Woods, while dollars, like legions without a central command, continue to dominate the currency transactions of the world." The "Community's

---

118 See note by von Loeck, AA, dated Feb. 7, 1978, on the conversation between Schmidt and Barre during the French-German consultations on Feb. 6, 1978, 1/HSAA006712.
119 Diary entry, Feb. 28, 1978: Jenkins, *European Diary*, 224.
120 Protocol by the Office of the Speaker of the German Government, confidential conversation between Schmidt and journalists in Copenhagen, Apr. 8, 1978, 1/HSAA006713.
121 Memorandum to the European Council, Copenhagen, Apr. 7–8, 1978, attached to a letter to Chancellor Schmidt dated Apr. 3, 1978, 1/HSAA006713.
122 Ibid., 2.

collective weight," by contrast, was "far greater than its monetary influence." This disparity should be changed not by establishing a full economic and monetary union immediately, Jenkins maintained, but by starting the process toward that goal.[123]

After the Copenhagen summit, Schmidt indicated cautiously to selected journalists that, depending on how the United States' fiscal, monetary, and oil policies developed, "new ideas" or "models" for a monetary system might be introduced later that year.[124] Referring to Jenkins's Florence speech, he said that the Commission president's remarks were perhaps too visionary but went in the right direction. "What is doable, that is what we are currently preoccupied with."[125] While refusing to say how West Germany would react to the dollar crisis, he made it clear that the solution discussed in Copenhagen had something to do with Europe. Although the dollar crisis was a grave problem, there was also a long-term objective, the construction of Europe. The world was interdependent, he observed, but the EC was even more so.[126]

Jenkins, Schmidt, and Giscard collaborated behind the scenes to secure the establishment of the European Monetary System (EMS). Schmidt made great efforts to bring as many participants on board as possible and to avoid creating a "two-speed Europe."[127] Bernard Clappier, the president of the Banque de France, and Horst Schulmann, the head of the Economics Department in the Chancellery, worked closely with Schmidt, Barre, and Giscard. Italian Minister of the Treasury Filippo Maria Pandolfi apparently also had considerable influence in shaping the details of the plan.[128] Pandolfi and Clappier often discussed matters directly with the chancellor, who, it appears, took primary responsibility for the project rather than delegating it to the Ministry of Finance.[129] The negotiations were by and large completed by December 1978. Some EC partners, like Tindemans of Belgium, were enthusiastic; others, like Italian Prime Minister Giulio Andreotti, had to be persuaded. Only Britain, as usual at the time, declined to participate.

Although Washington was not against a European monetary initiative in principle, Carter realized that it was largely a consequence of his policies. He got into a minor argument with Schmidt over the plans for EMS at the

123 Ibid., 2–3.
124 Protocol by the Office of the Government's Speaker, confidential conversation between Schmidt and journalists in Copenhagen, Apr. 8, 1978, 1/HSAA006713, 3.
125 Ibid., 4–5.   126 Ibid., 7.
127 "Vermerk über die Gespräche des Herrn Bundeskanzlers mit MP Andreotti am 1. November 1978 in Siena während des Mittagessens und nach dem Abendessen," Nov. 6, 1978, 1/HSAA006725, 7.
128 "Vermerk über die Gespräche des Herrn Bundeskanzlers mit MP Andreotti am 1. November 1978 in Siena während des Mittagessens und nach dem Abendessen," Nov. 6, 1978, 1/HSAA006725, 9.
129 Schulmann's papers might throw more light on the subject, but they are not yet open to researchers.

World Economic Summit in Bonn in July 1978. However, Andreotti, who was on good terms with Carter, successfully defended the EMS in a private conversation with him, which helped smooth the waters.[130] To appease Carter, Schmidt pledged to contribute to economic growth by increasing Bonn's budget deficit by as much as one percentage point. Bonn also supported Washington's efforts to liberalize trade in the GATT negotiations.[131] Carter, in turn, began to accept the advice of his colleagues and agreed to continue his efforts to reorient U.S. energy policies and curb oil consumption. He refrained from trying to intervene in the EMS negotiations.[132]

Schmidt was criticized at home because of the creation of the EMS and feared that his reputation was likely to suffer with every blow to the system once it became operative. Playing the nationalist card, opposition leader Helmut Kohl was not helpful.[133] What drove Schmidt to stake his reputation on the EMS? Schmidt told Andreotti that he feared "a collapse of the Common Market" and the potentially dangerous domestic and foreign policy consequences that might follow. To avert such a collapse, he had to "take risks." The EMS would stabilize individual member countries' currencies, reduce the danger of speculation against them, and create confidence. And if the EMS was successful, he speculated, it would help to "discipline the balance of payments policy of the United States."[134]

On December 6, 1978, acting in his capacity as president of the European Council, Schmidt sent a note about the plan for monetary cooperation to Washington, Tokyo, and Ottawa. He explained the reasons behind the establishment of the EMS in soft terms and expressed his hope that it would "turn out to be a European contribution to our common goal of worldwide economic and monetary stability."[135] The U.S. government did not respond officially to this announcement.

CONCLUSION

The EMS created the European Currency Unit (ECU) as a unit of account that made intra-European payments between central banks, governments,

---

130 Giulio Andreotti, *From the Atlantic Pact to Bush* (New York, 1992), 102.
131 May, "Weltwirtschaftsgipfel," 386.   132 Andreotti, *The U.S.A. Up Close*, 104.
133 Schulmann to Schmidt, Nov. 7, 1978, concerning summary of Schmidt's talks in Siena with the Italian, and in Paris, with the French government. 1/HSAA006725.
134 "Vermerk über die Gespräche des Herrn Bundeskanzlers mit MP Andreotti am 1. November 1978 in Siena während des Mittagessens und nach dem Abendessen," Nov. 6, 1978, 1/HSAA006725, quotations 5, compare 6, 8.
135 Personal message of Schmidt sent to Carter, Trudeau, and Fukuda, Dec. 6, 1978, after the European Council in Brussels, Dec. 4–5, 1978, Depositum BK Helmut Schmidt, 1/HSAA006727.

and the European institutions possible without resorting to the dollar. Entering into force in April 1979, the EMS was much better equipped to soften external shocks on the Common Market than the snake had been, and, above all, it reduced the exposure of the West European economies to U.S. monetary policy. In other words, the EMS was a defensive response to American policies perceived as damaging to Europe.[136]

In contrast to the old Bretton Woods System of fixed rates, which had assigned a privileged position to the dollar, the EMS's rules did not privilege a particular currency. Given that the central banks of hard currency countries were obliged to intervene on behalf of weaker currencies, any major currency strong enough to help others could in theory become the leader of the system.[137] In practice, the D-mark became the hardest major currency and therefore the system leader. Thereby the Federal Republic attained a certain hegemonic power, which, however, the Bundesbank sometimes found difficult to reconcile with its role as a national central bank. From 1979 onward, the Bundesbank found itself in much the same dilemma that the Federal Reserve had been from the 1950s until the end of the Bretton Woods system: it was a national institution with a national policy task, but it also bore substantial international responsibility.

West Germany's growing power in Europe was, however, not the consequence of a policy consciously and consistently pursued. As we have seen, European union was not a German concept, as Timothy Garton Ash implies, nor, as Schwammel argues, a concept that Bonn used to become a "great power."[138] Rather, European union was a multifaceted conceptual design developed by Europe's transnational political and administrative elites that was widely embraced by leading actors in European politics. It was a response to the discrepancy between the EC's economic weight and its political influence, and, in particular, to the asymmetries in transatlantic relations. Starting out as an Atlanticist, Schmidt initially supported European Union rather reluctantly and refrained from pushing it forward when transatlantic relations improved in 1975–76 and he realized that European Union was, for the time being, unrealistic. Similarly, his support for EMS stemmed not from a desire for a regional leadership role or monetary power for Germany but from concern for the European edifice.

---

136 Compare James, *International Monetary Cooperation*, 469; Miard-Delacroix, *Partenaires de Choix?* 184; and Schulz, "Vom 'Atlantiker,'" 203–8.

137 See Ungerer, *Concise History of European Monetary Integration*, 164.

138 Timothy Garton Ash argues, with qualified sympathy, that West Germany always wanted to mold Europe according to its own image and pursued national interests "in Europe's name": Garton Ash, *In Europe's Name: Germany and the Divided Continent* (New York, 1993), esp. 384–8; Schwammel, *Deutschlands Aufstieg zur Grossmacht*.

In fact, Schmidt expressed grave concern in his Marbella Paper about West Germany's "unwanted and dangerous rise" as a Western power second only to the United States.[139] He was afraid that NATO appeared more and more to be a German–American alliance disguised by a supranational command structure. The relative rise of West German military power, he feared, might, in conjunction with West Germany's currency reserves and status as a creditor nation, prompt envy or suspicion on the part of its allies as well as of the Soviet Union. To prevent such negative feelings from arising, Schmidt argued that West Germany, even if it could not really disguise its power, was strictly obliged to act as much as possible within the multilateral structures of the EC, the Atlantic alliance, and forums like the CSCE if it wanted to exert influence without causing concern in other capitals.[140] Schmidt's decision to opt for Europe in some cases – EPC, the European Council, and the EMS – and his advocacy of a broader concert like G-7 in others were motivated essentially by the same goals: to protect West German and European interests, especially when they seemed at risk from national U.S. policies, and to make German power more palatable to its neighbors and allies. Both also were instrumental in building a more equal partnership with the United States. Indeed, the multilateral embeddedness of West German policies allowed Schmidt the Atlanticist to take a tougher stance toward the United States on a number of issues than his predecessors had. Schmidt's decision in favor of a monetary Europe, the most far-reaching decision toward monetary union until then, took into account a growing readiness on the side of the West Europeans to assume full responsibility for their own well-being and to share global leadership at a time when the United States seemed insecure and focused on domestic issues.

---

139 Erwägungen für 1977, Jan. 5, 1977, 1/HSAA009302, 4.
140 Erwägungen für 1977, Jan. 5, 1977, 1/HSAA009302, 5.

14

The Quest for Leadership in a Time of Peace

Jimmy Carter and Western Europe, 1977–1981

JOE RENOUARD AND D. NATHAN VIGIL

> Your strength can compensate for my weakness, and your wisdom can help to min-
> imize my mistakes. Let us learn together and laugh together and work together and
> pray together, confident that in the end we will triumph together in the right.
>
> — Jimmy Carter, Inaugural Address, January 20, 1977

When Jimmy Carter fired this opening salvo of his presidency, he was
expressing hope that the American people would appreciate the honesty
and humility of a leader who wore as a badge of honor his inexperience in
Washington's corridors of power. But although Carter's words were ostensibly directed at the American people, they were also remarkably apropos
to the relationship he was soon to establish with the leaders of the Western
alliance. For Carter entered the international arena much as he entered
the White House: with a neophyte spirit of humility, cautious optimism,
and a willingness to learn from the experts. At the same time, however,
he brought an attitude toward governance – a combination of Wilsonian
moralism, an engineer's rationalism, and in British Prime Minister James
Callaghan's words, "a manifest dislike of horse-trading" – that would repeatedly hamstring his efforts to build and sustain cordial transatlantic relations.[1]

The relationship between the United States and its European allies in
the Carter years was generally characterized by the kind of goodwill that
had prevailed among the NATO allies since World War II. Americans
and Europeans continued to feel a common bond built around a shared
cultural heritage and fundamental agreement on trade and defense. But the
Carter years also witnessed serious tensions between Washington and the
European capitals, including some acrimonious personal debates that grew

---

1 James Callaghan, *Time and Chance* (London, 1987), 482–3.

into ugly, public confrontations. These disagreements grew largely out of the overriding concerns of national interest and conflicting responses to unexpected world events. Transatlantic tensions were further exacerbated by Carter's awkward negotiating style and his inexperience in world affairs and Washington politics.

Divergent national interests were a natural outgrowth of power inequalities in the Atlantic community. Europeans were anxious to assert their interests in the NATO alliance, and they worried about the deleterious effects of America's eroding economic might and its perceived post-Vietnam "loss of will" in defense matters.[2] European leaders also sought an active role in those East-West negotiations that directly affected their interests. British leaders, however, stood somewhat apart from the continental trends. As had been true for centuries, Britons in the 1970s stood both inside and outside Europe, anxious to be a part of the fledgling European Community but still ambivalent about their historical and cultural status as Europeans. So the governments of James Callaghan (1976–79) and, to a lesser extent, Margaret Thatcher (1979–90), cultivated a role as intermediary between the United States and the Continent, a role that benefited both London and Washington.[3]

Americans of the post-Vietnam era, meanwhile, wanted both a roll-back of international commitments and a strong reassertion of American principles. Carter tried to break this Gordian knot by proposing bold initiatives while also continuing his predecessors' most promising schemes. But although the mandate for change in American foreign policy was strong, Carter's support on both sides of the Atlantic was thin, and throughout his presidency, his inability to overcome his domestic critics was emblematic of his ongoing troubles with America's European allies.

We illustrate here the capricious nature of European-American relations in this period through a close examination of three areas of transatlantic consultation: Carter's defense policies, economic and monetary issues, and Carter's policy shifts in response to the shocks of 1979–80.

CARTER, NATO, AND EUROPEAN DEFENSE

Of all the transatlantic issues of this period, defense and security were, of course, of the utmost importance. For although East-West tensions had

2 Zbigniew Brzezinski, *Power and Principle: Memoirs of a National Security Advisor* (New York, 1983), 517.
3 Margaret Thatcher, *The Downing Street Years* (London, 1993), 65–9; Thatcher, *The Path to Power* (New York, 1995), 365–7; Jimmy Carter, *Keeping Faith: Memoirs of a President* (New York, 1982), 113.

lessened in the 1970s, U.S.-Soviet relations were still potentially explosive. For this reason, détente and the ongoing arms limitation talks were a constant source of tension on both sides of the Atlantic.

Four months into his presidency, in a speech at Notre Dame University, Carter laid out the "cardinal premises" of his foreign policy, most of which directly affected the European allies.[4] Regarding defense and NATO, he proclaimed a new vision for American policy based on closer cooperation among the industrial democracies, better relations with the Soviets, and a stronger conventional defense force. He also supported continuation of détente, as long as it led to progress that was "both comprehensive and reciprocal." Carter had long criticized Henry Kissinger for excluding Western Europe from the détente process, so his embrace of a more inclusive program was welcomed in Western European government circles. He went on to propose a comprehensive ban on nuclear testing, a new emphasis on human rights, a freeze on weapons modernization, and a substantial reduction in strategic weapons. As he put it, "Even if we cannot heal ideological divisions [with the Soviets], we must reach accommodations that reduce the risk of war." There was much in this speech for Europeans to applaud, for Carter seemed to have their best interests at heart.

But while Carter's defense proposals were widely admired, his contradictory decisions fed European fears of waning American resolve.[5] On the one hand, Carter claimed he wanted to continue to improve Western defense capabilities; on the other hand, he cut production of the B-1 bomber five months after taking office. He later achieved multilateral support for his proposed NATO conventional defense budget increase, but his statements on nuclear arms reductions confused many Europeans.

The issue of Western European nuclear capabilities was more pressing than concerns about conventional arsenals, especially considering the Soviets' deployment, beginning in 1977, of the SS-20 intermediate-range ballistic missile (IRBM) in the Eastern-bloc republics. The power, accuracy, and mobility of this weapon alarmed West German Chancellor Helmut Schmidt above all other European leaders, and he spearheaded a campaign to adopt an updated "dual-track" strategy to combat the menace.[6] Under

---

4 Jimmy Carter, "University of Notre Dame: Address at Commencement Exercises at the University, May 22, 1977," *Public Papers*, 1977, 957–62.
5 Schmidt, Callaghan, and Giscard all wanted Carter to continue détente. Thatcher, meanwhile, criticized the Carter administration's "overconfidence in the goodwill of the Soviet Union." Roy Jenkins, *European Diary, 1977–1981* (London, 1989), 123; Brzezinski, *Power and Principle*, 165; Thatcher, *Downing Street Years*, 65.
6 The original NATO dual "grand strategy" was jointly formulated in 1967. Helmut Schmidt, *Men and Powers: A Political Retrospective* (New York, 1989), 167.

such a plan, NATO would modernize its European tactical missile arsenal while also seeking to reduce the Soviet missile threat through arms control treaties. To this end, Schmidt and the other European Community leaders pressed the United States and NATO to announce in late 1979 what became known as the theater nuclear force (TNF) plan: new American Pershing II and ground-launched cruise missiles would be deployed in West Germany and Britain, while the Soviets would be pressed to reduce their SS-20s.

The Americans concurred with the TNF plan for the sake of European defense, while also assuming American support would facilitate European backing for the hotly debated U.S.-Soviet Strategic Arms Limitation Talks (SALT II). The SALT process fueled European leaders' defense anxieties because the Europeans were essentially spectators to a process that directly affected them. Although the Europeans agreed with arms reduction on principle, they worried that the Americans might pull too many missiles out of Europe. Furthermore, the Americans did not seem overly interested in pressing the Soviets to limit those missiles that threatened only Western Europe.[7]

European fears also improved at least one continental relationship. Britain and France were nuclear powers, which theoretically made possible a Franco-British nuclear axis. But such an arrangement was highly unlikely, and European leaders privately agreed that Franco-British nuclear cooperation could never be a substitute for American power in NATO.[8] Much more tenable – and evident – was the Franco-German friendship, fueled by mutual interests and mutual disillusionment with Carter and Callaghan. In 1977, Schmidt and French President Valéry Giscard d'Estaing found common cause on many issues, and though they did not have a strong vision for Europe, they could agree that, in European Community President Roy Jenkins's words, "They were rather hostile to Callaghan, whom they saw as semi-detached towards Europe, too attached to the unesteemed President Carter, and running an ineffective economy to boot."[9] Furthermore, although the leaders wanted American power on their side, they also accused Carter of eschewing a leading role. West Germany, said Schmidt, could not lead the Western alliance, and though "the United States almost effortlessly could . . . Carter shows no signs of doing so." As for Giscard, his fear that Carter's foreign policy was endangering détente also helped push France and West Germany closer together.[10]

---

7 Schmidt repeated this claim several times in his memoir, particularly regarding the Soviet SS-20 threat. Schmidt, *Men and Powers*, 70–1, 73–4, 188–92.
8 Peter Carrington, *Reflect on Things Past: The Memoirs of Lord Carrington* (London, 1988), 222.
9 Jenkins, *European Diary*, 22.   10 Ibid., 123, 169.

The Carter administration, meanwhile, consistently complained that the Europeans were not living up to their defense obligations. In January 1979, Carter met informally with Giscard, Schmidt, and Callaghan on the Caribbean island of Guadeloupe. Here the leaders discussed many issues, but Carter was most interested in pushing Europe to take more responsibility for its own defense. As he saw it, the key problem in the Atlantic alliance was that the Europeans seemed to want the United States to take the initiative on defense matters in order to minimize European domestic political losses. He later recalled, "I pointed out that we must meet the Soviet threat on intermediate-range missiles . . . but that no European leader had been willing to accept on their soil our neutron weapons, ground-launched cruise missiles, or the Pershing 2 medium-range missiles." Schmidt's obstinacy in this regard particularly rankled Carter because the chancellor had initiated the entire discussion of a European nuclear imbalance. Carter was clearly frustrated with this "typical" transatlantic situation, in which "the European leaders would let the United States design, develop, and produce the new weapons, but none of them was willing to agree in advance to deploy them."[11] The adoption of dual-track by the end of the year would solve some, but not all, of these conflicts.

Even on the issue of a conventional arms budget increase, the Americans felt they had to push their European friends to live up to their commitments. In his correspondence with Schmidt, Carter politely urged the chancellor to keep up with the agreed-on increase, while acknowledging that inflation was making such a commitment difficult.[12] Carter would later thank Schmidt for his efforts, but the issue afflicted German–American relations throughout his presidency. In a transitional meeting after the 1980 election, when Carter's secretary of state complained that most European nations were not living up to their budget increase agreements, Defense Secretary Harold Brown quipped, "The Allies . . . always rebuff us for putting too much pressure on them about defense contributions. . . . Only by chiding them do we get them to act."[13]

11 Schmidt remembered this exchange somewhat differently. He claimed he was at first reluctant because West Germany was not a nuclear power. He then agreed with Giscard that new deployments should only come if short-term negotiations with the Soviets failed. Carter, *Keeping Faith*, 234–6; Schmidt, *Men and Powers*, 189–90. Carter's presidential papers give little direct indication of Carter's personal views of the European allies. Perhaps he was wary, because of the lessons of Watergate, of having his thoughts recorded verbatim during meetings and conversations. At any rate, several other American and European sources assess the Carter administration's attitude toward the Europeans.

12 Note, Carter to Schmidt, Sept. 18, 1979, "Germany, Federal Republic of: Chancellor Helmut Schmidt, 6–10/79" folder, Box 7, NSA Brzezinski Material (hereinafter NBM), Jimmy Carter Library (hereinafter JCL); Telegram, Carter to Schmidt, 2/80, "Germany, Federal Republic of: Chancellor Helmut Schmidt, 6–10/79" folder, Box 7, NBM, JCL.

13 Memo, Brzezinski to Carter, Nov. 25, 1980, "Meetings – Miscellaneous Memos: 3/78–11/80" folder, Box 23, Zbigniew Brzezinski Collection (hereinafter ZBC), JCL.

All of these issues – arms reductions, defense obligations, détente, and friction between Carter and Schmidt – came to a head in the neutron bomb controversy, which saw the most acrimonious public exchanges of the Carter presidency. The Americans had been developing a neutron bomb, also known as an enhanced radiation warhead (ERW), since Gerald Ford's presidency.[14] The secret program predated Carter's arrival, but after a *Washington Post* reporter publicized it in 1977, Carter was put in the difficult position of having to justify the weapon.

The essential transatlantic issue here centered on political burden sharing, that is, who would take on the responsibility – or blame – for development and deployment of the neutron bomb. At the root of the controversy was the nature of the ERW. The neutron bomb was intended to kill human populations while leaving buildings intact, and so was quickly dubbed the "capitalist bomb" by Soviet propagandists. Carter pledged to develop and deploy the ERW only if the governments of Western Europe declared a need for it. The Europeans, meanwhile, tried to steer clear of the political flak that would follow such a request.

From the German perspective, this was a potentially explosive issue because the weapon was being skewered in the press and because Schmidt's political base was too weak to allow for bold moves. The left wing of his Social Democratic Party had moral concerns about the neutron bomb, while many moderates argued that it would make nuclear war more likely.[15] Furthermore, when Carter declared that development would only follow a European request for future deployment, he was reversing the traditional nuclear decision-making process in the Western alliance. And because Schmidt was no fan of the "unreliable" Carter, it was very easy for the West Germans to insist that the Americans make the initial production decision.

But Carter had his own domestic concerns. He had run for president on an arms reduction platform, so he was reluctant to add another component to the American nuclear arsenal. He therefore told his principal foreign policy advisers, Secretary of State Cyrus Vance and National Security Adviser Zbigniew Brzezinski, that he wanted the Europeans to shoulder the burden of neutron bomb deployment. "The President," Brzezinski recalled, "told us he did not wish the world to think of him as an ogre, and we agreed that we will press the Europeans to show greater interest . . . and therefore

---

14 Michael Broer, Frederick Donovan, and James Goodby, *The Neutron Bomb and the Premises of Power: President Carter's Neutron Bomb Decision* (Washington, D.C., 1995), 2.
15 Ibid., 3–4.

willingness to absorb some of the political flak."[16] But Brzezinski and Vance failed to realize that Carter was looking for an excuse to pull the plug on the program. Carter seems to have found the weapon too distasteful to develop, and this may have been at the heart of what soon became a major misunderstanding within the administration.[17]

When lengthy negotiations yielded a complex March 1978 agreement involving a future American production announcement, a NATO request for European deployment, and "linkage" of ERW production with arms reduction negotiations, Carter balked.[18] The terms of the agreement placed most of the burden on the United States, so without consulting his foreign policy advisers, Carter followed the advice of his domestic advisers and unilaterally decided against ERW development. These advisers swayed Carter with moral and domestic political logic, but they underestimated how much work had gone into the negotiations and how much of Carter's international prestige was at stake.[19] Carter's decision caused an immediate congressional outcry, sharp criticism from the European foreign policy community, and swift entreaties from Brzezinski and Vance that the president change his mind. Carter then modified his stance by deferring the production decision indefinitely.

Carter's two decisions on the neutron bomb – cancellation, then deferral – did immeasurable injury to his standing in international circles. They also irrevocably damaged the already caustic relationship between Carter and Schmidt, for Schmidt had concluded that the neutron weapon would be a valuable addition to the NATO arsenal and he had worked hard to get members of his own party to go along with the March agreement. The Callaghan government's respect for Carter also slipped somewhat, though the British were only mildly vexed because it was unlikely the weapon would have been deployed in Britain.[20] All things considered, although the Europeans consistently ducked responsibility for the neutron bomb, the lion's share of blame for the fracas must be placed at Carter's heels.

Although European-American defense issues could be contentious, the Anglo-American defense relationship was for the most part quite cordial. In fact, with the exception of Margaret Thatcher's ideological criticism

---

16 Brzezinski, *Power and Principle*, 302.
17 Brzezinski later wrote, "When the bureaucratic train was set in motion, I had assumed that we were fulfilling the President's requirements . . . I had underestimated the degree of Carter's reluctance to deploy this weapon." Ibid., 306.
18 Broer, Donovan, and Goodby, *The Neutron Bomb and the Premises of Power*, 9–10.
19 Ibid., 11.
20 David Owen later said he agreed with Carter's decision despite the Callaghan government's position favoring deployment. David Owen, *Personally Speaking to Kenneth Harris* (London, 1987), 136–7.

of Carter's human rights and détente aims, the "special relationship" was very much alive in the Carter years. Clearly, this relationship had its roots in linguistic and cultural ties as well as decades of close Anglo-American defense cooperation. But other factors were also at play. For starters, the continuing close relationship of the Carter years may have owed something to Britain's ambivalence regarding the EC, a position that gave both nations extra room to maneuver in transatlantic relations. At a more personal level, Carter and Callaghan forged a fond personal and professional relationship, as did their chief foreign policy advisers, Vance and British Foreign Secretary David Owen.[21] Callaghan was a committed Atlanticist, and he sought to move British foreign policy away from the European orientation pursued by the Conservative government of Edward Heath (1970–74). Indeed, on the Labour Party's accession to power in 1974, Callaghan had laid the foundation for this renewed relationship by saying, "We repudiate the view that Europe will emerge only after a process of struggle against America."[22] Later in Carter's term, when Thatcher replaced Callaghan, even the "Iron Lady" muted her earlier criticisms and publicly applauded Carter for his turn back to a tougher foreign policy.

British leaders may have overestimated their effect on the American policy-making process, but they nonetheless believed they had much to gain if they acted as an intermediary between the United States and continental Europe. That is, they believed they could use their geographical position and their unique understanding of their American and continental cousins to effectively translate each side's motives to the other. They saw this role as both instructive and as a fail-safe against intra-alliance misunderstandings. In Owen's words, the Anglo-American relationship "has been most valuable when it has poured oil on troubled waters."[23] One gets the sense here, especially from Owen and Roy Jenkins (who were anything but "anti-American"), that from the British point of view the Carter administration was much like an upstart member of the nouveau riche who needs his wise uncle's advice on the proper way to manage his capital. The Callaghan government came to this mildly paternalistic conclusion in part because Carter was new to the game of international diplomacy and because it saw Brzezinski as a rash, undiplomatic Cold Warrior. Moreover, the British diplomatic attitude had long fluctuated between a polite appraisal of the United States as a well-meaning but naive giant and a more rancorous assessment of the Americans as "oversexed, overpaid, and over here," as

---

21 Ibid., 90; Brzezinski, *Power and Principle*, 295.   22 *New York Times*, Mar. 20, 1974.
23 Owen, *Personally Speaking*, 77, 122.

the World War II gibe put it, and not quite deserving of their superpower status.

The Carter administration likewise seemed to think the British were allies worth consulting, and as a result the two nations found many points of agreement in these years. Neither side was above granting the other exceptional terms in bilateral arrangements, as when the Americans gave the British favorable concessions in the Anglo-American civil air agreement and in the renewal of nuclear exchange contracts. The British, meanwhile, were willing to lobby for the Americans in Europe. According to Owen, after Carter asked NATO nations to increase their conventional defense expenditures by 3 percent: "The example set by Britain in agreeing to pay the increase was enormously helpful in persuading Norway, Denmark, and the Benelux countries to do likewise."[24] The close Anglo-American relationship could also be seen in the Comprehensive Test Ban Treaty negotiations, in which the British were included largely because the Carter administration accepted Callaghan's initiative to join the talks.[25] Even when Anglo-American agreements were delayed, both sides were usually satisfied with the final terms. This was true, for example, of the Polaris-Trident arrangement, in which the Carter administration agreed to back American sales of the Trident missile system to the British.[26] So in the final analysis, the special relationship was strong, and the British were capable of mustering some influence in Washington. Nevertheless, the Western alliance as a whole could not avoid cultural, historical, and strategic misunderstandings.

ECONOMIC POLICIES

A significant rift developed between the United States and Western Europe over economic policy during Carter's first two years in office. This dispute stemmed largely from the unique characteristics of each nation's economy, and it further exacerbated tensions between Carter and Schmidt. The Europeans, especially France and West Germany, were livid over what they perceived as an American inclination to act entirely self-interestedly, while the Carter administration was frustrated by what it viewed as European protectionism and introversion. Meanwhile, as with defense issues, the Callaghan government carved out a niche as intermediary between the United States and Europe. A pattern emerged in these years whereby initial rhetoric toward cooperation was followed by disagreements, tough

24 Ibid., 140.   25 Ibid., 142.
26 Thatcher, *Downing Street Years*, 244–7.

diplomatic wrangling, and eventual compromise with a great deal of quid pro quo. As one would expect, Carter's decisions were based principally on domestic political interests, for however good his intentions vis-à-vis the allies were, he knew the Europeans could not vote him out of office.

Economic troubles were of paramount political and social significance in these years. Indeed, after Carter left office he claimed that the intractable American economy was the key factor in his 1980 loss to Ronald Reagan.[27] Carter inherited a shaky economy as a result of declining worker productivity rates, a growing trade deficit, deindustrialization, and Vietnam War debts, all of which combined to produce high unemployment levels and a wildly fluctuating inflation rate. Economists were baffled by what became known in contemporary parlance as "stagflation" (high unemployment and high inflation), for the orthodox view held that the problems were mutually exclusive. But as with many orthodoxies developed in mid-twentieth-century conditions, the 1970s forced a revision of the rules.

Of course, America's economic problems did not develop in a vacuum. Inflation and unemployment plagued all industrial nations in the 1970s, and most transatlantic economic conflicts stemmed from disagreements over the best means of slaying these twin dragons. The oil shock of 1973 had shown Western nations that they were not in complete control of the world economy, and the dissolution of the Bretton Woods par value system early in the decade further contributed to the confusion. President Richard Nixon's dramatic unilateral 1971 decision to take the United States off the gold standard effectively established a sea of free-floating currencies, and the industrial powers were still struggling with floating exchange rates when Carter entered the White House.[28] In economic historian W. Carl Biven's words, "The Carter Administration was presented with a new international monetary regime . . . whose workings were not yet fully understood."[29]

European leaders believed these "world" problems were aggravated by a combination of the Carter administration's economic mismanagement, the consumption habits of the American public, and a lack of American leadership. The West German and Japanese economies had grown tremendously since the war, and American economic hegemony was increasingly seen as a thing of the past. Yet the post–Bretton Woods void still needed to

---

27 W. Carl Biven, *Jimmy Carter's Economy: Policy in an Age of Limits* (Chapel Hill, NC, 2002), 1–2. Carter also cited the Iran hostage crisis and divisions within the Democratic Party.

28 Klaus Larres, "West Germany and European Unity in U.S. Foreign Policy," in *The United States and Germany in the Era of the Cold War, 1945–1990*, vol. 2, *1968–1990*, ed. Detlef Junker (Cambridge, 2004), 63.

29 Ibid., xi.

be filled, and Schmidt and Giscard did not see leadership coming from the United States. They were particularly rankled by the weak dollar, which hurt European exporters hoping to sell to the world's largest market. A falling dollar would become a commonplace in the decades that followed, but as European Commission president Roy Jenkins noted, "In the late seventies, when the era of dollar omnipotence was only a decade behind, [a falling dollar] seemed like a collapse of the verities."[30] The related American irritants of deficit spending and price caps on domestic fuel further miffed Schmidt and Giscard.[31]

Early in his tenure, Carter sought to revive the American economy through a stimulus package that would please his domestic constituents. He sent Vice President Walter Mondale to the allied capitals to press them to do the same. The "Mondale mission" to achieve joint expansion – whereby multiple nations would take measures to expand their economies for similar purposes (also known as reflation) – was based on the understanding of economic interdependence associated with the Trilateral Commission. Carter's Council of Economic Advisers believed that the United Kingdom was particularly interested in growth in world trade because of its recent productivity losses but that the West Germans and the French were cool to the idea.[32] Mondale's team nevertheless made it clear to the Europeans that the United States would engage in a stimulus program whether or not other G-7 nations followed.[33]

These issues were taken up midway through Carter's first year in office at the 1977 London G-7 summit. There, the American president pushed for higher growth targets and criticized European protectionism, while Schmidt emphasized fiscal restraint and existing growth forecasts. The West Germans and Japanese also pressed Carter to act more boldly to tackle the energy crisis.[34] Given these tough agendas, it is little wonder that none of the delegations got everything it wanted. For his part, Carter did not commit to fighting the energy status quo in America. Meanwhile, the West Germans and Japanese did not formally commit to an expansionary policy and insisted instead that their respective growth forecasts were well within reach.[35] But in the months that followed, the West German and Japanese economies grew more slowly than expected, bringing further inflationary

---

30 Jenkins, *European Diary*, 197.
31 Sir Robin Renwick, *Fighting with Allies: America and Britain in Peace and at War* (New York, 1996), 310–19.
32 Biven, *Jimmy Carter's Economy*, 98.   33 Ibid, 108.
34 Schmidt, *Men and Powers*, 361.
35 "Downing Street Declaration," http://www.g8.utoronto.ca/summit/1977london/communique.html. See also Biven, *Jimmy Carter's Economy*, 112.

pressure to bear on the dollar and thus further weakening it. To make matters worse, a verbal browbeating from Schmidt in London led Carter to put the word out that he might not attend any more such conferences.[36]

Because the G-7 economies were so closely entwined, we might ask why these differences of opinion were so pronounced. The example of the United States and the Federal Republic of Germany is particularly instructive, as these major trading powers appear at first glance to have had much in common. Both nations' economic policies followed a similar path, from applied Keynesianism in the 1960s and early 1970s to anti-inflationary policies in the 1980s and 1990s.[37] (The interim Carter years were a time of painful readjustment for both countries.) Their close economic ties were evidenced by their closely synchronized business cycles throughout this period. Furthermore, both the United States and the Federal Republic arguably had more to fear from the rising "Asian Tiger" economies than they had to fear from each other.[38]

But despite these similarities, each nation had its own set of priorities shaped by its particular economic situation. To begin with, Americans and West Germans saw their respective economies as two very different models. West Germans espoused the managed corporatism of "Rhineland capitalism" and Americans held to their distinctive understanding of the free market.[39] The Germans were also far more reliant on foreign trade, and thus more sensitive to the weak dollar, while higher unemployment levels in the United States pushed American policy makers to prioritize expansion.[40] Finally, the United States retained strength in its ability to use economic diplomacy in Western alliance defense policy negotiations, while West Germany's rising economic status made its leaders more willing than before to challenge American power.[41]

Powerful cultural and historical factors also hindered West German–American economic relations.[42] For their part, Americans were still haunted by visions of the Great Depression, when unemployment hovered in the double digits for more than a decade. Accordingly, the Democratic Party had made full employment its top priority since the New Deal. Carter

---

36 Callaghan, *Time and Chance*, 485–6.
37 Harold James, "Cooperation, Competition, and Conflict: Economic Relations between the United States and Germany, 1968–1990," in *United States and Germany*, 187–8.
38 Welf Werner, "Emancipation, Regionalization, and Globalization: German-American Trade Relations," in *United States and Germany*, 211.
39 James, "Cooperation, Competition, and Conflict," 187, 191–3.
40 Ibid., 189; Werner, "Emancipation, Regionalization, and Globalization," 211–12.
41 Monika Medick-Krakau, "Trojan Horse or Loyal Partner? West Germany as a Trading Power between the United States and the EC," in Werner, *United States and Germany*, 204.
42 This explanation comes from Biven, *Jimmy Carter's Economy*, 100.

realized inflation was a problem as well, and he would later take great pains to fight it, but in his first year in office, he followed the heart of his party in pursuit of lower unemployment figures. West Germans, meanwhile, were similarly haunted by the almost indescribable inflation of the years following World War I, a period that still serves as the standard textbook explanation of currency inflation gone horribly awry. An inflationary shock also followed World War II, and in the ensuing decades, monetary discipline became the foundation of West German economic orthodoxy. By the Carter years, West Germans were in no mood to brook American indifference on dollar-induced inflationary pressure.[43]

An exchange between Carter and Schmidt at the end of 1977 illustrates quite clearly the divergent priorities of West Germans and Americans. In the months that followed the London conference, the foreign exchange markets fluctuated with uncertainty, leading Schmidt to send Carter an urgent message regarding a proper Western response. The urgency of the memo underscored Schmidt's belief in the gravity of the situation – at least for West Germany – and his conviction that America could act to restrain the markets. He reminded Carter that a considerable portion of the U.S. current account deficit had been financed principally by European central banks rather than the reflow of capital to the United States by private financial markets. If these central banks were to change their policy, Schmidt warned, it would create the potential for even greater inflation. Perhaps fearing that Carter would see this as a purely European or West German problem, the chancellor eventually appealed to Carter's sense of common purpose with the alliance, saying, "I am deeply convinced that the necessary leading role of the United States and the strength of the American currency are inseparably linked with one another."[44]

Carter responded by agreeing that a stronger dollar was important, and he promised to fight devaluation by seeking legislation to cut taxes and reduce American dependence on foreign oil.[45] He then assured Schmidt that the United States would meet the growth targets stated at London. But in a more provocative passage, he went on to argue that the other industrial economies also needed to expand if the U.S. deficit were to be reduced, and he twice asserted that the EC must refrain from trade protectionism.[46]

---

43 Ibid., 116–17.
44 Memo, David Aaron to Carter, Dec. 22, 1977, "Germany, Federal Republic of: Chancellor Helmut Schmidt, 5-12/77" folder, Box 6, NBM, JCL.
45 Letter, Carter to Schmidt, Dec. 30, 1977, "Germany, Federal Republic of: Chancellor Helmut Schmidt, 5-12/77" folder, Box 6, NBM, JCL.
46 This point was echoed in ongoing negotiations with the British aimed at reducing tariffs. See Memo, Robert Strauss to Carter, Mar. 22, 1978, "3/23/78" folder, Box 77, Handwriting File, JCL.

Schmidt and Giscard took these differences of opinion to heart and began bilateral consultations that would eventually lead to the European Monetary System (EMS). They knew that such consultations might arouse suspicion, so they took pains to ease American and Japanese fears that Europe was turning inward.[47] As for the British, Callaghan agreed with the basic principle of EMS because he thought it would bring more order into the currency markets. Like his continental counterparts, he worried about the ramifications of the dollar's drop, and he was galled by the perceived lack of an American response to what the Europeans considered common economic interests. He implied as much in a paper he sent to Carter in 1977 titled "International Initiative on Growth and Currency." There, Callaghan pointed out that the dollar would not be able to serve as the world's sole reserve currency in the long term, and that "a depreciating dollar was not a matter for the United States to ignore or to treat as a purely domestic issue."[48]

But Callaghan's interest in the EMS was limited. Although he had come to agree in principle with Giscard and Schmidt by 1978, he nevertheless informed them that the United Kingdom would not join. He cited the improving fortunes of the British pound, but he also likely believed he could amass political capital by following the time-honored British tradition of keeping continental Europe at arm's length. Too many Britons still seemed suspicious of tying their nation's fortunes to those of Europe.[49]

Invariably, of course, Callaghan's major role in the transatlantic economic row was as an emissary for interests on both sides, and it appears that all parties accepted him in this capacity. In one particularly illustrative intra-alliance exchange in 1978, for example, Callaghan asserted that Schmidt "was exasperated" with Carter's economic policies, and "once again suggested that, in view of my good relations with Carter, I should visit him to encourage the United States to take a broader view."[50] Callaghan also worked with the Americans to pressure Europe when common Anglo-American interests were at stake.[51]

With the 1978 Bonn G-7 Summit on the horizon, the Carter administration felt the need to say something conciliatory about EMS as part of the preliminary summit bargaining. A memo to Carter from his summit assistant, Henry Owen, stated that the administration's economic concerns needed to be balanced against "our *political* stake in European integration,

---

47 Biven, *Jimmy Carter's Economy*, 166; Jenkins, *European Diary*, 225.
48 Callaghan, *Time and Chance*, 486, 490.   49 Ibid., 492–3.
50 Ibid., 487–8.
51 Memo, W. Michael Blumenthal to Carter, Mar. 21, 1978, "3/23/78" folder, Box 77, Handwriting File, JCL.

which would be advanced by European monetary cooperation," and "our *tactical* stake in being able to say something kind about European monetary cooperation, as part of the bargaining with Schmidt and Giscard at Bonn." Owen went on to say that such a statement would have to be phrased in a way that sounded both positive and prudent.[52] The administration thus remained cautiously diplomatic about EMS, but privately they were a bit concerned about what it could mean for the United States.

When the Bonn summit began, European leaders still sought to force the issue of the weak dollar, while Carter still wanted to discuss reflation, protectionism, and the aims of EMS. According to Jenkins, who was perhaps the most neutral observer among the major participants, things got off to a bad start when the Japanese prime minister criticized Carter for the weak dollar. Schmidt then threw fuel on the fire by speaking "too provocatively, and not persuasively, against the Americans."[53] Schmidt and Carter got into a sharp argument, after which Carter seemed to be very cool to the idea of EMS. But other American officials later assured EC representatives that the U.S. position on EMS was more favorable than Carter had implied. Eventually, despite Schmidt's public pronouncements to the contrary, the parties agreed to a joint reflation.[54] As for EMS, the final communiqué did not formally endorse the system; it noted only that EC representatives had announced it to the group.[55] Carter tacitly accepted EMS, and Schmidt understood this acceptance as a quid pro quo for implementation of a German reflation policy.[56]

But beyond Schmidt's desire for American acceptance of EMS, why did he finally agree to reflation? According to W. Carl Biven, Schmidt's attitude in Bonn was based on two conflicting needs: "He publicly resisted American pressure to adopt an expansionary policy in respect for the traditional German suspicion of exercises in demand management, while privately moving toward reluctant acceptance of a need to stimulate a lagging economy."[57] Schmidt also had personal and professional motives for remaining obstinate. In Biven's words, the former finance minister "is said to have expressed resentment at being lectured to by two inexperienced [American] academics."[58] Further domestic pressure to reflate came from German labor unions, the left wing of his Social Democratic Party, and the Bundesbank.[59]

---

52 Memo, Henry Owen to Carter, July 11, 1978, "1–12/78" folder, Box 23, ZBC, JCL.
53 Jenkins, *European Diary*, 294.   54 Biven, *Jimmy Carter's Economy*, 150–1.
55 "Final Communique," http://www.g8.utoronto.ca/summit/1978bonn/communique/index.html.
56 Biven, *Jimmy Carter's Economy*, 166–8.   57 Ibid., 150.
58 Ibid., 99. See also Letter, Schmidt to Carter, Apr. 9, 1979, "Germany, Federal Republic of: Chancellor Helmut Schmidt, 1–5/79" folder, Box 6, NBM, JCL.
59 Biven, *Jimmy Carter's Economy*, 150–1. The Germans were also pressured by the EC and the OECD.

For his part, Carter gave a nod to EMS while also lifting the American price ceiling on domestic oil and redirecting energy policy to get Americans to lower their energy consumption. These proposals had real promise at the time of the Bonn summit, but six months later the shah of Iran was overthrown, the world oil market spun into crisis, and ordinary Americans once again found themselves waiting in long lines for gas. Some observers later deemed the Bonn summit a failure because the decision to reflate was followed by a rapid rise in inflation. But this inflation would not have been so dramatic without the overthrow of the shah and the second oil price hike.[60] Economic conflicts continued for the rest of Carter's tenure, but they were largely overshadowed by two unexpected international events.

THE SHOCKS OF 1979–80

At the end of 1979, two crises overwhelmed the Carter administration. On November 4, militant Iranian students stormed the American embassy in Tehran and took sixty-nine American hostages. Then, on December 27, the Soviet Union sent its massive army across its southern border and into Afghanistan. The two crises dominated the attention of the Carter administration and determined the nature of transatlantic relations for the remainder of the Carter presidency.

The Iran hostage crisis significantly strained the relationship between the United States and Europe. For more than six months after the hostages were taken, the United States and its allies disagreed over how to properly respond. The disagreement stemmed from diverging national interests but was exacerbated by Carter's erratic policies, diplomatic gaffes, and unilateral actions.

Shortly after the hostage crisis began, Carter asked Thatcher, Giscard, and Schmidt to consider joining a trade embargo against Iran. According to Carter, Thatcher "promised her full backing," but Giscard and Schmidt promised only to issue supportive statements and to condemn Iran's actions.[61] Seeking more than words, Carter dispatched Vance to Europe. Vance asked the allies to support a concerted freeze against Iranian financial assets and, again, to join the United States in a trade embargo against Iran. When Vance's private appeals were met with resistance, the administration grew impatient. Defense Secretary Harold Brown publicly urged Europe to take immediate action, declaring, "It is now appropriate for our allies and friends, indeed for the world community, to reflect its disapproval through

60 Ibid., 178–9; Owen, 124.   61 Carter, *Keeping Faith*, 465.

concrete diplomatic and economic steps."[62] In January, the United States brought its desire for sanctions to the United Nations. When the matter was brought to a vote, the EC members voted unanimously in favor of sanctions. Their votes of support, however, were predictably overruled by a Soviet veto.

Although their efforts at the United Nations had failed, the United States continued to pressure its European friends to support economic sanctions. But while Europe had been willing to support United Nations–sponsored sanctions, they were unwilling to do so without the United Nations. By March, according to Vance, Carter was "angry about our allies' hedging on sanctions and putting strong political pressure on Iran."[63] On March 26, Carter wrote again to Thatcher, Schmidt, and Giscard, strongly requesting their support for sanctions. When these leaders continued to balk, Carter moved unilaterally. On April 7, he severed diplomatic relations with Iran and imposed full-scale sanctions.

With unilateral sanctions in place, the administration increased its efforts to bring Europe on board. The U.S. ambassadors in all the EC capitals delivered detailed lists of requests to the respective foreign ministers, and Vance met with numerous European ambassadors, stressing to them that "American patience was wearing thin."[64] On April 10, Carter repeated a familiar refrain in pointed remarks to Europe: "Nations ask us for leadership," he said, "but at the same time they demand their own independence of action. They ask for aid, but they reject any interference. . . . Some ask for protection, but are wary of the obligations of alliance."[65] On April 22, Europe finally gave America what it had been demanding. The foreign ministers of the nine EC nations voted to impose economic sanctions on May 17 unless decisive progress was made to free the American hostages.

Carter blamed Europe's delayed decision on selfish motives. "It soon became apparent," Carter later wrote, "that even our closest allies in Europe were not going to expose themselves to potential oil boycotts . . . for the sake of American hostages."[66] Carter's evaluation of European motives was partly correct, for the EC members had significant economic ties to Iran. West Germany, for example, had $1.2 billion in trade with Iran in 1979.[67] Even as late as April of 1980, six months after the crisis began, Germany was

---

62 *Washington Post*, Dec. 12, 1979.
63 Vance, *Hard Choices: Critical Years in America's Foreign Policy* (New York, 1983), 407.
64 Ibid.
65 Carter, "American Society of Newspaper Editors Remarks and a Question-and-Answer Session at the Society's Annual Convention, Apr. 10, 1980," *Public Papers of the Presidents*, 1980, 632.
66 Carter, *Keeping Faith*, 466.   67 *Washington Post*, Apr. 10, 1980.

receiving 12 percent of its oil imports from Iran, while Britain's monthly trade with Iran exceeded $40 million.[68]

But economic interests do not tell the whole story. European leaders also had serious doubts about the effectiveness of sanctions without UN support. They further questioned whether the Khomeini regime could be moved by rational calculations and feared that a Western trade embargo might drive Iran into the arms of the Soviet Union. When the EC members eventually committed to sanctions, they did so reluctantly. Horst Ehmke, a leading German Social Democrat, expressed this pessimistic view when he concluded, "Under certain circumstances, we have to support American policies even when we doubt they have much point."[69]

The erratic nature of American policy made it even more difficult for Europe to sacrifice its interests on behalf of the United States. Carter's position changed numerous times before sanctions were eventually imposed. After sending Vance to Europe in December to seek support for a trade embargo, Carter tabled sanctions on January 1 and decided to give UN Secretary-General Kurt Waldheim a chance to negotiate a diplomatic solution. Eleven days later, the United States asked the United Nations to vote on sanctions against Iran. Twelve days after that, Carter abandoned the sanctions idea again, this time in favor of working for a solution through two French lawyers who had connections in Iran. When this scheme did not work, sanctions were back on again. This vacillation prompted *Newsweek's* Paris bureau chief to write that Carter had "an Iranian strategy that oscillates between toughness and conciliation and haughtily requires the allies to follow each and every twist."[70] Theo Sommer, editor of *Die Zeit*, captured the uncomfortable predicament of European leaders as they began to realize that they would eventually have to back the American president: "No matter how amateurish, erratic and incompetent they may privately think he is, they know that in the last analysis they will have to go along with him in order to save the vital American connection."[71]

And Carter frequently did things that, in retrospect, appear "amateurish, erratic, and incompetent." In April, the president announced to a group of European television correspondents that he had sent EC leaders a "specific date" by which he expected them to approve sanctions and cut diplomatic ties with Iran. The correspondents immediately reported this announcement to their respective television audiences, and European leaders were

68 *Economist*, Apr. 19, 1980, 47; *Washington Post*, Apr. 10, 1980.
69 *Economist*, Apr. 19, 1980, 47; Apr. 26, 1980, 39.
70 *Newsweek*, May 12, 1980, 48.   71 *Economist*, Apr. 19, 1980, 47.

flooded with questions about the new Carter deadline. But when the European leaders were asked about Carter's "specific date," they did not know anything about it. Carter had failed to inform them of his plan before announcing it to the world media. Even Margaret Thatcher, America's staunchest ally during the period, had to publicly expose the president. "We have not been sent a date by which our American allies want us to act," she confessed to the press.

European leaders also took offense at Carter's ill-fated April 24 hostage rescue attempt. The botched attempt particularly stung the allies because just two days earlier the EC had agreed to levy sanctions on Iran, doing so in the belief that its decision would prevent the United States from taking any form of military action. In private correspondence with Carter, Schmidt had made clear that he strongly opposed any kind of military action.[72] But as U.S. demands for sanctions went unheeded in Europe, American officials repeatedly warned European leaders that the United States might resort to military force. "We warned them," Vance later wrote, "that without active support from our friends, unilateral action more severe than those the president had described to their heads of government would be forthcoming." The reaction to this warning, according to Vance, "was quite negative." European ambassadors in the United States "expressed grave reservations about the consequences if we should resort to force,"[73] and British Deputy Foreign Minister Douglas Hurd warned of "the immense, manifold dangers throughout the Islamic world of attempting to treat this matter in a military way."[74] When U.S. threats of force increased, however, the Europeans had to make a choice, and on April 22 they chose sanctions over force. Thus, it was a great shock when Carter sent U.S. helicopters into Iran two days later. "The timing was horribly bad," observed Pierre Lellouche, a strategy expert at the Institut Français des Relations Internationales. "May 18 would have been perfect, but doing it this way is really taking us Europeans for idiots."[75]

The rescue attempt was a wake-up call for Europe. Not only had Carter demonstrated a willingness to use force, but the rescue attempt had also triggered the resignation of Cyrus Vance, who was widely respected in Europe for his "quiet diplomacy and preference for negotiated solutions."[76] European leaders now realized that if they did not become more involved in the

---

72 Letter, Schmidt to Carter, Jan. 18, 1980, "Germany, Federal Republic of: Chancellor Helmut Schmidt, 6-10/79" folder, Box 23, ZBC, JCL.
73 Vance, *Hard Choices*, 407.   74 *Washington Post*, Apr. 25, 1980.
75 *BusinessWeek*, May 12, 1980, 26.
76 Following Vance's resignation, Schmidt told reporters that "regret in the circle of [European] heads of government and foreign ministers about the resignation of Cy Vance is general." *Washington Post*, Apr. 29, 1980.

formation of American policy, Carter might continue to make risky, uni-lateral decisions.[77] So after initial expressions of disapproval, both Giscard and Schmidt issued strong statements of support.[78] By expressing solidarity with America, West Germany and France hoped to obtain greater access to the American president. European leaders also decided to improve the transatlantic dialogue through bilateral Anglo-American contacts, such as an upcoming trip to Washington by British Foreign Secretary Lord Carring-ton, and through multilateral fora, such as the NATO council of foreign secretaries and the Venice economic summit. At the economic summit, the leaders issued public statements of mutual support, and soon thereafter the individual European nations finally passed various sanctions packages against Iran.

The other major event of the period, the Soviet invasion of Afghanistan, also heightened transatlantic tensions. Knowing that a sizable portion of the American public harbored strong anti-Soviet sentiments, struggling with a hostage crisis that daily made him appear helpless, and facing an election in which he was not even guaranteed the nomination of his own party, Carter seized on the Soviet invasion to demonstrate to the American people that he could be a strong leader.[79] Calling the Soviet invasion "the most serious threat to world peace since World War II," Carter took a number of steps to punish the Soviets, including a grain embargo, tighter controls on technology exports, the withdrawal of SALT II, and a boycott of the Olympics in Moscow. He also called for additional increases in U.S. defense spending and outlined a new blueprint for handling conflicts in the Persian Gulf region that came to be known as "the Carter Doctrine."[80]

The chief influences on Carter's reaction to Afghanistan were domestic political concerns, Carter's disillusionment with the Soviet Union, and the dominance of Zbigniew Brzezinski over the formation of American foreign policy. European leaders had no significant influence on Carter's decisions, but he still expected Europe's active support.[81] But, just as during the

---

77 Before the rescue attempt, Thatcher was the only European leader whom Carter had informed of his plans.

78 Associated Press, AM Cycle, International News, Apr. 28, 1980.

79 William Stueck, "Placing Jimmy Carter's Foreign Policy," in *The Carter Presidency: Policy Choices in the Post-New Deal Era*, eds. Gary M. Gink and Hugh David Graham (Lawrence, KS, 1998), 258.

80 Don Richardson, ed., *Conversations with Carter* (Boulder, CO, 1998), 182. Carter, "The State of the Union Address, Delivered before a Joint Session of Congress, Jan. 23, 1980," *Public Papers, 1980*, 194–203.

81 For a detailed list that includes all of the ways in which Carter expected the members of NATO to respond to the Soviet invasion, see Telegram, Carter to Schmidt, Mar. 27, 1980, "3-8/80" folder, Box 23, ZBC, JCL.

hostage crisis, America's allies had their own ideas and interests, and they responded to Carter's requests accordingly. Of the three leading European nations, France's response was the coolest, and Franco-American relations during this period were characterized by mistrust. Britain's response was by far the most positive, and Anglo-American relations remained strong throughout the final year of Carter's presidency. West Germany's reaction fell somewhere between that of France and Britain, but several Carter-Schmidt clashes ensured that German-American relations during this time would remain contentious.

Following the Soviet invasion of Afghanistan, Carter grew exasperated with the French. Two months after the invasion, Carter wrote critically in his diary of "the rapidly changing French foreign policy." He noted that France's public position had changed at least five times, and he concluded in frustration, "I don't know what's going on in France."[82] Carter's mistrust steadily increased, becoming so pronounced that he sought to avoid dealing with the French altogether. He even began excluding Giscard from telegrams that he sent to Schmidt and Thatcher. In one such telegram, Carter expressed reservations about convening a meeting of NATO members, because "a NATO summit would raise the now familiar problem of the level of French participation."[83]

France's chief East-West concern was the continuation of détente. An official French statement released shortly after the invasion read, "France does not intend to renounce the search for détente . . . whose alternative is the return to the Cold War." As a reflection of this policy, France collaborated with the United States in an international financial consortium to assist Pakistan but refused to join the Olympic boycott or declare economic sanctions against the Soviet Union. Foreign Minister Jean François-Poncet argued that it would be a "grave error" to "Westernize the Afghan affair."[84] In fact, rather than cut off diplomatic ties with the Soviets as the Unites States requested, Giscard met with Brezhnev on May 19. The following day the American secretary of state sharply scolded the French for arranging this meeting without consulting their allies, to which François-Poncet curtly replied that France did not need to seek anyone's "prior approval" for the way in which it dealt with the Soviets.[85]

By contrast, the British response to America's tough approach was, in Carter's words, "staunch and always helpful."[86] In addition to backing

---

82 Carter, *Keeping Faith*, 487.
83 Telegram, Carter to Schmidt, Mar. 27, 1980, "3-8/80" folder, Box 23, ZBC, JCL.
84 *Washington Post*, Jan. 10, 1980.   85 *New York Times*, May 22, 1980.
86 Carter, *Keeping Faith*, 486.

Carter's call for an Olympic boycott, Thatcher strengthened British relations with China, Turkey, and Pakistan and expanded British air and naval
capacities in the Indian Ocean.[87] Thatcher also reduced official contacts
between the Soviet Union and the United Kingdom, canceled military
exchanges between the two countries, and refused to renew Anglo-Soviet
credit arrangements.

Thatcher also sought to rally other European nations to America's
cause, calling the United States "the ultimate guarantor of European security."[88] When it became clear that the French were reluctant to back America's new Soviet policies, Thatcher firmly admonished them to do so. In a
rebuke of Giscard, Thatcher told the British House of Commons that she
remembered "the superb response that General de Gaulle gave to President
Kennedy's representative at the time of the Cuban missile crisis." De Gaulle
had said, "You may tell the President that France will support him," and
Thatcher concluded, "Europe should send the same message today."[89]

The West German response to Carter's Afghanistan policy fell somewhere between the policies of France and Britain. Schmidt shared many
of the French views regarding preserving détente and maintaining channels
of communication with the Soviets, but he also agreed with Thatcher's
position on an Olympic boycott, considering this issue "a matter of
morality."[90] Schmidt believed that allied solidarity was a critical prerequisite to effectively dealing with the Soviet challenge, and he assured Vance,
"We want to, and we will, be on board the American ship." "But," he cautioned, "the engine should not be fired up to full strength before knowing
where the journey is to lead."[91] Schmidt's statement highlights his central
concern during this period: he simply did not trust that Carter knew what
he was doing. "Though we had only minor objections to the individual
steps," Schmidt later wrote, "we saw clearly that there was no logical and
self-contained strategy for managing the crisis."[92] In fact, Schmidt seriously
questioned whether Carter was even sincere in his efforts to obtain a Soviet
withdrawal from Afghanistan. In his memoir Schmidt claimed to have asked
Carter what he would do if the Soviets remained in Afghanistan even after
an Olympic boycott. According to Schmidt, "Carter replied with disarming

---

87 Thatcher was unable, however, to deliver a British boycott of the Olympics. The British Olympic
    Committee sent the athletes against her wishes.
88 Margaret Thatcher, HC S, Feb. 28, 1980, *Margaret Thatcher: Complete Public Statements 1945–1990.*
    Database and Compilation (Oxford, 1999), UDN: 80_017.
89 Ibid.   90 Schmidt, *Men and Powers*, 78.
91 Vance, *Hard Choices*, 205.   92 Schmidt, *Men and Powers*, 203.

candor that he did not believe the Soviets would leave Afghanistan." Mortified by this reply, Schmidt went on to write, "I began to understand that what he was after was domestic prestige. For the sake of his prestige, Giscard and I were supposed to give up ours . . . [therefore,] I determined to make no more concessions."[93]

Ultimately, Schmidt did support Carter's decision to boycott the Olympics, but he remained bitterly convinced that Carter neither cared for Europe's interests nor appreciated Europe's sacrifices. Several times in the early months of the crisis, Schmidt asked Carter administration representatives whether the United States was planning a boycott. He was repeatedly told that there would be no boycott, and he informed the German Olympic Committee accordingly. "It was, then," wrote Schmidt, "a total surprise when Carter announced the boycott after all and, without consideration of the domestic humiliation he was causing his allies, demanded that they cooperate with his decision."[94]

The American policy with which Schmidt most disagreed was Carter's decision to cut off diplomatic ties with the Soviet Union. Shortly after the invasion, Schmidt had warned Carter that "we can only keep the current crisis . . . under control if communication is maintained with the Soviet Union." Only when allied positions were "unmistakably explained to the other side," Schmidt cautioned, "is there any prospect of understanding one another properly" and avoiding "the danger of escalation merely through misunderstanding."[95] Schmidt's belief in the necessity of clear communication led him to arrange a meeting with Brezhnev in June 1980. This planned meeting troubled Carter, for Schmidt had been publicly tossing around the idea of a three-year cessation of INF missile deployment. Concerned that Schmidt might inaccurately represent Western interests, Carter sent him a strongly worded letter, cautioning him against suggesting such a freeze to Brezhnev. The letter made Schmidt irate. He resented Carter's tone as a challenge to his integrity and loyalty to the alliance, and when the two men met in Venice later that month, sparks flew. Carter later claimed that his conversation was "the most unpleasant personal exchange" that he ever had with a foreign leader.[96] Although the two men emerged from their altercation with a positive statement for the press, they did not meet again during Carter's presidency.

---

93 Ibid., 207.   94 Ibid., 206.

95 Letter, Schmidt to Carter, Jan. 18, 1980, "Germany, Federal Republic of: Chancellor Helmut Schmidt, 6-10/79" folder, Box 23, ZBC, JCL.

96 Carter, *Keeping Faith*, 538.

CONCLUSION

Despite promising beginnings and some impressive public agreements, transatlantic relations in the Carter years were significantly strained behind the scenes. Carter's accession to the White House in 1977 was met with cautious optimism in European circles, and his attempts to bring morality to bear on American policy making were well regarded in much of the world. Furthermore, the Europeans were, for the most part, quite happy that he was not a trigger-happy cowboy cut from the Sunbelt mold of Lyndon Johnson and Barry Goldwater. But Carter's inexperience in world affairs and his inability to stake out a clear vision for the Western alliance vexed his more practiced European counterparts. When combined with differing national interests and the strain of two international crises, Carter's diplomatic shortcomings and erratic policies ensured that transatlantic relations were marked by significant discord.

The election of Ronald Reagan in November 1980 confirmed to some European observers the American public's support for Carter's harder-edged policies. World events and American domestic troubles had fully revived the Cold War during Carter's final year in office, and Reagan rode the tide of fear and discontent all the way to the White House. It is perhaps fitting, then, that Margaret Thatcher, who was the most vocal defender of Carter's tough turn, would also go on to be the most articulate champion of Reagan's conservative internationalism in the years to come. The events of the 1980s would be greatly influenced by the policies and personalities of this latest Anglo-American special relationship.

15

The United States, Europe, and the NATO Dual-Track Decision

JOACHIM SCHOLTYSECK

The debate over the deployment of intermediate-range nuclear missiles under the terms of the NATO dual-track decision of December 1979 acerbated ideological differences within the societies of Western Europe and resulted in large-scale social protests against political decision makers. It was seen on both sides of the East-West divide as literally a life-or-death struggle, as a choice between peace or war. The rallying cries "better red than dead" and "better dead than red" were more than a play on words.

The background to this debate was the waning enthusiasm for détente,[1] Soviet rearmament, and, in particular, the Soviet invasion of Afghanistan in December 1979,[2] which seemed to trigger a second Cold War. In retrospect, it is doubtful détente would have survived the invasion of Afghanistan. The United States was not willing to accept an expanded Soviet role in the world, and the Soviet Union was not willing to renounce its claim to broader worldwide influence. "The global processes in which both states existed made détente an unlikely option, unless fundamental adjustments took place in one or both of the two powers."[3] Consequently, the policy of nuclear deterrence, the backbone of strategic thinking during what Georges-Henri Soutou has dubbed the "Fifty Years' War," remained the foundation of East-West relations.[4] As John Lewis Gaddis, whose work has done so much to explain the underlying assumptions of deterrence, has summarized, "For

1 Richard Stevenson, *The Rise and Fall of Détente: Relaxations of Tensions in U.S.-Soviet Relations, 1953–1984* (Houndmills, U.K., 1985). See also Michael B. Froman, *The Development of the Idea of Détente: Coming to Terms* (London 1991); Richard Davy, ed., *European Detente: A Reappraisal* (London, 1992); John van Oudenaren, *Détente in Europe: The Soviet Union and the West since 1953* (Durham, NC, 1991).
2 Odd Arne Westad, "The Road to Kabul: Soviet Policy on Afghanistan, 1978–1979," in *The Fall of Détente: Soviet-American Relations during the Carter Years* (Oslo, 1997), 118–48.
3 Odd Arne Westad, "The Fall of Détente and the Turning Tides of History", in Westad, *Fall of Détente*, 3–33, 28.
4 Georges-Henri Soutou, *La guerre de Cinquante Ans. Les relations Est-Ouest 1943–1990* (Paris, 2001).

the Russians it made sense from the beginning not to initiate the use of nuclear weapons because the prospect of American retaliation was always present."[5] Even during the era of détente, when arms control talks had become an important arena for mutual reassurance, deterrence remained a cornerstone of the superpowers' strategies.[6]

This chapter analyzes the decision-making process during the missile debate, focusing on, on the one hand, the two superpowers and, on the other hand, the two Germanys. With the opening of some Eastern European archives since the end of the Cold War – access to Russian archives is still highly restricted – it has become possible to gain new insights into the meaning and the impact of NATO's dual-track policy.[7] Even today, the dual-track decision is not uncontested. In 2004, for example, Volker Zastrow called the dual-track policy "the biggest strategic mistake of the postwar era," as it allowed the Soviet Union to gain influence over the West's armament decisions.[8] It was not surprising that former West German Chancellor Helmut Schmidt strongly rejected Zastrow's interpretation and argued in response that the dual-track policy had been a successful team effort that laid the foundations for later disarmament agreements.[9]

The NATO dual-track decision came in response to Soviet rearmament. In the mid-1970s, the Soviet Union had begun constructing a land-based, intermediate-range nuclear ballistic missile system. The SS-20 missiles, as they were called in the West, replaced the older SS-4 and SS-5 missiles. Whereas the older missiles were equipped with only one warhead, the SS-20 had three warheads that could be independently targeted. The SS-20, powered by solid propellant, had a range of 5,500 kilometers and could be targeted to within 300 meters (as opposed to 2,300 meters with the SS-4 and SS-5). It was, moreover, mobile and therefore less vulnerable to enemy attack. One warhead had the explosive force of 150 kilotons of TNT. The

---

5 John Lewis Gaddis, *The Long Peace, Inquiries into the History of the Cold War* (Oxford, 1987), 146; John Lewis Gaddis, *We Now Know: Rethinking Cold War History* (Oxford, 1998).

6 Jennifer Sims, *Icarus Restrained: An Intellectual History of Nuclear Arms Control, 1945–1960* (Boulder, CO, 1990).

7 In addition, the works of Jonathan Haslam, Thomas Risse-Kappen, Helga Haftendorn, and Lothar Rühl, to mention just four examples, provided precise historico-political studies that were available earlier. Helga Haftendorn, *Sicherheit und Stabilität: Aussenbeziehungen der Bundesrepublik zwischen Ölkrise und NATO-Doppelbeschluss* (Munich, 1986); Lothar Rühl, *Mittelstreckenwaffen in Europa: Ihre Bedeutung in Strategie, Rüstungskontrolle und Bündnispolitik* (Baden-Baden 1987). For Haslam, see *infra* note 10, for Risse-Kappen, see *infra* notes 16 and 96.

8 Volker Zastrow, "Ein deutscher Albtraum," *Frankfurter Allgemeine Zeitung*, June 11, 2004. A similar argument can already be found in Christian Hacke, *Zur Weltmacht verdammt. Die amerikanische Aussenpolitik von Kennedy bis Clinton* (Berlin, 1997), 269.

9 Helmut Schmidt, "Der grosse Erfolg des Doppelbeschlusses," *Frankfurter Allgemeine Zeitung*, July 1, 2004.

SS-20 was tested for the first time in September 1975, and deployment began in March 1976. By 1987, the Soviet Union had 441 of the missiles in place.[10]

Was the testing and deployment of the SS-20 and the Tu-22 ("Backfire") bomber part of a routine weapons upgrade, as some scholars have argued, or should it be seen as an aggressive move on Moscow's part? This question remains the subject of debate to this day.[11] Some scholars have argued that the deployment was part of a "normal modernization program."[12] There is no question that it endangered the established Euro-strategic balance of power.[13] Historians still have to answer the question of why the Soviet Union deployed a weapon that "ultimately worsened Soviet security."[14]

The political leadership in Moscow was in an upbeat mood after the American defeat in Vietnam. Hoping to benefit from the decline of American prestige, the Brezhnev government confidently "adopted a more aggressive and rigid foreign policy."[15] But confidence gave way to overconfidence as the Soviet leaders obviously did not consider the potential impact that deployment of the SS-20 might have in the era of détente.[16] After the fall of the Soviet empire, scholars took a fresh look at the ideological zeal at the base of Soviet decisions. The Kremlin's "ideological arrogance," Vladislave Zubok and Constantine Pleshakov argue, "pushed the USSR down the road to economic overextension and, ultimately, imperial fatigue and decay."[17] Today, it appears that the decision to deploy the SS-20 was driven by a combination of ideology, defensive and technological considerations, and simple realpolitik. The Soviets and their allies were using détente for a systematic military buildup to alter the balance of power in the Warsaw Pact's favor.[18]

---

10 A detailed time line from testing to deployment can be found in Jonathan Haslam, *The Soviet Union and the Politics of Nuclear Weapons, 1967–87: The Problem of the SS-20* (Houndmills, 1989), 58–88.

11 Jost Dülffer, *Europa im Ost-West-Konflikt 1945–1991* (Munich, 2004), 93.

12 Raymond Garthoff, *Détente and Confrontation: American-Soviet Relations from Nixon to Reagan*, rev. ed. (Washington, D.C., 1994), 965; Robert Berman and James Baker, *Soviet Strategic Forces: Requirements and Responses* (Washington, D.C., 1982), 67; Klaus Wiegrefe, *Das Zerwürfnis. Helmut Schmidt, Jimmy Carter und die Krise der deutsch-amerikanischen Beziehungen* (Berlin, 2005), 165.

13 One of the first scholars to systematically form this argument was William Hyland, "The Struggle for Europe: An European View," in *Nuclear Weapons in Europe*, eds. William Hyland and Andrew Pierre (New York, 1984), 31.

14 Haslam, *Soviet Union*, x.

15 Ilya Giaduk, *The Soviet Union and the Vietnam War* (Chicago, 1996), 250.

16 Thomas Risse-Kappen, *Null-Lösung: Entscheidungsprozesse zu den Mittelstreckenwaffen 1970–1987* (Frankfurt am Main, 1988), 32.

17 Vladislav Zubok and Constantine Pleshakov, *Inside the Kremlin's Cold War: From Stalin to Khrushchev* (Cambridge, MA, 1996), 282. Cf. Melvyn Leffler, "Bringing It Together: The Parts and the Whole," in *Reviewing the Cold War: Approaches, Interpretations, Theory*, ed. Odd Arne Westad (London, 2000), 43–63, 45.

18 Jussi Hanhimäki, "Ironies and Turning Points: Détente in Perspective," in Westad, *Reviewing the Cold War*, 326–42, 330.

The hope of transforming military power into global political influence – a hope underlying the Soviet arms buildup since the time of Stalin – also played an important role in the SS-20 decision. Moscow calculated that

parity in strategic nuclear power could be used to advance claims to political equality in relation to the United States. Preponderance in conventional weaponry and forces and superiority in short and medium range nuclear systems could serve, not only to safeguard Soviet positions in Eastern Europe, but to change the domestic and foreign policies of the Western European countries in directions favorable to Soviet interests.[19]

This was a bold vision. In the 1970s, the high-technology sector emerged as a decisive strategic factor, and the increasingly "desperate efforts of the Soviet leadership to keep pace with the United States in military technology" imposed serious long-term burdens on the Soviet economy.[20]

By creating a "window of vulnerability," the Soviets had overstepped the boundaries of the superpower rivalry.[21] Soviet leadership had underestimated the extent to "which others were responding to its own behavior."[22] Pointing to later events, some scholars have argued that the SS-20 deployment did not unhinge NATO and therefore that Western fears were exaggerated.[23] This is certainly true in hindsight; but who in the late 1970s and early 1980s could have foreseen Mikhail Gorbachev's rise to power and the Kremlin's subsequent loss of determination to maintain the empire? Soviet nuclear policy, in combination with a considerable buildup of conventional forces, could be interpreted by the West as an indication of offensive intentions. In politics, it is necessary to keep worst-case scenarios in mind, and NATO had little choice but to suspect a further deterioration of East-West relations. The results of the Soviet deployment decisions were, in the end, dramatic. Even European détente, which had still been operative "when superpower détente was already dead on its tracks," was now coming to a standstill.[24]

When Jimmy Carter was elected president of the United States, the U.S. government did not attach much importance to the Soviet deployment. Initially, Carter wanted to take a fresh view of foreign policy. Looking back, he remarked: "To me the demonstration of American idealism was a

19 Hannes Adomeit, *Imperial Overstretch: Germany in Soviet Policy from Stalin to Gorbachev: An Analysis Based on New Archival Evidence, Memoirs, and Interviews* (Baden-Baden, 1998), 136–7; Gaddis, *We Now Know*, 221–2; Stephen J. Zagola, "Soviet/Russian Strategic Nuclear Forces, 1945–2000," in *The Military History of the Soviet Union*, ed. Robin Higham (New York, 2002), 209.
20 Aaron L. Friedberg, "The United States and the Cold War Arms Race," in Westad, *Reviewing the Cold War*, 207–31, 207.
21 Norman Friedman, *Conflict and Strategy in the Cold War* (Annapolis, MD, 1999), 376–7.
22 Haslam, *Soviet Union*, 92.   23 Wiegrefe, *Zerwürfnis*, 165.
24 Hanhimäki, *Ironies*, 333.

practical and realistic approach to foreign affairs, and moral principles were the best foundation for the exertion of American power and influence."[25] In his inaugural address, he pledged to do everything for the eventual elimination of nuclear weapons. European issues, in contrast, at first played virtually no role in Carter's foreign policy. Europe "was notably absent as a factor in Carter's education and experience, as were international issues as a whole."[26] It quickly became apparent that different factions within the administration were in disagreement on foreign policy and that Carter did not try to balance political priorities. In several speeches on foreign policy, Carter discarded the concept of containment policy, which had been the basis for U.S. foreign policy for more than thirty years. He called instead for a new American foreign policy based on moral values and an optimistic view of the future.

The European NATO allies regarded this reappraisal, which went hand in hand with a new interest in North-South relations, as an indication of weak leadership. This opinion was accentuated by the impression that Carter was not alarmed by Soviet advances around the globe. Moscow was not only in the process of rearming its Euro-strategic nuclear weapons at high speed but was also aggressively extending its influence in the Third World. Carter's "messianic vision" therefore reawakened anxiety among the Europeans. In the end, Carter's missionary zeal and human rights crusade made matters worse for everyone, even the Soviets, "who were far happier with the cynical realpolitik of Nixon and Kissinger rather than the flamboyant and self-serving ideologizing of Carter and Brzezinski, which set their teeth on edge."[27]

Friction within the Western alliance was, of course, nothing new; the strategy of flexible response had prompted a similar debate during the Kennedy administration. The establishment of NATO's Nuclear Planning Group in 1967 helped settle some of the recurring disagreements. The concept of flexible response was ambiguous. Whereas European leaders, with deterrence in mind, preferred a strategy that envisioned early use of nuclear weapons in the event of war, Washington preferred delaying a nuclear strike as long as possible, fearing that nuclear escalation would make the United States a primary target. In other words, European and American interpretations of NATO strategy diverged. During the period of détente, the

25 Jimmy Carter, *Keeping Faith: Memoirs of a President* (London, 1982), 212.
26 Gaddis Smith, "The SS-20 Challenge and Opportunity: The Dual-Track Decision and Its Consequences, 1977–1983," in *American Historians and the Atlantic Alliance*, ed. Lawrence S. Kaplan (Kent, OH, 1991), 116–34, 118.
27 Haslam, *Soviet Union*, 79.

ambiguity of flexible response had been a minor problem. In the late 1970s, however, disagreement over the strategy reemerged with a vengeance. The concept of flexible response was thus at the root of the problem between Carter and the Europeans. It created an atmosphere of mutual misunderstandings and undermined the sense of security in both the East and the West. The dynamics of the arms race in the 1970s seemed to be more than a mere side effect of flexible response.

The SS-20s were not even on the agenda of Carter's disarmament negotiations with Moscow in 1977. The Europeans tried to alter that decision but to no avail. What ensued could be characterized as a classical misunderstanding. The Europeans posed political questions; the Americans gave military answers.[28] Over the following months, the Europeans' worst fears were confirmed. Carter obviously had

set to sea with no experience in navigation, with only the vaguest notion of his destination, with a fractious and divided crew who, on taking turns at the wheel, were constantly altering course, and all of this at a time when, with squalls blowing and a major storm on the horizon, the surest sense of direction and the firmest hand were absolutely essentials.[29]

Carter's political overtures to the Soviets have been rightly characterized as a "near fatal combination of unrealistic expectations, tactless presentation, and lack of consultation with NATO Europe."[30]

It was the British and West Germans who "most vocally" expressed their concerns in 1977.[31] Helmut Schmidt's persistent fear of *Abkoppelung* – the possibility that the United States would decouple itself from Western Europe – was roused once again. He thus pushed to have the SS-20s included on the agenda of the ongoing Strategic Arms Limitation Talks (SALT). By the summer of 1977, London had aligned itself with Bonn in arguing for a European-based weapons system to counter the SS-20s. While their arguments for a close "coupling" of the United States to Western Europe in the event of an attack on the latter have caustically been labeled "esoteric"[32] and "metaphysical,"[33] it was obvious that, for the good of the Atlantic alliance, the European leaders' doubts about the reliability of the American security guarantee had to be quelled.

28 Wiegrefe, *Zerwürfnis*, 172.   29 Ibid., 85.
30 Haslam, *Soviet Union*, 79.
31 James Thomson, "The LRTNF decision: Evolution of U.S. Theatre Nuclear Policy 1975–79," *International Affairs* 60 (1984): 601–14, 604. See also James Callaghan, *Time and Change* (London, 1987), 552; Christopher Bluth, *Britain, Germany and Western Nuclear Strategy* (Oxford, 1995), 226–7.
32 Henry Kissinger, *Diplomacy* (New York, 1994), 777.
33 "Abschreckungsmetaphysik": Risse-Kappen, *Null-Lösung*, 72.

Although Carter's meandering was certainly not very helpful, there are several indications that he was not the only one who had lost track. Schmidt, too, did not always pursue a clear course. The chancellor's mixed signals – on the future of SALT and the way the SS-20 should be incorporated in the negotiations – were ill suited to persuading Washington to change its position.[34] This had as much to do with his strategic thinking as with domestic party politics. The widely held view of Schmidt as the "father of the dual-track policy" is inadequate because the idea of rearmament was at odds with his understanding of the importance of arms control.[35] It was partly inconsistent with his military-strategic and security policy considerations as he originally outlined them with the keywords "transatlantic coupling" or "continuum of escalation" in terms of "flexible response."[36] Schmidt was eager, on the one hand, to keep the process of European détente running; on the other hand, he was also anxious to maintain the balance of power in Europe, which had, in his view, been seriously undermined by the testing of the SS-20 and American SALT policy.[37] He was not keen on hearing lectures from Washington's emissaries about how the Western Europeans had to do more for their own defense. Nor did he trust much in Carter's abilities as a strategic thinker. Indeed, Schmidt later wrote that he sometimes had the impression that the Soviets understood his fears better than Carter did.[38]

The differences between the Western Europeans and Carter on NATO strategy and détente were slowly heightened by personal animosities and then reinforced by what scholars unanimously agree was a disastrous misstep on the president's part. In 1977, Carter proposed the construction and deployment of the neutron bomb to alleviate the Europeans' fears. But then, in early 1978, he changed his mind and made the "rather impulsive decision" to shelve the proposal without consulting the allies.[39] The Europeans were dismayed, and Schmidt extremely irritated. Carter's action damaged his relations with Schmidt beyond repair.[40] Today, Schmidt's constant lamenting about the president's weakness sounds rather self-righteous. Ironically, neither the Americans nor the Europeans wanted to be the ones responsible for the decision to deploy the neutron bomb, which many

---

34 Wiegrefe, *Zerwürfnis*, 175–80.   35 Risse-Kappen, *Null-Lösung*, 32.
36 Cf. Andreas Rödder, *Die Bundesrepublik Deutschland 1969–1990, München 2004, 59*; Garthoff, *Détente and Confrontation*, 942.
37 Helga Haftendorn, "Das doppelte Missverständnis. Zur Vorgeschichte des NATO-Doppelbeschlusse von 1979," *Vierteljahrshefte für Zeitgeschichte* 33 (1985): 244–87.
38 Helmut Schmidt, *Menschen und Mächte* (Berlin, 1987), 228.
39 Garthoff, *Détente and Confrontation*, 939.
40 Wiegrefe, *Zerwürfnis*, 201–6; Thomas Paes, *Die Carter-Administration und die Regierung Schmidt: Konsens und Dissens über die Sowjetunion-Politik 1977–1981* (Rheinfelden, 1991).

considered a particularly pernicious weapon.[41] Carter's National Security Adviser Zbigniew Brzezinski, obviously not sure who was to blame, prophesized that Carter's decision would "contribute to a sickness and then weakening of the alliance."[42] At one point, he turned a signed photo of Schmidt hanging in his office to face the wall as a sign of his annoyance with the chancellor.[43]

This dramatic rupture overlapped with other strategic discussions taking place at the time. In a much-quoted speech delivered at the London Institute for Strategic Studies, in October 1977, Schmidt pointed out that the imbalance of strategic nuclear weapons in Europe was alarming.[44] The imbalance, the chancellor warned, might lead Moscow to disrupt the very foundations of NATO and, thereby, the entire postwar order. Schmidt's London remarks have been labeled as bearing "the stylistic hallmarks of a last minute insert,"[45] but the repercussions were heard in Washington.

During the course of the summer of 1978, Carter decided that he could no longer ignore the fact that the Soviets were not cooperating in the disarmament talks, and another erratic and sudden shift in American foreign policy took place. In effect, Carter hijacked the position Schmidt had taken in his London speech. Although he thought that existing U.S. strategic weapons still had sufficient deterrent capacity and did not see the SS-20 missile as a qualitatively new armament, he did not want a repeat of the neutron bomb fiasco. Complying with the Europeans' urgent appeal to add the Soviet missiles to the disarmament agenda also served to counter the charge, leveled at home as well as in Europe, that Carter lacked leadership. Although the president continued to regard the additional threat posed by the SS-20s as a minor issue, he tried to adhere to his allies' wishes to reestablish the balance of power with respect to strategic weapons. "The SS-20s were as much an opportunity for the United States as a challenge. Substance was less important than the fact of doing something, anything at all, to demonstrate leadership."[46] Henry Kissinger put the matter even more bluntly in retrospect: "In its essence, the argument in favor of the intermediate range weapons was political, not strategic."[47] The reassessment of alliance necessities was in accordance with the demands of the strategic experts

41 Wiegrefe, *Zerwürfnis*, 181–206.
42 The quote can be found in Smith, *SS-20 Challenge*, 123.
43 Strobe Talbott, *Endgame: The Inside Story of SALT II* (New York, 1980), 150.
44 Helmut Schmidt, "Politische und wirtschaftliche Aspekte der westlichen Sicherheit. Vortrag des Bundeskanzlers in London," *Bulletin des Presse- und Informationsamtes der Bundesregierung*, no. 112 (November 8, 1977): 1013–20.
45 Smith, *SS-20 Challenge*, 120.   46 Smith, *SS-20 Challenge*, 124.
47 Kissinger, *Diplomacy*, 776.

on both sides of the Atlantic and of a "High Level Group" that had been appointed and had first met in November and again in December 1977.[48] In the end, Carter's volte-face of 1978 developed a momentum that was all but irreversible.

Ironically, Schmidt, who had been the one to propose the inclusion of the SS-20s on the arms talks' agenda, found himself in an unpleasant frontline position once again. He feared a setback to European détente and his own *Ostpolitik*, and he had to pay attention to the dissenters in his own party. His support for Carter's proposals was, therefore, hesitant and even dilatory. It has been suggested that Schmidt tried "to let the dual-track decision be imposed on him by the American government."[49]

In a meeting on the French Caribbean island of Guadeloupe in January 1979, Carter proposed reestablishing the balance of power by deploying American intermediate-range nuclear missiles. The nuclear partners, France and Great Britain, modified Carter's proposal and suggested engaging in disarmament negotiations with the Soviets.[50] It was agreed that deployment would begin in the event that negotiations failed. Schmidt, who needed some "persuasion," finally agreed to this linkage. Brzezinski was disappointed: "Throughout he was the one who was most concerned about the Soviet nuclear threat in Europe and the least inclined to agree to any firm response."[51] Egon Bahr, who disagreed with Schmidt's assessment of the situation, later labeled Guadeloupe a "Pyrrhic victory" for Schmidt and Europe.[52]

Schmidt's position was awkward indeed. Having brought the Americans around to his position, he now had to contend with his fellow Social Democrats[53] – much to the annoyance of his American counterparts, who feared he would not "hold firm."[54] Certainly he did not, in principle, forsake his loyalty to NATO. But he had to take into account the negative mood in his own party: it was only the tip of the iceberg when Bahr

48 On the "High Level Group," see Paul Buteux, *Strategy, Doctrine and the Politics of Alliance: Theatre Nuclear Force Modernization in NATO* (Boulder, CO, 1983).
49 Wiegrefe, *Zerwürfnis*, 261.
50 See Pierre Melandri, "La France et l'alliance atlantique sous Georges Pompidou et Valéry Giscard d'Estaing," in *La France et l'OTAN*, eds. Maurice Vaïsse, Pierre Mélandri, and Frédéric Bozo (Paris, 1997), 519–58.
51 Zbigniew Brzezinski, *Power and Principle: Memoirs of the National Security Adviser 1977–1981* (New York, 1983), 295. See also Carter's own recollection of Schmidt being "very contentious": Carter, *Keeping Faith*, 235.
52 Egon Bahr, *Zu meiner Zeit* (Munich, 1996), 505.
53 Anton Notz, *Die SPD und der NATO-Doppelbeschluss. Abkehr von einer Sicherheitspolitik der Vernunft* (Baden-Baden, 1990); Thomas Enders, *Die SPD und die äussere Sicherheit. Zum Wandel der sicherheitspolitischen Konzeptionen der Partei in der Zeit der Regierungsverantwortung 1966–1982* (Melle, 1987).
54 Brzezinski, *Power and Principle*, 308.

described the neutron bomb as a symbol of "the perversion of thinking." In 1977 and 1978, the chancellor resorted to a maneuver that by no means facilitated dialogue with Washington and that reawakened the perennial fear of German neutralism. The governing Social Democrats wished to continue their policy of détente and, to maintain their illusion of a "security partnership" with the East, heavily strained their policy concepts.[55] Carter's inconsistencies and Schmidt's wavering resulted in growing misunderstanding between Bonn and Washington. Relations between the United States and the Soviet Union deteriorated steadily after Guadeloupe. The signing of the SALT II Treaty in Vienna on June 18, 1979, did not end the arms race, and the Soviet invasion of Afghanistan later that year brought about the final turn in Carter's astonishing volte-face. As one scholar has noted, "The transition from Carter's emphasis on quiet confidence and moral values in the first year of his administration to the tough military posturing of the final years was far greater than the transition . . . between the Carter and Reagan administrations."[56]

The Western allies thus drew up plans to modernize their nuclear forces in the months following the signing of the SALT II Treaty. The number of missiles and cruise missiles was decided on "in a rather arbitrary and obscure series of guesses and compromises." The overall aim was to bolster the credibility of American "extended deterrence." "The Pershing II was billed as the ultimate theater weapon, greatly bolstering regional deterrence but not posing a strategic threat to the USSR," *Time* correspondent Strobe Talbot observed several years later. "It also had the cosmetic advantage as being distinguished in designation from the Pershing I only by a Roman numeral. That made it easier to advertise as an upgrade of an existing system."[57]

The decision to deploy Pershing IIs was officially adopted by Carter in early July 1979. Until the records from this period are opened to historians, it will be hard to determine whether defense contractors had any influence on the decision.[58] It has also been argued that this move was seen by Moscow as a "deliberate attempt to upset the balance."[59] Tentative efforts to sound out Moscow about a compromise led nowhere. In October 1979, Brezhnev offered to make a modest reduction in the number of

55 Frank Fischer, *"Im deutschen Interesse." Die Ostpolitik der SPD von 1969 bis 1989* (Husum, 2001), 377.
56 Smith, *SS-20 Challenge*, 126.
57 Strobe Talbott, *Deadly Gambits: The Reagan Administration and the Stalemate in Nuclear Arms Control* (New York 1984), 35.
58 On this subject, see Smith, *SS-20 Challenge*, 121.
59 Ibid., 124.

medium-range nuclear delivery systems, but this was "too little and too late."[60] The dual-track decision was approved by all NATO allies (with the exception of France) on December 12, 1979. While signaling their willingness to negotiate if Moscow withdrew the SS-20s, the NATO partners committed themselves to modernizing the West's intermediate-range missile systems within the next four years. Paragraph 7 of the communiqué issued by the foreign and defense ministers stated that "the deployment in Europe of U.S. systems comprising 108 Pershing II launchers... would replace older U.S. Pershing I-A, and 464 Cruise Missiles." A Pershing II, launched from West Germany could reach Moscow in less than eight minutes. A low-flying cruise missile would have been considerably slower but would have been able to carry a much larger warhead.

Two weeks after the dual-track decision, the Soviets invaded Afghanistan. At that point, even a Soviet offer to withdraw the SS-20s from Eastern Europe probably would not have been sufficient to change the course of events. It is open to doubt whether NATO "would have halted its progress towards a decision on deployment because the decision was as much a political as a military matter, as much a political gesture as an answer to military exigencies."[61] This was the main reason why, in 1979, the Western alliance was spared a fiasco like that of 1977. Schmidt and Carter were cooperating better than ever before by the autumn of 1979, and a failure of the dual-track decision would have had disastrous consequences for the alliance that neither government could probably have survived.[62]

About 125 SS-20s were in place when NATO decided on the dual-track strategy. In the following months, Schmidt grew more anxious. He had to take note of the fact that his government had acted against the central demand of a growing protest movement to abandon the deployment of the Pershing IIs and cruise missiles. Schmidt insisted vehemently on the agreed procedures and, at the same time, argued that West Germany should not be singled out for a special role as the only country where the new weapons were to be deployed. In June 1980, he floated the idea of a moratorium on theater nuclear weapons deployment. This rather ambiguous suggestion met with open opposition in Washington. Carter responded with a "toughly worded message" urging the chancellor to make no commitments without prior consultation. Brzezinski's journal entry for June 18, 1980, noted the tension between Bonn and Washington: "Schmidt is furious over the President's message no doubt, and the President will have a confrontation

---

60 Garthoff, *Détente and Confrontation*, 951. 61 Haslam, *Soviet Union*, 104.
62 Cf. Wiegrefe, *Zerwürfnis*, 274–5.

of sorts with him. . . . Even though every meeting produces declarations of friendship, Schmidt then follows up with back-sniping."[63] A meeting in Venice at the end of June ended with a "nasty confrontation," and relations between the president and the chancellor never recovered. Schmidt's visit on November 17, 1980, was "chilly and nonsubstantive."[64]

The United States and the Soviet Union opened disarmament negotiations in Geneva in late November 1981. During the following two years, as the talks proceeded inconclusively, the Soviets continued the SS-20 buildup. Fierce demonstrations against the dual-track decision took place throughout Western Europe, especially in West Germany, but the NATO allies did not change course. On October 1, 1982, the Schmidt government was brought down by a vote of no confidence, and Helmut Kohl became chancellor. Committed to continuity in security policy, he was determined to put an end to any doubts about West Germany's political orientation. Accordingly, on November 22, 1983, the Bundestag approved the deployment of new U.S. intermediate-range nuclear missiles on West German territory. One day later, the Soviet Union walked away from the Geneva disarmament talks.

The new Western weapons were deployed as planned in the wake of the events. A vigorous debate on the deployment took place across Western Europe. Huge demonstrations against the Pershings and cruise missiles took place in London, Paris, Brussels, and the Hague. The debate was especially fierce in West Germany, where the peace movement – part of the so-called new social movements that had emerged during the late 1960s – served as a vehicle of popular displeasure with the government's decisions. The fight against NATO's strategy was a catalyst in transforming the West German peace movement. Religiously motivated, mainly Protestant pacifists banded together with independent left-wing activists and members of the recently formed Green Party. They were eventually joined by Communist groups, which as will be shown below, were heavily supported and influenced by Moscow and East Berlin. The much weaker American peace movement did not really get into gear until 1983, much too late to have any influence.[65]

By that time, Carter had been voted out of office and succeeded by Ronald Reagan. While Carter had been seen by many in Western Europe as a somewhat sympathetic figure, the new president was widely regarded as the quintessential Cold Warrior. Even with the new administration in Washington, Schmidt's government continued to fight for exact adherence

63 Brzezinski, *Power and Principle*, 309.   64 Ibid., 311.
65 Smith, *SS-20 Challenge*, 131–2.

to terms of the dual-track decision, namely that deployment would proceed only if negotiations failed. Bonn soon found it more difficult to enter into dialogue with the opponents of arms control in Washington than with the peace movement at home. Schmidt's dilemma illustrates paradigmatically how alliance politics and Cold War strategy restrained the smaller allies, especially when Washington knew what it wanted. Reagan, who was not inclined to compromise, insisted on maximum demands in the negotiations with Moscow, and his administration expected the negotiations to end in failure.[66] It now became clear that the impression that political leadership within the Western alliance had shifted to Western Europe during the Carter presidency had been mistaken or was no longer the case.[67] The European NATO members ceased to have an important influence on the Soviet-American negotiations. Even when it looks as if the Geneva talks might bear fruit, the Europeans were simply ignored, Schmidt in particular.[68]

Reagan took it in stride when the Soviets walked out of the Geneva talks on intermediate-range missiles and, shortly thereafter, ended the START negotiations on long-range missiles. "They'd left the ballpark," he later wrote in his memoirs, "but I didn't think the game was over."[69] The new arms race that followed contributed to the weakening of the Soviet Union and finally to the collapse of the Soviet empire. At the time, many Western Europeans thought Reagan had no real understanding of détente or realpolitik. That rather one-sided view is giving way to a more nuanced assessment as Reagan has gained recognition for his strategic thinking.[70] Summarizing recent research, the *Economist* has noted, "There is a growing consensus the he was one of the most consequential presidents of the 20th century: in the same league as Franklin Roosevelt (his life-long hero) and Harry Truman, the architect of the cold war order that Mr. Reagan did so much to bring to an end."[71]

Does a look at East Germany shed any light on these crucial developments? It is much easier today to analyze East Berlin's position it was during the years Kremlinologists could offer only tentative speculation about strategic thinking in the East German capital. The country's Communist leaders agitated against the West's deployment of new nuclear weapons. At the same

---

66 Talbott, *Deadly Gambits*, 43–206.   67 Hacke, *Zur Weltmacht verdammt*, 271.
68 Rödder, *Bundesrepublik*, 63; Wolfram F. Hanrieder, *Deutschland, Europa, Amerika. Die Außenpolitik der Bundesrepublik Deutschland 1949–1989*, 2d ed. (Paderborn, 1995), 93; Herbert Dittgen, *Deutsch-amerikanische Sicherheitsbeziehungen in der Ära Helmut Schmidt. Vorgeschichte und Folgen des NATO-Doppelbeschlusses* (Munich, 1991), 258.
69 Ronald Reagan, *An American Life: The Autobiography* (New York, 1990), 586.
70 Cf. Paul Lettow, *Ronald Reagan and His Quest to Abolish Nuclear Weapons* (New York, 2005).
71 *Economist*, June 12, 2004, 25.

time, their actions were guided by the doctrine that "peace and progress in the world" could not "be achieved without the military predominance of the East."[72] Obviously, the East German leadership, which was interested in maintaining a certain level of confrontation between the blocs,[73] believed it could improve its own position during the resurgence of the Cold War, even if it paid lip service to the continuation of détente. Of course, the party leader Erich Honecker profited economically from the easing of the tensions in Europe.[74] East Berlin even benefited from NATO's deployment decisions. The Warsaw Pact's response to the dual-track decision helped narrow the gap between East Germany and the Soviet Union on the German question. East Berlin declared it was committed to peace in Europe at the same time that it publicly affirmed that its interests were identical to Moscow's and continued the militarization of East German society. Even in internal party debates, Honecker advocated "the Soviet Union's positions on security policy."[75] After talks with Soviet Foreign Minister Andrei Gromyko in December 1979, he was ready to accept Soviet deployment policy without further discussion. The arrival of Ronald Reagan in the White House in January 1981 caused concern in East Berlin that a further deterioration in East-West relations might jeopardize vital Western economic help. As we now know, the East German leadership gave careful consideration to the West's perceptions of security. During a consultation with the Soviet ambassador on February 9, 1982, Foreign Minister Oskar Fischer emphasized that East Germany would "not take up a different position" in any international disarmament negotiations than that which had already been agreed upon. The essential point, in his view, was to maintain the pressure on West Germany.[76]

The East German government subsequently tried to undermine the dual-track decision with appeals for peace aimed at strengthening the new social movements in West Germany. East Germany tried to gain influence mainly through the newly formed Green Party, which had grown out of the environmental and the peace movements, and in the wake of the public debate on the dual-track decision, was on the upswing. The documents from the East German archives show that several initiatives against NATO's

---

72 Fred Oldenburg and Gerhard Wettig, *Der Sonderstatus der DDR in den europäischen Ost-West-Beziehungen* (Cologne, 1979), 16.
73 Joachim Scholtyseck, *Die Aussenpolitik der DDR* (Munich, 2003), 44.
74 Herman Wentker, *Außenpolitik in engen Grenzen. Die DDR im internationalen System 1949–1989* (Munich, 2007). See also Hans-Hermann Hertle and Konrad Jarausch, eds., *Risse im Bruderbund. Die Gespräche Honecker – Breshnew 1974 bis 1982* (Berlin, 2006).
75 Heinrich Potthoff, *Im Schatten der Mauer. Deutschlandpolitik 1961 bis 1990* (Berlin, 1999), 176.
76 Quoted in Benno-Eide Siebs, *Die Aussenpolitik der DDR 1976–1989: Strategien und Grenzen* (Paderborn, 1999), 239.

rearmament plans – including the Krefeld Appeal and the mass demonstrations – were influenced by activists on the payroll of East Germany. Thus, one can speak of a "seduced peace movement."[77] At first, the East German tactics were successful in intensifying conflicts among the NATO members. The intense rearmament debates and waves of demonstrations had political consequences. In West Germany, they led to endless discussions about the legitimacy of nuclear deterrence. That, in turn, had repercussions in the United States. In the early 1980s, Washington anxiously watched for political shifts that might affect the Atlantic alliance. With the electoral victories of Margaret Thatcher and Helmut Kohl, the Labour Party in Great Britain and the SPD in Germany moved "far to the left and adopted platforms that [were] not just anti-deployment but very close to becoming anti-NATO."[78]

The East German leadership could not, however, permanently control the Western peace movements. Its efforts were unsuccessful in the end because the Greens were too heterogeneous to follow the lead of the ruling Socialist Unity Party (Sozialistische Einheitspartei Deutschlands). East Berlin replied to any references to human rights in the Eastern bloc and to diverging views on disarmament with a *fin de non reçevoir*.[79] Dissenting views were labeled false pacifist ideas that diverted attention from the real issues, namely the imperialism and revisionism of the capitalist powers. Some Western human rights activists tried to foster a common peace movement bridging the East and the West and approached East European dissidents.[80] Some groups within the Dutch peace movement, which was also receiving financial support from East Berlin, demonstrated against the Soviet deployment of nuclear weapons and the persecution of peace activists in East Germany.[81] Like Goethe's sorcerer's apprentice, who cried out in despair, "Those spirits I have summoned, I cannot get rid of them," the East German leadership could not control the forces it had unleashed.[82]

Although the leaders in East Berlin considered the West German Social Democrats the most suitable partner for cooperation on security, the change of government in Bonn in October 1982 did not have – contrary to expectations – dramatic consequences for relations between the two German

77 Udo Baron, "Die verführte Friedensbewegung. Zur heute nachweisbaren Einflussnahme von SED und MfS," *Die politische Meinung* 407 (October 2003): 55–61.
78 Strobe Talbott, *The Russians and Reagan* (New York, 1984), 43–4.
79 Udo Baron, *Kalter Krieg und heisser Frieden* (Münster, 2003).
80 Michael Ploetz and Hans-Peter Müller, *Ferngelenkte Friedensbewegung? DDR und UdSSR im Kampf gegen den NATO-Doppelbeschluss* (Münster, 2004), 319–43
81 Beatrice de Graaf, "Détente from Below: The Stasi and the Dutch Peace Movement," *Journal of Intelligence History* 3 (2003): 9–20.
82 "Die ich rief, die Geister/Werd ich nun nicht los," Erich Trunz, ed., *Goethes Werke, Hamburger Ausgabe in 14 Bänden* (Hamburg, 1969), 1:279.

governments. The Christian Democratic–Liberal coalition did not openly reject Honecker's proposed "coalition of reason." Nevertheless, in January 1983, Honecker complained that the new Chancellor Helmut Kohl was clearly an advocate of "the treacherous zero-option."[83] With the heated West European debate on NATO's deployment plans in mind, Honecker agreed in November 1983 to "cut the losses if possible" and acknowledged that the deployment of Soviet missiles in the GDR would "not draw cheers."[84] But these and other similar remarks should not be taken at face value. In early 1983, East Berlin could propose the creation of a nuclear weapons–free zone in Central Europe because it knew there was no risk that the West might take it up.

In East Berlin's view, the year 1983 was to be "decisive in the fight against the NATO missile resolution."[85] Given the resistance of large parts of the Western public, the East German communists kept hoping that the deployment of the Pershing and cruise missiles could still be prevented. If public protest was not successful, however, another course of action would follow. In line with Moscow and Prague, the East German leadership agreed that, "in case of the deployment of new American nuclear intermediate-range missiles in Europe, counteractive measures on the part of the socialist states will be unavoidable."[86] After the breakdown of the Geneva arms control and the Bundestag's approval of NATO's deployment plans, it was left to the Soviet Secretary General Yuri Andropov to announce the deployment of additional Soviet missiles in East Germany and Czechoslovakia.

In October 1985, Honecker claimed that the deployment of new American nuclear missiles in Western Europe would mean "not more, but less security."[87] Yet again, his statement has to be understood as an instrument to foster insecurity within the Western alliance. Although Honecker declared in the autumn of 1986 that an East–West agreement to remove this "Teufelszeug" – this "infernal stuff" – from East German soil was possible,[88] his remarks did not seem credible. It rather looked like another propaganda attempt to represent the regime in East Berlin as an honest broker eager to promote "peaceful coexistence." What the SED might have meant by "peaceful coexistence" is still open to interpretation. As we now know, the

---

83 "Rede Honeckers vom 4. Januar 1983 auf der Ordentlichen Tagung des Politisch Beratenden Ausschusses der Teilnehmerstaaten des Warschauer Vertrages am 4. und 5. Januar 1983 in Prag," Stiftung Archiv der Parteien und Massenorganisationen der DDR im Bundesarchiv, Berlin (hereafter SAPMO) DC/20/I/3/1908.
84 Quoted in Siebs, *Aussenpolitik*, 247.
85 "Bericht über die Ordentliche Tagung des Politisch Beratenden Ausschusses der Teilnehmerstaaten des Warschauer Vertrages am 4. und 5. Januar 1983 in Prag,"SAPMO DC/20/I/3/1908.
86 Ibid.
87 "Rede Honeckers am 22./23. Oktober 1985," SAPMO DC 20/I/3/2232.
88 *Neues Deutschland*, Nov. 22–23, 1986.

East German party leadership had "explicitly and aggressively" made the term a "a dialectic *double entendre*" that allowed them to portray their foreign policy as being "in accord with their principles" regardless of whether they pursued "relentless confrontation" or "compromise."[89]

Did the East German leaders seriously worry about collective security? Or, on account of East Germany's dependence on economic cooperation with the Federal Republic, did they merely employ the phraseology of détente?[90] Were Honecker's repeated peace overtures a serious effort to ensure a lasting peace or a propaganda ritual? It is still open to debate whether the East German regime was motivated primarily by "concerns for its own existence" or by ideology and realpolitik.[91] Of course, even dictatorships have a need for security – all the more so if they secretly fear that their political system might not be as solid and effective as they proclaim. Public discussion of the Soviet missile deployment was not possible within such a system. But nor is there any evidence that a debate on this issue took place behind closed doors. Except for some disputable statements made by former East German politicians in the 1990s, there is no indication that the regime's leaders had been troubled by a genuine feeling of threat.

While East Berlin supported the Western peace movement, it suppressed all East German peace initiatives that did not comply with its strict guidelines. Moreover, there is no evidence to support the view that Honecker was sympathetic to East Germany's unsanctioned peace movement on the missile deployments.[92] The sources suggest regime's peace rhetoric aimed at debilitating Western defense capabilities.[93] In the same vein, East German intelligence operations targeted the Atlantic alliance. Their emissaries

were certainly no "messengers of peace", as they were heralded by the . . . official propaganda and as they still often think of themselves. They may be more properly described as reckless gamblers – not only because of their unsavory personal double-lives but, more importantly, also because of the unpredictable results that the information they supplied could have had in the hands of both paranoid and reasonable Soviet leaders.[94]

89 Johannes Kuppe, "Die DDR und die nichtsozialistische Welt. Ein Essay zur Aussenpolitik der SED," in *Rückblicke auf die DDR*, ed. Gisela Helwig (Cologne, 995), 175–82, 181.

90 Karl-Rudolf Korte, *Deutschlandpolitik in Helmut Kohls Kanzlerschaft* (Stuttgart, 1998), 187.

91 Siebs, *Aussenpolitik*, 172.

92 Bernhard von Plate, "Die Aussenpolitik und internationale Einordnung der DDR," in *Deutschland-Handbuch. Eine doppelte Bilanz 1949–1989*, eds. Werner Weidenfeld and Hartmut Zimmermann (Düsseldorf, 1989), 589–604, 603.

93 Michael Ploetz, *Wie die Sowjetunion den Kalten Krieg verlor. Von der Nachrüstung zum Mauerfall* (Berlin, 2000), 146–55.

94 Bernd Schaefer, "The Warsaw Pact's Intelligence on NATO: East German Military Espionage against the West," Parallel History Project on Cooperative Security (PHP), http://www.php .isn.ethz.ch/collections/coll_stasi/intro_schaefer.cfm?navinfo=15296PHP (December 2008).

For the East German leadership, peace initiatives were little more than a means to portray West Germany as an aggressive power. The temporary success of that tactic came, however, at the cost of undermining the last hope of continuing détente. The so-called coalition of reason was virtually nonexistent.[95] One should not forget, however, that East Berlin was being closely watched by the Soviet Union. When Richard Burke, for example, tried to sound out the East German politicians Herbert Häber, Max Schmidt, Hermann Axen, and Claus Montag on their government's attitude toward the question of missile deployment in talks at East Germany's Institut für Internationale Beziehungen (Institute for International Relations), the Soviet leadership kept a close eye on the discussions to prevent, ab initio, any possible divergence on the part of their satellite state.[96]

Today, the dual-track decision seems to have faded into history and is mainly remembered by historians and those who participated in demonstrations against the deployment of nuclear weapons. Nevertheless, some questions are still worth discussing. Was the dual-track decision a landmark for the Atlantic alliance? I offer four final observations toward answering that question.

First, the decision itself had more political than strategic value. What would have happened if the NATO had not gone ahead with the missile deployment? The military consequences would probably not have been serious, but the change, of course, would almost certainly have created additional strain within the Western alliance. The question is purely hypothetical, however, as the Reagan administration supported the deployment plans. Although the Western European NATO allies acted like sovereign states, they still had to accept the restrictions imposed by Cold War strategy. Their sovereignty was not limited to the same degree as the Soviet Union's satellite states, but their influence on decisions within the Atlantic alliance was curtailed to an extent. This widely accepted view has, however, has been challenged. Thomas Risse-Kappen and, more vehemently, Klaus Wiegrefe have each argued, for instance, that European influence on American strategic decisions in the late 1970s was greater than most scholars have assumed.[97] Only when the archival records of this period are opened to research can this argument be proved – or disproved.

Second, did the disruption of 1968 challenge the legitimacy and prestige of world leaders in the long run? It has been argued that the great

---

95 Heinrich Potthoff, *"Die 'Koalition der Vernunft." Deutschlandpolitik in den 80er Jahren* (Munich, 1995).
96 Cf. the statement of Claus Montag in *DDR-Aussenpolitik im Rückspiegel. Diplomaten im Gespräch,* eds. Siegfried Bock, Ingrid Muth, and Hermann Schwiesau (Münster, 2004), 203–4.
97 Wiegrefe, *Zerwürfnis,* 18; Thomas Risse-Kappen, Cooperation among Democracies: The European Influence on U.S. Foreign Policy (Princeton, NJ, 1995).

powers – at least in the democratic societies of the West – had to take into account a growing protest movement: "Leaders now had to formulate policy against their constituents."[98] But it remains an open question as to how far so-called grassroots movements were capable of influencing alliance decisions. The events in the late 1970s and, even more so, early 1980s clearly show that once the decision had been made to proceed on the dual-track road, there was little chance that the peace movement's "War by Other Means"[99] would succeed.[100] Only the Soviets would have been able to alter the dual-track decision – but they refused to do so. They were confident that the decision was doomed to fail in the same way the neutron bomb had. Moscow was imaginative only in terms of propaganda measures, not in questions of military-strategic matters. The Soviets overestimated the impetus of the peace movement and of their own propaganda efforts.

The peace movement, overlooking the basic differences between dictatorships and democracies, turned its back on the Western consensus on the necessity of deterrence.[101] The high hopes of the protesters were crushed by the outcome of the March 1983 Bundestag elections in West Germany. This popular vote against the protesters and the ensuing implementation of the NATO dual-track decision proved disillusioning to the peace movement. Its clear defeat had remarkable consequences. From that point on, the new social movements turned away from foreign policy and security issues. Only time will tell whether any of the remnants of the different groupings within the peace movement will show renewed interest in the unsolved issues of global security.

Third, do we leave morality out of the discussion? Historians tend to avoid questions of good and evil whenever they can. But we should not forget that one actor in this instance was a dictatorship that had persistently oppressed its citizens and had only fifteen years before attacked a satellite state that had threatened to leave its orbit. The other actors, by contrast, were democratic states and societies that, in a sometimes-painful process, had come to terms with their deployment decision.[102]

---

98 Jeremi Suri, *Power and Protest: Global Revolution and the Rise of Detente* (Cambridge, MA, 2003), 212.
99 Jeffrey Herf, *War by Other Means. Soviet Power, West German Resistance and the Battle of the Euromissiles* (New York, 1991), 231.
100 Cf. Werner Link, *Frankfurter Allgemeine Zeitung*, July 20, 1991.
101 Peter Graf Kielmansegg, *Nach der Katastrophe: Eine Geschichte des geteilten Deutschland* (Berlin, 2000), 234–6. A dissenting view is offered by Lawrence S. Wittner, *Toward Nuclear Abolition: A History of the World Nuclear Disarmament Movement, 1971–Present* (Stanford, CA, 2003).
102 John Lewis Gaddis has pointed out the importance of the moral factor in Cold War history in his essay "On Moral Equivalency and Cold War History," *Ethics & International Affairs* 10 (1996): 131–48; for a different view, see Leo P. Ribuffo, "Moral Judgements and the Cold War: Reflections on Reinhold Niebuhr, William Appleman Williams, and John Lewis Gaddis," in *Cold War Triumphalism: The Misuse of History after the Fall of Communism*, ed. Ellen Schrecker (New York, 2004), 27–70.

Finally, from a broader perspective, the NATO dual-track decision is a fine example of the Atlantic community overcoming its strained relations and staying on its course. Certainly, the sometimes awkward maneuvering by Carter and his aides was detrimental to the alliance, and Schmidt's oscillations tested the limits of alliance loyalty. But in the end, the dual-track decision improved strategic deterrence, and the Western alliance proved stronger than the effects of miscalculations, misunderstandings, and personal ill will. Klaus Wiegrefe's conclusion, therefore, is well founded. From the point of view of alliance politics, the dual-track decision was "a great success."[103]

103 Wiegrefe, *Zerwürfnis*, 277. Cf. Hacke, *Zur Weltmacht verdammt*, 277: "successful alliance diplomacy."

PART FIVE

Epilogue

The Superpower and the Union in the Making

U.S.-European Relations, 1969–1980

MATTHIAS SCHULZ AND THOMAS A. SCHWARTZ

What can be learned from the case studies gathered in this volume? How does the new research presented here affect our understanding of post-war American diplomacy and Western European responses to American predominance (and relative decline) within the Atlantic alliance? Does the history of U.S.-European relations during the 1970s offer any lessons that might be of use to policy makers, advisers, or scholars at a time of uncertainty about the future of the Atlantic alliance?

The history of the 1970s reinforces a lesson often overlooked: there was never a golden age in the Atlantic alliance, a time when the United States and Europe cooperated in an atmosphere of complete mutual trust and harmony. From the very beginning, the alliance was marked by disagreements about strategies and the division of responsibilities. Issues such as German rearmament, nuclear weapons, and even chicken tariffs have prompted sharp exchanges across the Atlantic. If the title of this volume, *The Strained Alliance*, puts the emphasis on disputes and dilemmas – and some of the conflicts were clearly more intense and bitter than those of the 1950s and 1960s – a broader analysis of the relations between the United States and the major European countries of Britain, Germany, and France during the Cold War shows how these relations moved in cycles of cooperation and conflict.[1] The cycles were driven by a variety of factors, including, but not limited to, impending elections, domestic political alignments, events abroad, leadership personalities, bureaucratic politics, and economic developments. This cyclical paradigm did not follow a path that was mechanical, straightforward, or predictable. But as the analysis shows the cycles evolved within a larger

---

1 The official *NATO Review*, on the occasion of the alliance's twenty-fifth anniversary in 1974, gave reluctant equality to the downs in an article titled "Twenty Five Years of Ups and Downs." Lawrence Kaplan, *NATO and the United States: The Enduring Alliance* (Boston, 1988), 137.

international structure of constraints, which limited both how antagonistic as well as how harmonious they could reasonably become. At some point, certain self-correcting mechanisms would shift the pendulum of the U.S.-European relationship in the other direction, though not always as far, or with as lasting effects, as the initial push. The three most important constraints were the continuing relevance of the Cold War and the threat posed by the Soviet Union, the interdependence of the American and European economies, and the institutional framework through which the allies forced themselves to find agreement. The two most significant limits on the harmonious side of the relationship were, first, the process of European integration, with its creation of a separate, though relatively open, European market and a separate European identity, and second, the global commitments and resulting responsibilities of the United States (e.g., in the Middle East, Asia, and Latin America), which frequently separated American policy from the Europeans. These structural constraints and limits were fully in evidence during the long 1970s, swinging the alliance on the pendulum of relative crisis and relative harmony, within an international structure that seemed to be shifting as well, though not nearly as much as many contemporary observers believed – especially in light of the events of 1989, when the end of the Cold War marked a real transformation in the structure of international relations.

THE COLD WAR: THE SHORT AND SWEET LIFE OF DÉTENTE

Richard Nixon took office in January 1969 believing, as he had told the elite Bohemian Club in July 1967 that the Western alliance was "in deep trouble."[2] Later, at the Republican Party national convention in August 1968, he vowed to rebuild "the strength of our NATO alliance, which has been allowed to crumble and go to pieces during this Administration."[3] He blasted President Lyndon Johnson for not mentioning Europe in his 1968 State of the Union message and proclaimed, "It's time we begin paying Europe more attention. And if our ideals of Atlantic interdependence are to mean anything in practice, it's time we begin lecturing our European partners less and listening to them more."[4] Henry Kissinger's 1965 book *The Troubled Partnership* also portrayed an alliance in crisis: "for the first time since the war," Kissinger observed, "there exists an open challenge not

2 *Foreign Relations of the United States* (hereafter FRUS) 1969–1976, 1:3.
3 *FRUS*, 1969–1976, 1:50.
4 Radio address, Oct. 13, 1968 quoted in Lawrence Kaplan, *The Long Entanglement: NATO's First Fifty Years* (Westport, CT, 1999), 151.

just to the technical implementation of American plans but to the validity of American conceptions."[5] Such pessimism was greatly exaggerated. The Johnson administration's record on European matters was far more positive and constructive than Nixon and Kissinger contended. Under Johnson, the alliance had managed such contentious issues as the French withdrawal from the NATO command, the Kennedy Round trade agreement, and the costs of stationing U.S. troops in West Germany.[6] But with the extraordinary internal turmoil in all Western societies in 1968, the Vietnam stalemate, and the Soviet invasion of Czechoslovakia, Nixon's argument found a sympathetic audience. Nixon's decision to schedule a trip to Europe only a month after his inauguration was a sign of the importance he attached to the issue. By putting a visit with President Charles de Gaulle in Paris high on his itinerary, Nixon underscored his distance from the Johnson administration's hostility toward the French leader. In many ways, this visit can serve as a symbol for the Nixon approach to Europe.

By every account, the president's meeting with De Gaulle was a success. Nixon's admiration for de Gaulle's style of leadership was genuine. In their meetings, he assumed a very deferential tone and gave assurance that he, in contrast to his predecessor, would seek the general's advice. Nixon outlined in detail his own determination to follow de Gaulle's example and pursue détente with the Soviet Union, vowing to be "hard and pragmatic" in his dealings with the Soviets. What Nixon meant was that he wanted to connect improved relations with Moscow – particularly in the area of arms control – to Soviet cooperation on other issues, above all Vietnam. In effect, Nixon set out his controversial linkage strategy for dealing with the Soviet Union. This approach would be a clear departure from the Johnson administration's attempts to pursue talks on strategic arms despite Soviet-American disagreements on Vietnam and other issues. De Gaulle, enjoying Nixon's ostentatious flattery, downplayed his outspoken opposition to the Vietnam War and seemed to encourage Nixon's caution, telling him that he "should not rush to Moscow and lay out the red carpet before Brezhnev" and that he was "quite right in seeking to have adequate preparations made in advance" of a summit meeting.[7] De Gaulle also endorsed Nixon's idea of trying to develop parallel relationships with China and the Soviet Union, as, he maintained, Paris had already done.

5 Henry A. Kissinger, *The Troubled Partnership: A Re-appraisal of the Atlantic Alliance* (New York, 1965), 4.
6 Thomas A. Schwartz, *Lyndon Johnson and Europe: In the Shadow of Vietnam* (Cambridge, MA, 2003), 223–37.
7 *FRUS* 1969–1976, 1:62–3.

Nixon's hope that his talks with de Gaulle might be the start of a "new partnership" between the United States and Europe suffered a blow about a month later, when the general resigned from the presidency. A similar fate awaited Chancellor Kurt Georg Kiesinger, whom Nixon had met in Bonn during the same trip. Nixon, very much the disciple of Eisenhower, always argued, though not often in public, that "the highest priority American foreign policy objective must be . . . [keeping] Germany solidly on the Western side."[8] He was determined to visit Berlin but feared comparison to Kennedy's triumphal visit of 1963. Although the American embassy took care to try to drum up as large a crowd as the one that had turned out to see Kennedy, the six years separating the two occasions seemed like a lifetime.[9] Nixon and Kissinger recognized the relative decline in America's power, a decline often exaggerated in European assessments.[10] Grappling with Vietnam, the huge Soviet military buildup, and growing economic competition from Western Europe and Japan, the United States no longer seemed able to "pay any price, bear any burden," as Kennedy had promised. Although Kissinger still believed that "the prominent role that U.S. economic, diplomatic, and military power plays in the affairs of dozens of other states . . . refutes the frequent observations by contemporary analysts about the 'impotence of power,'" he was particularly hostile to any idea of resurrecting the "great days of the Marshall Plan," arguing that "nothing would sunder Atlantic relationships so surely as the attempt to reassert the notions of leadership appropriate to the early days of NATO."[11] Nixon and Kissinger formulated the Nixon Doctrine primarily to reflect America's decreased commitments in Asia, but the idea of reducing America's burdens also applied to Europe. Both men hoped that the Europeans would recognize that the Nixon Doctrine gave Europe priority in American foreign policy. Europe, Nixon explained in a February 1970 speech, "must be the cornerstone of the structure of a durable peace," as "America cannot – and will not – conceive *all* the plans, design *all* the programs, execute *all* the decisions and undertake *all* the defense of the free nations of the world." The United States, Nixon promised, "will help where it makes a real difference and is considered in our interest."[12] Europe was an area of American interest, but Nixon still expected the Europeans to do more both for their own defense and for Western interests around the globe.

8 *FRUS* 1969–1976, 1:5.
9 Andreas W. Daum, *Kennedy in Berlin*, trans. Dona Geyer (Cambridge, 2008).
10 Kaplan makes this argument in *NATO and the United States*; see 132.
11 *FRUS*, 1969–1976, 1:139, 32.
12 Nixon, Feb. 18, 1970, quoted in Kaplan *Long Entanglement*, 151.

Nixon and Kissinger also had domestic concerns in mind. They were worried that the mood of isolationism in the United States might put pressure on them to decrease the American military presence in Europe. Kissinger worried that a unilateral reduction in U.S. forces would not be offset by expanded military efforts on the part of the Europeans. As he told Nixon, "When big brother even appears to falter, the little brethren will not move forward courageously – as we seem to think – but, on the contrary, they will anxiously take several steps backwards."[13] Kissinger told Nixon about a West German leader who believed his country had to come to an accommodation with Moscow because he knew the Americans would ultimately withdraw their troops. The fear he expressed, Kissinger added, "is actually shared by virtually *all* Germans who do have opinions on foreign and world affairs."[14]

Nixon was angered by such fears, but he also thought it "a hard fact that the American military commitment of five-and-a-third or six divisions or whatever it is cannot continue ad infinitum." Nevertheless, his administration fought tenaciously against the Mansfield amendment, which would have cut U.S. troop strength in Europe by half. Former American NATO commanders as well as senior members of previous administrations such as Dean Acheson and George Ball were enlisted to voice opposition to the Mansfield amendment. Nixon even brought Lyndon Johnson into the fray.[15] The amendment was defeated by a Senate vote of 61–36 in May 1971, but critics nonetheless continued to call for cutbacks in the American military presence overseas. The administration scored a little-heralded success two years later when it succeeded in linking American troop levels in Europe to another product of détente, the Mutual and Balance Force Reduction (MBFR) negotiations with the Soviet Union. This linkage made Mansfield's position more difficult, and Nixon neutralized much of the domestic pressure for unilateral withdrawals.

This determination to remain a European power shaped the Nixon administration's approach to détente. The administration clearly wanted to move in the direction of better relations with the Soviet Union; Nixon himself had called for "an era of negotiation" in his inaugural address. Kissinger made it clear to Soviet Ambassador Anatoly Dobrynin, his back channel to Moscow, that "President Nixon takes into account the special interests of the Soviet Union in Eastern Europe, and does not intend to do anything there which could be evaluated in Moscow as a 'challenge'

---

13 *FRUS* 1969–1976, 1:119.
14 *FRUS*, 1969–1976, 1:119, emphasis in the original.
15 Kaplan, *Long Entanglement*, 153.

to her position in that region."[16] But as much as Nixon and Kissinger might have distanced themselves from the Eisenhower-era concept of roll-back, they saw no incompatibility between détente and containment. On the contrary, détente, they believed, was consistent with "the restraint of hostile Soviet moves or adventurism and the maintenance of allied strength and cohesion."[17] Any move toward better relations with the Soviet Union would, from their perspective, have to be led by the United States. Willy Brandt's dramatic steps in *Ostpolitik* were thus shocks to the system that required the Nixon and Kissinger to launch their own initiatives. After hav-ing given short shrift to relations with Europe and the Soviet Union because of its preoccupation with Vietnam in 1970, the administration rebounded with dramatic successes on several fronts in early 1971.[18] Together with the opening to China, the progress in the SALT negotiations and the Four Power talks on Berlin gave Kissinger occasion to claim that he had tamed the "beast of détente." Détente became an issue that both united and divided the Western allies. The Western Europeans wanted better superpower rela-tions but feared a Soviet-American condominium. The Americans wanted the stability detente offered but worried about the "Finlandization" of a Europe dependent on the goodwill – and resources of – the Soviet Union. Hence different priorities and a lack of consensus on détente plagued the alliance throughout the long 1970s.

ECONOMIC CONFLICT AND COOPERATION

In the economic realm, the Nixon administration ushered in a tougher approach to guard U.S. interests vis-à-vis a more competitive Europe. The Kennedy and Johnson administrations had, to some extent, recognized that American interest in access to European markets and European efforts to create a single market could not be easily reconciled — although the Community, except in agriculture, was not significantly more protectionist than the United States. Johnson was ultimately willing to make concessions to the Europeans — agreeing, for example, to leave tariffs on agricultural products untouched — for the sake of promoting free trade and European integration.[19] On monetary issues, Johnson and his advisers had worked through multilateral forums like the Group of Ten.[20] Nixon, by contrast,

---

16 Memorandum of Conversation, Dobrynin and Kissinger, June 12, 1969, quoted in Jeffrey Kimball, *The Vietnam War Files* (Lawrence, KS, 2004), 70–1.
17 *FRUS 1969–1976*, 1:137.
18 Kimball, *Vietnam War Files*, makes it clear how dominating the Vietnam issue was for the first two years of the administration: see 61–138.
19 Schwartz, *Lyndon Johnson and Europe*, 165–74.

was inclined from the very outset of his presidency toward a more unilateral approach and was less willing than his predecessors to make compromises for the sake of European interests. In a meeting in April 1969 to discuss trade issues, Nixon advised his commerce secretary to tell the Europeans, "Our mid-western friends here in America will stick with us on NATO but if we start fooling around with their soy beans, their votes are gone." Nixon stressed the problem of growing isolationism in America, and related it to the way the Europeans were constructing the European Economic Community: "If the American people get the impression that the European economy is turning inward, the Europeans can forget about political cooperation; no administration could survive supporting their case."[21] Nixon's most notorious expression of this sentiment came in March 1974, when he bluntly warned after the Middle East crisis, "The Europeans cannot have it both ways. They cannot have the United States' participation and cooperation on the security front and proceed to have confrontation and even hostility on the economic and political front."[22] While Kennedy and Johnson had similarly voiced exasperation with the Europeans – though usually in private – Nixon's evident willingness to act on this frustration was something new.

Changing economic and political circumstances prompted this shift in American policy. With the recession of 1969–70, a more nationalist economic policy gained domestic political support. Europe's traditional allies within the American government were also in eclipse. The State Department, mistrusted by Nixon and weakened by the Kissinger-Rogers feud, was less effective at making the case for full-scale support for European integration. The other cabinet departments dealing with Europe – especially Treasury and Commerce – asserted a much stronger line in negotiations. This trend reached its highpoint in the appointment of former Texas Governor John Connally, a Nixon favorite and a strong economic nationalist, as secretary of the treasury in 1971. The economic program Nixon announced in August 1971 – the decisions to severe the gold-dollar link once and for all, to abandon fixed exchange rates, and to impose a 10 percent surcharge on imports – came as a shock to the Europeans. As several essays in this collection make clear, the Nixon administration's actions encouraged greater European monetary cooperation, setting in motion the developments that led ultimately to the creation of the euro. The immediate aftermath of Nixon's abandonment of the Bretton Woods system, however,

20 Ibid., 174–81.
22 Kaplan, *Long Entanglement*, 157.

21 *FRUS* 1969–1976, 1:76.

was a prolonged attempt to negotiate a new international monetary system. A system of floating exchange rates was barely in place when the West was hit with the first oil crisis in the wake of the Yom Kippur War of October 1973. Unemployment and inflation rates reached double-digit figures in several Western European countries and, for a time, the United States.

If economic turmoil made cooperation among European and American leaders difficult at times, it also served to remind them of their interdependence. As Geir Lundestad notes, "the American–European economic relationship was flourishing, despite trade across the Pacific growing even faster than across the Atlantic."[23] Although both America and Europe had economic interests in other parts of the world, the connections between them remained strong. Europe accounted for 30 percent of all American foreign investment in 1970, and trade between the United States and Europe accounted for almost a quarter of America's imports and exports. Intense economic relations could help minimize political conflict, as Raj Roy's essay on the Anglo-American relationship in this volume makes clear. More generally, the extent of European–American economic ties reminded leaders of the Western nations that, much as they might be focused on the individual national interests, they were all in the same boat in the end. They remembered the lessons of the 1930s and recognized that economic antagonisms, left unchecked, could lead to political or even military conflict.

COOLING OFF ON EUROPE

If America's economic links with Europe created some sense of common problems, they also led to one of the most distinctive changes in U.S. policy during this era, namely the coolness toward European integration. Washington's enthusiasm for European integration was expressed in a variety of ways under Eisenhower, Kennedy, and Johnson – from applying pressure on the European allies to adopt the European Defense Community plan, to praising the Common Market Treaty and putting forward the misguided Multilateral Nuclear Force (MLF) proposal. Nixon and Kissinger took a very different stance toward European integration. While the administration echoed its predecessors in pledging support for greater European unity, it also made clear that the United States "will not inject [itself] into intra-European debates on the form, methods, and timing of steps toward unity." At first, this careful silence was constructive and probably contributed to the EEC's acceptance of Britain as a member in 1970. This nonintervention

---

23 Geir Lundestad, *The United States and Western Europe since 1945* (New York, 2003), 192.

was not limited, however, to not taking sides in intra-European debates. It went hand in hand with an insistence on dealing individually with the separate national governments in Europe as in the past. As Nixon once bluntly put it, "we have to work with the heads of Government in the various countries and not that jackass in the European Commission in Brussels."[24] Given American concerns about relative economic decline, Europe's increasing competitiveness, and the seemingly Gaullist tone of European foreign policy, it is little wonder that the Nixon administration did not embrace European unity with the same enthusiasm Washington had shown in the past.

It nonetheless remains an open question whether the failures of European integration during this era should be attributed primarily to American policy or to the continuing differences among the Europeans themselves. The essays in this volume on Kissinger's Year of Europe initiative raise this question and suggest that American policy was to blame. Certainly, 1973 saw something of a perfect storm in the convergence of circumstances and events that precipitated an extraordinary crisis in European-American relations.[25] After the outbreak of the Yom Kippur War, a more independent Europe had the opportunity to define itself in opposition to the United States. Europe's rejection of American policy during the war, its refusal of landing rights for American resupply planes to Israel, and its embrace of the Arab position on the war prompted the most serious crisis in transatlantic relations between the founding of NATO and the Iraq War. Washington's decision, without consulting its allies, to put its forces worldwide on nuclear alert in October 1973 raised tempers further on both sides of the Atlantic. As Kissinger later observed, "each side's unilateralism fed the other's and turned into a self-fulfilling prophecy."[26] Kissinger himself came to believe that his attempt in the Year of Europe to "give a new purpose to Atlantic relations" ran up against the fact that the allies "gave priority to constructing a united Europe" and believed "that both causes could not be advanced simultaneously."[27]

As serious as the 1973 crisis in transatlantic relations was, what is perhaps most striking is how quickly it was overcome. In Kissinger's dramatic and perhaps exaggerated telling, "when the democracies seemed to be returning

---

24 *FRUS* 1969–1976, 1:413.
25 See Daniel Möckli, "Asserting Europe's Distinct Identity: The EC Nine and Kissinger's Year of Europe"; Alastair Noble, "Kissinger's Year of Europe, Britain's Year of Choice"; and Fabian Hilfrich, "West Germany's Long Year of Europe: Bonn between Europe and the United States," in this volume.
26 Henry Kissinger, *Years of Upheaval* (Boston, 1982), 720.
27 Ibid., 726.

to the dark side of a history so filled with fratricidal strife, two events brought about a reversal."[28] The first of those events was a change in leadership in all of the major Western nations: Nixon, Heath, Pompidou, and Brandt were replaced, respectively, by Ford, Wilson, Giscard d'Estaing, and Schmidt. The second event was the Arab oil embargo. That this moment of crisis within the Atlantic alliance was relatively brief illustrates its exceptional nature and attests to the strength of the established transatlantic structures, including close Anglo-American ties and the U.S.-German security alignment, and the reservations about closer integration within the EC itself.

RENEWING THE INTERNATIONAL ARCHITECTURE

After the transatlantic crisis had subsided by the summer of 1974, the mid-1970s saw a consolidation of the alliance, which was enhanced by innovations in the international architecture that were supposed to improve transatlantic cooperation.

At the Washington Energy Conference of February 1974, it became clear that a majority of the EC member states, their efforts for dialogue with the Arab states notwithstanding, preferred to address the energy crisis in cooperation with the United States rather than let the West be divided by OPEC. To facilitate cooperation on energy policy, the Europeans and Americans created the International Energy Agency.

Second, British entry into the EC in 1973, the Labour Party's victory in the 1974 elections, and the changes of government in France and West Germany in the spring of 1974 strengthened the EC's commitment to transatlantic partnership, for the new European leaders were more pro-American, congenial, and pragmatic than were their predecessors. In March 1974, British Foreign Secretary James Callaghan expressly rejected "the view that Europe will emerge only out of a process of struggle with America."[29] London's renewed orientation toward the United States, and its lack of interest in closer European cooperation certainly contributed to the deceleration in the process of European integration in 1975–76. Another reason was that the French and German leaders were not ready to take Europe on the road toward federalism but were satisfied with strengthening Franco-German cooperation and the role of governments within the EC. Following a call

28 Henry Kissinger, *Years of Renewal* (New York, 1999), 605.
29 John Dumbrell, *A Special Relationship, Anglo-American Relations in the Cold War and After* (Houndmills, UK, 2001), 78. The Community's objective, agreed at the summit in the Hague in 1969 and reaffirmed in Paris 1972, to create a European union by the end of the decade, had, of course, not been the result of a struggle with America, but it is telling that the conflicts of the Year of Europe left someone like Callaghan with such an impression.

by the French intellectual Raymond Aron that "the autonomy of Europe demands a common defense even more than a common external tariff,"[30] Schmidt and Giscard d'Estaing also tried to lay a foundation for a European defense policy by intensifying Franco-German cooperation in weapons development and aerospace research,[31] but apparently neither of them saw the necessity – or, perhaps, the possibility – of pushing European integration any further. This was essentially a result of the strong improvement in U.S.-European relations under President Gerald Ford. In Ford, the Europeans found an interlocutor who was sympathetic to European concerns and was willing to make concessions to strengthen the alliance. As a consequence, cooperation on détente improved. Thanks to U.S. backing, the Europeans could, for the first time since the war, play a leading role in framing the rules regulating East-West relations and even go so far as to prescribe norms pertaining to the domestic order in Eastern Europe. In the context of the Conference for Security and Cooperation, the Western Europeans, supported by the United States, defined a "code of peace" and catalog of human rights to which the Soviets adhered with a view toward gaining technological and trade benefits. Western soft power, backed by U.S. hard power and readiness to make concessions, achieved a remarkable breakthrough in Helsinki in August 1975. Even though superpower détente quickly became fragile, the impact on East European societies was significant.

The improvement in U.S.-European relations was followed by institutional adaptations. By accepting Giscard d'Estaing and Schmidt's proposal for an economic policy summit of the governments of the leading industrial states, the Ford administration acknowledged the necessity of coordinating international economic policy with the other leading industrial market economies rather than acting unilaterally as Nixon had. This represented a concession to the Europeans, who hoped to exert more influence on American policy when they dealt with Washington in a multilateral framework. At the same time, it was an incentive for the Europeans to share in economic leadership. The inclusion of the president of the European Commission in the G-7 summits from 1977 onward gave the Community a stronger presence in world politics, especially as the G-7 moved from being a mere informal exchange on economic issues toward global coordination on economic and political issues. The creation and development of the G-7

---

30 Aron took part in a conversation on defense policy with the French president in 1974: quoted in *Le Monde*, May 23, 1975. Cf. Beatrice Heuser, *NATO, Britain, France, and the FRG: Nuclear Strategies and Forces for Europe, 1949–2000* (New York, 1997), 161.
31 Helmut Schmidt, *Die Deutschen und ihre Nachbarn: Menschen und Mächte II* (Berlin, 1990), 5; Pierre Gerbet, *La construction de l'Europe* (Paris, 1983), 412.

was thus an important step in enhancing the European Community's role in the structures of international governance and in transatlantic cooperation.

THE SECOND TRANSATLANTIC CRISIS AND THE DRIFTING
APART OF SOCIETIES

When Jimmy Carter became U.S. president in January 1977, everything seemed to point to further improvements in transatlantic relations. In a memo drafted shortly before the 1976 election, Cyrus Vance, at the time foreign policy adviser to the candidate Carter, had highlighted the need to develop new "methods for closer cooperation with our European allies." Coordinated Western action was particularly important in dealing with the developing world, Vance had argued, and if elected, Carter should not attempt to present the Europeans with "a proposed plan on which we expect them to sign off." "To do so," he warned, "would be to repeat the errors of the 'Year of Europe.'"[32] Indeed, Carter paid an early visit to the European Commission as well as to NATO headquarters in Brussels to underscore his respect for the European and Atlantic institutions. Later, he frequently received the president of the European Commission in Washington.

Yet the good intentions of the Carter administration did not prevent the eruption of another major crisis in European-American relations similar to the one in 1973 and 1974. This time, though, responsibility lay more squarely with Washington. Carter changed the tone and direction of several policies affecting Europe without consulting the European allies. Carter's focus on the domestic effects of his policies and his leadership style compounded the negative effects of such decisions. For example, his maladroit attempt to rescind the German-Brazilian nuclear technology deal of 1975, a treaty to which the United States was not a party, demonstrated both a lack of diplomatic tact and a problematic understanding of the United States' competence to set policies for other countries. His vacillation and change of position on the neutron bomb spurred grave misgivings among the Europeans and prompted many bitter exchanges. Schmidt could not forgive him, not least because the neutron bomb fiasco helped fuel the West German antinuclear movement, which was undermining Schmidt's domestic support. At the heart of the crisis, however, were the United States' economic problems, which were aggravated by the Carter administration's ill-designed fiscal, monetary, and energy policies. Like de Gaulle

---

32 Overview of Foreign Policy Issues and Positions, October 1976, memorandum reprinted in Cyrus Vance, *Hard Choices: Critical Year in American Foreign Policy* (New York, 1983), 446.

in the 1960s, but an Atlanticist by conviction, Schmidt found himself saying no to Washington at the 1977 World Economic Summit in London.[33] But whereas de Gaulle failed to change the international order in a constructive way, Schmidt, in collaboration with Commission president Roy Jenkins and Giscard d'Estaing, played an instrumental role in creating the European Monetary System. Again transatlantic tensions, this time triggered by Carter's policies, propelled European integration.

Carter learned the hard way that Washington had to take European interests into account if it wanted to draw on European support in times of need. He was confronted with a challenge to American prestige and a threat to the lives of American citizens in the Iran hostage crisis. The Soviet invasion of Afghanistan threatened the global balance of power. When Washington sought its allies' support in responding to these events, they were not particularly forthcoming.

Yet contrary to common European perceptions, Carter's presidency also featured some remarkable successes. Bringing peace to the Middle East was a major priority of his, and the Camp David accords were an important step toward that goal. His administration also contributed to the liberalization of world trade in the Tokyo Round of the General Agreement on Tariffs and Trade negotiations; close collaboration between Washington and Bonn played an important part in its successful conclusion. European-American cooperation prevented the rise of a new protectionism and helped reduce trade barriers when the second oil crisis hit at the end of the decade. The biggest success of the NATO alliance in this period – the dual-track decision of 1979 – was in some respects ambiguous. When the Soviets began to deploy a new generation of intermediate range nuclear missiles in Eastern Europe in 1976, some Western European governments were considering cuts in their defense budgets to gain room for maneuver in financing their social welfare programs. Schmidt was deeply concerned about this situation.[34] The dual-track decision, NATO's response to the Soviet missile deployment, was a demonstration of the alliance's unity on the political and strategic levels. Even France backed the dual-track decision. Achieving this compromise was very difficult, however, as was its implementation (i.e., the actual deployment of intermediate-range missiles). Western European governments came under increasing pressure from powerful peace movements

---

33 On de Gaulle's "power to say 'no'," see Frédéric Bozo, *Two Strategies for Europe: De Gaulle, the United States and the Atlantic Alliance* (Lanham, MD, 2001).
34 Helmut Schmidt, Erwägungen für 1977, Jan. 5, 1977, Depositum Bundeskanzler Helmut Schmidt, Archiv für soziale Demokratie, Bad Godesberg [hereafter Depositum Schmidt], 1/ HSAA009302, 40, 42.

capable of mobilizing up to several hundred thousand people for demonstrations. Opponents of the deployment and those on the Left throughout Western Europe, especially in West Germany, failed to see that the three-year time frame established in the dual-track decision gave priority to disarmament negotiations with the Soviets. Disregarding the Soviet Union's rearmament and its invasion of Afghanistan, the peace movement saw both the Soviet Union and the United States as imperialistic and potentially violent powers. Moreover, American society was increasingly seen by many in Western Europe as socially unjust, racially polarized (and this at a time when racial tensions in the United States actually declined), and insensitive to the environment.[35] The United States found itself with a serious image problem in Western Europe – a problem that persists to this day.

The Western European governments were likewise caught in a dilemma. They recognized the strategic need for the deployment of new intermediate-range missiles but, at the same time, saw détente as the only way to promote constructive change in Eastern Europe. Détente brought about an easing of travel restrictions; religious liberties were slowly extended in the Eastern-bloc states; and East-West family reunions were facilitated.[36] All these steps contributed to the gradual erosion of the Communist system from within. Dissident groups formed in Czechoslovakia, and 1980 saw the emergence of Solidarity in Poland, the Eastern bloc's first independent labor union. As long as détente was operative on the superpower level, it united the West Europeans and the United States in a common purpose. As it began to crumble and repressive policies became more pronounced in the East, stark differences between the Western Europeans and the United States emerged. Proximity to the iron curtain prompted the Western Europeans, especially the West Germans, to adhere much more strongly to the concept of confidence-building measures and negotiations than the Americans, who saw the East-West conflict primarily in terms of the arms race and the global struggle for supremacy. This made for increased tensions in the early 1980s as President Ronald Reagan employed a new Cold War rhetoric. When he launched the Strategic Defense Initiative, left-leaning Western Europeans became convinced that the United States had become as dangerous as the Soviet Union.[37] The Atlantic alliance weathered the protests that accompanied the deployment the Pershing II missiles in 1983, but the dual-track

---

35 Hans Tuch, 1967–1970, PAO [USIA] Berlin, interviewed by G. Lewis Schmidt, in "Germany Reader," comp. Teresa Allen, August 1993, Oral History Program, Georgetown University.
36 See the manuscript for Schmidt's speech before the National Press Club, June 30, 1977: Depositum Schmidt, 1/HSAA006699. It underlines the humanitarian impact of détente.
37 See Oskar Lafontaine, *Angst vor den Freunden: Die Atomwaffen-Strategie der Supermächte zerstört die Bündnisse* (Hamburg, 1983).

decision nonetheless accelerated the drifting apart of the societies of the United States and Europe. The United States had opted for a vigorous stance that relied on a nuclear deterrent, while many in Western Europe, especially among the younger generation, rejected this policy as a dangerous escalation that could lead all too easily to nuclear nightmare.

ADAPTING TO A CHANGING WORLD: THE EUROPEAN PROJECT AND THE ATLANTIC ALLIANCE

The United States and the European Community had to adapt to a changing global environment in the 1970s. As the OPEC countries were becoming steadily richer and more influential, the United States found itself grappling with a relative decline in its economic power. The Soviets had finally achieved parity with the West in the nuclear arms race. These developments made it necessary for the members of the Atlantic alliance to adjust their policies as well as the frameworks for monetary, economic, and security cooperation.

The process of adaptation was not easy for either side. On the European side, adaptation demanded innovation, as mechanisms had to be found to define common interests and to translate economic power into effective political influence. The slow but palpable progress of European integration in the 1970s suggests, first, that the Europeans were moving forward cautiously without knowing exactly which exact course to take and, second, that it was often by default that they opted for European integration. Although some observers at the time were critical of the slow pace of integration, others noticed a "silent revolution" that was "inadequately understood [in the United States]."[38]

The institutional innovations of 1974–75, which increased the weight of national governments vis-à-vis that of the Commission, were a disappointment for European federalists. Nonetheless, the EC did emerge as a global actor. The commitment on the part of the member states to play a shared role on the international stage rested on, as one senior West German official noted, the "political will to follow, after thorough discussion, the opinion of the majority, in order to bring about a common policy."[39] Even though that will was often not sufficient to resolve fundamental disagreements among the member states, the EC's successes – in supporting the establishment of

---

38 Fernand Spaak, "The U.S. and Europe: Partners at Last?" in *Drifting Together or Apart? U.S.-European Relations in the Paul-Henri Spaak Lectures, Harvard University 1981–1984*, ed. Richard Eichenberg (Lanham, MD, 1986), 30.

39 State Minister in the Auswärtiges Amt, Hans-Jürgen Wischnewski, in the debate on Europe in the Bundestag, Mar. 18, 1976; Tindemans-Bericht Heft 1, Depositum Schmidt, 1/HSAA006623.

democracy in Greece, Spain, and Portugal, for example, and their gradual integration into the Community – should not be overlooked.

In a 1978 memorandum to the European heads of state and government on plans for expanding the EC from nine to twelve members, Commission president Roy Jenkins warned that the EC's agenda was "littered with unadopted Commission proposals."[40] Jenkins's reminder points to the perpetual dilemma of the EC: while the Commission pushed forward, the national governments, especially London and Paris, were often reluctant on account of worries about sovereignty and national interest. Thus, Washington really did not need to attempt a divide-and-conquer strategy to retard European integration. Long before Donald Rumsfeld notoriously distinguished between an old and a new Europe divided on foreign policy, it was clear that disagreements within Europe were the main stumbling block to greater European integration and unity.

Although the new projects for European integration during the 1970s were not structurally directed against the United States, the conflicts analyzed in this collection show that problems within the transatlantic partnership could give new impetus to European integration. The European Monetary System developed in response to the weakness of the dollar, but its primary objectives were to preserve the Common Market and to prod Washington toward more stability-oriented policies. Eschewing competitive devaluation, the system put an end to the European reliance on American monetary leadership and opened a new chapter in international monetary policy that led ultimately to the adoption of the euro in 1999.

During the 1970s, European integration only occasionally appeared to be incompatible with the Atlantic alliance, as, for example, during the Year of Europe crisis. In trade relations, the area in which the EC had extensive jurisdiction, dealings between Washington and Europe were successful on the whole. Had Western Europe sought to build a common defense, it would most likely have done so within the framework of NATO. American complaints about the lack of European enthusiasm for defense spending were justified in so far as Washington continuously bore the brunt of the costs to defend the West, while the Europeans invested a large share of their national income in their generous social welfare systems.[41] Moreover, the Europeans were probably more comfortable relying on the American nuclear deterrent,

---

40 President of the Commission of the European Communities, Memorandum for the European Council, Copenhagen, Apr. 7–8, 1978, Depositum Schmidt 1/HSAA006713, 4.

41 Ronald Steel, "Europe: The Phantom Pillar," in *The American Century in Europe*, eds. R. Laurence Moore and Maurizio Vaudagna (Ithaca, NY, 2003), 66–78. Steel contends that the Europeans pledged in 1947–1948 to build up their military forces to complement the American military pillar as their economies grew.

backed up by the smaller French and British nuclear arsenals, than trying to create a European defense in which West Germany would have to possess nuclear weapons. Indeed, West Germany's commitment to nonproliferation in 1969 had been prerequisite for the relaunching of European integration at the Hague summit in the same year and was crucial for East-West détente. It also played an important part in restoring confidence in Germany among French political elites, who had been disturbed by Chancellor Ludwig Erhard's push for a transatlantic "multilateral nuclear force" in the mid-1960s.[42] Creating a European defense, in short, was simply not viable in the 1970s. Thus, the division of responsibilities within the Atlantic alliance was confirmed: the United Stats continued to provide a "nuclear guarantee," and the Western Europeans contributed a large share to the conventional defense of Western Europe.

Instead of developing a European security policy in the 1970s, the Europeans opted to increase their global commitments. The EC realized, as Fernand Spaak, chief of staff to the president of the European Commission, put it, "that the prosperity, and hence the political stability, of the Third World will be a key factor both for world peace and for our economic future." In Spaak's view, the United States did not fully acknowledge the EC's engagement in the developing countries as a contribution to the security of the West.[43] The "failure of the United States to keep pace with most European states in the share of national wealth transferred to developing nations" became a source of tension between the United States and Western Europe, as Cyrus Vance noted shortly after his tenure as secretary of state in the Carter administration.[44]

The United States, of course, did much more for Western security than the European Community and its member states for the developing world. And while the European contribution toward development was important, it also symbolized a flight from confronting the Soviet threat in Europe: the Western Europeans had little to counter the SS-20 missile except to ask the Americans for help and rely on U.S. leadership. Soft power had become Europe's preferred instrument for exercising international influence.

DIVERGENT DIPLOMATIC CULTURES?

Transatlantic conflicts in 1973 and 1978 arguably became more strident not only because of personality clashes between the major actors but also

42 See Matthias Schulz, "Integration durch europäische Atomstreitmacht? Ludwig Erhards Europaini-tiative im Jahre 1964," *Vierteljahreshefte für Zeitgeschichte* 53, no. 2 (2005): 275–314.
43 Spaak, "The U.S. and Europe: Partners at Last?" 30–1.
44 Vance, *Hard Choices*, 424–5.

because the United States and the European Community had developed increasingly different diplomatic cultures. The differences do not amount to a dichotomy between "paradise and power" – between Europe's reliance on international law and America's willingness to use military force – as Robert Kagan has provocatively argued.[45] Western European leaders, as the contributions by Schulz and Scholtyseck to this volume demonstrate, were as concerned as their American counterparts about the East-West balance of power during the 1970s and early 1980s. And with the exception of West Germany, numerous Western European countries took part in military operations within the framework of UN peacekeeping operations in the 1960s, 1970s, and 1980s. Some, most notably France, also used military force to intervene unilaterally abroad. Indeed, France was dubbed "gendarme of Africa" on account of its frequent interventions there.[46] These operations, as well as the Anglo-Argentine Falklands War, played a significant role in the power consciousness of European governments.[47] Even West Germany, though constrained by its constitution, did not eschew the use of force. In 1977, the West German government sent commandos to rescue passengers being held hostage in a hijacked plane in Mogadishu, Somalia. The army it maintained on the front line of the Cold War also attests to its recognition of the important role of hard power. Kagan conveniently ignores these facts. Still, it became clear in the 1970s that differences had developed between the Western European countries and the United States in how they formulated and pursued foreign policy.

As was seen in the 1970s, a change in presidential administrations usually means a change in U.S. foreign policy as well, given the accumulation of power in the person of the president. Nonetheless, American presidents tend to be more sensitive to domestic constituencies than are their European counterparts. Furthermore, the United States was less dependent on foreign trade than the EC member states and thus less dependent on cooperation with other countries. For these reasons, domestic politics generally had a larger influence on U.S. foreign policy, which made it subject to fluctuation in response to events and less open to influence by other countries.

By contrast, Western European governments were on the whole less prone to follow national interest groups than were the administrations in

---

45 Robert Kagan, *Of Paradise and Power: America and Europe in the New World Order* (New York, 2003).

46 Joseph Fitchett, "For France, Stakes in Zaire Run High, Plays Its Africa Card, Win or Lose," *International Herald Tribune*, September 25, 1991. France intervened, for example, in Chad (1969–1972, 1978–1980, 1983), in the Congo with Belgium (1964, 1978), and in the Central African Republic to depose the dictator Jean-Bédel Bokassa (1979).

47 Valéry Giscard d'Estaing, for example, stresses the importance of France's interventions abroad in his memoirs, *Le pouvoir et la vie* (Paris 1988).

Washington and more open to coordinating their policies with one another as well as with Washington. That was a consequence of the EC's dependence on foreign trade and the U.S. security guarantee as well as the limited, though growing, influence of lobby groups on Community policy. Moreover, during the period covered by this book, a culture of consultation and collective decision making in the area of foreign policy was developing as part of the process of European integration. A change of government in one EC member state, therefore, did not have nearly the same impact on EC policy as a change of administration in Washington did on American policy. European policies in the 1970s were thus more calculable and less reactive, more influenced by institutions than by personalities than were American policies, but the EC's slow-moving decision-making processes often left Europe incapable of responding quickly to international crises.

The 1970s were a pivotal decade for Western Europe as it took a more active role in shaping the international order than it had in the 1950s and 1960s. With the establishment of the Conference on Security and Cooperation in Europe and the G-7 summits, transatlantic cooperation was more strongly bound into institutions than ever before. That was a matter both of necessity in an age of increasing interdependence and, for the Europeans, of preference. Institutionalized cooperation enabled them to defend their interests more effectively than bilateral talks with the superpowers. The transatlantic conflicts of the late 1970s and early 1980s – over the decline of the dollar, the American hostage crisis in Iran, the consequences of the Soviet invasion in Afghanistan for détente, and the declaration of martial law in Poland – suggested, however, that the Western Europeans were no more satisfied with their part in transatlantic decision making than they had been a decade earlier. Indeed, writing shortly after his tenure as secretary of state, Cyrus Vance recognized that changing economic and political circumstances were making it increasingly necessary that the United States and Western Europe coordinate their polices and that the United States "be prepared to share the process of decision much more effectively than ever before."[48] Thirty years later and after the clash over Iran in 2003, the most serious transatlantic crisis since 1945, one can only concur with Vance's recommendation.

48 Vance, *Hard Choices*, 424.

Index